Dramatic Interactions in Education

Also available from Bloomsbury

Drama Education with Digital Technology, edited by Michael Anderson,
David Cameron and John Caroll
How Drama Activates Learning, edited by Michael Anderson and Julie Dunn
Lev Vygotsky, René van der Veer
MasterClass in Drama Education, Michael Anderson

Dramatic Interactions in Education

Vygotskian and Sociocultural Approaches to Drama, Education and Research

Edited by
Susan Davis, Hannah Grainger Clemson, Beth Ferholt,
Satu-Mari Jansson and Ana Marjanovic-Shane

Bloomsbury Academic
An imprint of Bloomsbury Publishing Plc

B L O O M S B U R Y
LONDON · OXFORD · NEW YORK · NEW DELHI · SYDNEY

Bloomsbury Academic
An imprint of Bloomsbury Publishing Plc

50 Bedford Square
London
WC1B 3DP
UK

1385 Broadway
New York
NY 10018
USA

www.bloomsbury.com

BLOOMSBURY and the Diana logo are trademarks of Bloomsbury Publishing Plc

First published 2015
Paperback edition first published 2016

© Susan Davis, Hannah Grainger Clemson, Beth Ferholt, Satu-Mari Jansson, Ana Marjanovic-Shane and Contributors, 2015

Susan Davis, Hannah Grainger Clemson, Beth Ferholt, Satu-Mari Jansson, Ana Marjanovic-Shane and Contributors have asserted their right under the Copyright, Designs and Patents Act, 1988, to be identified as Author of this work.

All rights reserved. No part of this publication may be reproduced or transmitted in any form or by any means, electronic or mechanical, including photocopying, recording, or any information storage or retrieval system, without prior permission in writing from the publishers.

No responsibility for loss caused to any individual or organization acting on or refraining from action as a result of the material in this publication can be accepted by Bloomsbury or the author.

British Library Cataloguing-in-Publication Data
A catalogue record for this book is available from the British Library.

ISBN: HB: 978-1-4725-7689-7
PB: 978-1-4742-9336-5
ePub: 978-1-4725-7690-3
ePDF: 978-1-4725-7691-0

Library of Congress Cataloging-in-Publication Data
Dramatic interactions in education : Vygotskian and sociocultural approaches to drama, education and research / edited by Susan Davis [and four others].
    pages cm
Summary: "A compendium of work from leading academics exploring sociocultural theory and research applications within the realm of drama and education"– Provided by publisher.
    Includes bibliographical references and index.
    ISBN 978-1-4725-7689-7 (hardback)
 1. Drama—Study and teaching. 2. Vygotskii, L. S. (Lev Semenovich), 1896-1934.
    I. Davis, Susan, 1961-
    PN1701.D725 2015
    371.39'9—dc23
    2014032003

Typeset by RefineCatch Limited, Bungay, Suffolk, UK

Contents

List of Contributors   vii
Foreword   *Vera John-Steiner*   xv

Introduction: Vygotsky, Sociocultural Concepts and Drama in and for Education   *Susan Davis, Hannah Grainger Clemson, Beth Ferholt and Satu-Mari Jansson*   1

Part I Vygotsky, Drama, *Perezhivanie* and the Unity of Development

1. Dramatic Interactions: From Vygotsky's Life of Drama to the Drama of Life   *Michael Michell*   19

2. Stanislavski and Vygotsky: On the Problem of the Actor's and Learner's Work   *Hannah Grainger Clemson*   39

3. *Perezhivanie* in Researching Playworlds: Applying the Concept of Perezhivanie in the Study of Play   *Beth Ferholt*   57

Part II Sociocultural Insights into Learning through Drama

4. Dialogue and Social Positioning in Dramatic Inquiry: Creating with Prospero   *Brian Edmiston*   79

5. Identity and Creativity: The Transformative Potential of Drama   *Harry Daniels and Emma Downes*   97

6. Constructing Identity and Motivation in the Drama Classroom: A Sociocultural Approach   *Richard Walker, Michael Anderson, Robyn Gibson and Andrew Martin*   115

Part III The Dynamics of Meaning Making through Drama Processes in the Classroom

7. Dramatic Play and Process Drama: Towards a Collective Zone of Proximal Development to Enhance Language and Literacy Learning   *Robyn Ewing*   135

8 Sociocultural Theory, Process Drama and Second Language
   Learning   *Penny Bundy, Erika Piazzoli and Julie Dunn*   153

9 Prolepsis and Educational Change through Drama: Bringing the
   Future Forward   *Patricia Enciso*   171

10 Interactive Drama with Digital Technology and Tools for Creative
   Learning   *Susan Davis*   189

Part IV Practice and Research Inspired by Sociocultural Approaches to
Drama, Education and Learning

11 A Theatre Company's Development, Cultural-historical Activity
   Theory and Developmental Work Research: Movement between
   Archetypes   *Satu-Mari Jansson*   211

12 How Environment Affects Learning: School Teachers Engaging with
   Theatre-based Pedagogies   *Anton Franks*   229

13 Drama, Theatre and Performance Creativity   *R. Keith Sawyer*   245

14 Building a Workplace Theatre: Forum Theatre and Developmental
   Work Research as Developmental Resources in Interventions
   Satu-Mari Jansson   261

Index   279

List of Contributors

Michael Anderson is Associate Professor in the Faculty of Education and Social Work at the University of Sydney, Australia. His research and teaching concentrates on how arts educators begin, evolve and achieve growth in their careers and how students engage with arts and technology to learn and create in arts education. This work has evolved into a programme of research and publication that engages with arts classrooms directly. His recent publications explore how aesthetic education is changing in the twenty-first century. These publications include *Partnerships in Education Research: Creating Knowledge that Matters* (with Kelly Freebody, 2014), *Masterclass in Drama Education* (2011) and *Drama with Digital Technology* (with John Carroll and David Cameron, 2009). The research reported in these books uncovers innovative linkages between drama education and theatre for young people that could significantly improve learning outcomes for students in the arts. Michael was a drama teacher and Creative Arts Consultant with the New South Wales Department of Education and holds senior positions in drama curriculum development and assessment with the New South Wales Board of Studies.

Penny Bundy is Associate Professor in the Applied Theatre team at Griffith University, Australia, where she convenes the Bachelor of Arts in Contemporary and Applied Theatre. In addition to being a Chief Investigator on the *TheatreSpace* project, Penny's other recent Applied Theatre research projects have included the use of drama to build resilience in newly arrived refugee communities and with adult survivors of childhood institutional abuse. Penny is co-editor (with John O'Toole) of the Intellect journal, *Applied Theatre Research*.

Harry Daniels is Professor of Education at the University of Oxford, UK. He has directed research of more than 40 projects funded by The Economic and Social Research Council (ESRC), various central and local government sources, The Lottery, The Nuffield Foundation and the European Union. He has recently completed two major studies of professional learning in and for multiagency work, one with Queen's University Belfast, UK, concerned with *Multiagency Work in Northern Ireland* and the other entitled *Learning in and for Interagency*

Working. Both were rated 'Outstanding' by ESRC and follow-up work has been funded by the practitioner/policy-making bodies such as The Local Government Association, Improvement and Development Agency (IDeA) and Local Authorities Research Council Initiative. He is also Adjunct Professor in the Centre for Learning Research at the Griffith University, Australia; Research Professor in the Centre for Human Activity Theory, Kansai University, Japan; and Research Professor in Cultural Historical Psychology at Moscow State University of Psychology and Education, Russia. His CV witnesses an extensive publication list including a series of internationally acclaimed books concerned with sociocultural psychology.

Susan Davis is Senior Lecturer in the School of Education and the Arts at Central Queensland University, Australia, with extensive experience in drama, theatre and education. Her research and creative practice interests include exploring the ways that creative processes (including digital technologies and drama processes) can be used for engagement and learning. In recent years she has initiated a number of practice-based research projects exploring sustainability and digital technologies. She was previously a drama teacher and Performing Arts Head of Department and created many youth theatre performances in collaboration with various industry partners. She has published extensively in the drama curriculum realm and currently sits on the Queensland Studies Authority Learning Advisory Committee for The Arts. Sue has presented her work at drama, education and sociocultural research conferences. She has written book chapters, scripts, was a writer for the textbook *DramaTexts* (2009), and has published in the leading drama and education journals. Her work is informed by sociocultural and activity theory research frames and in 2013 she also spent time as Visiting Scholar at the Centre for Research on Activity, Development and Learning (CRADLE) at the University of Helsinki, Finland.

Emma Downes has been teaching drama in the West Midlands, UK, for 12 years. She has experience of teaching at primary and secondary level. Emma has led Inset training using drama and is currently involved in a strategy to improve and develop teacher training in the West Midlands. Emma's interest in the subject of drama education was developed further through completion of the Masters course in 'Drama and Theatre Education' at the University of Warwick, UK. Her particular areas of interest are in the field of developing drama pedagogies as a means of empowering and removing barriers to learning, attainment and achievement.

Julie Dunn is Associate Professor at Griffith University, Australia, where she teaches in a range of undergraduate and postgraduate courses across the fields of arts education, applied theatre and educational communication. She is Program Convenor of the Master of Applied Theatre and Drama Education Degree, and has also taught in partnership with the Hong Kong Art School, Hong Kong. Her research is focused on improvised and playful forms of drama and the possible applications of these forms within school and community settings. Julie is currently a chief investigator on two major Australian Research Council funded grants: *Playful Engagement and Dementia: Assessing the Efficacy of Applied Theatre Practices* (2012–2015) and *Arrivals: Developing Refugee Resilience and Effective Resettlement through Drama-based Interventions* (2010–2013). Julie has recently taken up the role of editor of *NJ: The Journal of Drama Australia*.

Brian Edmiston is Professor of Drama in Education in the Department of Teaching and Learning at The Ohio State University, USA, where he teaches courses at the intersections of dramatic pedagogy with literacy, literature, inquiry-based education and ethical education. He grew up in Ireland, was an English teacher and Head of Drama in England, and an elementary teacher in the USA. The author of over 40 publications, the recipient of teaching and research awards, and an international presenter, his fourth book, *Transforming Teaching and Learning with Active and Dramatic Approaches: Engaging Students across the Curriculum* was recently published.

Patricia Enciso is Professor of Literature, Literacy and Equity Studies at The Ohio State University, USA, where she teaches courses in sociocultural theory, mediating multicultural literature, and conducts research in student learning through innovative arts-based pedagogies. She is co-editor of *Reframing Sociocultural Theory in Literacy Research: Identity, Agency and Power* (2007), and co-editor of *The Handbook of Research on Children's and Young Adult Literature* (2011), and has served as co-editor of *Language Arts*, the leading USA journal for teacher research and current issues in preK-middle grade literacy education. Patricia serves as incoming President for the Literacy Research Association and Research Director for the National Council for Research on Language and Literacy.

Robyn Ewing was formerly a primary teacher and is currently Professor of Teacher Education and the Arts and Acting ProDean in the Faculty of Education and Social Work at the University of Sydney, Australia. She is passionate about the role that the Arts can play in transforming learning and has a commitment to innovative teaching and learning at all levels of education. Robyn's teaching, research and extensive publications include a focus on the use of drama strategies with literature to enhance students' English and literacy learning. She particularly enjoys working with educators interested in reforming their curriculum practices. Teacher education, early career teachers, mentoring; sustaining curriculum innovation and evaluation; inquiry and case-based learning; and the use of arts informed narrative inquiry in educational research, are also current research interests. Robyn is working in partnership with the Sydney Theatre Company on the *School Drama* project to develop the confidence and expertise of primary teachers in using drama with literature. She is National President of the Australian Literacy Educators Association (ALEA), Vice President of the Sydney Story Factory Board and a Council Member of the Australian Film, Television and Radio School (AFTRS).

Beth Ferholt is Assistant Professor in the Department of Early Childhood and Art Education at Brooklyn College, City University of New York, USA. She is interested in imagination, play, emotional-cognitive development, creative early childhood educational practices, and in qualitative methodologies which allow us to study these phenomena. She currently studies these topics through a recently-emerging form of adult-child joint play, called playworlds. Beth is currently writing about the relationship between play and learning using findings from analyses of playworlds in Sweden and the USA. She has also done comparative analyses of Finnish and US playworlds, studied the impact of playworlds on early literacy development, and worked to understand playworlds as a method of research in which human development and learning can be studied without separating cognition from emotion.

Anton Franks is Associate Professor in Creative Arts and Education at the University of Nottingham, UK. He is interested in learning in the arts and culture, in and out of school, particularly in social, cultural and historical approaches to 'whole person learning' involving thought, emotion and the body. Before coming to the University of Nottingham, he taught drama and English in London schools and then was a teacher educator and researcher at the Institute of Education, UK. Publications include: 'Drama, desire and schooling' in *Changing English* 4:1; 'The meaning of action in learning and teaching' in *British Educational Research Journal* 27:2; 'School drama and representations of war and terror ...' in *Research in Drama Education* 13:1; 'Drama in teaching and learning, language and literacy', in *Routledge International Handbook of English, Language and Literacy Teaching*; and *English in Urban Classrooms* with Kress *et al.*

Robyn Gibson is a Senior Lecturer in the Faculty of Education and Social Work, University of Sydney, Australia. She has been a primary-school teacher, art/craft specialist and tertiary educator in Australia and the USA. Robyn writes about primary-school education in the visual and creative arts. In 2011, she published (with Robyn Ewing) *Transforming the Curriculum through the Arts*. She is currently engaged as the evaluator for *School Drama* – an initiative between the University of Sydney, Australia, and the Sydney Theatre Company. Recently, as part of a large ARC project, she has been examining the role of arts education in academic motivation, engagement and achievement. Her other academic research – which utilises interdisciplinary methodologies such as arts-informed inquiry and art/o/graphy – concerns creativity and creative teaching, art as research/research as art, particularly the connection between clothes and memory. Robyn has assumed roles such as Program Director of the Bachelor of Education (Primary) programme, Associate Dean of Undergraduate and Preservice Programmes, and currently, Associate Dean, Learning and Teaching.

Hannah Grainger Clemson is Research Fellow at the University of Warwick, UK, working with the Institute of Advanced Study on a range of interdisciplinary projects and the Centre for Educational Studies in Drama in Education. Her current research interests are in the construction of cultural narratives, and the notion of 'hybrid spaces', where technology and digital media are embedded in artistic and cultural experiences. She is also interested in research methodologies and publishing, working as an editor for a number of journals. She is passionate about the education of young people and about intercultural and international partnerships and dialogue, and has recently worked for the Directorate General Education and Culture at the European Commission in Brussels.

Satu-Mari Jansson is currently collaborating with Finnish actors, directors and stand-up comedians at TheatreWorks Training Ltd. Working with professional actors, she is using applied theatre methods and Forum Theatre to develop workplaces and organizations. She combines research-oriented development methods in her theatrical interventions and produces case descriptions and data to be utilised in her research work. She became familiar with activity theory and developmental work research in 2001 while working with professors Yrjö Engeström and Jaakko Virkkunen at the University of Helsinki, Finland. During the following years, she worked at the Theatre Academy, Helsinki, on the activity development of Finnish institutional theatres and application of theatre-based training in workplace contexts.

Vera John-Steiner is Regents' Professor Emerita of Language, Literacy and Sociocultural Studies and Linguistics at the University of New Mexico, USA, where she has been engaged in interdisciplinary teaching and research, and is a visiting lecturer. She has published in psycholinguistics, cultural historical theory, creativity, collaboration and bilingualism. Vera co-edited Vygotsky's *Mind in Society* (1978), a text that has been very influential in educational, psychological, and linguistic theory and practice. In *Notebooks of the Mind* (1997), she explores the development and diversity of thought processes and creative endeavours. The book received the William James Award in 1990. In *Creative Collaboration* (2006), she documents the impact of working partnerships in the human sciences. Her most recent publication, *Loving and Hating Mathematics* (2011), is co-authored with Reuben Hersh. Her honours include a Fellowship at the Centre for Advanced Study in the Behavioural Sciences, a Lifetime Achievement Award from the American Educational Research Association, and a Sussman Distinguished Visiting Professorship at Teacher's College, Columbia University, USA. She has taught and lectured in Latin America, Europe and the United States of America.

Ana Marjanovic-Shane is Associate Professor of Education at Chestnut Hill College, Philadelphia, USA. She is developing a sociocultural approach to education grounded in the key aspects of creative activities: play and drama, imagination and the arts. In developing her analysis of play and drama and her vision of education, Ana uses a Bakhtinian dialogic approach and an ecological orientation to understand the dynamics of events, the ways participants act and relate to each other through act-deeds (*postupok*), how they deeply experience these events (*perezhivanie*) and ways in which they create meanings. In Ana's view, events and processes in education should be approached and understood as creative praxis of meaning making. In this view, teaching should be regarded as an art rather than a technology. Both learning and teaching need to be designed contexts of meaningful practices that share the key aspects of play, the arts and especially the performing arts, and where experiences of the drama in education studies should be interwoven into the instructional design. She is one of the editors of the book *Vygotsky and Creativity: A Cultural-historical Approach to Play, Meaning Making, and the Arts* (2010).

Andrew Martin is Professor of Educational Psychology at the University of New South Wales, Australia, specializing in motivation, engagement, achievement and quantitative research methods. He is also Honorary Research Fellow in the Department of Education at the University of Oxford, UK, Honorary Professor in the Faculty of Education and Social Work at the University of Sydney, Australia, Fellow of the American Educational Research Association, and President Elect of the International Association of Applied Psychology's Division 5 Educational, Instructional, and School Psychology. Andrew is in the Top 25 of International Rankings of the Most Productive Educational Psychologists (*Contemporary Educational Psychology*, 2010). He has written over 250 peer reviewed journal articles, chapters and papers in published conference proceedings, written 3 books for parents and teachers (published in 5 languages) and has won 12 Australian Research Council (and National Health and Medical Research Council) grants as well as international funding (e.g. Spencer Foundation). He is Associate Editor of *British Journal of Educational Psychology*, immediate-past Associate Editor of *Journal of Educational Psychology*, and on Editorial Boards of four journals, including two international journals, *Journal of Educational Psychology* and *Contemporary Educational Psychology*.

Michael Michell is Research Fellow at the School of Education, University of New South Wales, Australia, where he is currently involved in a research and development project on teacher-based classroom assessment of English as second language learning. He lectures in language and literacy education, sociocultural perspectives on learning, and sociopolitical perspectives on education policy. Previously, Michael worked as an English as a Second Language (ESL) teacher and consultant in the New South Wales Department of Education, Australia, leading curriculum, assessment and research projects and policies aimed at improving ESL teaching and learning. He worked on two classroom-based, university partnership research projects, investigating 'scaffolding' in ESL and literacy pedagogy (2001–2003), and exploring high challenge/high support pedagogy for ESL students (2005–2007). From 2003 to 2008, he led action learning programmes with primary and secondary teacher teams, applying and integrating research findings and practice, and developing a school-based model of teacher professional learning. His research interests include application and development of Vygotskian, sociocultural and activity theories to student engagement and learning.

Erika Piazzoli is a Lecture at Griffith University, Australia. Her research has focused on engagement through a sociocultural framework, using process drama while teaching Italian as a second language. Currently, Erika teaches Italian, arts education and process drama for the School of Education and Professional Studies at Griffith University, Australia.

R. Keith Sawyer is Morgan Distinguished Professor in Educational Innovations, University of North Carolina at Chapel Hill, USA. He studies creativity and learning in collaborating groups. His approach is inspired by his early empirical studies of the interactional processes in jazz ensembles, improvisational theatre groups, and children at play. Sawyer connects these phenomena to learning within a theoretical framework, in the tradition of sociocultural psychology and distributed cognition, which he has called 'collaborative emergence'. He has studied collaborative learning groups in classrooms and other settings, and collaborative creativity in teacher teams and in business organizations. In his current research, he is studying how teaching and learning are organized in professional schools of art and design, with the goal of identifying a core set of features that can be used to design more effective learning environments.

Richard Walker is Associate Professor in the Faculty of Education and Social Work at the University of Sydney, Australia. He teaches educational psychology at undergraduate and postgraduate levels. His research interests have centred on ways of enhancing the learning, motivation and academic achievement of students at all educational levels. In recent years an interest in sociocultural theory has led him to investigate student learning in electronic environments designed to support collaborative and cooperative interactions amongst students; the use of textbooks and other learning resources; after school homework support; and identity formation. His most recent research activities have focused on the development of sociocultural approaches to the understanding of motivation, identity formation, and learning through homework activities.

Foreword
Vera John-Steiner

Drama is an excellent lens through which to view Vygotsky's theories of learning, development, language and creativity. As a young man, he was deeply involved with the theatre in his native hometown of Gomel in Belarus. His first publication, *The Psychology of Art* (1925), deals extensively with *Hamlet* within the context of a broader theory about the transformative value of art. Central to his theory, first developed in this early work, was his understanding of drama, film, painting and writing as deeply social processes. One of his most significant comments is that:

> Art is the social within us, and even if its action is performed by a single individual it does not mean that its essence is individual... Art is the social technique of emotion, a tool of society which brings the most intimate and personal aspects of our being into the circle of social life.
>
> (Vygotsky, 1971: 249)

In this view, the artist, even when engaged in solitary endeavours, is shaped and is shaping social artifacts that are shared by others. The creative process is not polarized into the individual and the group but is a process that integrates them in many different ways. Solo and shared activities combine like water from different sources into a mighty river.

Vygotsky approached the topics of his concern by viewing them developmentally. When exploring imagination, he first examined play as the means by which the growing child attempts to fulfil desires that are not attainable in reality. In early play, the child is inspired by interaction with caregivers who imitate the child's early groping gestures and give meaning to them by seeing the broader implications of what the child is attempting to accomplish. Stories, toys and small adventures are introduced into the child's life by his or her siblings or parents, and they provide the helpful artifacts which broaden the scope and pleasure of children's imaginative activities. These socially constructed artifacts are akin to the use of props that actors rely upon in their construction of a character in a play. While imagination is scaffolded in early development, its role is central to human adaptation. There is a growing literature on play, based in part on Vygotsky's ideas, including some excellent chapters in this volume.

Drawings and images are crucial to children's early expression of their emotions, but in play several modalities are engaged: children move while exploring musical instruments, they also speak and sing, developing their imagination more fully. Marjanovic-Shane (2010) describes the relational, emotional and transformative nature of play as a means by which stress, fears and aspirations have the potential to evolve into collective meanings through playful activity. In language, as children learn from storybooks, they can reach for 'the not here, the not now, the not real' (Connery and John-Steiner, 2012: 140). Dramatic play is facilitated by adults who demonstrate to children how a broom can be a dancing partner (Smolucha and Smolucha, 1986) or, as Vygotsky famously noted, a stick can become a rocking horse. Such object substitutions occur already in the second year of life and expand into more complex constructions through block play, dress up, musical explorations, and the dramatization of the texts of children's stories. Through play, children first exercise their imagination. 'By dragging a child into a topsy-turvy world, we help his intellect work because the child becomes interested in creating such a topsy-turvy world for himself in order to become more effectively the master of the laws governing the real world' (Vygotsky, *The Psychology of Art*, as quoted in Moran and John-Steiner, 2003: 69). Thus, play both expands and provides meaning to children's experiences. It is cathartic, and through expressing themselves in imaginative activities, children can also channel their emotions by these activities; a child with a working mother frequently dresses up with a purse and heels while enacting the goodbye scene of the parent leaving for her employment. Adults provide both models and encouragement for such ordering of painful or ambivalent feelings.

One of the most influential concepts in Vygotsky's theory is that of the zone of proximal development (ZPD). It is 'distance between the actual developmental level as determined by independent problem solving and the level of potential development as determined through problem solving through adult guidance or in collaboration with more capable peers' (Vygotsky, 1978: 86). This notion of support and modelling from more experienced others, which results in progress in learning and in independent performance, is widely quoted. Several authors have argued that it cannot be fully understood without situating it within the broader theoretical framework of Vygotsky's writings (Del Rio and Alvarez, 2007), that framework links learning and development not in a predetermined way, but 'it [learning] creates the area of potential development' (Vygotsky, 1934/1956: 452). When learning is open and dynamic – as in dramatic interactions – the internal, developmental processes of change and growth are complex processes that build on past experiences in all their varied forms. This is a subtle point in Vygotsky's theory, and it is often misrepresented. It is frequently viewed more rigidly. The variations in the process of appropriation of the culturally developed means and content of learning and the differing ways in which individuals explore and add to them are often underestimated. As Del Rio and Alvarez point out, Vygotsky viewed development as an open process (Del Rio and Alvarez, 2007: 280). This leads to variations in how individuals synthesize and shape what they have learned; they subsequently externalize their knowledge through imaginative constructions and problem-solving skills. Every developing person is a participant in a shared and complementary human process, thus the ZPD needs to be considered both from an internal and an external perspective (Vygotsky, 1934: 282). Development is the ongoing, dynamic outcome of multiple influences that become the basis of new, and frequently creative, outcomes.

Crucial to this process is the role of culturally constructed artifacts. These can be objects such as the stool on which the small child stands, eager to reach a tap, or the powerful semiotic means of language or algebra. These artifacts are the mediational tools humans use without which 'people would be buffeted about by stimuli they happened to encounter as they went about in the world. Instead, semiotic mediation provides the means for humans to control, organize, and re-signify their own behaviour' (Holland and Lachicotte, 2007: 115). In the course of dramatic interaction we can notice a whole range of such artifacts: the playwrights' or improvisers' reliance on live language with its musical, metaphoric and emotional power; the skilful use of gestures, intonation, body language and props by actors; books, films and historical events that provide a background for novel productions. Some of these artifacts are tangible, such as a pencil or a computer, and are frequently referred to in cultural-historical literature as tools. Others are less immediate; they are signs that stand for an object, such as musical notation or words, but they, too, are socially produced and have their material features of sound and shape.

The whole range of socially constructed artifacts and their transformation into internal resources is distributed across different participants. Each of us is just a subset of the totality of human experience at any particular time. Children vary in what they are drawn to and what they master, whether in visual, musical or verbal domains, and they may start their specialization in certain activities when quite young. Such choices contribute to the beginnings of division of labour, which may emerge even in dramatic play. The appropriation of semiotic means and artifacts that characterize a domain (i.e. music) requires the transformation of a shared process into an internalized, personal one. In writing about tools and symbols, Vygotsky differentiates between those aimed at transforming nature and others 'aimed at the transformation of the mind' (Holland and Lachicotte, 2007: 290).

But the process does not end there. Internalization is one phase of a dialectical process that moves from past learning acquired and expressed in social contexts to new appropriations of artifacts and semiotic means, which once integrated with past knowledge is ready to be externalized. The full dynamics of these cycles of learning, acting, development, transformation and expression are hard to specify. But the illustrations of 'process drama' and dramatic interactions described in this book provide vivid insights into the ways in which skills and knowledge are apprehended, transformed and creatively expressed.

In dramatic performances we see highlighted additional aspects of Vygotsky's developmental systems theory. One of these is the unity of cognition and emotion. Holzman (2009) quotes him when she writes:

> He believed that the separation of intellect and affect was 'one of the most basic defects of traditional approaches to the study of psychology,' and those who do so are left with thinking as 'divorced from the full vitality of life, from the motives, interests, and inclinations of the thinking individual.'
> (Vygotsky, 1987: 50 in Holzman, 46)

Increasingly, cultural-historical theorists recognize the role of emotion in externalized meanings and behaviours of learners engaged in creating discourse and play. For instance, a recent, special issue of the journal of this community of scholars is devoted to *Psychology of the Emotions and Cultural Historical Activity Theory* by Vadeboncoeur and Collie (2013: 210) who quote Vygotsky when presenting a conceptual framework and empirical studies, emphasizing that:

> Thought has its origins in the motivating sphere of consciousness, a sphere that includes our intonations and needs, our interests and impulses, and our affect and emotions. The affective and volitional tendency stands behind thought. Only here do we find the answer to the final 'why' in the analysis of thinking.
> (Vygotsky, 1987: 282)

In their description of feeling, Vadeboncoeur and Collie provide a developmental account in early childhood when the infant experiences the naming of his/her bodily and emotional experiences by caregivers and the subsequent differentiation of these into more nuanced expression and awareness. The dialectical relationship between thinking and feeling that Vygotsky emphasized is effectively captured in several chapters in this book, presenting dramatic processes among school-age children. Language expressed in scripted roles, spontaneous comments and appropriated as private speech becomes quite significant during these years in the lives of young learners. The authors further write that:

> Dialogue, oral or written, becomes an occasion for moving between thought, feeling, and word, for engaging in the 'living process of verbal thinking' and feeling (Vygotsky, 1987: 249) ... Feelings are shaped by the cultural understanding that constitutes the norms and expectations in social environments regarding how to feel, how to respond to events and experiences, how to express feelings, how others feel, and how to respond to those feelings.
>
> (Vadeboncoeur and Collie, 2013: 217)

Adults further refine their modes of thought and emotion while engaged in their work, in their various communities, and in their family lives. In my own early work, I emphasized language, learning and cognition while neglecting emotion. Then, more recently, when exploring people's lives committed to creative projects in the arts and sciences, I discovered the power of feelings in motivating them (John-Steiner, 1997). This shift prompted me to read Vygotsky more thoroughly and discover, together with many of my colleagues, his notion of the dialectical unity of thought and feeling.

Another of his concepts that has come to the fore in more recent Vygotskian scholarship is *perezhivanie*, which has been translated by some as lived emotional experience. Others add that this event occurs in a social context but may affect participants differently based on their culturally patterned experiences, their family values and practices, and their roles in the classroom or at work. In his essay on *The Problem of the Environment* (Van der Veer and Valsiner, 1994) Vygotsky explores how to find:

> ... the particular prism through which the influence of the environment on the child is refracted, i.e. it ought to be able to find the relationship which exists between the child and the environment, the child's emotional experience (*perezhivanie*), in other words, how a child becomes aware of, interprets, and concurrently relates to certain events.
>
> (Van der Veer and Valsiner, 1994: 341)

Perezhivanie was a notion Vygotsky encountered in the work of the Russian theatre director Stanislavsky in his interactions with actors, and it is productively used by some of the authors in this book. Perezhivanie is linked to imagination which builds on lived experiences – both direct and fictional. It combines and recombines aspects of these experiences as they are expressed in creative outcomes in everyday problem solving, artistic products, dramatic dialogues and scientific results. This concept is of particular importance to theorists and practitioners engaged in dramatic processes in the classroom.

In writing about creativity, Vygotsky did not restrict it to domain-transformative events but noted that: 'No accurate cognition of reality is possible without a certain element of imagination, a certain flight from the immediate, concrete, solitary, impressions in which this reality is presented' (Vygotsky, 1987: 349). The tracing of this creative path is increasingly possible through the use of notebooks, interviews, video-tapes and films documenting the co-construction of the embodiment of imagination.

The dramatic process is a collaborative one. Vygotsky's deeply social theory of learning and development supports the co-construction of spontaneously produced or scripted dialogue; performing arts programmes; problem-solving activities engaged in by peers; and long-term collaborative partnerships. In examining carefully documented, sustained collaborations, my colleagues and I have identified a variety of ways in which partners teach what they know and achieve mutual appropriation. Whether the exchange is short-lived, like in many improvisational activities, or whether the joint endeavours are sustained over years, they are built on the principle mentioned above: that each person is but a subset of human possibilities at any point in time. We draw upon our interdependence to broaden our limitations, whether by the use of socially developed semiotic means, including texts, face-to-face discourse, scientific concepts and strategies, or by consciously pooling our efforts in carefully organized joint projects. I characterize the latter in my book *Creative Collaboration*: 'Collaboration thrives on diversity of perspectives and on constructive dialogues between individuals negotiating their differences while creating their shared voice and vision' (John-Steiner, 2000: 6). This volume gives voice to this adventure by many gifted teachers, artists, children and researchers who have succeeded in creating live drama in classrooms. They bring the experiences and words of young learners where it is most needed, in school rooms that they can, through their magic, claim as their own.

References

Connery, C. and John-Steiner, V. (2012), 'The Power of Imagination: Constructing Innovative Classrooms through a Cultural-Historical Approach to Creative Education', *Learning Landscapes*, 6(1): 129–54.

Del Rio, P. and Alvarez, A. (2007), 'Inside and Outside the Zone of Proximal Development: An Ecofunctional Reading of Vygotsky', in H. Daniels, M. Cole and J. Wertsch (eds), *The Cambridge Companion to Vygotsky*, Cambridge, UK: Cambridge University Press, 276–303.

Holland, D. and Lachicotte, W. (2007), 'Vygotsky, Mead, and the New Sociocultural Studies of Identity' in H. Daniels, M. Cole and J. Wertsch (eds), *The Cambridge Companion to Vygotsky*. Cambridge, UK: Cambridge University Press, 101–35.

Holzman. L. (2009), *Vygotsky at Work and Play*, London: Routledge.

John-Steiner, V. (1997), *Notebooks of the Mind: Explorations in Thinking* (2nd edition), New York: Oxford University Press.

John-Steiner, V. (2000), *Creative Collaboration*, New York: Oxford University Press.

Marjanovic-Shane, A. (2010), 'From Yes and No to Me and You: A Playful Change in Relationships and Meanings', in M.C. Connery, V.P. John-Steiner and A. Marjanovic-Shane (eds), *Vygotsky and Creativity*, New York: Peter Lang, 41–62.

Moran, S. and John-Steiner, V. (2003), 'Creativity in the Making: Vygotsky's Contemporary Contribution to the Dialectic of Development and Creativity', in R.K. Sawyer *et al.* (eds), *Creativity and Development*. Oxford, UK: Oxford University Press, 61–90.

Smolucha, L.W. and Smolucha, F.C. (1986), 'L.S. Vygotsky's Theory of Creative Imagination', *SPEIL*, 5(2): 299–308. Frankfurt, Germany: Verlag Peter Lang.

Vadeboncoeur, J.A. and Collie, R.J. (2013), 'Locating Social and Emotional Learning in Schooled Environments: A Vygotskian Perspective on Learning as Unified', *Mind, Culture, and Activity*, (20)3: 201–25.

Van der Veer, R. and Valsiner, J. (eds) (1994), *The Vygotsky Reader*, Cambridge, MA: Blackwell Publishers.

Vygotsky, L.S. (1925/1971), *The Psychology of Art*, Cambridge, MA: The MIT Press.

Vygotsky, L.S. (1934/1956), *Izbrannie psikhologicheskie issledovaniya*, Moscow: Akademii Pedagogicheskikh Nauk.

Vygotsky, L.S. (1978), *Mind in Society: The Development of Higher Psychological Functions*, M. Cole, V. John-Steiner, S. Scribner, and E. Souberman (eds). Cambridge, MA: Harvard University Press.

Vygotsky, L.S. (1987), 'Imagination and its Development in Childhood', in R.W. Rieber and A.S. Carton (eds), *The Collected Works of L.S. Vygotsky*, vol. 1, translated by N. Minick, New York: Plenum Press, 339–50.

Introduction: Vygotsky, Sociocultural Concepts and Drama in and for Education

Susan Davis, Hannah Grainger Clemson, Beth Ferholt and Satu-Mari Jansson

The entire future of humanity will be attained through the creative imagination; orientation to the future, behaviour based on the future and derived from this future, is the most important function of the imagination. To the extent that the main educational objective of teaching is guidance of school children's behaviour, so as to prepare them for the future, development and exercise of the imagination should be one of the main forces enlisted for the attainment of this goal. The development of a creative individual, one who strives for the future, is enabled by creative imagination embodied in the present.

(Vygotsky, 1930/2004: 87–8)

Introduction

Education and research, like drama, are primarily concerned with experience, learning, knowing and understanding. It is also the belief of many that, as Vygotsky argued 85 years ago, approaches to education should be concerned with the function of imagination and behaviour informed by a vision for the future, to enable learners to act in and on the present. Vygotsky clearly recognized the importance of the arts and creative education as essential for productive human development, even going so far as to identify the important role that drama could play in helping students and learners take the everyday material of human existence, in order to have experiences which could change identity, their worlds and futures.

While drama and performance practices have existed within cultures since ancient times, the inclusion of drama within school and other educational programmes, and the study of drama and theatre within the academy, are much more recent pursuits. The scholarly legacies that are drawn upon can be transdisciplinary in their nature, although they predominantly come from philosophical and humanistic traditions, with a focus on frameworks and explanations that shed light on how humans interact, think, create, communicate and learn – all key concerns for the revolutionary scholar and thinker Lev Vygtosky.

Given Vygotsky's personal interest in theatre and even explicit writing and theorizing about theatre (Vygotsky 1971, 1932/1998), and about drama and creativity (Vygotsky, 1930/2004, 1931/1998), it is surprising that he has been drawn upon less often in drama education research, compared to other educational theorists such as Dewey, Gardner and Bruner. In fact, Roper and Davis (2000) proposed that Vygotsky should be a key theorist for drama researchers to draw upon. They highlighted the relevance of his work to drama, with his understanding of the ways that sign and symbol systems are used to create and mediate reality and human consciousness through interactive processes. In contemporary drama education research, a number of key concepts are drawn from Vygotsky's work; however, these concepts have been referred to without a wider consideration of the conceptual landscape of his work.

The relatively slow uptake of Vygotsky's work in drama education research is most likely because of the way that his work, when it finally was translated and became available in the West in the early 1960s (published in English in 1962), was translated by and largely introduced and promulgated to the West through the fields of linguistics and psychology, before subsequently having a large impact on educational thought (Britton, 1987; Daniels, 2001; Vygotsky, 1962). However, drawing on his early passions and through considering the development of a child's thinking, Vygotsky focused a considerable body of work on the concept of 'creativity', the importance of the arts in education, and even the specific role of drama and child-constructed drama in education. In his work *Imagination and Creativity in Childhood*, he examined the nature of learning in different arts areas and specifically discussed the nature of dramatic creativity and even the special qualities of improvised drama created by children:

> ...drama, which is based on actions, and, furthermore, actions to be performed by the child himself, is the form of creativity that most closely, actively, and directly corresponds to actual experiences...Thus the dramatic form expresses with greatest clarity the full cycle of imagination.
> (Vygotsky, 1930/2004: 70)

He saw drama as building on children's play, which is the original form of drama. He believed that the most creative forms of dramatic activity for children were those where they were involved in creating the drama themselves. While these might be based on an existing piece of literature or story, he believed that works that were 'created and improvised by [children] are more compatible with children's understandings' (Vygotsky, 1930/2004: 72). Through these processes they are able to experiment and implement imaginative activity. This is perhaps why Vygotsky claimed, 'Thus, drama is the most syncretic mode of creation, that is, it contains elements of the most diverse forms of creativity' (Vygotsky, 1930/2004: 71).

Vygotsky also saw a link between onstage drama and the drama of everyday life (Smagorinsky, 2011), where dramatic tensions exist, and how thinking and learning is defined by affect, motive and emotional experiences. These ideas had some impact on educational thought but still have great relevance to practice and research concerning drama education and potential for much wider application. On the other hand, educational researchers have only recently become more interested in the Vygotskian work, which is more directly focused on explicating the importance of the affective domain to his theories of learning: how imagination works; the individual and social nature of creativity; and the specific concept of *perezhivanie*. Therefore, we believe the work shared through this book will be of interest and value to a diverse range of theorists, researchers and practitioners across the drama, theatre, performance, applied theatre, school education, educational psychology and educational research fields.

This new publication has its origins in research dialogues at the International Drama in Education Research Institute (IDIERI) and the International Society for Cultural and Activity Research (ISCAR) conferences. We discovered a growing number of drama researchers who had been independently exploring the application of Vygotskian and post-Vygotskian concepts and methodologies in various drama and education contexts. We also found other researchers who were well-known in educational and psychology fields, but also interested in the possibilities for drama education in realizing sociocultural and cultural-historical principles in practice. This book therefore draws together some of this boundary crossing work for the first time.

We begin with Vygotsky's early background and parallels with Stanislavski's work in post-revolutionary Russia, gradually moving through to twenty-first century applications of Vygotskian concepts in digital learning and contemporary work environments. While drama education and applied theatre researchers may be familiar with several of Vygotsky's key concepts such as zone of proximal development (ZPD) (Vygotsky, 1978), dual affect and the importance of play (Vygotsky, 1933/1966), here we also explore other less commonly cited work about art and drama (Vygotsky, 1971), creativity and imagination (Vygotsky, 1930/2004, 1931/1998) and perezhivanie (Vygotsky, 1935/1994) – variously translated as something akin to an 'emotionally lived experience'.

Methodological applications of Vygotskian and post-Vygotskian approaches to drama, applied theatre and education research will be presented, such as *playworld* analysis (Connery *et al.*, 2010), activity theoretical analysis (Engeström, 1987, 2003; Engeström *et al.*, 1999), and developmental work research (Engeström, 2001, 2005, 2009). Bakhtin's work is also drawn upon to further explicate the significance of dialogic relationships crucial for understanding dramatic play and creative practice (Bakhtin, 1981, 1990). Specific research projects are introduced as innovative research paradigms for analysing and understanding collective creative practice, change and meaning making.

Key Concepts and Developments in Sociocultural and Cultural-historical Theory of Relevance to Drama and Education

It is important to note that there is a wide spectrum of theoretical positions and approaches that may be clustered under the broad umbrella of sociocultural and cultural-historical theory and research. The work of Vygotsky and his associates is foundational work in this realm, and has in itself given rise to other branches of theory and practice.

Cole and Engeström (1997) root cultural-historical theory in particular Soviet psychology developments of the 1920s and 1930s, and the work of early twentieth-century Russian social scientists such as Leontiev and Luria was also particularly influential on contemporary thought on human interaction (Daniels *et al.*, 2007). A central premise of this work is that the historical development of human beings is not governed by the same laws as biological evolution. The theory of mind that they developed highlighted the importance of cultural mediation and tools for enabling humans to engage with and act upon the environment and themselves. Minick (2005) identifies the first phase of Vygotsky's thinking as focusing on a 'unit of activity mediated by signs that are used as tools … to control behaviour' (Minick, 2005: 33). In external speech, thoughts manifest themselves in words and in external signs that are then internalized both by the subject and by others. One becomes aware of the social implication of the signs that one creates:

> I am aware of myself only to the extent that I am another for myself, i.e. only to the extent that I can perceive anew my own responses as new stimuli.
> (Vygotsky, 1979: 30)

Shane, 2011). Lindqvist (1995) used playworlds to explore what she described as the common denominator of play and art, but playworlds have been adopted by scholars in Sweden, Serbia (the former Yugoslavia), Japan, Finland, Lithuania and the United States, to study many areas, from narrative competencies and creativity to agency motivation. These scholars have been, like Lindqvist, inspired by Vygotsky's theories of both play and art, as well as by diverse theories and traditions of play and art creation (Marjanovic-Shane, 2011).

Drama processes are also used in non-school settings for educational purposes, often referred to as Applied or Participatory Theatre and widely used in different contexts such as health and welfare sectors, and for various training purposes (Ackroyd, 2000; Nicholson, 2005; Taylor, 2003). Common features include working with role, narrative and engaging participants in exploring different problems and perspectives. Work of this nature often has a specific intention related to emancipatory and egalitarian agendas or change processes. The development of tools and processes by practitioners such as Augusto Boal has been particularly influential as the means for engaging audiences as participants and actors.

Boal developed his Invisible Theatre and Forum Theatre forms in Brazil, influenced by the work of educationalist Freire, whose *Pedagogy of the Oppressed* (Freire, 1996) was first published in 1970 (Boal, 1979). Audiences were invited to participate in the drama in order to feel empowered to change their situation. Boal's Forum Theatre was originally used in factories and workplaces, but quickly spread to other areas of society. In practice, the dramatic action may be frozen, discussed, re-run – with audience members stepping in – and reflected upon in order to seek new possibilities, 'which in adapted form offered methods by which young people could exert more control over the problem-solving process' (Jackson, 1993: 28). This work has been influential around the world, including the UK's Theatre in Education movement in the 1970s (Grainger Clemson, 2011). Crucially, for all forms of drama education, this brings us to the important considerations about the nature of the drama and human experience. Drama and theatre art forms are based on human experience and also draw attention to human experience; our motives, attitudes, experiences, our actions, consequences of our actions and different ways we may interact with others and our world. The experience of drama though shifts the frame for many educational experiences, from that of outside observer and analyst, to that of participant and 'actor'. Boal states that:

> ...all human beings are Actors (they act!) and Spectators (they observe!). They are Spect-Actors... Everything that actors do, we do throughout our

Within education, a key form that has emerged is *process drama* (Bolton, 1992; Bowell and Heap, 2001, 2005; Haseman, 1991, 2001; Heathcote, 1975; O'Neill, 1995; O'Toole, 1992; Wagner, 1976). It is a form of drama which is referred to throughout a number of chapters and which, we would argue, embodies the principles of Vygotskian and sociocultural theory in practice. With process drama there is often no intention of creating a performance or piece of theatre as such. The learning relates more to exploring human experience through dramatic form and episodes. Process drama in a classroom context may be used synonymously, though not exclusively, to refer to 'experiential learning' or 'imaginative enquiry' (Bowell and Heap, 2010) and dramatic inquiry (Edmiston, 2014). A key aspect includes the notion of 'role-taking', with the leader or teacher often acting in-role alongside their students, managing and extending the process both in-role within the drama and out-of-role outside the drama.

In process drama the concept of narrative is generally driven by the introduction of dramatic tension, inviting the participants to investigate and problem solve. This often requires an active engagement, with participants co-constructing the dramatic action, investigating, problem-solving and creating dramatic encounters, and extending their own learning and understanding. While there may be a final performance product to such a process, the focus is mainly on the meaning making and experience of participants. Together they help build fictional worlds, taking on various roles within specific frames with participants creating the text through a structured but open process. The expectation is also that the group take part in reflection and feedback, with these experiences being crucial to the synthesis and meaning-making process (O'Neill and Lambert, 1990).

Other process-driven forms of drama that embody sociocultural concepts that are discussed in this book include 'dramatic play' and this can be seen to have significant overlap with the practice of 'playwords' that has emerged through the sociocultural realm. The term playworld was developed by Swedish scholar Gunilla Lindqvist (1995) to name the activity that is a central component of her creative pedagogy of play. This can be described as advocating 'forms of adult and child joint play involvement that are respectful of the child's culture, creativity and spontaneity, in a way that promotes her emotional, cognitive and social development' (Baumer, 2013: 1).

Playworlds consist of adults and children creating a common fantasy together through a combination of adult forms of creative imagining, which require extensive experience, and children's forms of creative imagining, which require embodiment of ideas in the material world (Ferholt, 2009, 2010; Marjanovic-

The history of how drama came to be introduced into schools and educational curriculum contexts is specific to different countries and education authorities, but in general occurred through two ways. Influenced by progressive education arguments, drama was seen as a set of pedagogical tools that could provide opportunities for children to develop their self-knowledge and creative expression. In the United Kingdom and beyond, this was influenced by the practice and writings of Way (1967) and Slade (1954) and later by leading drama in education proponents such as Dorothy Heathcote (Heathcote and Bolton, 1995; Johnson and O'Neill, 1984; Wagner, 1976), Gavin Bolton (1979, 1984, 1992) and John O'Toole (1992) among others. The second key driver for including drama in school education was more through the recognition of theatre as a specific art form with its own related traditions, forms and texts. The introduction of drama and theatre specific discipline areas within schools and universities has been most often associated with the study of theatre forms, genres, texts, production aspects and performance in various modes.

There is often a distinction made between drama and theatre and the origins of the two words signal some of these differences. While drama draws on the Greek word *draō* for 'action', theatre is from the Greek *theatron* – 'seeing place'. Going beyond action and enactment, *theatre* suggests a prepared presentation in a defined space and of the dramatic genre (Pavis and Shantz, 1998). The actors share their rehearsed final product and the audience have culturally-mediated expectations of the presentation to evoke feelings such as amusement, joy or sorrow along with a common understanding of the conventions of theatre. The performance is both a prepared and a unique event (Pavis and Shantz, 1998). These events are distinct from drama experiences which may focus on a process of discovery, rather than performance.

A key feature of the process and art form of drama and theatre is that participants commit to the world of 'what if?' and to what Coleridge called a 'suspension of disbelief'. This means that participants are able to explore human roles, worlds and experiences that are fictional. Aspects may reflect real life and impact on real life, but there is a distinction and that can provide a safety net and potential for exploration and learning (Bolton, 1984; Davis and Lawrence, 1986; O'Toole, 1992). While the use of drama and theatre processes in different contexts – within and outside of educational settings – may not explicitly acknowledge or 'teach' dramatic form, it has been argued that factors such as suspension of disbelief, emotional involvement, dramatic tension, actor/audience relationship, and the expressive use of voice and the body are characteristic of this type of work (Prendergast and Saxton, 2009; O'Toole and Lepp, 2000).

Sociocultural perspectives on human behaviour can be linked to the development of naturalistic drama in Western Theatre. The significant shift at the end of the nineteenth century was to 'return to the analysis of character ... ordinary people in their natural setting, and ... examine the physical and social influences that made them what they were' (Styan, 1981: 9). Made popular by the work of Russian practitioner Stanislavski, though not exclusive to his pursuit for onstage 'truth', was a rehearsal process that explored characters and meanings through practical tasks (Grainger Clemson, 2011). The conventions of drama – of role, space and time – are used to discover different perspectives on characters and situations (Neelands, 1997). As problematized by Vygotsky (1932), the portrayal of a character is dependent on the socio-historical experience of the actor, and here we clearly see again the crucial intersection of theatrical, psychological and pedagogical thought.

While there are many developments in post-Vygotskian theory, of specific relevance to this book is that in the realm of Activity Theory and Cultural-Historical Activity Theory (CHAT) (Cole and Engeström, 1993; Engeström, 1987, 2001, 2003). Langemeyer and Nissen (2011) identify three important historical dimensions in CHAT:

- first, an 'all-encompassing history' in which aspects of behaviour such as learning and play have been developed throughout the existence of humanity;
- second, the 'cultural-history' of an issue, such as forms of learning following particular education reforms; and
- third, the 'specific histories' of live communities, which form the approach to data (Langemeyer and Nissen, 2011: 21).

CHAT places emphasis on mediation and tools, and in CHAT, the emphasis moves 'from the individual to collective subjects' (Ellis *et al.*, 2010: 3).

Key Concepts in Drama Education

Like sociocultural theory, drama education can be conceived of as a spectrum of theory and practice. Drama education can be described as pedagogical strategies to be used for achieving diverse learning goals, as a subject or discipline area studied in its own right, as a form of co-curricular activity with participants/students creating and sharing theatrical events and a toolkit or set of practices for engaging participants in organizational learning and change.

lives, always and everywhere. Actors talk, move, dress to suit the setting, express ideas, reveal passions – just as we do in our everyday lives. The only difference is that actors are conscious that they are using the language of theatre, and are thus better able to turn it to their advantage, whereas the woman and man in the street do not know that they are speaking theatre.

(Boal, 1992)

He draws attention to the way that communicative tools are used by humans in their interaction, but in the drama space the actions take on a particular force in that they have been purposefully selected. Returning to Vygotsky and his concern with the creativity of the child, we note his similar claim that 'the dramatic form expresses with greatest clarity the full cycle of imagination' (Vygotsky, 1930/2004: 70). In these 'Dramatic Interactions' we constantly create spaces for, facilitate and explore the way learners relate to this collaborative meaning making and the understandings that are developed through that social process. Here, in these chapters we offer a detailed examination of many of these related theories, key concepts and instances of contemporary research and practice.

Overview of the Chapters

This book is organized into four sections, beginning with a more detailed introduction to Vygotsky's life and concepts, moving on to other sociocultural insights into learning through drama. The third section explores the dynamics of meaning making through drama processes in the classroom, and the book concludes with broader examples of practice and research inspired by sociocultural approaches to drama, education and learning.

The first part begins with Chapter 1, in which Michael Michell uncovers Vygotsky, the pre-Moscow psychologist theatre critic – through a detailed analysis of a selection of his theatre reviews originally published between 1922 and 1923. Based on an analysis of newly available texts, notebooks and unpublished material made available from the Vygotsky family archives, and specially commissioned translations of Vygotsky's 1922/23 weekly theatre reviews, the chapter examines recurring themes and preoccupations in Vygotsky's early work, with reference to that of theatre director Stanislavski. Hannah Grainger Clemson takes this on to the next stage in Chapter 2. Here she examines the socio-political historical context in which Vygotsky was developing his work, and the aligned practice of Stanislavski. With both shedding light on the other, the intersection of their practices and published material reveals its influence on modern drama and pedagogical thought.

To conclude this part, Chapter 3 by Beth Ferholt explores perezhivanie in the context of playworlds (Lindqvist, 1995), which is a form of adult-child joint play that makes imagination and creativity available for empirical study. A composite definition of perezhivanie is described working from a sociocultural context drawn from Vygotsky (1994) and Vasilyuk (1988), but also drawing from an interdisciplinary group of scholars and writers. Findings are presented from a playworld experience conducted in a United States elementary school on a military base.

Part 2 begins with Chapter 4, in which Brian Edmiston introduces and applies core Vygotskian and Bakhtinian concepts to reveal the impact of dialogue and social positioning in relation to meaning making. These concepts are explored through dramatic inquiry processes related to workshops focused on Shakespeare's *The Tempest*. This case demonstrates that children may not only actively engage in social activities but also in dialogue with peers and adults to begin to develop social and academic understanding beyond what they might ordinarily do in a classroom.

In Chapter 5, Harry Daniels and Emma Downes, a performing arts teacher, are concerned with creativity, the identity of disadvantaged students and the transformative potential of drama lessons in secondary schooling. They explore understandings of the mutual shaping of figured worlds, and identities in social practice, aligning Vygoskian theory to examples of classroom drama practice.

Chapter 6 by Richard Walker *et al.* takes a sociocultural discourse approach (Gee, 2001; Gee and Green, 1998) and the view that people have multiple identities that derive from their performances in social contexts and the way that they are consequently recognized by other people. They fuse this with a sociocultural psychological approach (Penuel and Wertsch, 1995), taking the view that identity formation is dynamic and involves complex interactions amongst cultural tools and resources, and the sociocultural and institutional contexts of action. The chapter examines a sample of responses from a drama classroom in New South Wales, Australia, in the context of sociocultural approaches to drama learning, motivation and identity formation.

Part 3 begins with Chapter 7, in which Robyn Ewing examines how dramatic play and the introduction of process drama strategies across the early childhood and primary curriculum can facilitate work in the collective ZPD and link directly to enhancing children's language and literacy learning. In particular, the chapter looks closely at two snapshots of how drama strategies and experiences can enable students to engage in creative thinking and problem-solving by enabling children to make emotional connections and develop and extend their understanding of narrative.

Chapter 8 is a collaboration between Penny Bundy, Erika Piazzoli and Julie Dunn. Their focus is on a philosophical and practical alignment between sociocultural theory, the pedagogy of process drama, and additional language teaching and learning. They examine a case study to support their exploration of four Vygotskyian concepts: ZPD, dual affect, the cycle of imagination and perezhivanie, to understand engagement and learning as related to additional language learning and process drama experience. The case involved a class of newly arrived refugee children (with minimal, and in some cases, no English language) in a Brisbane primary school. In particular, they examine how the drama created meaningful contexts for the learners to communicate in a way that might not normally be available to them.

Patricia Enciso describes the meaning and practice of 'bringing the future into the present' in Chapter 9. She describes work with students in a Midwest USA middle school and a process whereby teacher-researchers invented and enacted 'new futures' with their students, through a dramatic inquiry which opened spaces for collective voices and inquiry about bigotry and advocacy among immigrant and non-immigrant youth.

In Chapter 10, Susan Davis outlines research that explored student learning and creative practice using Information and Communications Technologies (ICTs), in a secondary school drama education context. Vygotskian theoretical frames and, more specifically, CHAT were drawn upon to analyse data and understand the impact of an intervention. What emerged were key contradictions, which are identified through the short narratives of two students. These contradictions highlighted potential shifts which were possible to achieve development and learning, but also the different creative preferences of students and what they value about the 'typical' drama experience.

Part 4 begins with Chapter 11, where Satu-Mari Jansson demonstrates how CHAT can be utilized to investigate learning and developmental processes within a professional theatre setting. The subject of the study is a regional theatre company in Finland which has introduced an audience development and applied theatre function. Jansson provides a micro-historical narrative of The Rovaniemi Theatre in Finland, and draws from Development Work Research (DWR) to analyse data and identify the importance of two theoretical concepts: the organizational archetype and contradiction. Analysis shows how contradictions were experienced between established forms of activities and the new, more hybrid types of activities by the theatre's curatorial staff and outreach artists.

In Chapter 12, Anton Franks focuses on the nature of the interaction between environment and learning in drama and theatre education. He draws from a research project that looked at a teachers' professional education scheme run by the Royal Shakespeare Company in the United Kingdom. Two related questions guide the inquiry: 'How can the learning environment in drama and theatre education be characterized and conceptualized from sociocultural and cultural historical points of view?' and 'What is the relationship between activity and environment – that is, how do particular socio-spatial environments affect learning? Goffman's work on interaction and frame analysis assists in defining the characteristics of social environments in relation to socially organized activity. Social semiotic and multimodal methods are also used to focus down on the surfaces of bodily action and the embodied activity of socially organized persons.

R. Keith Sawyer reviews a range of performance traditions in drama and theatre in Chapter 13. He explores the creative interactions that are to be found in improvised performances to more ritualized and structured performances, and explains how the social and interactive dynamics of these processes promote some of the highest forms of creativity. Examples reviewed include Chicago improvisational theatre, oral traditions around the world, as studied by linguistic anthropologists, and the performance of scripted plays.

In Chapter 14, Satu-Mari Jansson studies relationships between Augusto Boal's Forum Theatre and the methodology of DWR. She focuses on an intervention, which was used for the purpose of developing the actions of managers in a work context. She asks how can Forum Theatre and the methodology of DWR be used as intertwined developmental resources? The study documents the process of building a narrative and 'anti-model' as a form of mirror data that concretized experienced contradictions.

Suggestions for Readers and Future Research

Whilst each of the chapters stands alone, they come together to represent subtle variations in sociocultural and cultural-historical perspectives in drama and educational contexts. We hope that readers will enjoy the opportunity to explore these ideas, concepts and approaches, grouped as they are into sections, but that our readers will also make comparisons across the different bodies of literature and across different practices. We hope that this book will be a catalyst for further exploration and research in drama and education, both in terms of practical action and in terms of offering new lenses for analysis. In this volume we chart the development of ideas concerning theatre, psychology and education over more than a century, and yet we would consider this field to be still relatively new and emerging. What is required now is for others to contribute experiences and perspectives to this dialogue, to further develop the potential of the theoretical work and research in action, to reflect upon the dramatic interactions that are present in their contexts, and that may be required to create the kind of future we, like Vygotsky, might aspire to.

References

Ackroyd, J. (2000), 'Applied Theatre: Problems and Possibilities', *Applied Theatre Researcher*, 1.

Bakhtin, M.M. (1981), *The Dialogic Imagination: Four Essays*, translated by C. Emerson and M. Holquist, Austin: University of Texas Press.

Bakhtin, M.M. (1990), *Art and Answerability: Early Philosophical Essays*, translated by M. Holquist and V. Liapunov, Austin: University of Texas Press.

Baumer, S. (2013), 'Play Pedagogy and Playworlds', *Encyclopedia on Early Childhood Development*, publisher online, accessed 5 November 2012, at: *http://www.childencyclopedia.com/documents/BaumerANGxp1.pdf*

Boal, A. (1979), *Theatre of the Oppressed*, London: Pluto Press.

Boal, A. (1992), *Games for Actors and Non-Actors*, London and New York: Routledge.

Bolton, G. (1979), *Towards a Theory of Drama in Education*, London: Longman.

Bolton, G. (1984), *Drama as Education: An Argument for Placing Drama at the Centre of the Curriculum*, Harlow: Longman.

Bolton, G. (1992), *New Perspectives on Classroom Drama*, London: Nelson Thornes Ltd.

Bowell, P. and Heap, B. (2001), *Planning Process Drama*, London: David Fulton.

Bowell, P. and Heap, B. (2005), 'Drama on the Run: A Prelude to Mapping the Practice of Process Drama', *Journal of Aesthetic Education*, 39(4): 58–69.

Bowell, P. and Heap, B. (2010), 'Drame is not a Dirty Word: Past Achievements, Present Concrens, Alternative Futures', *Research in Drama Education: The Journal of Applied Theatre and Performance*, 15(4): 579–92.

Britton, J. (1987), 'Vygotsky's Contribution to Pedagogical Theory', *English in Education*, 21(3): 22–6.

Cole, M. and Engeström, Y. (1993), 'A Cultural-Historical Approach to Distributed Cognition', in G. Salomon (ed.), *Distributed Cognitions: Psychological and Educational Considerations*, New York: Cambridge University Press, 1–46.

Cole, M. and Engeström, Y. (1997), 'Cultural-Historical Approaches to Designing for Development', in J. Valsiner and A. Rosa (eds), *The Cambridge Handbook of Sociocultural Psychology*, Cambridge: Cambridge University Press, 484–505.

Connery, M.C., John-Steiner, V. and Marjanovic-Shane, A. (eds.) (2010), *Vygotsky and Creativity: A Cultural-historical Approach to Play, Meaning Making, and the Arts*, New York: Peter Lang.

Daniels, H. (2001), *Vygotsky and Pedagogy*, Abingdon, UK: RoutledgeFalmer.

Daniels, H., Cole, M. and Wertsch, I.V. (2007), *The Cambridge Companion to Vygotsky*, Cambridge: Cambridge University Press.

Davis, D. and Lawrence, C. (eds) (1986), *Gavin Bolton: Selected Writings*, London, Longman.

Edmiston, B. (2014), *Transforming Teaching and Learning with Active and Dramatic Approaches: Engaging Students Across the Curriculum*, New York and London: Routledge.

Ellis, V., Edwards, A. and Smagorinsky, P. (2010), 'Introduction', in V. Ellis, A. Edwards and P. Smagorinsky (eds), *Cultural-Historical Perspectives on Teacher Education and Development*, Abingdon: Routledge, 1–10.

Engeström, Y. (1987), 'Learning by Expanding: An Activity-Theoretical Approach to Developmental Research', accessed 4 March 2013, at: *http://lchc.ucsd.edu/mca/Paper/Engestrom/expanding/toc.htm*

Engeström, Y. (2001), 'Expansive Learning at Work: Toward an Activity Theoretical Reconceptualization', *Journal of Education and Work*, 14(1): 133–56.

Engeström, Y. (2003), 'Cultural-Historical Activity Theory, the Activity System', available online, accessed 2 March 2009, at: *http://www.edu.helsinki.fi/activity/pages/chatanddwr/*

Engeström, Y. (2005), *Developmental Work Research: Expanding Activity Theory in Practice*, Berlin: Lehmanns Media.

Engeström, Y. (2009), 'Expansive Learning: Toward an Activity-Theoretical Reconceptualization', in K. Illeris (ed.), *Contemporary Theories of Learning*, Abingdon and New York: Routledge.

Engeström, Y., Miettinen, R. and Punamaki, R. (eds) (1999), *Perspectives on Activity Theory*, Cambridge: Cambridge University Press.

Ferholt, B. (2009), *Adult and Child Development in Adult-Child Joint Play: The Development of Cognition, Emotion, Imagination and Creativity in Playworlds*, San Diego: University of California.

Ferholt, B. (2010), 'A Multiperspectival Analysis of Creative Imagining: Applying Vygotsky's Method of Literary Analysis to a Playworld', in C. Connery, V. John-Steiner and A. Marjanovic-Shane (eds), *Vygotsky and Creativity: A Cultural-Historial Approach to Play, Meaning-Making and the Arts*, New York: Peter Lang.

Freire, P. (1996), *Pedagogy of the Oppressed*, revised edition, London: Penguin.

Gee, J. P. (2001), 'Identity as an Analytic Lens for Research in Education', in W.G. Secada (ed.), *Review of Research in Education*, vol. 25. Washington, DC: American Educational Research Association, 99–126.

Gee, J.P. and Green, J.L. (1998), 'Discourse Analysis, Learning, and Social Practice: A Methodological Study', in P.D. Pearson and A. Iran-Nejad (eds), *Review of Research in Education*, vol. 23, Washington, DC: American Educational Research Association, 119–70.

Grainger Clemson, H. (2011), *The Social Drama of a Learning Experience*, Unpublished thesis, University of Oxford.

Haseman, B. (1991), 'Improvisation, Process Drama and Dramatic Art', *London Drama*, July: 19–21.

Haseman, B. (2001), 'The "Leaderly" Process Drama and the Artistry of 'Rip, Mix and Burn', in B. Rasmussen and Anna-Lena Stern (eds), *Playing Betwixt and Between: The IDEA 2001 Dialogues*, Bergen, Norway.

Heathcote, D. and Bolton, G. (1995), *Drama for Learning: Dorothy Heathcote's Mantle of the Expert Approach to Education*, Portsmouth, NH: Heinemann.

Jackson, T. (1993), *Learning through Theatre: New Perspectives on Theatre in Education*, London and New York: Routledge.

Johnson, L. and O'Neill, C. (eds) (1984), *Dorothy Heathcote: Collected Writings on Education and Drama*, Evanston, IL: Northwestern University Press.

Langemeyer, I. and Nissen, M. (2011), 'Activity Theory', in B. Somekh and C. Lewin (eds), *Theory and Methods in Social Research*, 2nd edition, London: SAGE Publications Ltd, 182–9.

Lindqvist, G. (1995), *The Aesthetics of Play: A Didactic Study of Play and Culture in Preschool*, vol. 62, Uppsala: Acta Universitatis Upsalensis.

Marjanovic-Shane, A. (2011), 'You are "Nobody"! The Three Chronotopes of Play', in E.J. White and M. Peters (eds), *Bakhtinian Pedagogy: Opportunities and Challenges for Research, Policy and Practice in Education Across the Globe*, New York: Peter Lang Publishers, 201–26.

Minick, N. (2005), 'The Development of Vygotsky's Thought: An Introduction to Thinking and Speech', in H. Daniels (ed.), *An Introduction to Vygotsky*, Abingdon, UK: Routledge.

Neelands, J. (1997), *Beginning Drama 11–14*, London: David Fulton.

Nicholson, H. (2005), *Applied Theatre: The Gift of Drama*, New York: Palgrave Macmillan.

O'Neill, C. (1995), *Drama Worlds: A Framework for Process Drama*, Portsmouth: Heinemann.

O'Neill, C. and Lambert, A. (1990), *Drama Structures: A Practical Handbook for Teachers*, Cheltenham, UK: Nelson Thornes.

O'Toole, J. (1992), *The Process of Drama: Negotiating Art and Meaning*, London and New York: Routledge.

O'Toole, J., and Lepp, M. (eds) (2000), *Drama for Life*, Brisbane: Playlab Press.

Pavis, P. and Shantz, C. (1998), *Dictionary of the Theatre: Terms, Concepts, and Analysis*, Toronto: University of Toronto Press.

Penuel, W. and Wertsch, J. (1995), 'Vygotsky and Identity Formation: A Sociocultural Approach', *Educational Psychologist*, 30: 83–92.

Prendergast, M. and Saxton, J. (eds) (2009), *Applied Theatre: International Case Studies and Challenges for Practice*, Bristol and Chicago: Intellect.

Roper, B. and Davis, D. (2000), 'Howard Gardner: Knowledge, Learning and Development in Drama and Arts Education', *Research in Drama Education: The Journal of Applied Theatre and Performance*, 5(2): 217–33.

Slade, P. (1954), *Child Drama*, London: University of London Press.

Smagorinsky, P (2011), 'Vygotsky's Stage Theory: The Psychology of Art and the Actor under the Direction of *Perezhivanie*', *Mind, Culture, and Activity*, 18: 319–41.

Styan, J.L. (1981), 'Modern Drama in Theory and Practice', vol. 1, *Realism and Naturalism*, Cambridge, UK: Cambridge University Press.

Taylor, P. (2003), *Applied Theatre: Creating Transformative Encounters in the Community*, Portsmouth, NH: Heinemann.

Vasilyuk, F. (1988), *The Psychology of Experiencing*, Moscow: Progress Publishers.

Vygotsky, L.S. (1930/2004), 'Imagination and creativity in childhood', *Journal of Russian and East European Psychology*, 42(1): 7–97.

Vygotsky, L.S. (1931/1998), 'Imagination and Creativity of the Adolescent', translated by M J. Hall, in R. Reiber (ed.), *The Collected Works of L.S. Vygotsky*, vol. 5, *Child Psychology*, New York: Plenum Press.

Vygotsky, L.S. (1932/1998), 'On the Problem of the Psychology of the Actor's Creative Work', in R. Reiber (ed.), *The Collected Works of L.S. Vygotsky*, vol. 6, New York: Plenum Press.

Vygotsky, L.S. (1933/1966), 'Play and its Role in the Mental Development of the Child, *Voprosy psikhologii*, 6.

Vygotsky, L.S. (1935/1994), 'The Problem of the Environment', in R. Van der Veer and J. Valsiner (eds), *The Vygotsky Reader*, Oxford: Blackwell.

Vygotsky, L.S. (1962), *Thought and Language*, Cambridge MA: MIT Press.

Vygotsky, L.S. (1971), *The Psychology of Art*, Cambridge, MA: MIT Press.

Vygotsky, L.S. (1978), *Mind in Society: The Development of Higher Psychological Processes*, Cambridge MA: Harvard University Press.

Wagner, B.J. (1976), *Dorothy Heathcote: Drama as a Learning Medium*, Washington DC: National Education Association of the United States.

Way, B. (1967), *Development through Drama*, London: Longman.

Part I

Vygotsky, Drama, *Perezhivanie* and the Unity of Development

1

Dramatic Interactions: From Vygotsky's Life of Drama to the Drama of Life

Michael Michell

Introduction

The greatest challenge a reader of Vygotsky's works faces is gaining an understanding of his theoretical system as a whole. Such understanding is an 'architectural' one that requires tracing the foundations and development of his theoretical concepts, identifying the relationships between them, and interpreting them within the argument structure in which they are expressed. In this respect, Vygotsky's theoretical system illustrates his notion of scientific knowledge as an organized system of abstract concepts, general propositions and dialectical thinking (Vygotsky, 1987), an interconnectedness Karpov (2005) identifies as the key to understanding Vygotsky's work as a whole.

Moreover, Vygotsky's system of thinking was itself in a continual state of evolution (Yaroshevsky and Gurgenidze, 1997). The development of his cultural psychology over the last decade of his life reflected the same internal change dynamics that he used to describe the self-transformational structures and processes of his object of study – the psyche. Understanding Vygotsky's developing thought therefore rests on knowledge of the status and chronological periods of his text production, critical to assessing the meaning and significance of his work as a whole.

There have been long-standing issues of the completeness and chronology of his six volume *Collected Works* (Vygotsky, 1987–1999), access to unpublished material, defective original texts, and poor editing and translations (van der Veer and Yasnitsky, 2011a,b). This situation has led *Dubna Psychological Journal* to collect and make available online Vygotsky's complete works and invite translation, analysis and commentary on these texts from international scholars (Yasnitsky, 2012a). In this context, a textual-historical analysis and reassessment of Vygotky's work based on an 'archival revolution' (Yasnitsky, 2010) is currently taking place in the recovery, reconstruction and publication of his texts. Initial analysis of new texts, notebooks and published and unpublished material made available from the Vygotsky family archives is giving new insights into the development and trajectory of Vygotsky's thinking and has located the origins of some of his later mature theories in his early texts (van der Veer and Zavershneva, 2011a,b; Vygotsky, 2010; Zavershneva, 2010a,b,c, 2012). With this understanding has come a new appreciation of the periodization of Vygotsky's work; the importance of his early writings on literature, theatre and art, and their influence on his later mature theories in his last and most productive period 1932–34 (Gonzalez Rey, 2011; Miller, 2011; Yasnitsky, 2012b), following his 'cognitive, instrumental period' of the second half of the 1920s. Understanding of the evolution of Vygotsky's thinking therefore requires an understanding of this periodic structure, bookended by his literary themes and preoccupations.

This chapter explores the lesser known connections and interactions between Vygotsky's life of drama and his psychology by employing a 'textological' approach to Vygotskian studies (Yasnitsky, 2010). It draws on recent developments in the recovery and publication of Vygotskian texts, in particular a first-time translation of Vygotsky's 1922/23 weekly theatre reviews, and aims to identify important connections that framed his theory of the sociocultural development of human psyche as a 'drama of life'.

Before becoming a psychologist in Moscow in 1924, Vygotsky's doctoral thesis on *Hamlet* formed the centrepiece of his 1925 work, *The Psychology of Art*. Two key ideas are fundamental to understanding his drama and psychology – the dialectic and the emotions. In *The Psychology of Art*, Vygotsky applied Marxian-Hegelian dialectics to understand a psychology of art animated by contradictions or collisions of literary form and content, and reader affect and intellect, to produce the transformational aesthetic-emotional release (synthesis) of catharsis:

> Aesthetic experience is the product of the influence of form on content, more specifically, of their collision in the work of art, the collision of the contradictory emotions generated by each which produces the annihilation of feeling, transforming the nature of the affects to produce the emotional release known as catharsis.
>
> (Lima, 1995: 418)

Vygotsky identified this cathartic, 'aesthetic reaction' (West, 1999: 53) as the mechanism by which art works on the human psyche; the literary text is the source and stimulus of aesthetic affect; and art itself functions as 'the social technique of emotion, a tool of society which brings the most intimate and personal aspects of our being into the circle of social life' (Vygotsky, 1925/1971: 249). While the concept of 'catharsis' does not appear again in Vygotsky's work, the role of the dialectic and the emotions move to centre stage in his evolving account of the drama of psychological development.

Vygotsky's Life of Drama – *Our Monday* Theatre Reviews

From 1917 to 1924, during the upheavals of the Russian Revolution and civil war, Vygotsky lived and became a prominent cultural leader in his native town of Gomel. As well as organizing forums on classical and modern literature, he was head of the theatre section of the Gomel Department of People's Education, where he took an active part in selecting the theatre repertoire, directing plays, and writing and editing for the theatre section in the Gomel newspaper *Nash Ponedel'nik* (*Our Monday*) (West, 1999), with some 67 of his theatre reviews originally published between 1922 and 1923 (Yasnitsky 2012c). It is apparent that he saw himself as a cultural agent, mediating the audience's experience and critical understanding of new and old theatre:

> It has always been my calling to build up 'an air bridge of criticism' between the audience and the stage ... but not to put a stamp of 'good' or 'bad', not to give diplomas of talent or mediocrity, but to help the spectator to build his own critical perception of the performance – 'The Author of Theatre Reviews', *Our Monday*, #28
>
> (Vygotsky, 1923/2012: 172)

Vygotsky's cultural mission of giving praise to 'the minor poetry of ephemeral, sweet, small, local art' (Vygotsky 1923/2012) was just as important for Gomel's '16 candles of the provincial stage' (Vygotsky 1923/2012) as for the established urban centres of Russian theatre. The early years of the Russian Revolution affected all aspects of society, art and culture, accelerating developments in drama and introducing a new theatrical language. For Vygotsky, mastering this new theatrical language was essential to being able to break away from the artistic constraints of the old culture. This artistic revolution made Vygotsky's role as a 'facilitator' of the audience's understanding of the new language all the more necessary:

> To express new ideas, new art has to master a new language. What happened before us is like an echo of the search for a new theatrical language. Every

> form of art, including the theatre, is in its essence a language, a form to express new ideas. It takes time to understand this language. Spectators may fail to comprehend it at once, so this process should be facilitated. The very fact that this new language takes us away from the flatness of a suffocating culture and spirit of the last century, entirely justifies using it – 'The First Swallow', *Our Monday*, #32,
>
> (Vygotsky, 1923/2012: 174)

The reviews are necessarily brief, typically half to one-and-a-half pages in length. First, Vygotsky typically locates the play – its plot, characters, themes and performance style – in the context of the original literary meaning ('essence'), reflecting his strong cultural historical approach to artistic analysis and appraisal. Second, Vygotsky typically evaluates the production – its acting and staging – from the perspective of how well it realizes the meaning and dramatic potential of the original play. Here, Vygotsky draws heavily on a 'Stanislavskian template' of organic as opposed to representational acting as his main criteria of theatrical success.

To understand Vygotsky's theatre reviews, an understanding of the concept of *perezhivanie* as the deep onstage psychological connection between character, actor and audience, promoted by contemporary theatre director Konstantin Stanislavski, is essential. As the 'genuine penetration of a psychic state in a represented character' (Carnicke, 1998: 149), perezhivanie conveys the 'inner life of the character' through the actor's 'communication of that life onstage in an artistic form' (Stanislavski, 2008: 19). With perezhivanie, the actor convincingly 'lives the role'; without it, the actor merely 'plays the part'. The hallmark of Stanislavski's system is this distinction between *organic acting* (experiencing) expressing 'inner truth' and *representational acting* (pretending) reflecting 'theatrical falseness' (Gillett, 2012: 2). While organic acting grasps universal depths of human experience, representational acting reflects 'stock-in-trade' acting conventions such as merely reciting lines and mechanical clichés for indicating feelings.

This Stanislavskian binary pervades all Vygotsky's reviews. His review of the Red Torch Troupe's choice of dated repertoire at first appears unpromising, however:

> ...our theatre succeeded in getting real sparks of artistic theatrical life out of these cold flints. Both original literary works were adequately translated into the dramatic form of stage performance. After the first performance of the Moscow Studio, I wrote, 'that it seemed, that the very life of a soul, not just its image, was torn open, disclosed for the audience; the same psychological insight, the same full integration with the role, amazing

transformation of the experience of the artist, the same profound intimacy and external rigor and elegant simplicity of execution, which infects the audience and creates deep intimacy uniting the audience with what is opening up on the stage' – 'Tour of the Red Torch Theatre', 'The Green Ring', 'Mladost', 'Monna Vanna', *Our Monday*, #40.

(Vygotsky, 1923/2012: 195)

Found throughout many of Vygotsky's reviews, the first perspective is the sharp division he draws between the repertoires and forms of the old and new theatre. The collision between the two is indicative of the significant changes which Russian theatre was undergoing during this revolutionary period, as well as of Vygotsky's new self-appointed pedagogic role in this great cultural transformation. A second perspective is his interest in literature-drama transitions, in particular how well literary works translate into dramatic form and fulfil their artistic potential on the stage.

Underpinning these two perspectives is Vygotsky's ideal of living theatre and acting that 'reaches the souls of the audience' (Vygotsky, 1923: 19), which he uses to evaluate the quality of this and other performances. In this context, it is worth noting that the phrase Vygotsky uses to describe the psychological connection between actor and audience – 'infects the audience' – is a direct borrowing of Tolstoy's description (Tolstoy and Maude, 1930) of the theatrical impact of perezhivanie. Two themes identified from the excerpt – old and new theatre, and the Stanislavskian ideal of living theatre – are now further examined in Vygotsky's reviews.

Old and New Theatre

For Vygotsky, the acting of the new theatre is characterized by a new naturalism ('neo-realism') in order 'to develop a national theatre, whose repertoire will be able to reflect real life, rich in colours, sounds and smells' (Vygotsky 1923/2012: 171). This naturalism, it is hoped, will replace prefabricated, 'stock in trade' acting of the pre-revolutionary era:

> With neo-realism all the naturalistic, dramatically wrong patterns and stamps are finally eliminated from the stage. Characters became deeper, their gestures more precise, voices – quiet and thoughtful. Some actors still bear something from the decadence epoch, others remind us of Satyricon.
> – 'Theatre Miniatures', *Our Monday* #28.

(Vygotsky, 1923/2012: 170)

Even Stanislavski's neo-realism was not beyond falling into its own 'patterns and stamps' like the old theatre. Vygotsky maintains a critical perspective on the Stanislavskian theatre, despite his evident regard for it:

> Stanislavsky's system strives to replace the art of portraying emotions by the art of living these emotions (perezhivanie). The author called it a spiritual naturalism. Stanislavsky's system was based on the emotive subtext, each actor was supposed to convey by paralinguistic and linguistic means.
>
> The actor must live the feeling that he is playing, rather than just portray it. Stanislavsky's system was created as a means to combat empty theatrical artificially created patterns and stamps. Remarkably, it has been repeatedly pointed out by the critics that any system inevitably leads to the creation of new stamps. The very possibility of such a reproduction of artificially created patterns is an extremely important factor. – 'Red Torch Performance Tour': 'Cricket on the Hearth', *Our Monday*, #38.
>
> (Vygotsky, 1923/2012: 190)

Here, Vygotsky adds an important critical historical perspective which recognizes the importance of the transition and translation of artistic forms and conventions, and with it, the potential for Stanislavkian theatre to succumb to the ossifications of its own performance traditions, its own 'patterns and stamps'. This socio-historical perspective achieves full articulation in Vygotsky's later drama theory in *The Problem of the Psychology of the Actor's Creative Work*.

The Stanislavskian Ideal of Living Theatre

When reviewing particular dramatic productions, Vygotsky invariably invokes Stanislavki's ideal of living theatre:

> This life on the stage is surely not a real life, but a special life, which, as opposed to a picture, should shine through the eyes of the portrait. And the creation of this special life is a great creative act of theatre. – 'Tour of the Red Torch Theatre', 'The Green Ring', 'Mladost', 'Monna Vanna', *Our Monday*, #40.
>
> (Vygotsky, 1923/2012: 196)

The reviews usually devote considerable space to evaluating actors' performances. Whenever Vygotsky considers the quality of acting in a play, it is always from the perspective of this Stanislavkian binary of 'living on the stage' as opposed to 'playing a role'. Vygotsky's comments on acting and the actor in his review of

'Praise to the Jewish Theatre', is a typical example, echoing the language of Stanislavki's own theatre manuals:

> An actor should live on the stage to render this character, this psychological portrait in such convincing details. A typical mistake actors make is to try to play the character without living it, without being taken by his passions, without feeling pain and joy. This is not the case in this play. Her voice is expressive, her gestures full of life, she plays with her soul, not with her mind. There are actors that sketch roles, as though wearing masks. This actress is different. She gives us a spiritual diary of his roles. This is, without a doubt, an intimate and psychological game. – 'Praise to the Jewish Theatre', *Our Monday*, #36.
>
> (Vygotsky, 1923/2012: 173)

The 'mask' metaphor used in the review plays a significant role in Vygotsky's appraisals. Vygotsky uses the word and associated metaphors of 'image' and 'portrait' to describe the un-involved, non-living nature of representational acting, 'The actor is not playing a character portrayed by the author, not a human being, but a stage image, created for this play, without merging with it, staying always beyond and above it' (Vygotsky 1923/2012: 175). Such criticism echoes Stanislavski's injunctions to actors to wholly identify with the life of the character and not be guided by a visual or ideational mental representation of the character:

> One should not act an image ... Carry out all your planned actions correctly, penetrate into and sense all the thoughts contained in your role while you are on the stage, analyse your attitude ... and as a result of all that you will achieve an image. Don't force yourself into any schematic form on the stage.
>
> (Stanislavski and Rumyantsev, 2013: 105)

In describing representational acting in terms of 'wearing a mask' in contrast to creating inner life on the stage, Vygotsky articulates Stanslavski's ideal of living theatre as:

> ... something that I would define as an ability not just to pose before the audience, but live on the stage, a genius to apply his own inner world to perform as opposed to wearing a mask of the stage. – 'Theatre Miniatures', *Our Monday* #28.
>
> (Vygotsky, 1923/2012: 170)

Similarly, Vygotsky's use of related 'puppet' and 'marionette' metaphors to describe the un-involved, character-distancing nature of representational acting in contrast to living drama is an extension of the Stanslavskian aesthetic:

It will definitely take a while for the actors to learn to live on the stage, not to be marionettes moved by the strings without any feeling of what is going to happen. Each actor, no matter how insignificant is his part, should be a part of a whole, not playing his part separately, but living a drama, crying, laughing and making the audience believe that it is all real. – 'Silva', 'Mann Sollte Mann Sein', *Our Monday*, #30.

(Vygotsky, 1923/201: 171)

It is clear then that Vygotsky's theatre reviews owe much to Stanislavsky's system and language. These review excerpts are illustrative examples of the influence of the Stanislavskian binary of organic acting ('living the part') and representational acting ('playing the role') on Vygotsky's views as to what counts as good or bad theatre. The nature and extent of this binary throughout the reviews is summarised in Table 1.1 below.

The Problem of the Psychology of the Actor's Creative Work

After an interval of eight years, Vygotsky's 1932 paper, *The Problem of the Psychology of the Actor's Creative Work*, marks a resumption of his life of drama, this time as a social theorist of drama rather than a drama critic. In the light of his earlier theatre reviews, analysis of the paper represents a development in Vygotsky's thinking about 'theatrical psychology' (Vygotsky, 1999b: 237) and its connections between character, actor, audience and society. Once again, Stanislavsky's system is a key reference in Vygotsky's theorizing, though this time, instead of being a frame of reference for experiencing theatre, it becomes an object of cultural historical analysis, and a token in his cultural historical

Table 1.1 Stanislavskian binaries in Vygotsky's theatre reviews

'playing the role'	versus	'living on the stage'
portraying emotions		living emotions
fake, forced		real, natural
empty theatrical artificiality		spiritual naturalism, neorealism
puppets, marionettes, pulling strings		live on the stage
masks, rehearsal before the main performance		living a drama
patterns and stamps, image, stereotypes		life of a soul
posing		inner life

argument about changing social-psychological systems of consciousness. In this late text, then, we see a major shift in focus from audiences' lived experiences of theatre to an expanded historical perspective on the development of artistic consciousness and emotion through time and social space.

The Marxian-Hegelian dialectic which structured the thesis of *Vygotsky's Psychology of Art* makes a return, driving Vygotsky's cultural historical argument and analysis. Vygotsky poses the initial problem (thesis) of the actor's psychology in his reiteration of Diderot's 'paradox of the actor': 'must the actor experience what he portrays, or is his acting a higher form of "aping", an imitation of an ideal prototype?' (Vygotsky, 1999b: 239). Vygotsky highlights Diderot's paradox by noting two fundamentally contradictory 'systems of performance' (Vygotsky, 1999b: 240); one being the representational acting Diderot supported where actor and passions were distinct, and the other, Stanislavski's acting system where actor and passions merged. In Vygotsky's argument, Stanislavski's system represents *par excellence* the contemporary antithesis, or negation, of Diderot's representational conception of acting. Far from merely endorsing Stanislavski's system over Diderot's, however, Vygotsky advances his argument by a series of negations of the 'Stanislavskian negation'. This negation takes two basic forms: negation by incorporation within a larger unity, and negation of its own entity through multiplicity. These 'negations of negations' are an integral part of the logic structure of Marxian-Hegelian dialectic (Bottomore, 1991: 287) and, as such, are essential to understanding Vygotsky's argument as a whole.

As a first move in his argument, Vygotsky uses negation by multiplicity to localize, personalize and relativize the Stanislavsky acting system within a diverse field of theatre practices, styles and agents:

> Many who were active in the theatre produced extremely complex systems of the actors' performance in which they found concrete expression not only of purely artistic aspirations of their authors, not only canons of style, but also systems of practical psychology of the actor's creative work.
>
> (Vygotsky, 1999b: 237)

In a second move, Vygotsky then further negates the *internal* identity and stability of Stanislavski's system by drawing attention to its diversified form and expression at the hands of Stanislavsky's pupil, Vakhtangov:

> We see how the internal technique of Stanislavski and his mental naturalism come to serve completely different stylistic tasks, opposite in a certain sense to the one that they served at the very beginning of development. We see

how certain content dictates a new theatrical form, how a system proves to be much broader than the concrete application it is given.

(Vygotsky, 1999b: 242)

By propounding the view that Stanislavki's system is neither immutable nor universal, but subject to larger historical forces of artistic evolution and development, Vygotsky highlights the historical contingencies of Stanislavkian theatre in a way that recalls the socio-historical perspective of his earlier theatre reviews.

Connected to Vygotsky's negation by multiplicity argument is his negation by incorporation argument, which challenges the identity of the Stanislavski system by subsuming it within a broader system. The passage below marks a key transition from negation by multiplicity – which identifies Stanislavskian theatre as one among many particular stage systems – to negation by incorporation, which locates Stanislavskian theatre as part of a larger unified, historical social-psychological system:

> Stage systems, from the actor, from theatrical pedagogy, from observations of rehearsals, and during performance, which are usually enormous generalizations of the producer's or actor's experience, set specific, unique features of experience inherent only in the actor, as being of paramount importance, forgetting that ... that the actor's psychology comprises only a part of the total psychology in both the abstract-scientific and the concrete-life significance of this word.
>
> (Vygotsky, 1999b: 238)

As part of the move to reframe Stanislavskian theatre as a concrete instance of a larger unified, historical social-psychological system, Vygotsky identifies its fundamental limitations in terms of its individualistic focus on the psychology of the actor:

> We must not forget that the emotions of the actor, since they are a fact of art, go beyond the limits of his personality and make up a part of the emotional dialogue between the actor and the public. The actor's emotions ... become understandable only if they are included in the broader social-psychological system of which they are a part. In this sense one must not separate the character of the stage experience of the actor, taken from the formal aspect, from the concrete content that includes the stage image, and relation to, and interest in, that image from the social-psychological significance and from the function that it fulfils in the given case of the actor's experience.
>
> (Vygotsky, 1999b: 241)

This move to reposition Stanislavskian theatre experience within a larger sociocultural frame involves a certain negation of, and distancing from, the original phenomenon in question: 'In order to explain and understand experience, it is necessary to go beyond its limits; it is necessary to forget about it for a minute and move away from it' (Vygotsky, 1999b: 243). The end result of all these negations is an expanded perspective on, or synthesis of, 'art as the social technique of emotion' constituted through artistic reformulations of emotion, and interaction between audiences' theatre experience 'of the actor's embodiment' and wider 'social consciousness' (Vygotsky, 1999b: 241).

The synthesis of the dialectic argument reframes the original problem from one focused on the individual psychology 'of the actor's creative work, which changes from epoch to epoch and from theatre to theatre' (Vygotsky, 1999b: 239) to one encompassing the social psychology of theatre cultures over time. The paradox of the actor is then 'converted into an investigation of historical development of human emotion and its concrete expression at different stages of social life' (Vygotsky, 1999b: 244). A higher cultural–historical perspective is reached which is able to conclude that:

> ... the psychology of the actor expresses the social ideology of his epoch and ... it also changes in the process of the historical development of man just as external forms of the theatre and its style and content change. The psychology of the actor of the Stanislavsky theatre differs much more from the psychology of the actor of the Sophocles epoch than the contemporary building differs from the ancient amphitheatre.
>
> (Vygotsky, 1999b: 240)

This conclusion concerning the cultural–historical nature of theatre psychology is finally viewed as part of a higher enterprise 'to study the order and connection of affects' (Vygotsky, 1999b: 244). Such affects, however, cannot be studied as isolated mental processes, but need to be viewed as 'new alloys of mental functions and unities of a higher order ... in connections combining emotions with more complex psychological systems' (Vygotsky, 1999b: 244).

Vygotsky's Drama of Life

As we consider Vygotsky's late psychology, we can observe a reverse influence in which the cultural resources from his life of drama inform his theory of human developmental psychology as a drama of life. This influence can be detected in three ways – drama as metaphor, drama as meta-frame and drama as medium.

Drama as Metaphor

Drama is a guiding metaphor framing the formulation of one of Vygotsky's fundamental theoretical constructs – the social mediation of his general genetic law of cultural development. In his annunciation of the law, in his 1931 monograph, *The History of the Development of Higher Mental Functions*, both direct and indirect theatre metaphors are highlighted:

> We can formulate the general genetic law of cultural development as follows: every function in the cultural development of the child *appears on the stage twice*, in two *planes*, first, the social, then the psychological, first between people as an *intermental category*, then within the child as an *intramental category*. This pertains equally to voluntary attention, to logical memory, to the formulation of concepts, and to the development of will.
>
> (Vygotsky, 1999a: 106)

In his analysis of this passage, Veresov (2004, 2007) draws attention to Vygotsky's use of the theatre language of Russia's pre-revolutionary 'silver age'. Here, 'planes' refers to back and front stage performance areas, while 'category' is a specific theatre term referring to a 'dramatic event, collision of characters on the stage' (Veresov, 2007: 4). A theatrical understanding of these terms therefore changes the meaning of Vygotsky's social mediation from what appears to be a passive process of internalization of the social to an interactive, conflicted emotional struggle between inner and outer forces. In light of this, Veresov explicates the dramatic interaction inherent in Vygotsky's law:

> The social relation he means is not an ordinary social relation between two individuals. This is a social relation that appears as a category, i.e. as [an] emotionally coloured and experiencing collision, the contradiction between two people, the dramatic event, a drama between two individuals. Being emotionally and mentally experienced as social drama (on the social plane) it later becomes the individual intra-psychological category.
>
> (Veresov, 2007: 4)

Dramatic interaction therefore lies at the heart of Vygotsky's mediational process. This interaction manifests as inter- and intra-personal collision, conflict, contradiction and crisis in a struggle towards self-transformation – all of which are hallmarks of a dialectic process which Vygotsky saw at work in the unfolding development of the human psyche.

Drama as Meta-Frame

In the same 1931 monograph, drama moves from metaphor to meta-frame in Vygotsky's theorization of the cultural development of the child and human psyche (personality). The concept of drama itself becomes a higher-order perspective that encompasses all the contradictory, dialectic processes of development described above. Child development is seen as a dialectic outcome of interacting biological and cultural processes where 'what is unfolding is . . . the greatest drama of development – a collision of the innate and the social-historical' (Vygotsky, 1999a: 222). The concept of drama provides Vygotsky with a rich framework for describing the interplay of biological and cultural forces that go to make up the messy, non-linear path of human development, of 'revolutionary changes, regression, gaps, zig zags, and conflicts, in order to see that introducing the child into the culture is development in the true sense of that word' (Vygotsky, 1999b: 221).

Having applied processes of dramatic interaction as a meta-frame for describing and explaining child ontogenesis, Vygotsky also extends the frame to understanding what he considered to be the psychical entity driving this process of development – personality. For Vygotsky, personality was much more than an individual configuration of personal traits, but rather a dynamic cultural historical formation of a developing system of human consciousness resulting from sustained interactions between a person's motive forces of behaviour and their mastery of the cultural tools and means of their lived, social environment (Vygotsky, 1999b: 242).

Central to the development of personality in childhood was the emergence and activity of new psychological formations of consciousness, self-reflection and self-awareness, in particular the 'acting "I"' of early childhood (Vygotsky, 1999b: 248) and the 'reflecting "I"' of adolescence (Vygotsky, 1998: 181). In his 1930/31 handbook, *Pedology of the Adolescent*, Vygotsky represented the period of adolescence as the culmination of this development of reflexive human consciousness with its advent marking the interaction with (antithesis) and integration of (synthesis) the acting 'I' and the reflecting 'I' (Vygotsky, 1998: 181). Vygotsky captures the agentive, 'self-shaping' (Vygotsky, 1998: 180) qualities of this period of ontogenesis in terms of a new actor on life's stage:

> Here a new acting persona enters the drama of development, a new, qualitatively unique factor – the personality of the adolescent himself. We have before us the very complex structure of this personality.
>
> (Vygotsky, 1998: 180)

As well as being used to describe the development of personality from infancy to adolescence, Vygotsky also applies the drama meta-frame to consider the personality's internal developmental dynamics. The clearest indications of his thinking in this regard are found in an unpublished manuscript written in 1929 and later published in a Russian psychological journal as *Concrete Human Psychology* (Vygotsky, 1986). As the editor notes, these private notes were a preliminary sketch for *The History of the Development of Higher Mental Functions*, and provide a valuable window on Vygotsky's developing thinking in relation to some of the basic postulates of his cultural-historical theory from his classical works of the early 1930s (Vygotsky, 1986).

Of particular relevance to our argument, is that *Concrete Human Psychology* contains a number of new ideas and reflections about developmental dynamics of personality that were not dealt with until his later works. In the text, these ideas are often expressed, with related references, in elliptic, telegraphic sentences reminiscent of the abbreviated character of inner speech Vygotsky described in his last chapter of *Thinking and Speech* (Vygotsky, 1987: 274). The internal drama of development of personality is a recurring theme throughout the text, for example, '*A drama truly full of internal struggle is impossible in organic systems*: the dynamic of the personality is drama' (Vygotsky 1986: 67, original italics). These dramatic internal interactions are identified as either higher mental functions, or internalized but conflicting social roles. In the course of the text, it appears that application of the drama meta-frame leads Vygotsky to reconceptualizing the nature and interaction of his higher mental functions, stating that, 'They [the higher functions] can be most fully developed in the form of *drama*' (Vygotsky 1986: 59, original italics), as well as a reframing of the concept and development of personality 'as a participant in a drama. The drama of personality' (Vygotsky 1986: 68).

Concrete Human Psychology is a valuable example of writing as a 'thinking tool' for the incubation and development of ideas. Vygotsky's repeated references to Politzer and his idea of concrete psychology as a drama (Nakamura, 2000) clearly reflected his own interests, but also suggest that he was resolving to conduct further research along these lines in the future. New ideas about the internal drama of development of personality and the unified and generative character of the psyche sit uncomfortably alongside existing material from

Vygotsky's 'instrumental, cognitive period' and, in true dialectic manner, challenge, reframe and potentially transform them. It is worth noting that the nascent drama meta-frame evident in this text subsequently developed into a generative theoretical tool for further psychological research. Russian and Spanish researchers in the Vygotsky-Leontiev tradition have continued this trajectory of Vygotsky's examination of the human drama of development through developmental and psychodynamic research on 'personality' (Bozhovich, 2004a,b, 2009; Bozhovich and Slavina, 1968; Vasilyuk, 1991) and 'subjective sense' (Gonzalez Rey, 2002, 2004, 2007, 2008, 2009).

Drama as Medium

The third dramatic influence on Vygotsky's late psychology goes beyond using drama as psychological metaphor or meta-frame to using drama as a medium for psychological theorizing. This describes Vygotsky's use of Stanislavski's concept of subtext as both a model and a method for examining individual motives that lie behind and drive human thinking and speech, outlined in his 1934 publication, *Thinking and Speech*. This investigation involved identifying the internal dynamics of personal sense and meaning in addition to sign mediation through social interaction as 'thought is not only mediated externally by signs. It is mediated internally by meanings' (Vygotsky, 1987: 282). Vygotsky identified the new psychological unit of analysis encompassing this transition from thought to speech as 'verbal thinking', and characteristically highlighted its developmental significance in terms of a drama meta-frame:

> We carried our analysis from the most external to the most internal plane. In the living drama of verbal thinking, movement takes the reverse path. It moves from the motive that gives birth to thought, to the formation of thought itself, to its mediation in the internal word, to the meanings of external words, and finally to words themselves.
>
> (Vygotsky, 1987: 283)

Conducting such 'analysis of the internal planes of verbal thinking' (Vygotsky, 1987: 282), however, is extremely difficult before availability of speech recording technology and data transcription methods. In the absence of such resources, Stanislavski's theatre concept of subtext offered Vygotsky a way of 'examining the unexaminable' by providing both a concrete conceptual model and interpretative method. Vygotsky recognized that the theatre, specifically Stanislavskian theatre, provided the model for psychology in this area:

> The theatre faced this problem of the thought that lies behind the word earlier than psychology. In Stanislavski's system in particular, we find an attempt to recreate the subtext of each line of the drama, to reveal the thought and desire that lies behind each expression.
>
> (Vygotsky, 1987: 281)

As shown in Chapter 3, Vygotsky, in the last pages of *Thinking and Speech*, exemplified his concepts of motive and verbal thinking in action by directly applying Stanislavsky's notes 1916–1920, to selected lines from a 1906 Stanislavski production. This provides a clear example of Vygotsky's conscious use of drama as a textual medium and mediating tool for modelling new psychological concepts and developing new interpretative method. Given the theoretical significance of this dramatic interaction, we wonder whether Vygotsky's scheme of egocentric and inner speech might not also have its origins in his early thesis on *Hamlet*, a play chiefly performed through soliloquy, or 'speech for oneself' (Vygotsky, 1987: 71, 257, 259).

Conclusion

This historical analysis of Vygotsky's drama-related texts has highlighted a two-way dramatic interaction between Vygotsky's 'life of drama' and his 'drama of life'. The first has drawn our attention to the literary foundations of his early work as a resource for his life-long investigation into the nature and development of human consciousness. The second has drawn our attention to his specific understandings of drama as a lens for envisaging a 'concrete human psychology' capable of explicating the unfolding drama of development of the human psyche. Smagorinsky (2011) neatly captures this cross-over of life, psychology and art:

> Vygotsky sees personality, with its psychological foundation, and art, with its dramatic origins, as interrelated. The development of personality is fundamentally dramatic and the phenomenon of art is at its heart psychological, suggesting the necessity of both in the development of consciousness.
>
> (Smagorinsky, 2011: 335)

This dramatic interaction has also highlighted drama as a cultural resource for Vygotsky's psychological theorizing. Drama is represented in Vygotsky's work in two complementary ways: as unfolding stages of personal development (ontogenesis) and as conflictual interaction driving development (sociogenesis). Underpinning both is a dialectic drama of development involving sociocultural agency, transition, transformation and generativity.

References

Bottomore, T. (ed.) (1991), *A Dictionary of Marxist Thought*, Oxford: Blackwell.

Bozhovich, L. (2004a), 'Developmental Phases of Personality Formation in Childhood', *Journal of Russian and East European Psychology*, 42: 35–54.

Bozhovich, L. (2004b), 'L.S. Vygotsky's Historical and Cultural Theory and its Significance for Contemporary Studies of the Psychology of Personality', *Journal of Russian and East European Psychology*, 42: 20–34.

Bozhovich, L. (2009), 'The Social Situation of Child Development', *Journal of Russian and East European Psychology*, 47: 59–86.

Bozhovich, L. and Slavina, L. (1968), 'Soviet Psychology of Character Training', *Russian Education and Society*, 11: 3–15.

Carnicke, S.M. (1998), *Stanislavsky in Focus: An Acting Master for the Twenty-first Century*, Abingdon, UK: Routledge.

Gillett, J. (2012), 'Experiencing or Pretending – Are We Getting to the Core of Stanislavski's Approach?' *Stanislavski Studies*, 1, available online, accessed 11 April 2014 at: *http://stanislavskistudies.org/issues/issue-1/experiencing-or-pretending-are-we-getting-to-the-core-of-stanislavskis-approach/*

Gonzalez Rey, F. (2002), 'L.S. Vygotsky and the Question of Personality in the Cultural-Historical Approach'. in D. Robbins and A. Stetsenko (eds), *Voices within Vygotsky's Non-classical Psychology: Past, Present, Future*, New York: Nova Science, 129–42.

Gonzalez Rey, F. (2004), 'Subjectivity in Communication: Development of Personality', in A. Branco and J. Valsiner (eds), *Communication and Metacommunication in Human Development*, USA: Age Publishing, 249–70.

Gonzalez Rey, F. (2007), 'Social and Individual Subjectivity from an Historical Cultural Standpoint', *Critical Social Studies*, 9: 3–14.

Gonzalez Rey, F. (2008), 'Subject, Subjectivity, and Development in Cultural-Historical Psychology', in B. Oers, W. Wardekker, E. Elbers and R. van der Veer (eds), *The Transformation of Learning:Advances in Cultural-Historical Activity Theory*, Cambridge: Cambridge University Press, 137–54.

Gonzalez Rey, F. (2009), 'Historical Relevance of Vygotsky's Work: Its Significance for a New Approach to the Problem of Subjectivity in Psychology', *Outlines: Critical Practice Studies*, 11: 59–73.

Gonzalez Rey, F. (2011), 'A Re-examination of Defining Moments in Vygotsky's Work and their Implications for his Continuing Legacy', *Mind, Culture, and Activity*, 18: 257–75.

Karpov, Y.V. (2005), *The Neo-Vygotskian Approach to Child Development*, Cambridge: Cambridge University Press.

Lima, M.G. (1995), 'From Aesthetics to Psychology: Notes on Vygotsky's Psychology of Art', *Anthropology and Education Quarterly*, 26(4): 410–24.

Leach, R. (2004), *Makers of Modern Theatre*, Abingdon, UK: Routledge.

Miller, R. (2011), *Vygotsky in Perspective*, Cambridge: Cambridge University Press.

Nakamura, K. (2000), 'On L.S. Vygotsky's Conception of Concrete Human Psychology: In Relation to G. Politzer', *The Report of Tokyo University of Fisheries*, 35: 131–40.

Smagorinsky, P. (2011), 'Vygotsky's Stage Theory: The Psychology of Art and the Actor under the Direction of *Perezhivanie*', *Mind, Culture, and Activity*, 18(4): 319–41.

Stanislavski, K. (2008), *An Actor's Work: A Student's Diary*, Abingdon, UK: Routledge.

Stanislavski, C. and Rumyantsev, P. (2013), *Stanislavski on Opera*, Abingdon, UK: Routledge.

Tolstoy, L. and Maude, A. (1930), *What is Art and Essays on Art*, London, New York and Toronto: Oxford University Press.

van der Veer, R., and Yasnitsky, A. (2011), 'Vygotsky in English: What still needs to be done', *Integrative Psychological and Behavioral Science*, 45: 475–93.

van der Veer, R., and Zavershneva, E. (2011), 'To Moscow with Love: Partial Reconstruction of Vygotsky's Trip to London', *Integrative Psychological and Behavioral Science*, 45: 458–74.

Vasilyuk, F. (1991), *The Psychology of Experiencing: The Resolution of Life's Critical Situations*, Hemel Hempstead, UK: Harvester.

Veresov, N. (2004), 'Zone of Proximal Development (ZPD): the hidden dimension?' in Ostern, A. and Heila-Ylikallio, R. (eds), *Sprak som kultur – brytningar I tid och rum – Language as Culture – Tensions in Time and Space*, vol.1, Vasa, 13–30.

Veresov, N. (2007), 'Sign Mediation: Magic Triangle: Sign-mediated Action and Behind', in *ISCAR 2007, Fourth Nordic Conference on Cultural and Activity Research*, Oslo, Norway, 15–17.

Vygotsky, L.S. (1923/2012), Nash podenel'nik [*Our Monday*], Weekly Theatre Reviews, Issues 21–58, Gomel, *Dubna Psychological Journal, No. 3c*, translated by Olga Ignatova) Accessed 29 October 2014, at: *http://www.psyanima.ru/journal/2012/3/2012n3a6/2012n3a6.1.pdf*;

Vygotsky, L.S. (1925/1971), *The Psychology of Art, Scripta Technica*, Cambridge, MA: MIT Press.

Vygotsky, L.S. (1986), 'Concrete Human Psychology', *Psychologiya*, 14(1): 51–64.

Vygotsky, L.S. (1987), 'Thinking and Speech', in R. Rieber and A. Carton (eds), *The Collected Works of L.S. Vygotsky*, vol. 1, New York: Plenum Press.

Vygotsky, L.S. (1998), 'Part 1: Pedology of the Adolescent', in R.W. Rieber (ed), *The Collected Works of L.S. Vygotsky*, vol. 5: *Child Psychology*, New York: Plenum Press.

Vygotsky, L.S. (1999a), *The Collected Works of L.S. Vygotsky*, vol. 4: *The History of the Development of Higher Mental Functions*, R.W. Rieber and A.S. Carton (eds), New York: Plenum Press.

Vygotsky, L.S. (1999b), 'On the Problem of the Psychology of the Actor's Creative Work', in R.W. Rieber (ed.), *The Collected Works of L.S. Vygotsky*, vol. 6: *Scientific Legacy*, New York: Plenum Press, 237–44.

Vygotsky, L. (2010), 'Two Fragments of Personal Notes by L.S. Vygotsky from the Vygotsky Family Archive, Prepared for Publication and with Comments by E. Zavershneva', *Journal of Russian and East European Psychology*, 48: 91–6.

West, D.W. (1999), 'Lev Vygotsky's Psychology of Art and Literature', *Changing English*, 6(1): 47–55.

Yaroshevsky, M. and Gurgenidze, G. (1997), 'Epilogue', in R.W. Rieber and A.S. Carton (eds), *The Collected Works of L.S. Vygotsky*, vol. 3: *Problems of the Theory and History of Psychology*, New York: Plenum Press, 345–69.

Yasnitsky, A. (2010), ' "Archival Revolution" ' in Vygotskian Studies? Uncovering Vygotsky's archives', *Journal of Russian and East European Psychology*, 48: 3–13.

Yasnitsky, A. (2012a), 'The Complete Works of L.S. Vygotsky: PsyAnima Complete Vygotsky Project', *Dubna Psychological Journal*, 3: 144–8.

Yasnitsky, A. (2012b). 'Vygotsky as an Art and Literary Scholar', in V.V. Maltsev, The Soviet theatre of 1920s in Vygotsky's Assessment Kotik-Friedgut, B. The Seeds that Sprout: An Overview of Early Journalistic Essays of L.S. Vygotsky (1916–1923), and Other Papers'. *Dubna Psychological Journal*, 1: 154–5.

Yasnitsky, A. (2012c), 'Vygotsky's Early Works: Literary and Theatrical Reviews in Newspaper 'Nash ponedel'nik' [Our Monday] (Gomel), 1922/1923', *PsyAnima, Dubna Psychological Journal*, 1: 226–7.

Zavershneva, E.I. (2010a), 'The Vygotsky Family Archive (1912–1934)', *Journal of Russian and East European Psychology*, 48: 14–33.

Zavershneva, E.I. (2010b), 'The Vygotsky Family Archive: New Findings', *Journal of Russian and East European Psychology*, 48: 34–60.

Zavershneva, E.I. (2010c), 'The Way to Freedom', *Journal of Russian and East European Psychology*, 48: 61–90.

Zavershneva, E.I. (2012), 'The Key to Human Psychology', *Journal of Russian and East European Psychology*, 50: 16–41.

2

Stanislavski and Vygotsky: On the Problem of the Actor's and Learner's Work

Hannah Grainger Clemson

At a lecture, the well-known Professor of the Institute speaks:

'The milkmaid is afraid that her cow will be confiscated; the peasant is afraid of compulsory collectivization; the Soviet worker is afraid of the endless purges; the Party worker is afraid that he will be accused of deviating from the Party line; the scholar is afraid that he will be accused of idealism... Fear compels talented members of the intelligentsia to renounce their mothers, to falsify their social origin, to wiggle their way into high positions... Fear stalks everyone.'

(Afinogenov, 1935: 451)

Introduction

In this depiction of contemporary society, Afinogenov's hugely successful play, *Fear* (*Strakh*), produced by the Moscow Art Theatre in 1931, is indicative of the crossovers between artistic, scientific, social and political endeavours occurring at that time in early Soviet Russia. In the play, Professor Borodin's efforts to research behaviour away from politics have been challenged by a new, young Bolshevik researcher from the country. His plan to undermine this challenge and expose the Soviet system of control is betrayed by close associates and he is arrested after the lecture and interrogated. Sometime later he returns to his institution, where his rivals are now in charge. They offer him a position and, broken, old and apologetic, he accepts.

Within the fictional onstage world, social and political tension is created by the insecurity of a human's motivations, whilst in the world of the actor the tension is a matter of both personal psychological interpretation and stylistic physical portrayal. First, what are the subtextual – or inner motivational – voices of these characters? Second, how much should be revealed to the audience at each given point as they make sense of the world they are presented with (Wolfson, 2006)? These kinds of questions lie at the heart of sociocultural perspectives and were also taken up by the two early twentieth-century Russian figures that are the focus of this chapter: Konstantin Stanislavski (born Konstantin Sergeyevich Alekseiev), theatre director and one of the founders of Naturalist acting in Western theatre, and Lev Vygotsky, a Jewish Byelorussian psychologist with a passion for theatre, literature and philosophy (Blanck, 1992). This chapter explores the historical context of their psychological, scientific and artistic thought and practices, and moves towards a deeper understanding of the development of their ideas. The work of one sheds light on the other, and reveals an intersection of their practices and published material that created important fault lines of modern drama and pedagogical thought.

It was Stanislavski's beloved Moscow Art Theatre that staged one of the first productions of Afinogenov's controversial play. This was at the same time as Lev Vygotsky was Head of Research at the Moscow Institute of Defectology, Vygotsky also having a strong association with cultural and literary activities, both in his upbringing and the acquaintances he later kept (Van der Veer, 2007a), including the poet Mandel'shtam and film director Eisenstein (Van der Veer, 2007b). Both held thought and motivation at the core of their understanding of human behaviour; internal processes that manifested themselves externally and physically in the world. This influenced their concurrent investigations into the work of the actor and of the learner, which both responded to and challenged the ideology of the society they were in. It is unclear how often, if at all, they might have met and discussed their ideas. Might they have acknowledged each other as they passed in the street or even taken a stroll in the Aleksandrovsky Garden, near both their institutions, overshadowed by the walls of the Kremlin?

Much has already been documented about their separate careers through their own writings, including Vygotsky's Theatre Reviews (Chapter 1), and subsequently through the writing of others. In this chapter, I focus on the parallels in their terminology and expression of ideas, in order to explore how their work developed and eventually overlapped in the same complex and rapidly-changing ideological society. The other purpose of this chapter is to contribute to an understanding of the term *perezhivanie* – 'lived through' as a close approximation of the meaning of this word – and what it meant to both Stanislavski and Vygotsky as their perspectives developed over time. For both, the concept of perezhivanie was an ongoing practical investigation into the motivation and interpretation of human behaviour. It was a period of focus on motivation and problem-solving, and on tools and logical action; however, the term has been variously interpreted in subsequent years. I draw in particular from *On the Problem of the Psychology of the Actor's Work* (Vygotsky, 1999a,b) as a key text to chart the development of the 'systems' of both men, and take a loose chronological journey to explore the self within the environment, units of human internal motivation and external action, and the communication with the self and others.

The Internal and External Self within the Environment

Vygotsky proposed the term perezhivanie in 'On the problem of the environment', a lecture published in 1934 (although he had worked on the concept many years previously), as a unit of analysis to explore how one's environment affects one's psychological development; in other words, an emotional experience that is at the same time both personal and situational (Van der Veer and Valsiner 1994). He is understood to have attempted 'to capture the process through which children make meaning of their social existence'; how emotional experiences are internalized and understood, which can be different for individuals (Mahn, 2003: 129). Daniels reinforces this concept by explaining how Vygotsky 'understood perezhivanie as the integration of cognition and affective elements, which always presupposes the presence of emotions' (Daniels, 2008: 43). There are also distinct clues as to his understanding of the term that are evident in the language that he uses when he is writing about the theatre, as discussed later in this chapter.

Stanislavksi's use of the term has also been emphasized as a process for the actor (Smeliansky, 2008) and as an experimental scientific approach (Pitches, 2005). Stanislavksi's published records of rehearsal methods describe a concern that an actor attends to experience – perezhivanie – thus contributing to the internal state of the actor in the preparation and convincing performance of a role and the external theatrical state – *voploscenie*. Efreimov, who ran the Moscow Art Theatre for 30 years, reiterates the ongoing endeavour of the actor both to realize the character in action and to constantly (re)create life onstage in a spontaneous fashion (Smeliansky, 2008). This endeavour was in reaction to the prevailing style of theatre at the end of the nineteenth century that Stanislavski in particular felt was devoid of 'truth'.

He wanted to establish rational decision-making by the actor, in order to achieve more believable action onstage – 'inwardly well-founded, in proper, logical sequence and possible in the real world' (Stanislavski, 2008: 48) – rather than merely showing off to an audience in the 'bad habits' of older companies (Styan, 1981). Stanislavski asked 'What might be ... "if" ...' of his actors to begin the process of establishing such logical action. For example, one might move towards a door differently if a madman were thought to be behind it. The 'Given Circumstances' – the situation as imposed by the dramatist – were seen to be crucial, when coupled with the actor's imagination, in giving rise to genuine, living human passions and feelings. Thus the actor's own personal experiences are revealed themselves in actions and the audience 'judge the people being portrayed ... understand who they are, through their deeds and actions' (Stanislavski 2008: 55). In rehearsal, Stanislavski devised tasks for his actors that helped create the external world around the characters, increasing their sense of 'being', of 'living through'.

Texts were to be thoroughly researched and discussed before any practical work and actors were trained to have complete command of mental and physical states. The production as a whole also attended to the complete sense of the fictional world to aid the imagination, with highly detailed and accurate theatrical sets and costumes. Achieving this sense of 'truth' was encouraged by the emergence of plays written by Chekhov, amongst others, who focused on the minutiae of everyday interaction.

The Artistic and Scientific Laboratory (1917–1923)

During the Russian Civil War (1917–23) between the Bolshevik Red Army and its opposition forces, Stanislavski remained in Moscow but focused his efforts on establishing the First Studio for young actors. In 1922/23, his company toured America and were praised for joining the experimental theatre movement (Gray, 1964); however, when passing through Paris they were also criticized as being once revolutionary but already old-fashioned and 'conservative' (*Time*, 1923).

Feeling a loss of the original theoretical basis of his work when he returned to Moscow, Stanislavski quickly reorganized his studio and company in order to refocus the actor's training and rehearsal work on the *psychological* process. There followed 34 productions in the next 2 years, many of them Chekhov revivals but in 1924 also a few original works, including the psychological drama, *In the Grip of Life*, by Knut Hamsun. Although successful, he also alienated himself from other directors wishing to work in different styles (Gray, 1964) and so it should not be assumed that the productions were either mainstream or popular pioneering works of the time. Whether or not his artistic work was a purposeful turn to the work of scientific psychologists, what is certain is that a more 'systematic' approach was developing.

One of the terms Stanislavski used was *throughaction*: the bringing together of all the elements of a role in a continuous thread, as the character follows his 'inner drive' from one event to the next (Stanislavski, 2008). With a concern for the historical context, Stanislavski would ask his actors to extend their own characters' throughaction by imagining what events occurred before and after the action of the play itself, thereby extending the logic and purpose of the character. This transforms a sense of perezhivanie from being a present sensation to also reaching into the past and future. In his writing there is perhaps an attempt to conform to the more state-sanctioned Soviet psychological terminology by using alternative terms such as 'representation', 'appraisal' and 'will-feeling' (Benedetti, 2008). All contribute to an understanding of the function of throughaction as discovering the strength of impulses that beat at the heart of a character, of a human being. Discovering this would connect with the inner truth of a role, rather than merely imagining and reconstructing the external world.

At this time, Vygotsky returned from Moscow to his home in Gomel to become something of an educational and cultural leader. He taught a variety of subjects at local institutions and established himself as a critic and cultural advisor, which involved bringing touring theatre companies to Gomel. Eventually he was permitted to set up a laboratory where he was teaching and began to focus on psychological processes. He included art, diagrams and maps in his consideration of sociocultural psychological tools, demonstrating his continued reflection on the visual as influential in human activity. It is likely that contemporary designers such as Craig had also been influential in their visual representation of the human psyche and his favouring of semiotics, Wertsch and Tulviste (2005) believe, was probably influenced by Saussure at this time.

Minick (2005) identifies this phase as Vygotsky focusing on the *instrumental act*, 'mediated by signs that are used as tools ... to control behaviour' (Minick, 2005: 33). In the spirit of investigation, but also allying himself with the prevailing political climate, Vygotsky quoted Marx in his essay *Problems of Method*: 'if the essence of objects coincided with the form of their outer manifestations, then every science would be superfluous' (Vygotsky, 1978: 63). Here he is suggesting that external/physical representations are not as obvious or direct as their internal/mental counterparts. He emphasized his method as a focus on process rather than product; one that sought to differentiate seemingly similar (external) acts by further investigating their nature to see where they may relate to different (internal) processes.

Taking Stanislavski's work to assist in our understanding of Vygotksy – and vice versa – there is a clear recognition of the complexity of human behaviour, and the belief of both men that to understand external action, we must understand the psychological process, which involves desires and goals.

For Vygotsky 'mediated action' is the most basic action, and where acts involve cultural tools, of which a principal one is language. Nevertheless, the individual is never in isolation and never just a present incarnation of themselves. There will inevitably be differences from previous instances of that action, a creative event being one where an existing action pattern is transformed in a new context. Vygotsky states:

> To study something historically means to study it in the process of change ...
> To encompass in research the process of a given thing's development in all its phases and changes – from birth to death – means to discover its nature, its essence, for it is only in movement that a body shows what it is.
>
> (Vygotsky, 1978: 64–5)

Here we get a definite sense of such actions being 'organic'; this word also appearing in Stanslavski's terminology for the acting process and the life of the character (Gorchakov, 1974).

In recognizing the shift in theatre practice, and the practical application of such theoretical perspectives by Stanislavski and his actors, we can further appreciate Vygotsky's consideration of human behaviour through art, literary and theatre works. A conceptual belief in the external influences on internal thought that subsequently resulted in external physical action is clear in the work of both of them, and continued to develop within an ever-changing sociopolitical climate, over the course of the next decade.

Bureaucracy and Investigating Behaviour (1924–1930)

During this period, there was tight Communist Party control over both culture and science, but those who worked in these fields were also in conflict with each other (Kozulin, 2005). Psychologists made the distinction between objectivist and subjectivist perspectives, presumably not only in describing their work but to state their allegiance to, or critique of, Soviet ideology. Contemporaries would often use terms such as 'materialist' or 'idealist' to discredit others (Van der Veer, 2007b), as depicted in the play, *Fear* (described above). On the opening of his new Institute of Psychology in 1912, Chelpanov had been congratulated by Pavlov for his undertaking of the 'formidable' task of brain study, the reason Pavlov (known for his experiments on stimulus-response with dogs) had banned 'subjective' perspectives in his own laboratory (Kozulin, 1985: 25). Chelpanov sought to distinguish 'self-observation' from 'internal perception' in addition to keeping a 'neutral' experimental field from a Soviet ideological one (Kozulin, 1985). His criticism of materialism, however, only served to weaken his position and he was fired in 1923. Work in the field of psychology was a risky business, depending on one's allegiance to State-sanctioned opinion.

In 1924, whilst psychologists like Pavlov and Bekhterev continued to work on physiological mental processes, Vygotsky returned to Moscow. First living with his family in the basement of the Institute, he then moved to a small apartment on Serpuchovskaia, on the other side of the river, where students such as Leontiev and Luria would squeeze into the small room to discuss their research (Harré, 2006). In his early work at the Institute, Vygotsky's focus was on voluntary attention and goal-directed thought, not necessarily on social interaction. Minick believes this was an attempt to differentiate his work from that on conditioned reflexes and investigate his interest in semiotics without wholly rejecting the stimulus-response unit as the 'basic building block of behaviour' (Minick 2005: 40). In order to identify the unit of analysis, Vygotsky used the term *edinitsy* – directly translated at 'units' and perhaps better related to his scientific, experimental endeavours. This does not mean a separating of independent psychological functions but, again, an understanding of the complex relationships between mental functions; connections which change over time.

Previous translations of Stanislavksi from his Russian notes into English prose, most notably by American writer and translator Elizabeth Reynolds Hapgood, have also used the word 'unit' to describe a section of the text or an event of varying size that could be more thoroughly analysed, making the actor's work easier. On the surface this seems like a concrete link between Vygotsky and Stanislavski regarding their practical approach. However, by understanding Vygotsky's conceptualizing of the relationships and through a different contemporary translation of the original Russian texts, we see clearly a concern for breaking down the mental functions and yet making connections between them in order to discover a person's – or fictional character's – motivations and relationships with the world through action.

A related concept also partially lost in translation was 'objective', implying in English that it might mean the end goal of a person's action. It was, and is, frequently coupled with 'unit' to signify what an actor believes the character was motivated by at that point. Instead of 'unit', Stanislavski in fact used the word *kusok* – bit (as in of meat) – but with a similar connotation. The Russian word translated as 'objective' was *zadacha* – actually meaning task or problem – and which, rather than being the fixed entity that 'objective' implies, was framed as a question, to be fulfilled by *diestvie* (action):

> Tasks are the lights which . . . stop you losing your way . . . These are the basic stages in a role which guide the actor during the performance.
> (Stanislavski, 2008: 143)

Even by moving on to a new 'bit', the character's 'task' might not disappear in the next scene, but may be consumed into a new one. The crucial element in the process of experiencing a role was the setting of a problem, which gives life to both actor and character. This problem-setting and problem-solving is the key to achieving a spontaneity onstage that adds to the sense of truth. An actor must have here both the 'lived' experience of feeling the natural impulse to further action as well as having a consciousness slightly separate to the character that knows and moves forward to the next impulse. The actor will discover and rehearse these steps and then re-live it again in each performance.

In his introduction to *An Actor's Work* (Stanislavski, 2008), Donnellan describes his favourite anecdote about a dog that slept in the corner of Stanislavski's rehearsal room but 'just before the actors were to finish, the dog would already be at the door, leash in mouth, waiting to be taken home' (Donnellan, 2008: ix). This puzzled Stanislavksi who could not find an obvious reason for this regular occurrence.

Given the alternate behavioural theories by psychologists such as Pavlov, and the social and political moods at the time, we might suppose for a moment the dialogue about the dog's movement that might have ensued:

'Did someone ring the luncheon bell?'

'I think it was the prayer call of the little temple on the other side of Tverskaya'

'Or maybe he senses the censoring Glavrepertkom[1] gathering outside. . .'

In actual fact, as Donnellan relates:

> Finally, Stanislavski figured it out. The dog could hear when the actors started talking like normal human beings again. The difference between the fake and the living was ... sharp.
>
> (Donnellan, 2008: ix)

Stanislavski was immediately prompted to question the authenticity of his actors' verbal expression.

In 1925, Vygotsky wrote, 'I am aware of myself only to the extent that I am another for myself, in other words only to the extent that I can perceive anew my own responses as new stimuli' (Vygotsky, 1979: 30). This perspective can be equally meaningful to an actor. First, it relates to the self as operating on a continued line of its own action and subsequent new impulse. Second, in the social real and fictional worlds, it relates to how people/characters relate to one another and considers the interpretation and effect of one's own actions by and on others. Third, where a human might be more consciously aware of themselves as speaker to another, what Stanislavski may have found in the episode with the dog is another example of the continued struggle for the actor to maintain their sense of 'audience': aware of an interpretation of their verbal action whilst fighting against unnaturalness in the expression itself, so as to conform to onstage belief. This layering of goal-oriented action is important to consider when applying it to sociocultural theoretical frameworks.

Subtext and Social Signs (1930–1931)

An appreciation of the actor's negotiation of real and imagined worlds can be paralleled with Vygotsky's investigation into the development of a child's imagination. Minick (2005) identifies two later shifts, around 1930, in Vygotsky's consideration of the 'psychological system' and a new relationship between mental functions, including experiments concerning the development of word meaning, linked to the development of concepts. In *An Experimental Study of Concept Formation* he writes that a child's imagination and play are the key to understanding the link between their cognitive and social development. Where play in the early years might be reproduced experiences, the development of abstract thought in an imagined space, where thought and meaning are liberated from their origins, allows the child to substitute one object for another – for example, a stick for a horse (Minick, 2005).

In *On the Problem of the Psychology of the Actor's Creative Work*, published in 1932, Vygotsky fully confronts the significance of his work in relation to dramatic form – an old 'research problem' with new possibilities – where he attempts to resolve:

- the actor's ability to externally portray emotions and the audience to 'feel';
- the actor's inner feelings being coaxed from experience and generated 'artistically'; and
- the actor within a socio-cultural historical context.

Smagorinsky (2011) undertakes a rich and useful exploration of Vygotsky's various perspectives relating to art and theatre, drawing a link between his investigation into emotion with the work of the actor and his understanding of expression rooted in cultural context:

> An actor's ability to portray an emotion does not follow solely from the ability to produce tears or to construct an expression, but is dialogically related to genres and conventions of expression through which the culture of that expression realizes its ideology, social future, sources of emotions, and other situated aspects of appropriate emotional gesture.
>
> (Smagorinsky, 2011: 334)

Such a concept is best explored, as Vygotsky himself does so, through the idea of subtext. For Stanislavski, the subtext (*podtext*) was the images and words relating to the character's experiences, held in the mind of the actor in a constant stream throughout the performance. Whereas previous work focused on physical action, stirring feelings and experiences, now 'inner mental images are a decoy for feelings and experiences in words and speech' (Stanislavski 2008, 411). Reminiscent of Bakhtin's concept of dialogue as social transactions between speaker and listener (Voloshinov, 1973), Stanislavski was concerned with actors having conversations as they would do in life, requiring them to transmit, pause, receive. The pause indicates where the other person – the 'object' – needs to have time to decode the subtext or mental images that are being portrayed (Stanislavski, 2008: 407).

> There should be no soulless, emotionless words in the theatre. Neither should there be unthinking, actionless words. Words must excite all manner of feelings, wants, thoughts, intentions, creative ideas, aural and visual images, and other sensory experiences in the actors and their partners and, through them, the audience.
>
> (Stanislavski, 2008: 402)

Vygotsky believed that 'the living phrase, spoken by the living person, always has its subtext; there is always a thought hidden behind it' (Vygotsky, 1999a: 281), but he also acknowledged the nature of interpretation, open to actors; that multiple subtextual phrases could be ascribed to the same line, with very different meanings. To illustrate the relevance of theatre to his work, Vygotsky selects an extract from Griboedov's, *Woe from Wit*, performed at the Moscow Art Theatre in 1906, together with the 'Motives' as described by Stanislavski in his *Notes 1916-1920*. Berducci (2004) seems to mistakenly believe that Vygotsky assigned the motives in the chosen passage (and groups Stanislavki loosely with 'other literary figures' (Vygotsky, 2004: 344)), which highlights how little the two have been connected. It is perhaps Berducci but also Vygotsky who may not have fully appreciated the concept of defining the task or subtext at a given point. Its function is not only increasing one's awareness of the character's mindset but also giving the actor portraying them a problem, an ongoing spark to ignite vocal and physical action and a dynamic, lived experience.

> We come now to the last step in our analysis of verbal thought. Thought itself is engendered by motivation, that is, by our desires and needs, our interests and emotions. Behind every thought there is an affective-volitional tendency, which holds the answer to the last 'why' in the analysis of thinking. A true and full understanding of another's thought is possible only when we understand its affective-volitional basis. We shall illustrate this by an example already used: the interpretation of parts in a play. Stanislavsky, in his instructions to actors, listed the motives behind the words of their parts. For example:

Text of the Play – from Act One	Parallel Motives
SOPHYA:	Tries to hide her confusion.
O, Chatsky, but I am glad you've come.	
CHATSKY:	Tries to make her feel guilty by teasing her.
You are glad, that's very nice;	
But gladness such as yours not easily one tells.	'Aren't you ashamed of yourself?'
It rather seems to me, all told,	Tries to force her to be frank.
That making man and horse catch cold	
I've pleased myself and no one else.	Tries to calm him.
LIZA:	Tries to help Sophya in a difficult situation.
There, sir, and if you'd stood on the same landing here	
Five minutes, no, not five ago	

> You'd heard your name clear as clear.   *Tries to reassure Chatsky.*
> You say, Miss! Tell him it was so.   'I am not guilty of anything'
> SOPHYA:
> And always so, no less, no more.
> No, as to that, I'm sure you can't reproach me.
>
> – From *Thought and Language*, translated in Kozulin (1986);
> similar, though not identical, to Rieber (1999)

Vygotsky was curious as to the more complex relationship between the internal and external functions. Here, by analysing the work of the actor on subtext and dialogue, he seems to have found at least an artistic ally to his psychological questions:

> To understand another's speech, it is not sufficient to understand his words – we must understand his thought. But even that is not enough – we must also know its motivation. No psychological analysis of an utterance is complete until that plane is reached.
>
> (Vygotsky, 1986: 252–3)

Both Stanislavski and Vygotsky were concerned with the notion of the dramatist's construction of the characters' context, with the justification of action based on a logical sequence of human behaviour, and the connection between the inner emotional and external physical states. These processes are analysed by taking each goal-directed action and investigating both the social circumstances and the tools used to solve each task, which we recognize as forming the basis for other sociocultural theoretical frameworks subsequently developed by others. Whereas actions may be interpreted from a singular perspective, the challenge for the onstage actor in constructing the logical inner life of a character highlights the fact that in reality, too, human action may be governed by many different inner motives, which may only be revealed subtly. However, what is also a key part of the process is the interpretation by others of that individual's actions as signifiers of inner thought and emotion, dependent on their mutual social experiences and understanding.

'Fear' and Ending the Tale (1931–1938)

With Afinogenev's *Fear* already playing in Leningrad in 1931, the artistic pressure was on the Moscow Art Theatre's own production to 'produce a modern Soviet spectacle' (Wolfson, 2006: 96). Having been previously attacked for its relatively conservative style, not least by the playwright who himself was an officer of the

Russian Association of Proletarian Writers, the company was 'enjoying' a 'state sanctioned prominence' once more (Wolfson, 2006: 95). This play is an example of the cultural context crucial to our understanding of the work of contemporary artists and scientists. It offers another perspective on the complex psychological and social processes in human behaviour, and the matter of audience interpretation and their own sense of lived experience.

Interestingly, the set design differed between the productions. In Leningrad the stage floor sloped and the non-verbal gestures became more potent in their symbolic meaning for the audience (Wolfson, 2006), and suggest an acknowledgement by theatre practitioners at the time of the power of visual symbolic signs onstage. The Moscow version was nowhere near as abstractly realized, but even so, the demand for authenticity is typified in a startlingly knowing report sent from the Glavrepertkom (central censorship board) chairman:

> The ... interrogation scene is done in an entirely unacceptable fashion. A windowless room with dirty walls, with black doors ... which open without a sound – all this creates an unacceptably distorted representation of the way in which ... interrogations actually take place.
>
> (Wolfson, 2006: 116)

The play deals with the central issue of interpretation of behaviour, precisely the concern of psychologists of the time: reconciling – or not – the consciousness with action and emotion. The main character of Professor Borodin has been described as a composite of the reflexologists Bekhterev and Pavlov, the latter critical of the Bolsheviks until the Nazis came to power (Rosenthal, 1997). In the plot Borodin is arrested but manages to recommence his work by admitting his former errors in pretending to steer clear of politics whilst deliberately seeking to undermine the 'progressive' work of his assistant and the ruling authorities. Characters conceal their 'true' identity for fear of betrayal but their inner thoughts are hinted at through subtle non-verbal gestures and facial expressions – a subtext – that the audience can witness but other characters appear not to (Wolfson, 2006).

From an actor's perspective in the Stanislavskian tradition, the creative decision is how far to reveal the underlying motive or 'task' at a given moment in order to be both faithful to his character and allow the audience to appreciate this moment-by-moment discovery. This is 'the lived-through' experience of investigation just as the characters do in the play and the authorities do on-stage and in the world outside.

How 'regulated' human spontaneous social behaviour can be was a core question for the audience to have had presented to them, but in the context of

Soviet society this question is perhaps more pertinent. Vygotsky's writing on Imagination and Play seems a daring claim when one thinks that acceptable forms of children's play were distinguished by the People's Commissariat of Enlightenment, including the fact that fairy tales and 'frivolous' bourgeois toys were actively discouraged (Kelly, 2006). It is perhaps even more incredible that such ideas on imagination – the very core of the art form – could survive such public scrutiny.

In the 'social process' of theatre, Vygotsky states:

> The actor creates on the stage infinite sensations, feelings, or emotions that become the emotions of the whole theatrical audience. Before they became the subject of the actor's embodiment, they were given a literary formulation, they were borne in the air, in social consciousness.
>
> (Vygotsky, 1999b: 241)

The task of the actor highlights the complex and dynamic relationship between internal and external processes. What the audience in the play would have witnessed was action that was highly regulated, following months of intensive rehearsals. This is not regulated in the political sense, but in the context of a deep psychological system for the theatre, developed over decades. The onstage act is not as spontaneous as it is in its first instance of creation; however, the preceding development of the nuances of motivation and action is crucial. Vygotsky states:

> In the process of social life, feelings develop and former connections disintegrate; emotions appear in new relations with other elements of mental life, new systems develop, new alloys of mental functions and unities of a higher order appear within which special patterns, interdependencies, special forms of connection and movement are dominant ... The experience of the actor, his emotions, appear not as functions of his personal mental life, but as a phenomenon that has an objective, social sense and significance that serves as a transitional stage from psychology to ideology.
>
> (Vygotsky, 1999b: 244)

In the play, Professor Borodin's daughter, Valia, creates an abstract sculpture for a competition, but is given a harsh lecture by the judges about representing concepts in a simple manner to generate 'pure' thoughts. This event is meaningful not only in reflecting the drive for socialist realism but also the tension, dramatically and scientifically, between authenticity and complexity:

> Within the world of the play, the urgency of revealing the true motivation of every character is underscored by the fear of not possessing sufficient

information for distinguishing friends from enemies. Stage realism links sufficiency to complexity, to the tension between text and subtext. On the one hand, the play insists on the complexity of human motivations; on the other it insists on the transparency of artistic representation. This contradiction ... lies at the core of the theatrical method that manipulates the feelings and thoughts of the spectators by expressly seeking to capture on stage a picture of the world they will find authentic.

(Wolfson, 2006: 101–2)

How we perceive the world of the everyday and that of the artistic or scientific are not separable, as typified in the events that followed. Just three years later, Vygotsky contracted tuberculosis and died in 1934, aged 37. Though premature, this perhaps saved him from a worse fate at the hands of the authorities. His books were banned and his family kept his unpublished manuscripts under the bed in their apartment (Gindis, 1999). Three years later, Bakhtin, a writer and philosopher, fled to Moscow having already served in labour camps and six years in exile. Sheltered at a friend's house without residence permits, he wrote about laughter under the shadow of fear (Hirschkop, 1999). Similarly, Meyerhold was unemployed and under great threat but was looked after by Stanislavksi and given the reins to the theatre when Stanislavski died in 1938, aged 74. However, that year, Meyerhold – the surviving link between these two men, as a former student of Stanislavski and teacher to Zaporozhets, a student of Vygotsky – was himself arrested, tortured and shot.

Legacy in Western Thought and Practice

The immediate onset of the Second World War delayed publication of both men's works, and the varying translations and interpretations since this time have had a bearing on the dissemination of ideas and the development of key concepts in different directions. Nevertheless, the parallels are still evident and have implications for our perception of artistic and scientific concepts. Whilst Stanislavski was concerned with the individual within their social world as presented to a theatrical audience, Vygotsky also concerned himself with the human born of, but also acting upon, the world, and both acknowledged the power of emotion to motivate a being into action.

The actor's gradual release of external hints at the internal workings of the character went hand in hand with a concern for developing the audience's understanding and adding to the dramatic tension. Making the process of human behaviour transparent yet subtle was the key to onstage 'truth' and was dependent upon an audience being capable of reading such social signs. Similarly, human development in the everyday can be conceived of as a process that is inherently social in what both constrains and motivates us. Such concepts and practices have a long legacy in the training, rehearsal and performance of modern Western theatre.

Vygotsky's perspective on external language as part of the process of an individual's understanding highlights the importance of communicative tools in developing understandings and new perspectives, a creative event being one where an existing action pattern is transformed in a new context (Moran and John-Steiner, 2002). However, according to Vygotsky, the act of artistic creation cannot be taught (Oreck and Nicoll, 2010) and so the pupil must gradually acquire a way of communicating ideas and approach the task by directly acting upon the object of enquiry. Vygotsky's problematizing of the processes involved in imaginative activity continues to offer perspectives on contemporary educational practices and curricula that demand such abstract thought, acknowledging the importance of the transformation of thinking by reason into intellectual imagination as part of the preparation for future adult life (Vygotsky, 2004). Some 40 years after Vygotsky's original publication that introduced the term perezhivanie into his own body of psychology work, many Western educationalists called for pupils to 'take an active part in learning' (Barnes, 1976: 28), with exploratory talk and the negotiating of different ideas and experiences helping to form new understandings. This signalled a shift in focus to the language of the classroom, and the area of teacher and pupil talk (Edwards and Mercer, 1987; Edwards and Westgate, 1994; Mercer, 2000, 1995), and later to the development of learning tasks that facilitate empathy, which in many cases has included drama-based tasks that stimulate 'imaginative enquiry' (Bowell and Heap, 2010). This has led to a revised reading of Vygotsky's work in terms of emotion and bodily action, and research into the process of externally communicating internal psychological states in classroom settings. As Wright and Rasmussen state, students can be:

> ... taught to use their bodies as centres of perspective, in sight, reflection, motivation and agency. Students, therefore are taught to both listen to, and be 'in' their bodies, in order for them to express and be able to go 'out' of them.
> (Wright and Rasmussen, 2001: 227)

From uncertain beginnings of artistic and psychological experimentation, and political controversy, the legacy of perezhivanie is a concept that is at once artistic, scientific, social and psychological, and may yet be termed educational.

Note

1 Главрепертком – *a commission for approval of performers' repertoires*

References

Afinogenov, A. (1935), 'Fear (*Strakh*)', in E. Lyons (ed.), *Six Soviet Plays*, London: Gollancz, 393–469.
Benedetti, J. (2008), 'Endnotes', in K. Stanislavski, *An Actor's Work*, Abingdon: Routledge, 613–74.
Berducci, D. (2004), 'Vygotsky Through Wittgenstein', *Theory and Psychology*, 14(3): 329–53.
Blanck, G. (1992), 'The Man and his Cause', in L. Moll, *Vygotsky and Education: Instructional Implications and Applications of Sociohistorical Psychology*, Cambridge: Cambridge University Press.
Daniels, H. (2008), *Vygotsky and Research*, Abingdon, UK: Routledge.
Donnellan, D. (2008), 'Introduction', in K. Stanislavski, *An Actor's Work*, Abingdon, UK and New York: Routledge, ix–xiv.
Edwards, A. and Westgate, D. (1994), *Investigating Classroom Talk*, London: Routledge.
Edwards, D. and Mercer, N. (1987), *Common Knowledge: The Development of Understanding in the Classroom*, Abingdon, UK: Routledge.
Gindis, B. (1999), 'Introduction of Dr Gita L. Vygodskaya', *Remedial and Special Education*, 20: 329.
Gorchakov, N.M. (1974), *Stanislavsky Directs*, Connecticut: Greenwood Press.
Gray, P. (1964), 'Stanislavski and America: A Critical Chronology', *The Tulane Drama Review*, 9(2): 21–60.
Harré, R. (2006), *Key Thinkers in Psychology*, London: SAGE.
Hirschkop, K. (1999), *Mikhail Bakhtin: An Aesthetic for Democracy*, New York and Oxford: Oxford University Press.
Kelly, C. (2006), 'Shaping the "Future Race": Regulating the Daily Life of Children in Early Soviet Russia', in C. Kiaer and E. Naiman (eds), *Everyday Life in Early Soviet Russia: Taking the Revolution Inside*, Bloomington: Indiana University Press.
Kozulin, A. (1985), 'Georgy Chelpanov and the Moscow Institute of Psychology', *Journal of the History of the Behavioural Sciences*, 21(1): 23–32.
Kozulin, A. (2005), 'The Concept of Activity in Soviet Psychology', in H. Daniels (ed.), *An Introduction to Vygotsky*, 2nd edition, London and New York: Routledge.
Mahn, H. (2003), 'Periods in Child Development: Vygotsky's Perspective', in B.G.A. Kozulin, *Vygotsky's Educational Theory in Cultural Context*, Cambridge: Cambridge University Press.
Mercer, N. (1995), *The Guided Construction of Knowledge: Talk Amongst Teachers and Learners*, Clevedon, UK: Multilingual Matters Ltd.

Mercer, N. (2000), *Words and Minds: How we Use Language to Think Together*, Abingdon, UK: Routledge.
Minick, N. (2005), 'The Development of Vygotsky's Thought', in H. Daniels, *An Introduction to Vygotsky*, 2nd edition, London and New York: Routledge.
Pitches, J. (2005), *Science and the Stanislavky Tradition of Acting*, Abingdon and New York: Routledge.
Rosenthal, B. (1997), *The Occult in Russian and Soviet Culture*, Ithaca and London: Cornell University Press.
Smagorinsky, P (2011), 'Vygotsky's Stage Theory: The Psychology of Art and the Actor under the Direction of *Perezhivanie*', *Mind, Culture, and Activity*, 18; 319–41.
Smeliansky, A. (2008), 'Afterword', in K. Stanislavksi, *An Actor's Work*, Abingdon and New York: Routledge.
Stanislavski, K. (2008), *An Actor's Work*, translated by J. Benedetti, Abingdon and NewYork: Routledge.
Styan, J. (1981), *Modern Drama in Theory and Practice: Realism and Naturalism*, Cambridge: Cambridge University Press.
Time (1923), 'Theater: Theater Notes', 7 April 1923, accessed 17 September 2009, *Time*, available from: *http://www.time.com/time/magazine/article/0,9171,715269,00.html*
Van der Veer, R. (2007a), *Lev Vygotsky*, London and New York: Continuum.
Van der Veer, R. (2007b), 'Vygotsky in Context: 1900–1935', in H. Daniels, M. Cole and J.V. Wertsch, *The Cambridge Companion to Vygotsky*, New York: Cambridge University Press.
Van der Veer, R. and Valsiner, J. (1994), *The Vygotsky Reader*, Oxford: Blackwell.
Voloshinov, V.N. (1973), *Marxism and the Philosophy of Language*, translated by L. Matejka and I.R. Titunik, New York: Seminar Press.
Vygotsky, L.S. (1978), *Mind in Society: The Development of Higher Psychological Processes*, Cambridge, MA: Harvard University Press.
Vygotsky, L.S. (1979), 'Consciousness as a Problem of Psychology of Behaviour', *Soviet Psychology*, 17: 5–35.
Vygotsky, L.S. (1986), *Thought and Language*, translated by A. Kozulin, Cambridge, MA: MIT Press.
Vygotsky, L.S. (1999a), *The Collected Works of L.S. Vygotsky*, vol. 1: *Problems of General Psychology*, R.W. Rieber (ed.), New York: Kluwer Academic/Plenum Publishers.
Vygotsky, L.S. (1999b), *The Collected Works of L.S. Vygotsky*, vol. 6: *Scientific Legacy*, R.W. Rieber (ed.). New York: Kluwer Academic/Plenum Publishers.
Vygotsky, L.S. (2004), 'Imagination and Creativity in Childhood', *Journal of Russian and East European Psychology*, 42(1): 7–97.
Wertsch, J. and Tulviste, P. (2005), 'Contemporary Developemental Psychology', in H. Daniels (ed.), *An Introduction to Vygotsky*, New York: Routlege.
Wolfson, B. (2006), 'Fear on Stage', in C. Kiaer and E. Naiman, *Everyday Life in Early Soviet Russia: Taking the Revolution Inside*, Bloomington: Indiana University Press.
Worrall, N. (1996), *The Moscow Art Theatre*. London and New York: Routledge.

3

Perezhivanie in Researching Playworlds: Applying the Concept of Perezhivanie in the Study of Play

Beth Ferholt

Introduction

Cognition and emotion are still, often, separated in the social scientific study of development and learning. Vygotsky wrote of this separation that it is 'a major weakness of traditional psychology' and explained that this separation 'makes the thought process appear as an autonomous flow of "thoughts thinking themselves", segregated from the fullness of life, from the personal needs and interests, the inclinations and impulses, of the thinker' (Vygotsky, 1986: 10). The concept of *perezhivanie* overcomes the dichotomy between cognition and emotion. The concept of perezhivanie thus allows teachers and researchers to approach cognition and emotion as parts of a whole and to understand the relations between these processes without losing the complexity and fluidity of these relations.

This chapter focuses on *preschool didactics*, a field in which education and play (which is not drama, but is closely related to drama) are both central. Most preschool teachers do not need to be told that the 'fullness of life' is what matters most to the children in their classrooms, to themselves, and even to the majority of the guardians of the children they teach. Over the past decade, I have introduced the concept of perezhivanie to many preschool teachers and many have told me that they were already thinking about this phenomenon.

However, these same teachers have asked me to explore this concept further in our research and teaching projects together. They value perezhivanie in their practice and they appreciate that a theory of perezhivanie may be able to help them to strengthen this aspect of their practice. Perhaps such a theory could also help to refocus the field of preschool didactics away from individualism and I will return to this thought in my conclusion.

In this chapter I build a working definition of perezhivanie that draws from several different fields and genres. I build this definition while applying the concept of perezhivanie in analysis of an event in a *playworld*. I conclude with a brief discussion of how this concept could be useful to both teachers and researchers at this particular time within the field of preschool didactics.

Playworlds

The term playworld was developed by Swedish scholar Gunilla Lindqvist (1995), but has been adopted by scholars in Sweden, Serbia (former Yugoslavia), Japan, Finland, Lithuania and the United States (see Marjanovic-Shane *et al.*, 2011 for references to relevant studies). These scholars have been, like Lindqvist, inspired by Vygotsky's theories of both play and art (Vygotsky, 1971, 1978, 1987, 2004), as well as by diverse theories and traditions of play and art creation (Marjanovic-Shane *et al.*, 2011). In the *Encyclopedia on Early Childhood Development*, Lindqvist's *creative pedagogy of play*, in which playworlds is the central component, is described as advocating 'forms of adult and child joint play involvement that are respectful of the child's culture, creativity and spontaneity, in a way that promotes her emotional, cognitive and social development' (Baumer, 2013: 1).

In playworlds (Lindqvist, 1995), adults and children create, enter and exit a common fantasy together. They do this through a combination of adult forms of creative imagining, which require extensive experience (disciplines of art and science), and children's forms of creative imagining, which require embodiment of ideas in the material world (play) (Ferholt, 2009a; Marjanovic-Shane *et al.*, 2011). A playworld creates an opportunity for children to encourage adults to participate with them in play, while adults are engaged in encouraging children to participate in arts and sciences.

The ideal of modern Western childhood, with its emphasis on the innocence and malleability of children (Aries, 1962; Fass, 2007), has combined with various social conditions to promote two categories of play. Playworlds do not fall into either of the categories: in playworlds adults do not direct children's play towards adult-determined developmental goals; nor do adults in playworlds protect children's play from adult interference. Instead, in play worlds adults actively enter into the fantasy play of young children (Ferholt, 2010a; Marjanovic-Shane *et al.*, 2011).

Due to the ambiguity of play (Sutton-Smith, 1997), there is much debate about what defines a playworld activity as such. In the playworlds of the study that I will describe below, adults and children worked together to bring a work of literature to life (Lindqvist, 1995: 72) through joint scripted and improvisational acting, costume and set design, and multi-modal rehearsal and reflection. They shaped their classroom into a world inspired by a book.

The Playworld of this Study

In the playworld of this study the class with which we worked was a kindergarten and first-grade class that was located within a public elementary school on a military base in the United States. The participants included the 20 students of the class and their teacher, as well as myself and three other researchers from the Laboratory of Comparative Human Cognition at the University of California, San Diego. The book on which the playworld was based was C.S. Lewis's *The Lion, the Witch and the Wardrobe* (Lewis, 1950).

Over a single academic year, the first half of the novel was read aloud to the children and then the children became more and more active participants in the acting of the story until they collectively wrote and directed their own resolution to the novel's central conflicts. Playworld sessions occurred weekly, lasted approximately two hours, and included reflection upon the enactments in the form of discussion, free play or art activities. Most of these sessions included all four researchers playing the child heroes of the playworld. The teacher joined halfway through the sessions, playing the evil White Witch. The children joined during the sessions following the arrival of the White Witch, in-role as themselves, and the children were the primary planners of the final playworld sessions.

All of these playworld sessions involved set pieces and props created by both the adults and children, including some props that were designed to appeal to the participants' senses of touch, smell and sound. By the time that half of the sessions were completed the teacher, who had been moving the set pieces to the side of the classroom at the end of each playworld session, began to leave the set pieces in place throughout the week. The classroom was filled with the large, colourful structures and the teacher conducted all of his classroom activities in and around a cardboard dam, cave, castle and so on.

We videotaped all classroom activities related to the playworld project as well as adult rehearsals, adult planning meetings and individual interviews with adult and child participants. In addition, we collected field notes from all the adult participants and the many e-mail correspondences among adult participants.

Data analysis referred to in this chapter includes two types of analysis: analysis of discourse and communicative exchanges using transcriptions from the video and audio recordings, and the juxtaposition of the material of a playworld with poetic representations of this playworld (see Ferholt, 2010a, for a description of this second type of analysis). The description is excerpted from Ferholt (2010a); see also Baumer et al. (2005); Ferholt (2009a) and Ferholt and Lecusay (2010) for further details.

Building a Working Definition of Perezhivanie while Applying the Concept

The concept of perezhivanie allowed us to make sense of one child's unexpected behaviour during one event in this playworld, and helped us to make sense of the event as a whole. With this sense-making we came to understand that the playworld session that provoked this unexpected behaviour, which we had thought was one of the less useful sessions for the children, was actually very important to at least some of the children. This in turn shaped how we created subsequent playworld sessions with the children. We decided that the teacher should continue to play the role of the Witch. The concept of perezhivanie thus helped, in part, with data analysis during this playworld activity, and so shaped this playworld activity.

The following is a description (excerpted from Ferholt, 2009a, 2010a) of a few moments from this year-long playworld. This event took place when Michael, the teacher, entered the playworld for the first time by dressing as the White Witch in front of the children.[1] Preceding this event, the children had been wondering for many weeks who would 'be the White Witch' in their playworld. Milo is the pseudonym of the child whose reaction to his teacher, I will argue, may be understood using the concept of perezhivanie.[2]

The Event

>Michael is putting on his gloves in front of the children. Milo is holding his own right arm. He holds his arm while his finger points to Michael, joining his classmates in response to Michael's questions: 'So, who do you think is the White Witch?'
>
>Then, all of a sudden, Milo's right arm breaks free and starts to point back to himself. At this point Milo's face moves from what we researchers describe

as bored wariness to joy and pride. A second child who is sitting next to Milo, named Luke, then takes Milo's arm himself and moves it down, ending the pointing.

Luke falls into Milo from the side, embracing him, while another child who is next to Luke, Maya, also leans in. Heads touching, faces turned upward, the three children turn to look to Michael. Then Milo, who now has what we describe as an exhausted, ecstatic look on his face, raises his arm slightly and, with Luke still holding his arm, knocks his own chest with his fist, thumb up.

About a minute later, Michael reaches down for his white fur coat, which Luke is holding. As his teacher's white hands and arms move down toward Luke, Milo's own hands and arms reach up towards his teacher. Then Milo's hands open and fall to his lap, palms up, mirroring his teacher's hands. We describe Milo's facial expression as, at this point, showing great peace.[3]

Perezhivanie

I will first turn to some of the technical uses of perezhivanie within the disciplines of theatre (Schechner, 1985; Stanislavski, 1949) and psychology (Bozhovich, 1977; Vasilyuk, 1988; Vygotsky, 1994). I will then expand my definition of the term by drawing from the work of a range of scholars and artists whose studies of the properties of perezhivanie converge, often without their using, or possibly even being aware of, the term perezhivanie. While I will discuss the work of several key theorists of perezhivanie, I will not make a comprehensive survey of the growing body of literature on perezhivanie here.

Perezhivanie [pâr-uh-jhi-von-yuh] the Russian word, not the term, is commonly used and can be translated simply as 'experiencing'. *Pere* means 'again' and *zhivanie* comes from the verb stem *zhit*, meaning 'to live'. The verb, *pereivat* (*perezhivat*), does not have an exact translation in English but refers to the process of worrying or empathically suffering things through. Smagorinsky and Daigle write that *pereit* is one of the most frequently used words to describe emotion in Russia (Smagorinsky and Daigle, 2011, drawing from the work of Viktoria Driagins).

Robbins writes that perezhivanie 'is difficult to understand for those of us outside of Russian, because it really captures the "Russian soul" in so many ways' (Robbins, 2007a). Translation of perezhivanie into English (and many other languages) is indeed difficult in great part, because the English language itself separates emotion and cognition. Of course this difficulty in translating the word will inform but not hinder my project of creating a working definition of the term.

Origins of the Term

As explored by Michell and Grainger Clemson in the preceding chapters, perezhivanie was first used as more than an everyday word in the dramatic system of Konstantin Stanislavski (1949). For Stanislavski, perezhivanie is a tool that enables actors to create characters from their own re-lived, past lived-through experiences. Actors create a character by revitalizing their autobiographical emotional memories and, as emotions are aroused by physical action, it is by imitating another's, or a past self's, physical actions, that these emotional memories are relived.

The Dynamic Relationship between Emotion and Cognition, the Relationship between the Individual and the Environment, and the Unit of Analysis

Vygotsky himself described perezhivanie thus:

> The emotional experience [perezhivanie] arising from any situation or from any aspect of his environment, determines what kind of influence this situation or this environment will have on the child. Therefore, it is not any of the factors themselves (if taken without the reference of the child) which determines how they will influence the future course of his development, but the same factors refracted through the prism of the child's emotional experience [perezhivanie].
>
> (Vygotsky, 1994: 338–9)

In this way Vygotsky explains, generally, how cognition and emotion are dynamically related. We cannot ask what a child learned from a situation without taking into consideration the child's emotions in that situation.

Vygotsky then follows this statement with two mandates that describe the import of this observation. He first makes more explicit that perezhivanie *is* the relationship between individual and environment, and therefore that this phenomenon is central to his theory of development: 'It [psychology] ought to be able to find the relationship which exists between the child and its environment, the child's emotional experience [perezhivanie]' (Vygotsky, 1994: 341).

Vygotsky then explains that perezhivanie is methodologically essential in the study of human development. Perezhivanie avoids the loss of those properties that are characteristic of the whole, and thus makes possible analysis through units rather than elements:

> In an emotional experience [perezhivanie] we are always dealing with an indivisible unity of personal characteristics and situational characteristics, which are represented in the emotional experience [perezhivanie]. That is why from the methodological point of view it seems convenient to carry out an analysis when we study the role the environment plays in the development of a child, an analysis from the point of view of the child's emotional experiences [perezhivanie].
>
> (Vygotsky, 1994: 342)

Bozhovich (1977) argues that, 'for a short period of time Vygotsky considered perezhivanie as the "unity" of psychological development in the study of the social situation of development' (Gonzalez-Rey, 2002: 136, cited in Robbins, 2004). Despite the fact that perezhivanie was a key concept for one of the most significant scholars of human development, it remains a relatively obscure concept within preschool didactics.

Using the concept of perezhivanie, the event described above can be understood as Milo revitalizing his autobiographical emotional memories by imitating another's physical actions. Milo appears to experience himself as the White Witch, when asked who is the White Witch, and it is his hand that seems to do his remembering for him. (His hand is like Dr Stangelove's hand, as it escapes his grip to point to him, in the Stanley Kubrick film of that name (1964)). Later Milo's hands mirror Michael's hands as Michael reaches for his fur coat.

In this process Milo's cognitive and emotional engagements are inextricable. The relationship between Milo and his teacher becoming the White Witch *is* what we are looking at. The wider picture is that Milo is having a very difficult year and that his relationship with his teacher and his relationship with the role of the White Witch – his identification with the person of Michael and his role – gives him great strength in the face of his trials.

Overcoming Despair

Vasilyuk (1988) adapts Vygotsky's use of the term perezhivanie to describe a form of inter-subjectivity in which we insert ourselves into the stories of others in order to gain the foresight that allows us to proceed. He describes perezhivanie as an internal and subjective labour of 'entering into', which is not done by the mind alone, but rather involves the whole of life or a state of consciousness. And although, for Vasilyuk, perezhivanie is the direct sensation or experience of mental states and processes, another person is needed for this experience. It is this inclusion of another that allows a person to overcome and conquer despair through perezhivanie.

Working from within the framework of cultural historical activity theory, Vasilyuk (1988) gives us at once a broader and more specific definition of perezhivanie than does Vygotsky. But he has not actually moved further from the non-technical definition of the word 'perezhivanie.' As Robbins explains:

> '(P)erezhivat' means, if you look at it closely, that you have passed as if above something that had made you feel pain ... There, inside of a recollection that we call an 'again living' – lives your pain. It is the pain that doesn't let you forget what has happened. And you keep on coming back to it in your memory, keep living through it over and over again, until you discover that you have passed through it, and have survived.
>
> (Robbins, 2007a)

In the event described above, Milo is inserting himself into the story of others in order to gain the foresight that allows him to proceed. We also know that Milo is including another, Michael/the White Witch, as an important source of his perezhivanie. And, although we have no other evidence, I believe that it is a look of despair that we see flutter across Milo's face between the other expressions that I have described above. I think it is accurate to say that he appears to 'pass as if above something that had made (him) feel pain ...' (Robbins, 2007a).

Performance as 'Twice-behaved Behavior' or being 'Beside Myself'

Schechner integrates the work of the psychoanalytic play theorist D. W. Winnicott, Victor Turner and Gregory Bateson (in his discussion of the *play frame* (1972)) with his own work as a theatre director (Schechner, 1985). He claims that the underlying processes of the ontogenesis of individuals, the social action of ritual and the symbolic/fictive action of art are identical (Schechner, 1985), and he supports this claim by describing, in concrete detail, the process of perezhivanie. He does not use the term itself although he is, of course, familiar with Stanislavski's work.

For Schechner performance is perezhivanie. He writes, 'Performance means: never for the first time. It means: for the second to *n*th time. Performance is "twice-behaved behavior"' (Schechner, 1985: 36). Schechner calls this 'restored behaviour' and adds: 'Put in personal terms, restored behavior is "me behaving as if I am someone else" or as if I am "beside myself", or "not myself", as when in a trance' (Schechner, 1985: 37). Here we have Vasilyuk's (1998) form of intersubjectivity in which we insert ourselves into the stories of others in order to gain the foresight that allows us to proceed.

In the event under analysis, Milo is strikingly behaving as if he is 'someone else' or 'as if (he is) "beside (him)self", or "not (him)self"' (Schechner, as quoted above). It is part of a trance that '(w)hile performing, a performer experiences his own self not directly but through the medium of experiencing the others' (Schechner, 1985: 111–112), and through the pointing to himself and his inward-looking facial expressions it appears that Milo is certainly experiencing himself through his experience of Michael. Both Milo and Michael are 'not not' the White Witch, as will be discussed in more depth, below.

Prolepsis and Stages of Perezhivanie

The essence of Schechner's argument is that there are three parts to the process of performance, not two, and that in performance time flows in more than one direction:

> Although restored behavior seems to be founded on past events ... it is in fact the synchronic bundle (of three parts) ... The past ... is recreated in terms not simply of a present, ... but of a future ... This future is the performance being rehearsed, the 'finished thing' to be made graceful through editing, repetition, and intervention. Restored behavior is both teleological and eschatological. It joins first causes to what happens at the end of time.
>
> (Schechner, 1985: 79)

In this process we do not have one behaviour that is repeated. Instead of just remembering what came before, that which came before is shaped by a vision of the future. Specifically, the way that the flow of time becomes multidirectional is that 'rehearsals make it necessary to think of the future in such a way as to create a past' (Schechner 1985; 39). As Schechner explains, 'In a very real way the future – the project coming into existence through the process of rehearsal – determines the past: what will be kept from earlier rehearsals or from the "source materials"' (Schechner, 1985: 39).

Vasilyuk is describing the same phenomenon when he writes of the proleptic nature of perezhivanie in the development of Raskolnikov, the main character in Dostoevsky's *Crime and Punishment*:

> Although the given schematism 'fault – repentance – redemption – bliss' is formally expressed as a series of contents following one another in time, this

does not mean that the later elements in the series appear in consciousness only after the earlier stages have been traversed. They respond to one another psychologically and all exist at once in consciousness, as a Gestalt, though it is true they are expressed with varying degrees of clarity as the series is gone through. Bliss is conferred even at the beginning of the road to redemption, as a kind of advance payment of emotion and meaning, needed to keep one going if a successful end is to be reached.

(Vasilyuk, 1988: 190–1)

Vasilyuk outlines four stages of perezhivanie to describe its proleptic nature: fault, repentance, redemption and bliss. Schechner outlines three stages of this phenomenon and explains that they culminate in the public performance: tabula rasa, initiation or transition, and reintegration. Schechner describes these stages as follows:

The workshop-rehearsal process is the basic machine for the restoration of behavior ... [whose] primary function ... is a kind of collective memory-in/of-action. The first phase breaks down the performer's resistance, makes him a tabula rasa. To do this most effectively the performer has to be removed from familiar surroundings. Thus the need for separation, for 'sacred' or special space, and for a use of time different than that prevailing in the ordinary. The second phase is of initiation or transition: developing new or restoring old behavior. But the so-called new behavior is really the rearrangement of old behavior or the enactment of old behavior in new settings. In the third phase, reintegration, the restored behavior is practiced until it is second nature. The final part of the third phase is public performance.

(Schechner, 1985: 113–14)

These stages closely match those stages of perezhivanie that Vasilyuk presents, even though Schechner's and Vasilyuk's terms differ.

I argue elsewhere (Ferholt, 2009a) that it is the juxtaposition of 'temporal double sidedness' (Cole, 2007[4]), growing back and towards the future and the past simultaneously, with these stages, that creates perezhivanie. We are growing back and forward, but still somehow moving from past to future: the foresight allows us to *proceed*. Schechner argues that this juxtaposition provides the rhythm that allows us to raise ourselves up and hover, suspended momentarily in a state of being simultaneously ourselves and not ourselves; of being our past and future selves. I find it helpful to think of a spiral, as a spiral keeps moving outward but passes over the same spot again and again. I will return to this complicated point in a discussion of the 'present moment,' below.

Our example with Milo and Michael illustrates particularly well the idea that, '(i)n a very real way the future – the project coming into existence through the process of rehearsal – determines the past: what will be kept from earlier rehearsals or from the "source materials"' (Schechner, 1985: 39). We can surmise that something about himself will be kept, or become more 'real', now that Milo has seen this something in Michael's and Milo's own future as the White Witch. In other words, the White Witch as a character resonates with both Michael and Milo and they each become more themselves as they develop this role.

Furthermore, Milo's initial look of joy and pride at the start of the event shows us 'Bliss ... conferred even at the beginning of the road to redemption, as a kind of advance payment of emotion and meaning, needed to keep one going if a successful end is to be reached' (Vasilyuk, 1988: 190–1). Milo perseveres through this clearly difficult as well as joyful experience (we know it is difficult if only from the physical support we see him receiving from his friends) after he has a grand look of joy on his face, at the very start of the event. And, in conjunction with this early arrival of bliss, Milo spends the rest of the event growing back and towards the future and the past simultaneously: moving faster towards a future peace as he looks backwards towards the former bliss.

In this event, Milo experiences his unique response to the White Witch's arrival amongst the excitement and fear of his classmates. As we focus on Milo, centred on the screen in our video data of the event, he also merges into the dance of gestures and facial expressions around him: 'Art is the social technique of emotion, a tool of society which brings the most intimate and personal aspects of our being into the circle of social life' (Vygotsky, 1971: 249). We are not making sense of an individual's behaviour with our application of the concept of perezhivanie, but are instead making sense of experiencing in this classroom (Dewey, 1934, 1938).

The Potential Space of 'Not Not Me'

Winnicott writes of play:

> Whereas inner psychic reality has a kind of location in the mind or in the belly or in the head or somewhere within the bounds of the individual's personality, and whereas what is called external reality is located outside these bounds, playing and cultural experience can be given a location if one uses the concept of the potential space between the mother and the baby.
>
> (1971: 53, cited in Schechner, 1985: 110)

According to Schechner, this potential space of play and cultural experience which lies between the internal and the external is the workshop-rehearsal. Schechner explains this as 'not not' or 'double negativity':

> The most dynamic formulation of what Winnicott is describing is that the baby – and later the child at play and the adult at art (and religion) – recognizes some things and situations as 'not me.' By the end of the process 'the dance goes into the body.' So Olivier is not Hamlet, but he is also not not Hamlet. The reverse is also true: in this production of the play, Hamlet is not Olivier, but he is also not not Olivier. Within this field or frame of double negativity, choice and virtuality remain activated.
>
> (Schechner 1985: 110)

Schechner explains a central component of the formation of this doubleness by referring to Winnicott's (1971) transitional object (the blanket or stuffed animal that is the first 'not-me,' representing the mother (primary caretaker) when she (he) is absent). In perezhivanie the paradox of the potential space of double negativity is that you become more yourself the more you become the other, and visa-versa. This happens because, as discussed above, perezhivanie is the relationship between the individual and the environment.

Shechner (1985) makes this point as follows:

> Restored behaviors of all kinds ... are 'transitional.' Elements that are 'not me' become 'me' without losing their 'not me-ness.' This is the peculiar but necessary double negativity that characterizes symbolic actions. *While performing, a performer experiences his own self not directly but through the medium of experiencing the others*. While performing, he no longer has a 'me' but has a 'not not me,' and this double negative relationship also shows how *restored behavior is simultaneously private and social*. A person performing recovers his own self only by going out of himself and meeting the others – by entering a social field. The way in which 'me' and 'not me,' the performer and the thing to be performed, are transformed into 'not me ... not not me' is through the workshop-rehearsal/ritual process.
>
> (Schechner, 1985: 111–12, author's italics)

The workshop-rehearsal process allows one to use another person/fictional character as a pivot[5] to detach emotions that are personal from the self and to relive them through another. This is the process that allows one to be that which one could not imagine without this process.

As stated above, Vygotsky also takes us past the dichotomy between personal and social, as he takes us past the dichotomy between emotion and cognition. In *The Psychology of Art*, he clearly does this in tandem with Schechner's argument:

> Art is the social technique of emotion, a tool of society which brings the most intimate and personal aspects of our being into the circle of social life. It would be more correct to say that emotion becomes personal when every one of us experiences a work of art; it becomes personal without ceasing to be social.
>
> (Vygotsky, 1971: 249)

The potential space of not not me and not not Hamlet, of not not personal and not not social, shows the fractal nature of this working definition of perezhivanie that I am creating. This is one aspect of perezhivanie that captures the whole.

The Present Moment

Another aspect of perezhivanie that captures the whole is the sensation of being at the centre of this workshop-rehearsal process. This is what Schechner calls an experience of the 'present moment'[6]. He describes this experience using powerful metaphors:

> During performance, if everything goes right, the experience is of synchronicity as the flow of ordinary time and the flow of performance time meet and eclipse each other. This eclipse is the 'present moment', the synchronic ecstasy, the autotelic flow, of liminal stasis. Those who are masters at attaining and prolonging this balance are artists, shamans, conmen, acrobats. No one can keep it long.
>
> (Schechner, 1985: 112–13)

Schechner also describes this phenomenon through experience in the space of performance:

> A performance 'takes place' in the 'not me . . . not not me' between performers; between performers, texts and environment; between performers, texts, environment and audience. The larger the field of 'between', the stronger the performance. The antistructure that is performance swells until it threatens to burst. The trick is to extend it to the bursting point but no further. It is the ambition of all performers to expand this field until it

includes all beings, things and relations. This can't happen. The field is precarious because it is subjunctive, liminal, transitional: it rests not on how things are but on how things are not; its existence depends on agreements kept among all participants, including the audience. The field is the embodiment of potential, of the virtual, the imaginative, the fictive, the negative, the not not. The larger it gets, the more it thrills, but the more doubt and anxiety it evokes, too.

(Schechner 1985: 113)

Here we have arrived at the centre of perezhivanie. The phenomenon is temporally double-sided, yet we proceed. This is because another has helped us to create an eye in the storm by allowing us to be not-not-them, and so not-not-ourselves. The sensation of this eye is that of being in the present moment. And the eye itself we will call an anchor or a constant, for reasons that will be discussed in the following section of the chapter.

In our example with Milo and Michael, it is in the personal social space that time stands still. Again, the sensation of being at the centre of the workshop-rehearsal process is what Schechner calls an experience of the *present moment*, '... the synchronic ecstasy, the autotelic flow, of liminal stasis ... No one can keep it long' (Schechner, 1985: 112–13). Milo experiences the 'anchor in the fluidity of life' (Robbins, 2007b), the 'Life stand still here' (Woolf, 1927: 240), and what is particularly fascinating in the video data is that his movements make him appear slower than his classmates as his hand escapes himself to pound his chest, the chest of not not Milo and the chest of the not not White Witch.

The Anchor, the Constant or Under the Firmament of You

Robbins describes this 'present moment' and 'field of between' of twice-behaved behaviour, created in the juxtaposition of temporal double-sidedness with the progressive stages of the workshop-rehearsal process, as the 'anchor' of perezhivanie. She writes, '*Perezhivanie* ... is an anchor in the fluidity of life, it represents a type of synthesis (not a concrete unity of analysis), but an anchor within the fleeting times we have on this earth, dedicated to internal transformation and involvement in our world' (Robbins, 2007b).

Michael, the teacher, uses the term 'constant'[7] instead of 'anchor'. When a constant is formed:

> The movement back and forth, from one world to another and back again – again and again and in this swinging way that almost makes you nauseous ... like a pendulum rushing to the center and then slowly coming back out

again, is what is driving the motion through this spiral so that you seem to pass the story inside itself. *When you stay still it all disappears* [italics added].

(Ferholt, 2010b)

Michael describes a constant concretely as 'someone who helps you reflect back on what you yourself did ... [a] constant helps you remember your own experience and this person may/may not have experienced anything you did.' He adds, 'A constant is sort of like a beacon ... guiding you back on course. But, also giving you hope.' And Michael also explains how a constant works in practice: 'When all is chaotic (in my classroom) and I need something to "right my ship" I think of (my constant)' (Ferholt, 2009b).

Buber (1970) corroborates Michael's findings when he writes of the I-You (I-Thou) relationship. He writes, 'As long as the firmament of the You is spread over me, the tempests of causality cower at my heels, and the whirl of doom congeals' (Buber, 1970: 59). Buber's description includes both the stillness that 'rights the ship' and temporal double-sidedness that proceeds.

The concept of perezhivanie thus allows us to return to the 'fullness of life', to the 'personal needs and interests, the inclinations and impulses, of the thinker' (Vygotsky, 1986: 10). Robbins, Michael and Buber are all defying Cartesian dichotomies that allow us to imagine 'an autonomous flow of thoughts thinking themselves' (Vygotsky, 1986: 10).

In summary, the working definition of perezhivanie that I have built through discussion and analysis, above, includes the following components:

- revitalizing autobiographical emotional memories by imitating another's (or a past self's) physical actions;
- cognition and emotion are dynamically related;
- the relationship between individual and environment *is* the event;
- a form of inter-subjectivity in which we insert ourselves into the stories of others in order to gain the foresight that allows us to proceed (in the face of despair);
- an internal and subjective labour of 'entering into', which is not done by the mind alone, but rather involves the whole of life or a state of consciousness;
- another person is needed for this experience;
- you keep on coming back to something in your memory, keep living through it over and over again, until you discover that you have passed through it, and have survived;
- 'twice-behaved behaviour';
- time flows in more than one direction;

- potential space of 'not not me';
- experiencing the self, not directly but through the medium of experiencing the others;
- the eclipse is the 'present moment', the synchronic ecstasy, the autotelic flow, of liminal stasis: no one can keep it for long.

Conclusion

The concept of perezhivanie may be especially useful to both teachers and researchers at this particular time within the field of preschool didactics because we are in the midst of an international movement that is making early childhood education/care look more and more like childhood education. In the face of the increasing emphasis in preschools on cognitive learning in academic subjects, which comes with this downward movement, we have few theoretical buttresses. Now more than ever we conceptually divide cognitive development from the personal needs and interests, and the inclinations and impulses of children and also teachers, in preschools, in part because we do not have robust theoretical alternatives.

Dewey (1934) started us down a useful path in this regard with his *Art as Experience* and the concept of perezhivanie can help us to develop a comprehensive theory that takes into account experiences in the preschool classroom. Furthermore, the subfield of relational pedagogy is providing a fundamental challenge to the aforementioned trend, and the concept of perezhivanie might be able to find a broader audience within the field of preschool didactics from within this subfield. For instance, Aspelin (2011) proposes a 'two-dimensional conception of education', which is also informed by Martin Buber's I-You (I-Thou) relational conception. Co-existence is one of two fundamental types of relationships within Aspelin's conception of education, and it appears to be closely related to the concept of perezhivanie.

By placing concepts such as *co-existence* and perezhivanie in dialogue, and in dialogue with Dewey's theories of experience, we may be able to contribute towards reorienting the field of preschool didactics away from individualism. Such a reorientation could allow teachers and researchers to address the separation of cognition and emotion in both the practice and theory of preschool didactics. It could allow teachers and researchers to approach cognition and emotion as parts of a whole and to understand the relations between these processes without losing the complexity and fluidity of these relations.

Notes

1. I have chosen this event in part to put this chapter in dialogue with my (2010) discussion of perezhivanie.
2. I will include descriptions of Milo's facial expressions, below, which participating researchers have agreed upon. We have not yet conducted a micro-analysis or coding of facial expressions in this study, and the observations of these expressions are not necessary to the core of my argument. However, I left these observations in the text because they make the description of the event richer and, I believe, no less accurate.
3. A film of this event could not be included but can be viewed upon request of the author.
4. Cole (2007) has used the term 'temporally double sided' to describe this phenomenon of growing back and towards the future and the past simultaneously while discussing Dewey's relation of the notion of object to prolepsis.
5. I am referring broadly to Vygotsky's 1978 use of the term 'pivot' when writing on play.
6. Daniel Stern (2004) does not refer to Schechner but expands upon this theory of the present moment.
7. The term 'Constant' is derived from an episode of the fifth series of the television show 'Lost' (American Broadcasting Company 2004–2010).

References

Aspelin, J. (2011), 'Co-existence and Co-operation: The Two-dimensional Conception of Education', *Education*, 1(1): 6–11.
Aries, P. (1962), *Centuries of Childhood*, New York: Alfred A. Knopf.
Bateson, G. (1972), *Steps to an Ecology of Mind: Collected Essays in Anthropology, Psychiatry, Evolution, and Epistemology*, San Francisco: Chandler Publishing Co.
Baumer, S. (2013), 'Play Pedagogy and Playworlds', *Encyclopedia on Early Childhood Development*, published online, accessed 5 November 2012, at: *http://www.childencyclopedia.com/documents/BaumerANGxp1.pdf*
Baumer, S. Ferholt, B. and Lecusay, R. (2005), 'Promoting Narrative Competence through Adult-Child Joint Pretense: Lessons from the Scandinavian Educational Practice of Playworld', *Cognitive Development*, 20: 576–90.
Bozhovich, L. (1977), 'The Concept of the Cultural-Historical Development of the Mind and its Prospects', *Journal of Russian and East European Psychology*, 16(1): 5–22.
Buber, M. (1970), *I and Thou*, New York: Scribner.
Cole, M. (2007), Online Discussion forum: XMCA, available at: *http://lchc.ucsd.edu/mca/* accessed 29 April 2009.
Dewey, J. (1934), *Art and Experience*, New York: Perigee Books.

Fass, P. (2007), *Children of a New World*, New York: New York University Press.
Ferholt, B. (2009a), *Adult and Child Development in Adult-Child Joint Play: the Development of Cognition, Emotion, Imagination and Creativity in Playworlds*, San Diego: University of California.
Ferholt, B. (2009b), Email received 15 March 2009 from teacher 'Michael'.
Ferholt, B. (2010a), 'A Multiperspectival Analysis of Creative Imagining: Applying Vygotsky's Method of Literary Analysis to a Playworld', In C. Connery, V. John-Steiner and A. Marjanovic-Shane (eds), *Vygotsky and Creativity: A Cultural-Historical Approach to Play, Meaning-Making and the Arts*, New York: Peter Lang.
Ferholt, B. (2010b), Author's Words in a Written Dialogue about the Properties of a Constant with Teacher 'Michael', 16 March 2010.
Ferholt, B. and Lecusay, R. (2010), 'Adult and Child Development in the Zone of Proximal Development: Socratic Dialogue in a Playworld', *Mind Culture and Activity*, 17(1): 59–83.
Lewis, C.S. (1950), *The Lion, the Witch and the Wardrobe*, New York: Macmillan Publishing Co.
Lindqvist, G. (1995), *The Aesthetics of Play: A Didactic Study of Play and Culture in Preschool*, vol. 62, Uppsala: Acta Universitatis Upsalensis.
Marjanovic-Shane, A., Ferholt, B., Nilsson, M., Rainio, A. P. and Miyazaki, K. (2011), 'Playworlds: An Art of Development'. In C. Lobman and B. O'Neill (eds), *Play and Culture*, Association for the Study of Play (TASP).
Robbins, D. (2004), 'Guest Editor's Introduction', *Journal of Russian and East European Psychology*, 42(4): 3–6.
Robbins, D. (2007a), Online Discussion forum: XMCA, available at: *http://lchc.ucsd.edu/mca/* accessed 1 December 2013.
Robbins, D. (2007b), Online Discussion forum: XMCA. Available at: *http://lchc.ucsd.edu/mca/* Accessed 29 December 2013.
Schechner, R. (1985), *Between Theater and Anthropology*, Philadelphia: University of Pennsylvania Press.
Smagorinsky, P. and Daigle, E.A. (2011), 'The Role of Affect in Students' Writing for School', in E. Grigoreno, E. Mambrino and D. Preiss (eds), *Handbook of Writing: A Mosaic of Perspectives and Views*, New York: Psychology Press.
Stanislavsky, K. (1949), *Building a Character*, New York: Theatre Arts Books.
Stern, D. (2004), *The Present Moment in Psychotherapy and Everyday Life*, New York: W.W. Norton & Company.
Sutton-Smith, B. (1997), *The Ambiguity of Play*, Cambridge, MA: Harvard University Press.
Vasilyuk, F. (1988), *The Psychology of Experiencing*, Moscow: Progress Publishers.
Vygotsky, L.S. (1971), *The Psychology of Art*, Cambridge, MA: MIT Press.
Vygotsky, L.S. (1978), *Mind in Society: The Development of Higher Psychological Processes*, Cambridge, MA: Harvard University Press.
Vygotsky, L.S. (1986), *Thought and Language*, Cambridge, MA: MIT Press.

Vygotsky, L.S. (1987), 'Imagination and its Development in Childhood', In R.W Rieber and A.S. Carton (eds), *The Collected Works of L.S. Vygotsky*, vol. 1, New York: Plenum Press, 339–50.
Vygotsky, L.S. (1994), 'The Problem of Environment', in R. Van der Veer and J. Valsiner (eds.), *The Vygotsky Reader*, Oxford: Blackwell, 338–54.
Vygotsky, L.S. (2004), 'Imagination and Creativity in Childhood', *Journal of Russian and East European Psychology*, 42(1): 7–97.
Winnicott, D.W. (1971), *Playing and Reality*, New York: Basic Books.
Woolf, V. (1927), *To the Lighthouse*, London: Hogarth Press.

Part II

Sociocultural Insights into Learning through Drama

4

Dialogue and Social Positioning in Dramatic Inquiry: Creating with Prospero

Brian Edmiston

Introduction

At the close of a performance of *The Tempest*, Prospero addresses the audience directly,

> Gentle breath of yours my sails
> Must fill, or else my project fails.

Through the consciousness of the magician Prospero, Shakespeare draws our attention to the fact that the boat Prospero has conjured to take him back to Naples from the island, where he has been marooned for 12 years, can only sail in the collective, living, creative imagination of the audience. In the theatre, the dramatic illusion of an island world will soon be ended with the applause that Prospero now requests:

> ...release me from my bands
> With the help of your good hands.

In a classroom, applause is either unnecessary, or only transitory, when teachers and students use drama to explore possible meanings of a play, or any other text or topic. As the drama in education scholar, Gavin Bolton (1979) argues, 'though participants in classroom drama may at any time perform for one another they do not expect an ovation. In a performative mode, as part of collaborative meaning-making, people share ideas with everyone in a group, not a separate audience: the structure ... operates for [all] the participants, heightening their experience ... and understanding' (Bolton, 1979: 74–5). Rather than only interpreting other people's words, as audiences and actors do with a theatre production, or individually interpret texts, as most readers of books do, students can be more active in their meaning making. With teacher direction and involvement, by using dramatic inquiry young people can be more socially engaged and dialogic as they collaboratively create learning environments and understandings about texts.

In this chapter, using examples from work on *The Tempest*, I illustrate educational reasons for bringing a narrative world to life for students through dramatic inquiry. First, a teacher may work with participants to create playful environments for inquiry where learning may occur beyond what would be likely without adult guidance and participation. Second, a teacher may carefully plan and structure activities in which people may create understanding that is more dialogic because of how he or she positions and dialogues with participants.

I analyse practical examples of dramatic inquiry from my research in an elementary classroom and in a professional development workshop. I apply two core concepts, dialogue and positioning, that guide my participatory action research (McIntyre, 2007) when I work with teachers. Like the authors of previous chapters, I begin with assumptions that learning and understanding are the products of predominantly social, cultural and imaginative meaning-making activities.

Dramatic Inquiry

The widely-used term *process drama* (O'Neill, 1995) highlights dynamic, artistically structured and theatrical dimensions of classroom drama. In contrast, my term *dramatic dialogic inquiry*, or more succinctly *dramatic inquiry* (Edmiston, 2014), foregrounds how dramatic pedagogy may be used to structure meaning-making through dialogic learning and teaching in planned sequences of tasks focused by inquiry. Whatever text is the subject of inquiry may be more at the edges of activities that contextualize learning and teaching or towards the centre, as it was in the examples used in this chapter (Wolf et al., 1997).

In Dramatic Inquiry Adults Play with Participants

A key sense in which dramatic inquiry is *dramatic* is that participants are playing. They make meaning by interacting as if they are inside a fictional or drama world (O'Neill, 1996). Using Jerome Bruner's (1986) terms, this is a 'possible world' that may be the subject of inquiry as people explore, experience and reflect upon imagined events in ways resembling how we inquire in the 'actual' everyday world. It has long been recognized (Bolton, 1986) that, like young children pretending in informal situations, people participate in any classroom use of drama via a dramatic playing mode (as well as a performative mode). In 'the "as if" mode for oneself and one's fellow participants' (Bolton, 1986: 14), people imagine the individuals, groups, spaces and actions in a fictional world as they collaboratively improvise interactions not composed by the author of any text, create images using words from a text and dialogue to make meaning about events in the world of a narrative.

Vygotsky (1976) argues that in play people 'act independently of what they see' (Vygotsky, 1976: 545). When people play, their experience of the literalness of the everyday world and its social rules recedes as an imagined reality with new social rules takes precedence for participants who may play together not only with objects but also with meaning. In playing, an abstracted shared social *meaning* of objects and actions in a particular context 'determines behaviour' and shapes experience because it 'dominates' over an individual's sensory perception of movements or things (Vygotsky, 1976: 547). Participants are more intentional in their actions and interpretations because they are 'relying on internal tendencies and motives, and not on incentives supplied by external things' (Vygotsky, 1976: 544). For example, how people choose to interact as if they were shipwrecked on an island would be different from how children would normally behave in a classroom.

The meaning that young people make without adult involvement may be extended in dramatic inquiry when a teacher-leader plays collaboratively with participants. Vygotsky stresses the connection between play and imagination when he argues that 'play is imagination in action' (Vygotsky, 1976: 539). When people play collaboratively they access and use what Maxine Greene (Ayers, 1995) calls 'shared and public ... social imagination' as they 'imagine a world as if it could be otherwise' (Ayers, 1995: 322). When an adult helps children learn to work together and introduces events (such as a tempest) and tools (such as a model ship) that young people would ordinarily not access, they may extend their imagining possibilities, for example, how they might act and interact if, like characters in the world of *The Tempest*, they too had been marooned on an island or tossed there in a storm. Furthermore, and extending what I have argued elsewhere (Edmiston, 2003), repeatedly under the direction of a teacher-leader participants collectively or individually 'step in' to imagine 'what IF?' spaces in a fictional world and 'out' to make meaning as they reflect in the everyday world of 'what IS.'

When I observed Lorraine Gaughenbaugh as she worked collaboratively with nine- and ten-year olds (Edmiston, 2014), she began her work on *The Tempest* with dramatic playing in which the children could experience as if they had been on the Elizabethan sailing ship in the storm that begins the play. She had told me how intentional she had been in building social practices of collaboration in the classroom and this was evident: With both direction and participation by Lorraine, everyone moved seamlessly in and out of a gradually forming imagined space of a ship at sea in a storm. The practices she had promoted and the objects Lorraine provided the children with were pivotal. Children passed around and moved a model ship, and then used a sheet, plastic bags and an open area that invited movement, along with some of Shakespeare's phrases, all as mediating tools for meaning making. Using social imagination the children delighted in flapping the sheet-as-a-sail and using the plastic bags along with their collective voices to make the sounds of a gale. They also shouted, moved and talked as if they were sailors and passengers on a ship buffeted by the waves and then tossed into the water as they feared the ship was about to split in two. When invited to do so by Lorraine they reflected on their socially imagined experiences: 'That was fun,' 'I was terrified,' 'I held on to a piece of wood in the water.'

Dramatic Inquiry is Dialogic Inquiry

In dramatic inquiry, participants' meaning-making reflections are extended into dialogic inquiry guided by a teacher-leader. In inquiry-based pedagogy, participants – young people with adults – create understanding collaboratively, guided in their dialogic explorations of narratives or topics by explicit or implicit inquiry questions. For example, initially the children in Lorraine's classroom focused on the following question: What might it have been like to be on a sailing ship in a tempest?

Whereas Vygotsky's writings have frequently been interpreted to stress the difference between what learners and teachers know or can do, Lois Holzman (2010) has stressed that 'what is key ... is that people are doing something together ... in collective activity' (Holzman, 2010: 29). Similarly, for Gordon Wells (2000), inquiry is dialogic when it is collaborative as young people and adults are 'attempting to make sense with and for others', while at the same time 'we make sense for ourselves' (Wells, 2000: 58). In Lorraine's classroom the children worked collaboratively to make sense when they moved and spoke with one another. All could choose where they might have been on the ship as the storm arose, several flapped the sheet-as-a-sail, some reached out to others as they imagined being tossed about or falling into the water, while many called out their own or some of Shakespeare's words, such as 'fall to,' 'we run ourselves a ground' and 'we split, we split.'

In dramatic inquiry, teacher and students adopt a dialogic inquiry stance. As Wells (2000) shows, when people are inquiring their dialogue generates 'real questions' that are 'taken over and owned by the students' engendering a 'desire to understand' (Wells, 2000: 64). Maureen Boyd and William Markarian (2011) argue that for teachers to promote dialogic inquiry they must adopt a 'dialogic stance' intended to 'encourage students to articulate what they know and position them to have interpretive authority' add Boyd and Markarian, 2011: 519). In Lorraine's classroom, as the children created images of a ship in a tempest, some shared relevant experiences of storms or ships and all had parallel but differing interpretations of the dangers for sailors in facing a tempest at sea ranging from 'Why were they so close to the rocks?' to 'There was nothing else the captain could have done.'

Creating Environments for Learning and Development

For Vygotsky (1976), playing is educationally significant as 'the leading source of development' (Vygotsky, 1976: 537). In play, it is as though people are 'a head taller' as each 'behaves above his [or her] daily behavior' (Vygotsky, 1978: 102). In Lorraine's classroom, the children's lived experiences and meaning-making potential were continually being extended in dramatic playing, for example as they pretended to interact as if they were adult characters in the narrative.

Vygotsky theorizes how children's conceptual understanding develops in relation to learning in meaningful social interactions that lead development. 'Learning awakens a variety of internal development processes that are able to operate only when the child is interacting with people in his environment and in cooperation with his peers' (Vygotsky, 1978: 90). For Vygotsky, people learn in what he describes as a 'zone of proximal development' or ZPD:

> ...the distance between the actual developmental level as determined by independent problem solving and the level of potential development as determined through problem solving under adult guidance, or in collaboration with more capable peers.
>
> (Vygotsky, 1978: 86)

Vygotsky identifies the need for problem solving, which for me is a synonym for inquiry. As Holzman (2010) stresses, a ZPD is not an entity but 'a process...

and an activity ... the simultaneous creating of the zone (environment) and what is created (learning-leading-development) by social units' (Holzman, 2010: 30). In other words, Vygotsky shifts focus from individual learning to the process of adults and children collaboratively creating environments in which learning (that leads development) for everyone in a group can happen. When participants create images and share experiences in a fictional world of dramatic inquiry, all are creating a potentially rich learning-leading-development environment.

Creating environments for learning, as Mercer (1994) argues and as I illustrate throughout this chapter, requires carefully 'planned and designed' activities and tasks (Mercer, 1994: 101). Planning for 'guided participation' (Rogoff, 1990) by a more knowledgeable adult or peer is widely accepted as promoting cognitive development in a ZPD. Using Vygotsky's (1986) terms, a primary intent of learning is to develop more culturally agreed 'scientific' conceptual understandings (e.g. of a tempest) beyond any idiosyncratic 'spontaneous' meanings children have already developed. As in Lorraine's classroom, when children desire information or clarification, teachers can provide this via instruction contextualized as part of ongoing inquiries in playful collaborative activities which may, or may not, be very physically active. When the children participated in a brief discussion about tempests, one child said he had thought the word 'tempest' meant 'someone in a temper'. Teacher and peers provided information, for example by comparing tempests with tornadoes and sharing stories of their destructive power while connecting with their imagined experiences on the ship.

Creating Understanding in Dialogue

Bakhtin approaches social interactions from a different though complementary viewpoint to Vygotsky's conceptualization of understanding as 'developing'. For Bakhtin, people create, or author, understanding in dialogic interactions: each person experiences dialogue as 'open' in the sense that for each it is 'able to reveal ever newer ways to mean' (Bakhtin, 1981: 346). People dialogically create meaning and shape their understanding not just by talking with other people but when they dialogue with other perspectives and consciousnesses that may be experienced not only externally in the face-to-face utterances of social interactions but also as internal dialogue (Bakhtin, 1981: 427). Whereas dialogic interactions open up meaning making, monologic interactions are 'passive' and close down meaning making because they 'contribute nothing new' to a person's understanding (Bakhtin, 1981: 281). In schooling, the more students are expected to follow other people's directions and accept unquestioned interpretations of texts by others, the more their classroom experiences are monologic and the less authorship they have of meaning. This can happen whether or not people use dramatic pedagogy.

Vygotsky (1978: 96) stresses the importance of one person having a more complex understanding than another, so that in a social interaction one person may guide another towards constructing new or more nuanced meaning that builds on their existing understanding. For Bakhtin, the significant difference between one person and another is not their relative age or the extent of their knowledge or prior experience, but rather that in dialogue each person is able to think about, respond to, and thus understand the same events *differently*.

When a person acts intentionally they do so with a distinctive perspective, voice, viewpoint or consciousness (using terms that Bakhtin employs throughout his writings). Because everyone has 'a uniqueness that does not repeat itself anywhere' (Bakhtin, 1993: 38), a child's thoughts and deeds should not be viewed as lesser than that of an adult. And because a person's consciousness arises from their unique prior experiences, values, beliefs and assumptions, each person sees, speaks, acts and evaluates their own and other people's situations, words and deeds differently when they dialogue.

As young people inquire they need to encounter, and have opportunities to dialogue with, viewpoints of every person in the classroom and with the consciousness of any character in a fictional world. Using additional terms of Bakhtin (1986, 1990), in dialogue one person 'addresses' one or more other people expecting in 'response' to be both 'answered' and addressed by others in a potential back-and-forth ongoing dialogic exchange in which each person authors new understanding. As Bakhtin (1981) puts it, 'understanding comes to fruition only in the response' (Bakhtin, 1981: 282).

The children were dialoguing in Lorraine's classroom. As they moved the model, their bodies, the sheet and the plastic bags to make the sounds of a storm, the children were addressed by Lorraine when she invited them to move and speak their thoughts. One boy answered by calling out, 'I hope everyone can swim.' And as if to stop her being swept overboard, a girl was holding on to her friend who had cried 'Help', while another girl was grasping her imagined jewels. The cry for help by one child anticipated a response that came from her real-life friend. The children were creating meaning dialogically.

Social Positioning

How people position one another makes a difference to the meaning they make. Positioning theory (Harré and Langenhove, 1999) provides a social constructionist conceptualization of 'positionality'. In different social situations, as people interact and engage in discursive social practices over time, each is doing so from different 'positions'. As Harré and Langenhove (1999) put it, 'a position is a complex cluster of generic personal attributes ... which impinges on the possibility of ... action' (Harré and Langenhove, 1999: 1). As people position one another, each assumes or accepts more or less authority to act and interpret their situation that they view as part of a particular narrative or 'storyline' (Langenhove and Harré, 1999: 17). Using dramatic inquiry, I work within a storyline of a collaborative exploration of topics or texts. As much as possible, as a teacher I position myself and all the young people as having the authority to act, interpret and inquire.

In everyday social interactions, teachers as well as students are never acting independently but rather one person is always positioning others so that each either tends to accept an assumed subject position (first-order positioning) or resist such positioning (second-order positioning) (Langenhove and Harré, 1999: 20).

Adding a Bakhtinian perspective to positioning theory, positioning can be considered an aspect of how one person addresses and answers another. Dialogic positioning by teacher or student opens up dialogue about a topic as people either accept how each is being positioned or negotiate new positions. Conversely, monologic positioning closes down meaning making about a topic: People are not in dialogue either because one or both resists how they are being positioned or they are unable to negotiate new relative positions. Ideally, teachers consistently position students as dialogic inquirers and students accept that positioning.

As people position one another in social interactions, I argue that people are always answering an implicit positioning question addressed to them: 'Who am I and who are you in relation to others in this event?' Lorraine positioned the young people, and herself, as dialogic inquirers who shared the authority to act and interpret events. In creating the imagined environment of the storm, all could choose how they moved and what they said as they dialogically made sense of the opening scene in *The Tempest*.

In dramatic inquiry, a person's answer to the 'Who am I?' question is more complex than in classrooms where people are not in dialogue as if they are other people. When I pretend in fictional events to be another person I may act and interpret events with more (or less) authority than 'I' actually have in everyday situations. For example, I-as-a-duke may issue commands that may have life-and-death consequences for others-as-my-subjects. Put another way, in dramatic inquiry people can both play with how they position one another and inquire into the meaning of the social consequences of such positioning. Furthermore, in dramatic inquiry, using Bakhtin's (1981) term, positioning is always 'double-voiced' (Bakhtin, 1981: 324) – people position one another in the everyday classroom world of 'what IS' at the same time as they do in the fictional world of 'what IF?' Each person's language and movement 'expresses the direct intention of the character who is speaking and the refracted intention of the author' (Bakhtin, 1981: 324).

Significantly, how adults and young people position one another in the fictional world can be negotiated in the everyday world. In teacher-mediated dialogic positioning in the everyday world, how young people might play with highly monologic positioning in a fictional world can be agreed upon and subsequently interpreted. In the dramatic inquiry focused on *The Tempest*, in addition to consistently acting from subject positions as dialogic inquirers, young people could choose to take up multiple fictional subject positions ranging from dialogic sailors to monologic monarchs. Each fictional positioning opened up alternative ways to take action in relation to others, and thus additional dimensions to creating understanding both about events in the lives of fictional characters and how that understanding might relate to their own everyday lives.

Contextualized Themes and Inquiry Questions

As I have conceptualized dramatic inquiry, the collaborative exploration of narrative events is focused by questions with social, cultural and ethical dimensions formed from themes contextualized in a fictional world (Edmiston, 2014). A major theme of *The Tempest* is introduced in the event following the opening scene when Prospero tells his daughter, Miranda, aged almost fifteen, his story of what had happened to them before coming to the island. From her prior knowledge of the children's concerns, Lorraine identified this event as illuminating a theme that would likely interest the children – relationships between siblings.

Prospero's tale is significant because now on the island are the very people, including his own brother Antonio, who had usurped him as Duke of Milan

12 years earlier, abandoning him and Miranda to a boat so unseaworthy that, as he puts it, 'the very rats instinctively had quit it.' Understanding Prospero's perspective on what happened previously is crucial for interpreting how – and why – Prospero later acts (or could act) towards these new arrivals on the island.

Narratives may be conceptualized as comprised of sequences of events. Like the storm conjured by Prospero that opens the play, what previously happened in Milan, as Elizabeth Ellsworth (1997) argues, was an event since there was a 'rupture of continuity' in which 'normal life' and 'the *status quo* is disturbed' (Ellsworth, 1997: 150). Prospero, having previously experienced what Victor Turner (1974) describes as a 'breach' of norms, is now faced with the possibility of taking 'redressive action' in response to the escalation of the 'crisis' caused by the imminent arrival of his brother and his accomplice, the King of Naples (Turner, 1974: 38–9). What should Prospero do? As he retells what had happened he asks Miranda the following central question that frames his view of his brother, Antonio:

Mark his condition and the event; then tell me
If this might be a brother?

In planning, Lorraine and I restated Prospero's words as questions:

- How should brothers and sisters treat one another?
- Why do people treat others badly?
- Should people, including Prospero, forgive or seek revenge?

Written on a white board the questions were successfully used as an initial guide for inquiry with the children over several hour-long sessions, when I was not present.

I used the same questions on a subsequent occasion in a 75-minute professional development workshop for teachers on dramatic inquiry that I led at a national conference. My planning was based on tasks Lorraine had already introduced in her classroom. In the workshop I began with the event when Prospero tells Miranda his story of what had happened a dozen years earlier. The initial sequence of tasks was designed to build on participants' prior knowledge and introduce minimal information so that they could begin to imagine the Elizabethan world that contextualizes the inquiry: city states, castles, dukes, kings and servants. What follows is a list of the planned tasks:

- Discuss what we know about where rich people and servants lived in the time of Shakespeare.

- Walk as if we are each a servant in a castle/manor carrying something the lord/duke/king might need to a place where you use it.
- You-as-servants show us what servants might be doing. Reflect on why and connect with the world of *The Tempest*.
- Walk as if you are a duke/duchess or king/queen in one of the places already imagined. Reflect on what noblemen like Duke Prospero in Milan (and his younger brother Antonio) and King Alonso in Naples might have been doing.
- Note Shakespeare does not mention wives or parents. Reflect on what might have happened and the laws of inheritance.

In the first sequence of tasks, as people imagined they were 'in a castle/manor' they were additionally playing with fictional positionings as servants in relation to nobles. Throughout, and in reflective dialogue (in whole group and in pairs), participants were dialogically positioned to make meaning about their fictional experiences.

The second sequence of tasks was designed so that participants might extend their understanding of the socio-political context of the relationship:

- Discuss possible meanings of how Prospero describes Naples: 'inveterate enemy'.
- Introduce how tapestries could record events. In self-selected groups of 4–5 with one as director/narrator, prepare still images as if of tapestries showing what might have happened to make Naples an 'inveterate enemy' of Milan.
- Show still images to the whole group to interpret from Prospero's perspective. How might Prospero act, knowing Antonio assisted Naples to attack Milan?
- Reflect on what differing views on the same events tapestries in Naples might show.

Presentness and Eventness

I argued above that in dramatic inquiry participants' positioning is doubled. So too is their experience of events. Bakhtin (1990) conceptualizes people's experience of everyday life as an 'open event of being', and like readers people also experience 'events' in the lives of fictional characters (Bakhtin, 1990: 97–9). Participants in dramatic inquiry position one another in the everyday classroom events at the same time as they position one another as if they are people in fictional events. As Morson and Emerson (1990) summarize, Bakhtin proposes two key dimensions of the live experience of events, whether in life, or in narratives: 'presentness' and 'eventness' (Bakhtin, 1990: 46–7). Both are significant factors affecting whatever understandings readers or participants in dramatic inquiry create as they inquire into the meaning of events in a narrative.

Presentness

When a person experiences what happens to characters as if it is happening here-and-now (including what is or may be about to happen) they feel present. When people experience minimal presentness in the events of their everyday life or in the events of a narrative, the meaning they make will be diminished. For Bakhtin, 'time is open and each moment has multiple possibilities ... the potential to lead in many directions' (Morson and Emerson, 1990: 46–7). 'Now and imminent time', a well-known phrase of the legendary drama in education practitioner and scholar, Dorothy Heathcote (Johnson and O'Neill, 1984: 161), captures the sense of presentness in a fictional narrative event felt as tension between what is happening to characters and what feels inevitable or likely to happen to them in the future.

I designed the third sequence of tasks for participants to experience, among other things, presentness in the event Prospero narrates. Initially, I wanted participants to feel present in the sort of interactions that siblings (as children of an Elizabethan duke) might engage in. The images created in the first tasks were interpreted using the inquiry questions. I also invited participants to make connections with their own past experiences of siblings and with their beliefs about how they ought to act.

To further contextualize the brothers' relationship, I distributed selected phrases of Shakespeare's text for interpretation by participants in small groups. Again, with one as director/narrator, they created and then performed still/moving images as if in Prospero's memory:

Antonio, my brother '... of whom, next thyself [Miranda], of all the world I loved'
I was 'rapt in secret studies' in my 'library' that 'was dukedom enough'
I 'put the manage of my state' to my brother
I was a 'stranger to the state ... neglecting worldly ends'
I was 'all dedicated to closeness and the betterment of my mind'

My brother, Antonio, 'He did believe he was indeed the duke'
Naples, an 'inveterate enemy' of Milan, 'a treacherous army levied'
'They hurried us aboard ... a rotten carcass of a boat ... the very rats instinctively had quit it.'

Participants reflected to develop some understanding of Prospero's viewpoint on his brother's actions. Using a handout of an edited version of Prospero's speech, I asked people to stand in a circle to read the text collaboratively from one punctuation mark to the next (Berry, 2008: 39). Reading again, we stopped to interpret words such as 'Absolute Milan' meaning Antonio took the title of Duke of Milan. Focused on the inquiry questions, people shared more about how siblings ought to treat one another, including interpretations tempered by the context: 'Antonio was tired of being taken advantage of' and 'Prospero wasn't given a choice by his brother.'

The more people feel present, the deeper the experience and the richer the meaning made about an event. Just as the children-as-sailors, pretending they were in a storm, could immediately feel present while moving and calling out, the adults were also able to 'step in' to experience and dialogue within present moments in the narrative world and then 'step out' again into the everyday world to dialogue as themselves. Participants were making meaning about what was happening in the narrative event and inquiring into its significance both for the characters and for themselves.

Eventness

For Bakhtin (1984), eventness is 'played out at the dialogic meeting between two or several consciousnesses' (Bakhtin, 1984: 88). It is significant because the more people experience eventness the more possibilities for dialogue: they can interpret whatever is said and done from multiple available competing viewpoints.

In the next sequence of tasks, the focus was especially on eventness. Using the strategy of Continuum to explore responses to the third inquiry question (Should people, including Prospero, forgive or seek revenge?) I placed cards with words Forgiveness and Revenge on opposite sides of the room, inviting the participants to 'stand along an imagined line between these words standing closest to the idea you feel will guide Prospero's actions more.'

I asked participants to put a finger on a word or phrase from the extract they had just read that suggested a reason for why they were standing where they were. I invited people to share their thinking with those around them and then with the whole group. Some spoke as if they were characters and others as teachers. There was extended dialogue about the significance on the one hand of Prospero saying of his brother to Miranda, 'next thyself, of all the world I loved', while on the other hand Antonio had put them 'in a rotten carcass of a boat' that all agreed could easily have sunk. Finally, I asked if our conversation had made a difference and if so to move along the continuum, which many did.

Participants' meaning-making potential was doubled as dialogic inquirers were experiencing events and positioning one another in the everyday *and* fictional worlds. Everyone was positioned as able to move and dialogue with one another, not only from their own subject positions as teachers in the room but also in the world of *The Tempest* from the subject positions of Prospero and Antonio as well as Miranda and Alonso.

Teaching as Polyphonic Dialogic Positioning

As I have outlined above, Bakhtin theorizes that understanding is created in dialogue among people. Furthermore, Bakhtin (1990) argues that individuals dialogically create understanding internally as they both empathize with characters and contemplate their experience from a distance.

In analysing dramatic pedagogy, Dunn and O'Toole (2011) have argued that 'being involved' in dramatic action lies on a 'continuum'. Involvement lies 'between empathy (the emotional identification with the character and the dramatic situation) and distance ... the gap between the participants and the roles/characters they are playing and the degree to which participants can view the situation and their roles from outside the action.' (Dunn and O'Toole, 2011: 29).

Bakhtin (1990) conceptualizes that it is not enough for actors or children to enter into a different consciousness, as he or she 'in feels' and 'co-experiences' with a character (Bakhtin, 1990: 62). It is essential to move 'outside' to engage in 'active and creative contemplation'. Bakhtin likens this to viewing like an 'author-director-spectator' (Bakhtin, 1990: 75–9). As Bakhtin (1986) clarifies elsewhere, for a person 'to understand it is immensely important to be *located outside* the object of his or her creative understanding – in time, in space, in culture. For one cannot even really see one's own exterior and comprehend it as a whole' (Bakhtin, 1986: 7). In reflecting from 'outside' as a spectator on an 'utterance' made as part of physical movement by a participant-as-a-character, any participant can 'author' some meaning in a 'finalized wholeness' of their own or another's utterance

(Bakhtin, 1986: 76). However, such finalization is only provisional, since in dialogue people speak 'assuming a responsive attitude' (Bakhtin, 1986: 76).

In my dialogic positioning as a teacher, following Bakhtin, I am cognizant that dialogue may happen both internally (within a person) and externally (between people). In addition, I plan for polyphonic dialogue. Niculin (1998), applying Bakhtin's concepts, contrasts 'polyphonic dialogue' with 'Platonic dialogue', dominant in most classroom discourse, where 'many voices display one idea' (often the teacher's). In contrast, as he puts it, 'in polyphonic dialogue every voice presents its own unique idea [and] multiple voices do not try to reach a synthesis' (Niculin, 1998: 393–4). The more polyphonic the classroom the more 'multiple voices' young people have opportunities to engage with in dialogue, each of which may affect their changing understanding (Depalma, 2010: 437).

The teaching described above was polyphonic dialogic positioning. It was planned and implemented to promote internal and external dialogue from as many viewpoints as possible. Though much of my teaching involved facilitation and instruction, in addition it was sometimes intended to promote or even provoke dialogue that would be unlikely to happen if participants were working without a leader. Drawing on Bakhtin (1981), I have characterized this teaching mode as intending to 'dialogize' prior understandings or current meaning being made by participants (Edmiston, 2014).

Teaching as Dialogizing

Whereas the previous tasks had been mostly facilitating participants to share existing views, the final sequence was intended to provoke people to respond with views that might dialogize whatever meaning had begun to settle for each person. As Holquist puts it, meaning is dialogized 'when it becomes relativized, de-privileged, aware of competing definitions for the same things' (Bakhtin, 1981: 427).

As the participants stood in a circle, I-as-Prospero re-read Prospero's speech but now listening-as-Antonio anyone could interrupt saying 'Stop' if they wanted to talk back to Prospero and give an alternative interpretation to his viewpoint on events. Almost immediately, a participant responded to Prospero's words 'and to him put the manage of my state' saying 'because you were inept in doing your job'. Another added, 'see – the people needed me to rule' when as Prospero I said, 'thus neglecting worlds ends'. After several minutes of dialogue I again used the strategy of the Continuum, inviting people who now stood in a different place to share their reasoning.

This teaching was planned to provoke and make visible changes in understanding about the relationship between the brothers and how Prospero might engage both with his brother whom he had 'loved of all the world' and with the 'treacherous' king of Naples. Many had shifted their position towards forgiveness, having identified more with Antonio's perspective; others moved in the opposite direction towards revenge.

Conclusion: Creating with Prospero ... and Others

Though adults and children created meaning with Prospero as they explored the world of *The Tempest*, they were not under his command. Prospero's view of events was introduced not simply to be comprehended by participants but rather to be encountered as one consciousness among many in the narrative events that were introduced as people created their own understandings in polyphonic dialogic interactions.

My intention was that meaning should not be fixed or finalized but rather kept in motion as people took up one position after another, played with how they positioned one another, and over time engaged in dialogue with many viewpoints. In both Lorraine's classroom and in the teacher workshop, participants created understanding in teacher/leader-mediated environments and dialogic interactions. Through dramatic inquiry they came to know more about not only physical realities, like a tempest, but also social relationships, cultural contexts, and ethical concepts like forgiveness and revenge. All did so as they engaged, and were positioned by us as teachers, to participate in an ongoing dialogue that ideally, as Bakhtin stresses, is never ending:

> To live means to participate in dialogue: to ask questions, to heed, to respond, to agree, and so forth. In this dialogue a person participates wholly and throughout his whole life: with his eyes, lips, hands, soul, spirit, with his whole body and deeds.
>
> (Bakhtin, 1984: 293)

References

Ayers, W. (1995), 'Social Imagination: A Conversation with Maxine Greene', *International Journal of Qualitative Studies in Education*, 8(4): 319–28.
Bakhtin, M.M. (1981), *The Dialogic Imagination*, M. Holquist, and V. Liapunov (eds), Austin, TX: Texas University Press.
Bakhtin, M.M. (1984), *Problems of Dostoevsky's Poetics: Theory and History of Literature*. C. Emerson (ed.), Minneapolis, MN: University of Minnesota Press.
Bakhtin, M.M. (1986), *Speech Genres and Other Late Essays*, C. Emerson, and M. Holquist (eds), Austin, TX: Texas University Press.
Bakhtin, M.M. (1990), *Art and Answerability: Early Philosophical Essays*, M. Holquist and V. Liapunov (eds), Austin, TX: Texas University Press.
Bakhtin, M.M. (1993), *Toward a Philosophy of the Act*, V. Liapunov and M. Holquist. (eds), Austin, TX: Texas University Press.
Berry, C. (2008), *From Word to Play*, London, UK: Oberon Books.
Bolton, G. (1979), *Towards a Theory of Drama in Education*, Harlow, UK: Longman.
Bolton, G. (1986), *Selected Writings on Drama in Education*, D. Davis and C. Lawrence (eds), Harlow, UK: Longman.
Boyd, M.P. and Markarian, W.C. (2011), 'Dialogic Teaching: Talk in Service of a Dialogic Stance', *Language and Education*, 2(6): 515–34.
Depalma, R. (2010), 'Toward a Practice of Polyphonic Dialogue in Multicultural Teacher Education', *Curriculum Inquiry*, 40(3): 436–49.
Dunn, J. and O'Toole, J. (2011), 'When Worlds Collude: Exploring the Relationship between the Actual, the Dramatic, and the Virtual', in M. Anderson, D. Cameron and J. Carroll (eds), *Drama Education and Digital Technology*, Sydney, Australia: Continuum, 20–37.
Edmiston, B. (2003), 'What's my Position? Role, Frame, and Positioning when Using Process Drama', *Research in Drama Education*, 8(2): 221–9.
Edmiston, B. (2014), *Transforming Teaching and Learning with Active and Dramatic Approaches: Engaging Students Across the Curriculum*, New York and London: Routledge.
Ellsworth, E. (1997), *Teaching Positions: Difference, Pedagogy, and the Power of Address*, New York: Teachers College Press.
Harré, R. and Langenhove, L.V. (1999), 'The Dynamics of Social Episodes', in R. Harré and L.V. Langenhove, *Positioning Theory: Moral Contexts of International Action*, Malden, MA: Blackwell Publishers, 1–13.
Holzman, L. (2010), 'Without Creating ZPD's there is no Creativity', in M.C. Connery, V.P. John-Steiner and A. Marjanovic-Shane (eds), *Vygotsky and Creativity: A Cultural-historical Approach to Play, Meaning-making, and the Arts*, New York: Peter Lang, 27–40.
Johnston, L. and O'Neill, C. (eds) (1984), *Dorothy Heathcote: Collected Writings on Drama and Education*, London, UK: Hutchinson.

Langenhove, L.V. and Harré, R. (1999), 'Introducing Positioning Theory', in R. Harré and L.V. Langenhove, *Positioning Theory: Moral Contexts of International Action*, Malden, MA: Blackwell Publishers, 14–31.

McIntyre, A. (2007), *Participatory Action Research*, Thousand Oaks, CA: Sage.

Mercer, N. (1994), 'Neo-Vygotskian Theory and Classroom Education', in B. Stierer and J. Maybin (eds), *Language, Literacy and Multilingual Matters: A Reader*, Clevedon, UK: The Open University, 92–110.

Morson, G.S. and Emerson, C. (1990), *Mikhail Bakhtin: Creation of a Prosaics*, Stanford, CA: Stanford University Press.

Niculin, D. (1998), 'Mikhail Bakhtin: A Theory of Dialogue', *Constellations: An International Journal of Critical and Democratic Theory*, 5(3): 381–402.

O'Neill, C. (1995), *Drama Worlds: A Framework for Process Drama*, Portsmouth, NH: Heinemann.

Rogoff, B. (1990), *Apprenticeship in Thinking: Cognitive Development in Social Context*, New York: Oxford University Press.

Turner, V. (1974), *Dramas Fields, and Metaphors: Symbolic Action in Human Society*, Ithaca, NY: Cornell University Press.

Vygotsky, L.S. (1976), 'Play and its Role in the Mental Development of the Child', in J.S. Bruner, A. Jolly, and K. Sylva (eds), *Play: Its Role in Development and Evolution*, New York: Penguin Books, 537–44.

Vygotsky, L.S. (1978), *Mind in Society: The Development of Higher Psychological Processes*, Cambridge, MA: Harvard University Press.

Vygotsky, L.S. (1986), *Thought and Language*, Cambridge, MA: MIT Press.

Wells, G. (2000), 'Dialogic Inquiry in Education: Building on the Legacy of Vygotsky', in C.D. Lee and P. Smagorinsky (eds), *Vygotskian Perspectives on Literacy Research: Constructing Meaning through Collaborative Inquiry*, Cambridge, UK: Cambridge University Press, 51–85.

Wolf, S., Edmiston, B. and Enciso, P. (1997), 'Drama Worlds: Places of the Heart, Head, Voice and Hand in Dramatic Interpretation', in J. Flood, S.B. Heath and D. Lapp (eds), *The Handbook for Literacy Educators: Research on Teaching the Communicative and Visual Arts*, New York: Simon & Schuster Macmillan, 492–505.

5

Identity and Creativity: The Transformative Potential of Drama

Harry Daniels and Emma Downes

Introduction

In this chapter we aim to bring a Vygotskian perspective on creativity to bear on one aspect of Drama in Education. In schools, children's identities are, to some extent, prescribed and often they are placed in categories of need and difficulty. Schools also differ in the extent to which they maintain relations of power and control, which are realized in 'status' relations witnessed in pedagogic practices. Children become 'pupils' or 'students' or become members of categories of attainment. Some may qualify for 'Free School Meals' (FSM), which is often taken as the prime index of poverty in the United Kingdom. Membership of this *group* is often, erroneously, assumed to be predictive of outcomes for a particular *individual*.

Pedagogic responses to children who are placed in categories associated with disadvantage are often characterized by increases in teacher control over the selection and sequencing of content, the pacing of progression through curriculum content, and the criteria of evaluation (Daniels, 2008). This is exemplified in a report of a comparison of low and high socio-economic status (SES) settings in Scotland, in which Duffield (1998) reports reduced levels of opportunity for discussion and the achievement of group consensus in low SES settings. She attributes this to teachers' anxiety about control and wariness about pupil autonomy in low SES settings. These low SES students are placed in pedagogic contexts which offer little by way of opportunity for engagement in the transformation of social relations, order and identity. The case description included in this chapter is an example of the way in which pupils who are on the FSM register can experience the transformative potential of drama in relation to identities within school and beyond. This represents a challenge to the understanding that drama allows you to 'express yourself'; rather it suggests that drama provides opportunities for the exploration of identities which are fictitious but may also impact on the 'actual'. As such it provides all participants with respite from the constraints of notions of 'self', which arise when membership of categories are allocated and pedagogies assume a focus on a narrow conception of learning.

Much has been made of the enduring poor attainment of pupils on the FSM register in comparison to their peers, whose identity of 'disadvantage in school' may shape attitudes and values towards school in general and specifically towards practices of learning (see Dolby and Dimitriadis, 2004 and *Challenge the Gap*[1]). In many schools they are now seen as vulnerable. The irony of the nature of this vulnerability appears to be lost. One response is that they are vulnerable to inappropriate pedagogies. In contrast to the rigid pedagogic practices that may operate within the rest of the curriculum, the drama classroom may offer a temporary lull through the creation of 'negotiated' identities and mediated relations of power and control. Drama is a powerful tool for creating contexts that may provide the opportunity to renegotiate identities.

Tools for Creativity

Above all, Vygotsky was seeking to develop a liberationist version of social formation in which rather than being pinioned by history, individuals contributed to the creation of cultural tools which they used to change the world. He developed accounts of human action and activity in which cultural artifacts, such as speech, mediate human engagement with aspects of the social, cultural historical situations in which they were located. These artifacts or tools are human products that are taken up, developed and transformed in the course of human activity. The emphasis is on the social production of artifacts that can be used as tools of both personal and social development and change. This cultural historical perspective on creativity has been summarized by Glăveanu:

> The new artefact (material or conceptual) is seen as emerging within the relation between self (creator) and others (broadly understood as a community), all three being immersed into and in dialogue with an existing body of cultural artifacts, symbols and established norms. This model is not structural but dynamic since it is in the 'tensions' between all four elements that creativity takes shape with the 'new artifact' becoming part of

'existing culture' (for self and/or community) and constantly alimenting the creative cycle.

(Glăveanu, 2010a: 12)

Social and cultural tools are historical products, and creativity involves their deployment in the cultural context of the here-and-now. Vygotsky (2004) started with a conception of creativity as 'a historical, cumulative process' (Vigotsky, 2004: 30). This sense of creativity capitalizing on the past is exemplified in the following, more recent statement: 'the most eminent are those creators who best utilize the social and cultural tools and best fit with the social and cultural expectations of their time' (Moran and John-Steiner, 2003: 80).

The concern has been to develop an account in which humans were seen as 'making themselves from the outside', rather than being dominated and controlled from the outside. Through acting on things in the world, they engage with the meanings that those things assumed within social activity. Humans both shape those meanings and are shaped by them. This understanding is exemplified in recent research on creativity when it is understood as 'studying the intrapersonal dynamics of creative processes in the context of the interpersonal relations that make it possible' (Glăveanu, 2010b: 63). From the perspective of learners who are deemed 'vulnerable', or whatever term is used to suggest low attainment, the question is as to whether they have access to the kind of interpersonal relations in the classroom that facilitate the intrapersonal dynamics of creative processes.

Creativity in Schooling

Vygotsky recognized the importance of the development of creativity through schooling and also rejected the notion of creativity as the product of sudden inspiration (Vygotsky, 2004). He argued that the active promotion of creativity was a central function of schooling:

> We should emphasize the particular importance of cultivating creativity in school-age children. The entire future of humanity will be attained through the creative imagination; orientation to the future, behaviour based on the future and derived from this future, is the most important function of the imagination. To the extent that the main educational objective of teaching is guidance of school children's behaviour so as to prepare them for the future,

development and exercise of the imagination should be one of the main forces enlisted for the attainment of this goal.

(Vygotsky, 2004: 87–8)

His analysis of the development of creativity is marked by an emphasis on interfunctional relations that resonates throughout his work. He argued that children are not necessarily more creative than adults; rather that they have less control and critical judgment over the products of their imagination. He suggests that as rational thought develops so does critical judgment, and that the tendency is for adolescents to become increasingly dissatisfied with the products of their imagination if they do not acquire appropriate 'cultural and technical factors' or tools with which to engage in creative activity.

Adults dismiss their creative output if they are not given the tools with which to be creative. In the context of this chapter, this position forces us to reflect on the ways in which lessons in drama can provide new tools for creativity, not least by virtue of their capacity to bring multiple perspectives explicitly into view. It also prompts concerns about the ways in which provision is constructed for those considered to be 'vulnerable'. Is this provision always conducive to the development and celebration of creativity or is more preoccupied with conformity and control?

Vygotsky argues that creativity is a social process that requires appropriate tools, artifacts and cultures in which to thrive. This position has been adapted by Wertsch and Tulviste (1996), who talk of creativity as 'transformation of an existing pattern of action, a new use for an old tool.' Wertsch (1991, 1998) reminds us that individuals' histories with regard to cultural tools are an important element in the development of mediated action. He argues that when Vygotsky uses the term *mental function* he does so with reference to social interaction and to individual processes. In this sense, mental functions may be seen to be carried by groups as well as individuals. He sees ability as the capacity to function with the tool and also talks of mind being socially distributed, belonging to dyads and larger groups who can think, attend and remember together (Wertsch, 1991, 1998).

Thus, a Vygotskian understanding of creativity acknowledges its pervasiveness, understands the centrality of tools for creativity and recognizes the importance of the social organization of pedagogy that promotes creativity. When brought together, these elements of practices that promote creativity have important implications for learning that transforms identities.

Creativity in the Zone of Proximal Development

Vygotsky developed his well-known but frequently misunderstood concept of the Zone of Proximal Development (ZPD) as a means of discussing the way in which social and participatory learning takes place and development is facilitated (John-Steiner and Mahn, 1996). This was integrated into his theory of play. It was argued that in play the child could temporarily become 'higher than his average age, higher than his usual everyday behaviour; he is in play as if a head above himself' (Valsiner and van der Veer, 1993: 44). This concept is often referenced in pedagogic initiatives which claim a Vygotskian heritage. However, a myriad of misinterpretations bedevil much of this literature. Chaiklin (2003) suggests that much of what has been discussed under the rubric of the ZPD misses the central theoretical insistence on social influences leading *development*. The distinction between microgenesis (in which small-scale steps take place) and ontogenesis (which involves qualitative differences in developmental development) is missed in what for Chaiklin are misinterpretations of the original formulation of ZPD in its instructional frame of reference.

The term scaffolding, which is often deployed as an operational derivation of the ZPD, could be taken to infer a 'one-way' process within which the 'scaffolder' constructs the scaffold alone and presents it for use to the novice. Sadly, this is so often the case with young people who schools see as vulnerable. Newman *et al.* (1989) argued that the ZPD is created through negotiation between the more advanced partner and the learner, rather than through the donation of a scaffold as some kind of prefabricated climbing frame. There is a similar emphasis on negotiation in Tharp and Gallimore (1988), who discuss teaching as *assisted performance* in those stages of the ZPD where assistance is required. The key question here seems to be with respect to where the hints, supports or 'scaffold' come from. Are they produced by the more advanced partner or are they negotiated? Vygotsky is unclear on this matter.

Chaiklin (2003) suggests that terms such as scaffolding should be reserved for practices which are designed to teach specific skills and subject matter concepts, as against instruction designed to serve explicitly developmental purposes (Chaiklin, 2003: 59). Cole and Griffin (1983) mount a strong criticism of the scaffolding metaphor based on the extent to which the child's creativity is underplayed. The argument that different settings and activities give rise to spaces within the ZPD for creative exploration rather than pedagogic domination, is at the heart of their position, stating that, 'Adult wisdom does not provide a teleology for child development. Social organization and leading activities provide a gap within which the child can develop novel creative analyses' (Cole and Griffin, 1983: 62). This carries important implications for pedagogic practice. The argument is that the creativity inherent in learning and transformation should be seen in dialogic terms rather than a skill to be transmitted. In the same way that Cole and Griffin caution against acts of pedagogic imperialism, Vygotsky urges us to recognize the centrality of creativity to the entire educational enterprise.

Creativity, Learning and Identity

Learning as a process is linked with identity formation, as in Brown and Duguid (2000), who see learning as demand driven, a social act, and as identity formation. Lave and Wenger argue that persons 'become' as they come to progressively involve themselves with the activities of a community. In this way learning means to move from peripheral participation to full membership within a knowledge community (Lave and Wenger, 1991). This theme is pursued by Wenger who theorized identity as a 'way of talking about how learning changes who we are and creates personal histories of becoming in the context of our communities' (Holland *et al.*, 1998: 5). Holland *et al.* also state that:

> Forms of personhood and forms of society are historical products, intimate and public, that situate the interactivity of social practices. It is in this doubly historical landscape that we place human identities. We take identity to be a central means by which selves, and the sets of actions they organize, form and re-form over personal lifetimes and in the histories of social collectivities.
>
> (Holland, *et al.*, 1998: 270)

In studying the development of identities and agency specific to historically situated, socially enacted, culturally constructed worlds, Holland *et al.* (1998) reference Bakhtin (1978, 1986) and Vygotsky as they develop a theory of identity as constantly forming. They conceive of a person as a composite of many often contradictory, self-understandings and identities, which are distributed across the material and social environment and are rarely durable (Holland *et al.*, 1998: 8). They draw on Leontiev in the development of the concept of socially organized and reproduced figured worlds, which shape and are shaped by participants and in which social position establishes possibilities for engagement. They also argue that figured worlds:

> [D]istribute 'us' not only by relating actors to landscapes of action (as personae) and spreading our senses of self across many different fields of activity, but also by giving the landscape human voice and tone.
>
> (Holland *et al.*, 1988: 8)

They deploy the Bakhtinian concept of the space of authoring to capture an understanding of the mutual shaping of figured worlds and identities in social practice. They also argue that multiple identities are developed within figured worlds and that these are 'historical developments, grown through continued participation in the positions defined by the social organization of those world's activity' (Holland *et al.*, 1998: 41). Identity formation is a social activity that may take place is the unseen minutiae of interaction. It is as much a collective activity in the here and now as it has been through history. Vygotsky writes:

> Just as electricity is equally present in a storm with deafening thunder and blinding lightning and in the operation of a pocket flashlight, in the same way, creativity is present, in actuality, not only when great historical works are born but also whenever a person imagines, combines, alters, and creates something new, no matter how small a drop in the bucket this new thing appears compared to the works of geniuses. When we consider the phenomenon of collective creativity, which combines all these drops of individual creativity that frequently are insignificant in themselves, we readily understand what an enormous percentage of what has been created by humanity is a product of the anonymous collective creative work of unknown inventors.
>
> (Vygotsky, 2004: 10–11)

This points to the importance of the cultures of the school which form the setting for collective creative working and activity, and the importance of the individual, the collective and the social in arriving at an understanding of the underlying processes and structures. The drama classroom provides a space for an experimental refiguring of the landscape of the social world of the young person. Arguably this is particularly important for someone who has been positioned in the institutions of schooling as vulnerable, disadvantaged or unacceptable.

Further questions relate to the ways in which the 'figured' world of the drama lesson impacts on the 'real' everyday world. More specifically, how do the participants in the drama renegotiate themselves and the relation of others to them in the world beyond the drama classroom? The exchange during in-role work creates the possibility for such reorientations to meaning and understanding of the self. After this moment of in-role work, participants are able to dissect, analyse and discuss. This has implications for all to extend their own maps of the world. Children are natural experts in this practice. From the moment they enter the school, they are shaped and formed by the social and cultural practices modelled by those already operating in that context.

This approach to a theory of identity in practice is grounded in the notion of a figured world in which positions are taken up, constructed and resisted. We will now move to a discussion of the ways in which these understandings of processes of social formation may be relevant to drama in secondary schools.

Reflections on a Transformative Moment in a Drama Lesson

What follows is an event drawn from the experience of teaching rather than a formal research project. It was selected in order to provide a glimpse of the way in which drama can provide the context for the exploration of reinterpretations of the past, re-signification in the present, and new possibilities for the future. The challenge is to co-create a context in which participants accept the possibility of transformation(s). In doing so, they may seek resolution or re-negotiation through the temporary 'role'. Bolton (1979) affirms the importance of creating fictional worlds that offer new perspectives on familiar worlds:

> Children can intellectually and emotionally exist simultaneously and effectually in two worlds; one real but suspended as far as necessary, and one that is fictional but it is the 'operational' world of the drama.
> (Bolton, 1979: 20)

A useful example of this moment would be an exchange through *improvisation* – a technique by which participants adopt a role different to the socially and formally agreed one identified at the beginning of the discourse. Participants are able to enter a temporary moment of transformation and it is in this moment that, following Holland *et al.* (1998), 'identities' can be negotiated through dialogue and action. In one sense, they engage in the process of 'rewriting' themselves and repositioning themselves in the narratives of their everyday life. They may engage in some form of learning through being placed in situations in which tensions that had previously been invisible are rendered visible and open to conscious reflection. They are both immersed in a context but also given the opportunity of distancing themselves from the events. This resonates with the view of development that Yaroshevsky (1989) attributes to Vygotsky.

Rather than understanding a stage of development through the 'ladder' metaphor associated with Piaget, Yaroshevsky suggests that Vygotsky had a dramaturgical notion in mind when he invoked the word *stage*. The idea was that of a stage where two planes – the personal and the social – were in play. When these two planes collided, as a result of incommensurability between personal understandings and social situations, then a reforming of both may occur. Yaroshevsky argues that it was through his early association with the dramatist Stanislavski and the poet Mandelstam, whose reading group he attended, that Vygotsky developed this understanding of *stage*. If it is the case that he was thinking in this way, it certainly opens the way for an understanding of identity work as the recognition, and possibly the understanding of tensions and contradictions and their on-going resolution. Drama lessons can provide settings in which participants can both immerse themselves in the action of a Vygotskian stage and also seek to understand the ways in which personal change can become possible. The tools of drama can be used as a means of 'seeing' the tensions that may exist in everyday social situations, but remain unseen by those who are given or take up particular social positions. It is through the opportunity of gaining new perspectives on the familiar that it can become 'strange' and open to a new form of engagement.

One key element in the construction of pedagogic settings that promote creativity is the conscious adjustment of relations of power and control. Many drama practitioners will recognize the layout of a circle as a starting position for the lesson. Immediately this configuration subverts the traditional layout of a classroom, which positions the teacher at the front of the class with the pupils facing towards them. In a circle, the participants are encouraged to be inclusive and equal, with both pupils and teacher sharing the space. Whilst it is still possible to identify the teacher as different and retaining the power(s) of a teacher, there is at least the potential for pupils to negotiate their role within this classroom.

This potential is further strengthened through the process of *contracting* – whereby the participants attempt to find a suitable paradigm for collaborative work. Neelands (2004) outlines four key conditions for distinguishing when *theatre* is taking place, which we can also use to understand the requirements and responsibilities for undertaking drama work (see Table 5.1).

In each of the four areas of contracting, the pupils have equal responsibility for the creation and maintenance of the context. This collective responsibility prepares the space for renegotiation of role and identities and does so in such a way that the individual is protected by the agreement of the group. This

Table 5.1 Four conditions of theatre (Neelands, 2004: 4)

1. An elected context		Theatre is by choice. It is bracketed off from 'daily life'. It is a mode of live experience that is special and different from our everyday experience. The 'choice' is often formalized by the spatial and temporal separation of theatre from life, so that performances are advertised to occur at a certain time within a designated performance space.
2. Transformation of self, time and place		Within the 'elected context' there is the expectation that a 'virtual present' or 'imagined world', which is representative of an 'absent' or 'other reality', will be enacted through the symbolic transformation of presence, time and space. The performance space, the experience of time and the actors all become something different for the duration of the performance.
3. Social and aesthetic rules/ frame		Theatre is a rule-bound activity. Certain rules are 'perpetual' – there must be a choice as to whether an event is experienced as theatre, for instance. Others are tied to particular paradigms, the rules and conventions of a particular form or period of theatre. These rules relate both to the art of theatre and also to the terms of the social encounter that is theatre; being silent or joining in, for instance.
4. Actor – audience interactions		There is always a performer function (the transformed self) and an audience function (reacting and responding to the performers actions). In some forms of theatre these functions are clearly separated – the audience comes to communicate with actors. In others, the separation is less defined – a group come together to communicate as actors and as audience. Whatever form theatre takes, there must be communication between performer and audience.

exemplifies the argument of the primacy of the social in the shaping of the individual. It also attests to the understanding of the space of authoring in the landscape of the social world discussed by Holland *et al.* (1998) and Vygotsky's understanding of creativity. This may be the only opportunity pupils have to participate in a genuinely dialogic pedagogic process during their time at school. As such, the pupil's role and identity becomes that of 'citizen' within a potentially democratic classroom. These negotiations may occur prior to any drama taking place, but are a social necessity in order to establish the explicit and tacit understandings for those who will participate. In *Other People's Children*, Delpit identified five aspects of this culture of power and stated, 'The rules of the culture of power are a reflection of the rules of the culture of those who have power' (Delpit, 1995: 24). In a traditional classroom, this may reflect the power that the teacher has over the pupils, in the role of a position of responsibility and dominance.

> If you are not already a participant in the culture of power, being told explicitly the rules of that culture makes acquiring power easier.
>
> (Delpit, 1995: 24)

In the drama lesson, the acquisition of power becomes possible as the participants become players in which the rules are made explicit through the sharing and distribution of influence. The culture of power through drama is that it enables existing social orders to be re-examined and negotiated through the lenses of multiple perspectives. Through participation or as a spectator, the traditional hegemonic structure is disrupted and may be permanently transformed. According to Leland and Harste:

> A change or reframing of an old perception occurs as students are able to arrange or alternate previous assumptions. The imagination works as a stage to play out our roles and juxtapose ideas giving us the ability to see the other side, to weigh alternatives, and use what some refer to as intuition.
>
> (Leland and Harste, 1994: 71)

Heathcote provides insights into how pupils might have the opportunity to experience transformation through engagement and participation within a drama lesson. It is possible to identify aspects of her work that can be aligned with the theories and beliefs of Vygotsky relating to how children learn. In *Contexts for Active Learning* (Heathcote, 2000), she proposes four theoretical models, one of which at least forms the framework for the exploration of transformative role(s), transitionary identities and empowerment:

> Drama used to explore people, their behaviour, their circumstances, their responses to events which affect them ... around this 'pure' form there have developed a network of other forms of exploring people and events invented by a variety of teachers to serve their own interests and beliefs ...
>
> (Heathcote, 2002: 31–32)

The following brief event is drawn from a lesson in a large secondary school in The Midlands. The city is the second largest in England, with a proud history in manufacturing and an ethnically diverse population. In the school in which this event took place there are significantly more boys than girls, primarily because there is a girls' school in the locality. The number eligible for FSM is well above the national average because the school is located in an area of social and economic disadvantage. Most students are of White British origin. The event is selected in order to provide an indication of how pupils are able to assume the position of authority, with power and status through interaction with Teacher in Role (TIR).

To set the scene, the teacher assumes the role of a young refugee whose son is unwilling to speak. Her attempts to settle peacefully in the local community are thwarted by the sustained attack on her and her family home. The dramatic pretext is identified as a bucket, cloth and cleaning spray. Prior to the start of the drama, the pupils share through discussion and analysis of the 'symbols' (props), what they believe may happen in the following dramatic moment.

The TIR as the refugee enters the dramatic space, collects the bucket and cloth and begins to scrub the wall which is covered with abusive graffiti. Turning directly to the audience she speaks:

'Why do you do this to me?'

It is at this point that the pupils are able to enter the drama – in a role(s) suggested and negotiated through the group. By assuming a role in the moment of fiction, the participants are able to explore possible responses in a way that protects them from the restraints of reality and 'self'. This enables individuals to voice thoughts, fears and concerns through the lens of 'role', which in turn reflects the everyday reality of life. The teacher poses the following question to the group: 'Who might witness this moment?' Individuals respond and then take on the role of the person they volunteered. Examples could include neighbours, police or a postal delivery person.

The child (as in role of neighbour) may offer tea and sympathy, exploring ways in which they may help. Alternatively, the role of the perpetrator may be presented. Through the protection of 'role', it is possible to examine ambiguities and conflicting moralities, to re-examine what these might mean in our shared reality. As Bolton states, 'Heathcote's assumptions underlying her drama praxis were, ... that participants engage with making meanings and those meanings relate to a human struggle' (Bolton, 1998: 78). This engagement has transformative potential.

Underpinning Heathcote's work are assumptions about the nature of learning, which echo those who have been influenced by Vygotsky, as outlined recently by Davis (2013). Learning involves the mutual shaping of person and setting. In schools, learning involves the active role of teachers and peers in the social co-construction of solutions to problems using the tools and signs that are made available. In the arts, these tools can activate the imagination and crystallize belief. The arts utilize form and structure to express ideas and emotions.

Here lies the importance of the potential of drama for (creative) learning and working with imagination(s). This rests on an understanding of the importance of both external human activity and internal interactions – and reflection – for learning. Drama, whether it be scripted or improvised, is a microcosm of events that reflect events and possible events in the real world. As such, participation in the drama provides opportunities for pupils to challenge or subvert the identities they normally assume, willingly or not. This is both emancipatory and provides temporary relief from the limited power that pupils hold within the socio-cultural relationships in the school. Drama offers the possibility for the construction of 'interrupts' in the ongoing flow of life in school. The refiguring of the landscape and the transformation of identity may result. This may entail voluntary or involuntary participation in trajectories that lead to contestation of the identities, donated through the ways in which processes of categorization operate within institutions and schooling.

The power structures evidenced in the traditional hierarchies of schooling may be reviewed, including those between the pupils themselves. During a drama lesson, pupils are able to observe each other and model alternatives for interpretation. As well as Heathcotian style process drama, other dramatic forms such as Boal's Forum Theatre offer opportunities for disrupting traditional school hierarchies and practices. Forum Theatre features the sharing of a play or scene, usually indicating some kind of oppression, which is shown twice (Boal, 2000). Participants are allowed to interrupt and exchange places with one of the oppressed characters. The intention is that they show how the situation may be changed to enable a different outcome and may explore several different alternatives. The remaining participants stay in character and improvise their responses, whilst a facilitator enables communication between the players and the audience. This strategy subverts and restructures traditional relationships between actors and audiences. It enables participants to develop and reflect on courses of action, which could be applicable to their everyday lives. This may promote the development of alternatives to established identities and newly shared understandings. This blurring of the boundaries between actor and spectator immediately creates the opportunity for dialogue and interaction, in both assumed and given identities.

This is evident in the development, sharing and exploration of participants' opinion, thoughts, feelings and values in the drama lesson. Through the lens or voice of the 'role', divergent or conflicting modes can be resolved or sustained.

Importantly, the opportunity to 're-play' the moment can serve to find alternative resolutions in which new identities may be created. This may well be evidenced in the dialogue and discussions pre and post the moment in which the drama occurs. During the exchange of dialogue, the extent to which the participant is able to create and develop the role or identity is dependent on how capable of using the tools the individual is. An example of this could be whereby a view that is contradictory to that held by the individual is shared through the lens of the role. Through negotiation and use of drama strategies, pupils are empowered to structure imagination so that their world(s) become meaningful in a shared reality. As O'Neill emphasizes:

> It is imagination that allows both teacher and students to devise alternative modes of action, alternative projects and solutions, and imagination is at the heart of this complex way of thinking.
> (O'Neill, cited in Heathcote and Bolton, 1995: viii)

Conclusion

Drama can provide a situation for the development of alternative ways of thinking and feeling about the world and one's position within it. Through the careful structuring of social encounters, the teacher can help young people to do the kind of 'identity work', which is absent from many other curriculum settings. To requote Holland *et al.* (1998):

> Cultural worlds are populated by familiar social types and even identifiable persons, not simply differentiated by some abstract division of labour. The identities we gain within figured worlds are thus specifically historical developments, grown through continued participation in the positions defined by the social organization of those world's activity.
> (Holland *et al.*, 1998: 41)

We argue that drama provides the opportunity for a form of social intervention that can help to subvert some of the 'positions defined by the social organization' (Holland *et al.*, 1998), and offer the possibility of a form of learning which enables them to experience a change in subject position and to reflect on that change. They are learning to see familiar landscapes from new positions. This is made possible through moments of collective creativity, which sow the seeds of personal change. They bring personal histories into new settings and have the opportunity of standing outside familiar trajectories in order to contemplate new realities. As Vygotsky and Bakhtin remind us, learning of this kind involves the mutual shaping of person and place in the world. In one sense Vygostky saw life as a progression through an ongoing series of dramatic encounters in which collisions between person and situation and their dialectical resolution were the very engine of existence. If education is supposed to prepare young people for later life, then drama lessons are a most important way of understanding the nature of experience that lies ahead. They stand in stark contrast to the predeliction for control and 'on-task' behaviour, where the task is reading or writing (Duffield, 1998) that so many low SES young people encounter, perhaps especially when they have entered the pedagogic world of 'being an FSM' pupil.

Note

1 Challenge the Gap is a UK programme managed by Challenge Partners which aims to accelerate the progress of disadvantaged pupils and break the link between poverty and performance. Further information is available via their website *www.challengepartners.org*

References

Bakhtin, M.M. (1978), 'The Problem of the Text', *Soviet Studies in Literature*, 14(1): 3–33.
Bakhtin, M.M. (1986), *Speech Genres and Other Late Essays*, translated by Vern W. McGee, C. Emerson and M. Holquist (eds), Austin: University of Texas Press.
Boal, A. (2000), *Theatre of the Oppressed*, London: Pluto Press.
Bolton, G. (1979), *Towards a Theory of Drama in Education*, London: Addison-Wesley Longman Limited.
Bolton, G. (1998), *Acting in Classroom Drama, a Critical Analysis*, Staffs, UK: Trentham Books Ltd.
Brown, J.S. and Duguid, P. (2000), *The Social Life of Information*, Boston: Harvard Business School Press.
Chaiklin, S. (2003), 'The Zone of Proximal Development', in 'Vygotsky's Analysis of Learning and Instruction', in A. Kozulin, B. Gindis, V. Ageyev and S. Miller (eds), *Vygotsky's Educational Theory in Cultural Context*, Cambridge: Cambridge University Press.

Cole, M., and Griffin, P. (1983), 'A Socio-Historical Approach to Re-mediation', *Quarterly Newsletter of the Laboratory of Comparative Human Cognition*, 5(4): 69–74.

Daniels, H. (2008), *Vygotsky and Research*, London: Routledge.

Davis, S. (2013), 'Transformative Learning: Revisiting Heathcote and Vygotsky for the Digital Age', Paper presented at the International Drama/Theatre and Education Association World Congress, Paris. Accepted for publication in 'Performance' No. 3, December 2014

Delpit, L. (1995), *Other People's Children*, New York: New Press.

Dolby, N., and Dimitriadis, G. (eds) (2004), *Learning to Labor in New Times*, London: Routledge.

Duffield, J. (1998), 'Learning Experiences, Effective Schools and Social Context', *Support for Learning*, 3(1): 3–8.

Glăveanu, V.P. (2010a), 'Creativity as Cultural Participation', *Journal for the Theory of Social Behaviour*, 41(1): 48–67.

Glăveanu, V. (2010b), 'Paradigms in the Study of Creativity: Introducing the Perspective of Cultural Psychology', *New ideas in psychology*, 28(1): 79–93.

Heathcote, D. (2000), 'Contexts for Active Learning', in *Drama Research*, vol. 1, London: Heinemann.

Heathcote, D. and Bolton, G. (1995), *Drama for Learning: Dorothy Heathcote's Mantle of the Expert Approach to Education*, Portsmouth, NH: Heinemann.

Holland, D., Lachiotte, L., Skinner, D. and Cain, C. (1998), *Identity and Agency in Cultural Worlds*, Cambridge, MA: Harvard University Press.

John-Steiner, V. and Mahn, H. (1996), 'Sociocultural Approaches to Learning and Development: A Vygotskian Framework', *Educational Psychologist*, 31(3–4): 191–206.

Lave, J. and Wenger, E. (1991), *Situated Learning: Legitimate Peripheral Participation*, Cambridge: Cambridge University Press.

Leland, C and Harste, J.C. (1994), 'Multiple Ways of Knowing: Curriculum in a New Key', *Language Arts*, 71(5): 337–45.

Moran, S. and John-Steiner, V. (2003), 'Creativity in the Making: Vygotsky's Contemporary Contribution to the Dialectic of Development and Creativity', In R.K. Sawyer, V. John-Steiner, S. Moran, R.J. Sternberg, D.H. Feldman, H. Gardner and M. Csikszentmihalyi (eds), *Creativity and Development*, Oxford: Oxford University Press.

Neelands, J. (2004), *Beginning Drama 11–14*, London: David Fulton Publishers.

Newman, D., Griffin, P. and Cole, M. (1989), *The Construction Zone: Working for Cognitive Change in School*, Cambridge: Cambridge University Press.

Tharp, R.G. and Gallimore, R. (1988), *Rousing Minds to Life: Teaching, Learning and Schooling in Society Context*, Cambridge: Cambridge University Press.

Valsiner, J. and Van der Veer, R. (1993), 'The Encoding of Distance: The Zone of Proximal Development and its Interpretations', in R.R. Cocking and K.A. Renninger (eds), *The Development and Meaning of Psychological Distance*, New Jersey: Erlbaum Associates, 35–62.

Vygotsky, L.S. (1978), *Mind in Society: The Development of Higher Psychological Processes*, Cambridge, MA: Harvard University Press.
Wertsch, J.V. (1991), *Voices of the Mind: A Sociocultural Approach to Mediated Action*, Cambridge, MA: Harvard University Press.
Wertsch, J.V. (1998), *Mind as Action*, New York: Oxford University Press.
Wertsch, J.V. and Tulviste, P. (1992), 'L.S. Vygotsky and Contemporary Developmental Psychology', *Developmental Psychology*, 28(4): 548–57.
Yaroshevsky, M. (1989), *Lev Vygotsky*, Moscow: Progress Publishers.

6

Constructing Identity and Motivation in the Drama Classroom: A Sociocultural Approach

Richard Walker, Michael Anderson, Robyn Gibson and Andrew Martin

Introduction

Well I walked into the room, the kids were milling around a bit and I asked them to form groups. We were working on characters that day and I asked them to take on different characters and work with each other to understand how the characters would react to each other. The characters working together in a given situation created the scenario, I think it was something like a dinner party. It gave us a really good start to the playbuilding process in the end because the kids were engaged I suppose by trying out new things in character and by pushing themselves and pushing the others in character. They enjoyed the thrill, I think, of living inside someone else's shoes and their characterizations got richer as they played off each other. I think they also enjoyed the opportunity to collaborate and be creative together.

(John[1] – High School Drama Teacher, Sydney[2])

The drama classroom is frequently characterized by practitioners and theorists as a place of learning where collaborative, creative learning takes place. John's reflections on his classroom (above) reveal processes of identity formation and motivation at work that are consistent with Vygotsky's view that:

> Every function in the child's cultural development appears twice: first, on the social level, and later, on the individual level; first, between people (interpsychological) and then inside the child (intrapsychological). This applies equally to voluntary attention, to logical memory, and to the formation of concepts. All the higher functions originate as actual relationships between individuals
>
> (Vygotsky, 1978: 57)

By its very nature, drama, and process drama in particular, focuses on understanding human experience through the taking on of identity in role and understanding the realities of that role through interaction with other characters. Vygotky's reflections on a child's cultural development occurring twice – first socially and then internally – reflects the kind of processes that happen routinely in drama classrooms and are consistent with the kinds of reflections John is making on his own classroom experience. The act of improvising a character and playbuilding requires students to engage directly with others, learn from them in and out of role, and reflect on their own actions and the actions of others, in and out of role.

An added layer occurs in the pedagogical feedback that drama teachers provide for students. This critique allows them to reflect on, and continue to develop, their skills as drama makers. In drama education, identity is understood as a process of socially and collaboratively negotiated creation in the form of role making and role taking, consistent with the Vygotskian perspective. Reflective processes that are usually undertaken individually in log books or similar help the student to consider the implications of the identities they have formed and how these identities have intersected with the identities of others, especially in character work. This approach to 'playing at identity' allows young people in a relatively 'penalty free zone' to experiment with and manipulate different kinds of identities to understand the implications of the choices they make. According to Dezuanni and Jetnikoff (2011), the creativity inherent in arts education is a fundamental aspect of the process of identity formation. Drama students' agency over the identity formation, although moderated by their fellow students, is strong in this situation where they have distance from their actual identity.

John's reflections also reveal the work of drama in developing motivation and engagement in students. Again, this motivation and engagement is socially mediated through the interaction of students with each other. In John's example, students were engaged and motivated to participate through their interaction with other students in character. He describes how the students motivate or, in his words, 'push' each other to deepen characterization. This scenario is typical of the ways drama educators work with their students to create socially mediated motivations to engage in learning.

The role of identity and motivation has, however, been under-emphasized in discussions of classroom practice in drama education; in particular, there have been few attempts to examine identity and motivation in the drama classroom from the perspective of sociocultural theories. This chapter does so and attempts to explain both in the context of Vygotskian and neo-Vygotskian theoretical concepts. Prior to this, we provide a brief account of a sociocultural approach to identity formation and construction. We then examine drama education practice and consider the relevance of classroom drama practices for identity formation and the construction of motivation. This includes teacher and student perspectives, taken from a recent qualitative investigation into motivation, and drama, learning and performance in three Australian high schools[3]. Finally, brief conclusions are drawn in relation to identity and motivation in the drama classroom.

Sociocultural Perspectives on Identity and Motivation

Identity Formation

Sociocultural approaches to identity formation take the view that identity is a social construction, which is shaped and formed through sociocultural, historical and institutional processes. In this regard, language is seen as playing a central role in identity construction and formation. As a consequence, approaches which emphasize language in identity formation have sometimes been referred to as sociocultural discourse approaches.

While there are many sociocultural discourse perspectives on identity formation, James Gee's (2001) work is perhaps the best known and will be briefly elaborated on here as a well-developed example of this perspective (Gee, 2001; Gee and Green, 1998), indicating that people have multiple identities which derive from their performances in social contexts and the way that they are consequently recognized by other people. He suggests four main ways in which people are recognized as certain kinds of people and identities are ascribed to them. First, identities develop from, or are ascribed, on the basis of natural states (N-Identity), such as being female or, in a school context, having a physical or mental disability. Second, identities are authorized by institutions (I-Identity) according to the positions that people hold in them. Institutions have rules, regulations and traditions which involve different positions and responsibilities and which cause people to be recognized as different kinds of people. Third, people are recognized as certain kinds of people and so acquire identities because of the discursive (D-Identity) or dialogic interactions in which they are involved; that is, the way that other people talk about and interact with a person leads to the discursive construction of identities.

These discursive interactions are based on the recognition of some characteristic of an individual or the ascription of some characteristic to an individual. For instance, in the school context, this might be the ascription of the term 'behaviour problem' to a student. Gee (2001) notes that both I-Identities and D-Identities may be considered to be on a continuum in relation to how actively or passively a person attempts to adopt or recruit them. Fourth, identities are created from shared participation in the practices of social or cultural groups, referred to by Gee (2001) as affinity groups (A-Identity). In a school context, an affinity group may share similar interests in music or dress, or in activities like playing chess or debating. Different societies may have tended to foreground different views of identity so that, for instance, N-Identities have been foregrounded in some societies, while different identities have also been foregrounded in different historical eras. Finally, views of identity require interpretive systems which allow the interpretation of nature, institutions, discourse and affiliative groups. These interpretative systems also mean that identities can be negotiated, contested or resisted (Gee, 2001). It is clear that N-, I-, D- and A-Identities are not separate and immutable categories (Gee, 2001). The categorization of these differing identities will depend upon a range of interpretive factors, and the categorization may change depending upon the perspective from which they are viewed.

Being recognized as a certain kind of person also depends upon Discourses (Gee, 2001), with a capital D. These are combinations of ways of speaking, acting and interacting, dressing, feeling, believing and valuing, and using objects, tools or technologies. For social or historical reasons these combinations allow one to be recognized in particular ways. These combinations are upheld or supported and maintained by groups of people or by institutions, or combinations of institutions, so that people continue to be recognized over time in certain ways and not others. Gee (2001) suggests that the meaning of terms *community of practice* and *discourse community* have much in common with the meaning of Discourse. Finally, Gee (2001) considers that people have Discourse trajectories which reflect their experiences within different Discourses and therefore their experience of being recognized in various ways. In addition to their experiences of Discourses, people also create their own individual narratives. While Discourses are social and historical, narratives are individual, though socially constructed.

Although Gee (2001) emphasizes that identity involves the recognition by others of an individual as being a certain kind of person, and therefore emphasizes the impact of others and Discourses on identity formation, he does make clear that individuals may actively 'bid' for certain identities, or attempt to 'recruit' particular identities. Identity formation from a sociocultural discourse perspective, therefore, involves more than the ascription of identities but also involves agency on the part of the person forming the identity. However, this perspective is silent on the issue of motivation, although inferences concerning motivation and identity might be made on the basis of Discourses and the four identities identified earlier.

Gee's notion of multiple personalities based on natural appearance (N), institutional (I) context and (D) dialogic interaction mirrors the identity experimentation process involved in dramatic role taking and characterization. Returning to John's statement at the opening of this chapter, we can see that Gee's identities are interacting in the dramatic play. For instance, students have the opportunity to subvert their natural characteristics by 'acting' taller or shorter. Students also have the opportunity to imagine themselves in different 'I' identities by situating themselves in different contexts. In John's case, his students decided to relocate themselves at a dinner party. John's reflection that they were unlikely to have experienced a dinner party highlights the opportunity for young people in these situations to 'play at' different I-identities.

This ability to manipulate and imagine different I-identities is significant for learning. In her drama research, Freebody (2010) used this technique to gain insight into how young people understood their current I-identity and their agency over it. The use of drama as a research tool gave her access to a flexible, imaginative capacity that allowed her to understand the way students perceived their social identity and how flexible that I-identity became when dramatic tools such as improvisation and characterization were applied. She found that young people coming to drama have fairly inflexible senses of their I-identity, but that they are able to imagine differently with use of dramatic techniques. In her work, identity was developed through role taking and negotiation, allowing it to be reframed and reformed consistently with Gee's D-identity where students interact constantly in imagined characters as a way of understanding the role they are taking and understanding the impact of the role on other roles.

Other Sociocultural Perspectives on Identity and Motivation

While attempts to develop a sociocultural theory of motivation are evident in the work of Sivan (1986), Hickey (1997, 2003) and Hickey and Granade (2004), the most comprehensive sociocultural approach has been developed by Walker and his colleagues (Walker, 2010; Walker et al., 2004. 2010). This approach has also been extended to consider both motivation and identity (Walker, 2007, 2008; Walker et al., 2010), who consider that identity formation and motivation are fundamentally social in nature and have their origins in social practices. Their approach involves a meta-theory which attempts to explain the relationship of the social world to the world of the individual. It also involves a theoretical explanation of the way that identities and motivational goals, standards, beliefs and expectations have their origins in various cultural practices, are transformatively internalized through collaborative engagement in these cultural practices, and are then transformatively externalized in collaborative or individual activity.

The sociocultural meta-theoretical perspective developed by Walker and colleagues endorses a social epistemology and accords analytical or theoretical primacy to the social world over the individual world, while recognizing that these worlds are closely interlinked and interdependent. According primacy to the social origins of identity and motivation does not, however, mean that explanations of individual identity or motivation can be reduced to social explanations or that social processes determine individual identity or motivation. Sociocultural reductionism (Martin, 2006) and social determinism are avoided in this approach to identity and motivation through theoretical notions, which explain how the social world is internalized and externalized by individuals. These assert that while there is a dynamic interdependence (Valsiner 1997a,b, 1998) between the social and individual worlds, they are distinguishable and qualitatively different from each other. This approach, while recognizing the social nature of identity and motivation, also recognizes that an individual's intra-psychological functioning is still relatively autonomous from the social world; the approach thus also recognizes the agency of the individual.

In developing their approach, Walker and colleagues have drawn together a number of ideas from sociocultural theorists including Vygotsky, Valsiner and Rogoff. While not all of these ideas will be discussed in the current chapter, they include the following:

- the enculturation of individuals into the cultural practices of particular communities;
- the zone of proximal development; the notions of internalization and externalization;
- the processes of canalization and self-canalization;
- the importance of interpersonal relations and intersubjectivity;
- and the ideas of inclusive separation and planes of analysis.

From this sociocultural perspective, identity formation and motivation are considered to have their origins in the academic practices of the school and are subsequently internalized by learners, as zones of proximal development are created through the process of enculturation into valued activities. The academic practices of schools are associated with various academic identities and the specific practices of reading, writing, mathematics, drama and other school subjects enculturating students into identities such as that of being a writer, performer or mathematician. Enculturation into specific cultural practices also involves enculturation into the motivational goals, standards, beliefs and expectations of particular cultural groups and communities of practice.

As the enculturation process takes place, practices and activities become increasingly valued and important to the individual, and the identities and motivational goals and standards associated with those practices are internalized. The process of internalization is transformative so that identities and motivational goals and standards are selectively constructed and are also transformed during the process of internalization. Furthermore, Sainsbury and Walker (2007) consider that the internalization of identity and motivation also depends upon the degree of intersubjectivity, or shared understanding, created as learners work collaboratively with each other. Sainsbury and Walker (2007) suggest that productive and good interpersonal relations lead to higher levels of intersubjectivity, while poor interpersonal relations lead to lower levels of intersubjectivity. Higher levels of intersubjectivity, in turn, are considered to enhance the internalization of identities and motivational goals and standards. In a study of a primary science classroom, Pressick-Kilborn (2011) found support for the role of intersubjectivity in identity formation and motivation. Her study suggested that high levels of intersubjectivity between the teacher and students in the classroom lead to high levels of student interest in science and to the construction of science-related identities.

Student identities, however, can also influence interpersonal relations, intersubjectivity and the subsequent processes of internalization. In research conducted with first-year pharmacy students and reported by Sainsbury and Walker (2007), some students with well established, competitive, academic identities, influenced the interpersonal dynamics of cooperative learning groups in detrimental ways which impacted on the subsequent learning of group members. This was in contrast to another group where interpersonal relations and intersubjectivity promoted the internalization and learning of group members. One student in the detrimental group, for instance, had obtained the highest university entrance score possible, and was very competitive, determined to achieve high grades on her own. This student was very committed to this competitive identity and her identity prevented her from engaging collaboratively in group activities. Her identity influenced her interactions with group members and lead to group dynamics, which made it harder for the group to develop shared understanding of group tasks, and this ultimately impacted on the understanding and learning of group members. In the group with productive social relations, however, student identities promoted long-term student learning and understanding.

The internalization of academic identities and motivational beliefs and standards may also be actively resisted by individuals. This process of resistance was demonstrated in an investigation conducted by Walker (2003), in which some pre-service teachers resisted the identities associated with learning with technology. However, once academic identities and motivation beliefs have been internalized, they are subsequently externalized in subsequent interactions with others. The process of externalization is also transformative so that the identities and motivational beliefs that are externalized may not be the same as those that are internalized. In her research, Pressick-Kilborn (2011) demonstrated inferential support for the internalization and externalization of science-related identities and motivation within the classroom context. That is, students appeared to internalize their science-related identities from their engagement in the science activities and practices of the classroom. Pressick-Kilborn (2011) also found strong support for the idea that identities are formed as a consequence of processes of canalization, which is the way that children are channelled in various directions. In her study, the channelling of student science activities by parents in the home was strongly related to student interest in, and valuing of, science activities in school, and to the construction of science-related identities. Pressick-Kilborn (2011) also found support for the contention that canalization processes, in conjunction with a person's valuing of, and identification with, particular activities and practices, leads to self-canalization processes on the part of students. She showed that where students were guided into science-related activities by their parents, they were much more likely to channel themselves into science activities in the classroom.

Identity and Motivation in Classroom Drama Practice

In drama education, identity construction is apparent in the process of learning as part of each participant's development of self and is acknowledged in curriculum documentation as a central learning objective. The rationale of the syllabus in the Australian state of New South Wales makes this orientation explicit:

> Drama encourages a cooperative approach to exploring the world through enactment. The collaborative nature of this art form engages students in a creative process of sharing, developing and expressing emotions and ideas. It is a form of action in which students take on a role as a means of exploring both familiar and unfamiliar aspects of their world. They portray aspects of human experience while exploring the ways people react and respond to different situations, issues and ideas.
>
> (NSW Board of Studies, 2003)

A key approach in drama education practice that allows identity 'exploration' is the process of *metaxis* (Boal, 1995). Metaxis is a pedagogical approach used in character formation where the student is encouraged to perform a character while simultaneously retaining a sense of themselves; in essence, maintaining their own identity while playing another. Researchers in drama education have claimed that metaxis grows and deepens empathic engagement in learning in this art form (O'Toole, 2004). For example, a student playing Romeo is metaxically engaging in the character of Romeo while simultaneously reflecting on that process as a student. This is a kind of reflection-in-action in which the student draws from their own dramatic skills while reflecting on the identities of other characters. Through metaxis, identity becomes critical as an exploration of the 'other', including other characters and other student identities within the class. As Peter Wright argues:

> This ability grows out of our own self-awareness as a reference point, that is, our own bodily presence and it is this self-awareness that allows us to infer the mental states of others. In other words, rationality is grounded in bodily experience and the embodied mind is intersubjectively constituted at its most fundamental levels.
>
> (Wright, 2011: 113)

Drama learning also provides a space for students to critically reflect on their own identity, and in a kind of penalty free zone experiment with different identities, in order to play at different identities or with different aspects of the student's own identity from within the safety of the role. This is true of both text-based drama and improvisational drama. The improvisation process is a kind of collaborative playwriting where all members of the group have the opportunity to contribute to the developing dramatic work. The improvisation process often throws up engaging moments that are used in the play building process. At the centre of the improvisation process is role taking. In role taking, students have the opportunity to improvise different kinds of characters and different characteristics of those characters. Initially, students inexperienced in drama adopt stereotyped characters that are often derived from their television or popular media consumption. The role of the teacher in facilitating improvisation is to deepen these characters and roles. Students do this by undertaking and experimenting with a range of roles and a range of behaviours related to those roles in the improvisation and play building process.

Collaborative work is at the heart of dramatic practice in the classroom. Students are required to work individually on performance pieces and drama-related tasks (director's portfolio, design assignments, written responses), but the majority of classroom time is taken up by collaborative group-based tasks. The concept of the ensemble is pervasive and persistent in professional theatre and also forms the basis for collaborative work in drama curricula in New South Wales and international drama curricula (Anderson, 2012). Collaborative practice is used by drama teachers to familiarize students with the discipline of working with ensembles in theatre. Drama educators also claim that this approach builds a pro-social orientation for students, developing democratic understanding and teamwork skills (Neelands, 2009). This is due in part to the nature of the art form, with the vast majority of theatre being ensemble work. However, it is also the case that teachers value this kind of work as a way to build intrapersonal and interpersonal understanding in students. Teachers scaffold group and collaborative work in several different ways. Text-based work is often approached with a fairly traditional rehearsal room approach where students are allocated roles and where a director blocks (arranges) movement and dialogue. This is especially true if students are involved in a public performance such as a musical. When students are improvising or play building, the process is often more facilitative with the teacher structuring the approach (as described earlier) and intervening where groups require support or inspiration for the development of their dramatic work. The scaffolding of collaborative and group work is a major task of the drama teacher and requires skills in facilitation and direction (often at the same time). While this process is aimed at developing new dramatic work through an understanding of the making and performing process, drama teachers are also attending to the learning of intrapersonal and interpersonal skills in their students.

A Brief Sociocultural Analysis of Classroom Drama Practice

The drama classroom has its own social, cultural and institutional traditions. These traditions are influenced by both the traditions of schooling and the traditions of the theatre and theatrical training, and in turn influence both identity formation and motivational beliefs, standards and expectations. In relation to identity formation, the drama classroom is concerned with both the identities of learning and the identities of theatrical performance and improvisation. As the sociocultural theories outlined earlier in the chapter have indicated, both kinds of identities are concerned with being recognized as a certain type of person and persuading oneself and others about who one is. In relation to motivation, as students are enculturated into the practices of the drama classroom, these practices become valued and important practices for students. As a consequence, these practices are likely to be motivating for students.

School classrooms are inherently social environments and this is especially true of the drama classroom with its considerable emphasis on collaborative and group activities. These collaborative drama practices, and the associated scaffolding provided by drama teachers, provide students with contexts in which identities and motivational standards, beliefs and expectations can be transformatively internalized and subsequently externalized. Collaborative and group drama activities, along with teacher scaffolding, create zones of proximal development (Vygotsky, 1978), which allow the processes of transformative internalization to operate. Collaborative and co-operative learning activities in the drama classroom are also more likely to lead to greater levels of intersubjectivity amongst those students in the groups and in the classroom as a whole. In turn, higher levels of intersubjectivity are likely to enhance the internalization of both identity and motivational processes. Identities and motivation may be externalized in the context of both collaborative and individual activity. When they are externalized in the context of collaborative activity, then the potential exists for the creation of zones of proximal development and for their subsequent internalization by other students.

Teacher and Student Perspectives on Motivation in the Drama Classroom

A recent mixed methods study (Martin et al., 2013) was designed to address substantive questions of relevance to students, educators, parents, policy makers and key stakeholder institutions about the role of the arts, including drama in academic motivation, engagement and achievement. The quantitative phase of the project to assess these questions used a longitudinal survey instrument. Classrooms identified as creating effective learning environments in this survey were then invited to be part of the qualitative phase of the research that aimed to report on what constituted 'best practice' learning and teaching in arts classrooms.

In the qualitative phase, data was collected in these high performing arts classrooms in the following ways:

- real-time student artifacts (using Personal Data Assistants), which included samples of students' work in dance, drama, music and visual arts. In some cases this included students reflecting, for instance in dance, on their choreography and then demonstrating it to the PDA through video of the dance;
- the generation of student and teacher interview data to better understand the specific classroom processes and practices that underlie the link between arts education and productive motivation. Amongst other things, the interviews examined student and teacher perspectives on:
  - which elements of arts education foster motivation and engagement;
  - if there some forms of arts education (e.g. drama) that are more closely associated with or supportive of broader engagement.

Here we report on research in drama classrooms in three high schools in New South Wales and the Australian Capital Territory (Munday, 2014). The first feature of the student and teacher research data was the overarching prevalence of collaboration as a factor in the development of motivation in the classroom. In some ways this is unsurprising, as the syllabus that governs and guides the teaching in these classrooms mandates collaboration and cooperation as part of the rationale for the learning that takes place in these classrooms. The following excerpts from interview data reveal the experience of drama teachers relating to collaboration and the role that collaboration plays in motivation:

> Well, it's the only subject where students are encouraged and indeed mandated to work together collaboratively. And really in the real world that's what they're going to have to do when they leave school. I mean it's, you know, everything is about teamwork and collaboration. So within the curriculum it gives you those skills, it gives you those skills to be able to collaborate, to negotiate, to be creative with other people and they're all getting excited about it. You can tell they're engaged.
>
> (Sasha – Teacher, Ashmore High School)

> You know, kids who start off really shy and seeing a group evolve over a year and become a team of collaborators and individual kids growing and developing in the course of a year and growing in confidence and growing in sophistication in terms of their practice. So yeah, it's a very rewarding field. I see the students motivated a lot of the time especially when I do playbuilding

and collaborative work with kids. You know, having a go at some of more physical theatre forms and that kind of work can be quite exciting and creative.

(Alice – Teacher, Croydon Grammar)

These teachers reveal a strong orientation towards motivating and engaging students in the drama classroom through collaborative activities. Sasha's comment, 'You can tell they're engaged', reveals a pedagogical judgement that her students are drawn in to the learning community by the act of collaboration. Alice's comment demonstrates that collaborative practices are central to drama learning and motivation.

These teachers' reflections are supported by the comments of students in their drama classes:

> But I would say that definitely, therefore, the [collaborative] culture of the drama class and the respect we have for each other and the commitment we put into the stuff really does inevitably affect our final performance.
>
> (Guy – Student, Ashmore High School)

> There is a lot of collaboration and really the only way to get over those conflicts and to get someone motivated is to talk through them. The problem with that [group] assessment task was that, no matter how much you talked to them, they wouldn't want to listen. So really, the only way to get over it would be to toughen up. To have to put in extra work on their behalf and just hope that everything falls into place by the end. It did. But the times – from beginning to basically the end, it was just so much hard work getting everyone motivated, getting everyone focused. It really just made uneffective [sic] working conditions. Like got nothing done in entire lessons.
>
> (Ginnie – Student, Ashmore High School)

These students' reflections provide a realistic view of the culture that pervades collaboration in drama learning. While Thomas identifies 'respect' as central to success in this community, Sarah has a more qualified view of the culture of collaboration, seeing it as a difficulty that needs to be navigated through talk and 'toughening up'. While these responses suggest this practice is a source of motivation and students identify readily with the collaborative process, they do sometimes see collaboration in more negative terms than their teachers, who in the main consider the collaborative process as a motivating factor in drama learning.

The second key theme to emerge is the role of performance in motivating students. Both teachers and students commented on the role of performance in motivating students and in building a sense of confidence in their personal capabilities, as noted by one of the drama teachers:

> Drama builds their self-confidence and they have to continue to develop as their skills of self-expression and to be able to get up in front of people and have the courage and the confidence in themselves to be able to express themselves ... I think at its essence, drama is about understanding people and life and delving into lives and delving into some of the truths that underpin life. And that encourages a very deep sort of learning.
>
> (Sasha – Teacher, Ashmore High School)

Students also expressed their belief that public performance was a motivating factor for them:

> And even from a self-perspective, it builds up your confidence. I mean especially for people who are a bit intimidated. Like stepping up in front of people, it kind of helps with other aspects of school. Maybe like English with speeches and that ability just to go forward and do whatever and it's all good, there's no repercussions you can just express yourself.
>
> (Jeff – Year 11 Student, Croydon Grammar School)

> That was – last time I did that was around Year 8 or something. Year 9. It was okay. Kind of just – basically what I did, it just gave me more confidence when I perform, which is nice. I was fortunate enough to actually go in a commercial for bike sales, which was pretty cool.
>
> (Brad – Student, Ashmore High School)

> It [the performance] kind of gives us a base that – hey, it's not working. Yeah, it gives us a base that we are able to achieve stuff. It gives us kind of motivation and confidence and knowing that we can actually achieve stuff. If we've done it before, then we can do it again. In a bigger scale even.
>
> (Charlie – Year 9 Student, Ashmore High School).

> I've never been one that's really excited and really enjoyed performing. I think it's just the feeling of being judged or something like that, but it's really built my self-confidence up through the arts.
>
> (David – Year 9 Student, Northern Grammar School)

The student reflections here clearly support Melinda's (the teacher's) claim that 'Drama builds their self-confidence'. Perhaps the most telling comment is David's suggestion that even though he did not like performing, his confidence was nevertheless built through these processes. While performance in the drama classroom is sometimes an individual activity, student performance often develops out of highly collaborative classroom activity and this has a powerful motivating effect, despite individual concerns of having one's identity 'judged'.

Conclusion

The drama classroom, with its emphasis on play building and character improvisation, is centrally concerned with the construction of identities and, as this chapter has demonstrated, sociocultural theories can provide important insights into the processes involved in such identity construction. Within these theoretical perspectives, collaborative processes are considered to play a pivotal role, not only in identity construction, but also in other learning and motivational processes. As with identity construction, motivation is considered to be social in nature, and this chapter indicates how the practices of the drama classroom provide a context for both identity formation and the social construction of motivation. Furthermore, the qualitative research reported in the chapter demonstrates the importance of collaborative and group drama activities and shows how collaborative learning has important motivational consequences.

Notes

1 All names of participants and schools in this chapter are pseudonyms.
2 This interview took place in September 2011 and was undertaken as part of the research for Anderson (2012).
3 This research was funded by the Australian Research Council and The Australia Council for the Arts. The research team included some of the authors of this chapter, as well as David Sudmalis, Marianne Mansour, Caitlin Munday, Arief Liem and Josephine Flemming.

References

Anderson, M. (2012), *Master Class in Drama Education: Transforming Teaching and Learning*, London: Continuum.

Boal, A. (1995), *The Rainbow of Desire: The Boal Method of Theatre and Therapy*, London: Routledge.

Dezuanni, M. and Jetnikoff, A. (2011), 'Creative Pedagogies and the Contemporary School Classroom', in J. Sefton-Green, P. Thompson, L. Bresler, and K. Jones, (eds), *The Routledge International Handbook of Creative Learning*, New York and London: Routledge.

Freebody, K. (2010), 'Exploring Teacher–Student Interactions and Moral Reasoning Practices in Drama Classrooms', *Research in Drama Education*, 15: 209–225.

Gee, J. P. (2001), 'Identity as an Analytic Lens for Research in Education', in W.G. Secada (ed.), *Review of Research in Education*, vol. 25. Washington, DC: American Educational Research Association, 99–126.

Gee, J.P. and Green, J.L. (1998), 'Discourse Analysis, Learning, and Social Practice: A Methodological Study', in P.D. Pearson and A. Iran-Nejad (eds), *Review of Research in Education*, vol. 23, Washington, DC: American Educational Research Association, 19–170.

Hickey, D.T. (1997), 'Motivation and Contemporary Socio-constructivist Instructional Perspectives', *Educational Psychologist*, 32: 175–93.

Hickey, D.T. (2003), 'Engaged Participation versus Marginal Non-participation: A Stridently Sociocultural Approach to Achievement Motivation', *Elementary School Journal*, 103: 401–29.

Hickey, D.T. and Granade, J B. (2004), 'The Influence of Sociocultural Theory on our Theories of Motivation and Engagement', in D.M. McInerney and S. Van Etten (eds), *Big Theories Revisited*, Greenwich, CN: Information Age, 223–47.

Martin, A., Mansour, M., Anderson, M., Gibson, R., Liem, A. and Sudmalis, D. (2013), 'The Role of Arts Participation in Students' Academic and Nonacademic Outcomes: A Longitudinal Study of School, Home, and Community Factors', *Journal of Educational Psychology*, 105: 709–27.

Martin, J. (2006), 'Social Cultural Perspectives in Educational Psychology', in P. Alexander and P. Winne (eds), *Handbook of Educational Psychology*, 2nd edition, Mahwah, NJ: Erlbaum, 595–614.

Munday, C (2014), 'Conceptualizing the Drama Classroom as Community: A Case Study Approach to Effective Learning and Teaching', Unpublished Doctoral Thesis, The University of Sydney.

Neelands, J. (2009), 'Acting Together: Ensemble as a Democratic Process in Art and Life', *RiDE: The Journal of Applied Theatre and Performance*, 14: 173–189.

NSW Board of Studies (2003), *Stage 6 Drama*, Sydney: Board of Studies.

O'Toole, J. (2004), *The Process of Drama: Negotiating Art and Meaning*, London: Routledge.

Pressick-Kilborn, K. (2011), 'Towards a Sociocultural Theory of Interest: Students' Interest in Learning Science and Technology in a Community of Learners', PhD Thesis, The University of Sydney.

Sainsbury, E. and Walker, R. (2007), 'Same Words, Different Meanings: Learning to Talk the Scientific Language of Pharmacy', in A. Brew and J. Sachs (eds), *Transforming a*

University: *The Scholarship of Teaching and Learning in Practice*, Sydney: Sydney University Press, 13–26.

Sivan, E. (1986), 'Motivation in Social Constructivist Theory', *Educational Psychologist*, 21: 209–33.

Valsiner, J. (1997a), 'Magical Phrases, Human Development and Psychological Ontology', in B.D. Cox and C. Lightfoot (eds), *Sociogenetic Perspectives on Internalization*, Mahwah, NJ: Erlbaum, 237–55.

Valsiner, J. (1997b), *Culture and the Development Children's Action: A Theory of Human Development*, 2nd edition, New York: Wiley.

Valsiner, J. (1998), 'Dualisms Displaced: From Crusades to Analytic Distinctions', *Human Development*, 41: 350–4.

Vygotsky, L.S. (1978), *Mind and Society: The Development of Higher Mental Processes*, Cambridge, MA: Harvard University Press.

Walker, R.A. (2006). 'Internalizing Motivation', Symposium (Chair: Sanna Jarvela and Dan Hickey), 'Where Social and Self Meet in Future Conceptualizations of Engagement. The Concept of Motivation and the Field of Motivation Research', The 10th International Conference on Motivation, Landau. Germany, 28–30 September.

Walker, R.A. (2007), 'Sociocultural Perspectives on Academic Regulation and Identity: Theoretical Issues', Symposium (Chair: Erica Sainsbury), 'Academic Regulation and Identity: Sociocultural Perspectives and Research'. European Association for Research on Learning and Instruction, Budapest, 28 August–1 September.

Walker, R.A. (2008), 'A Sociocultural Approach to Identity Formation', Invited Symposium (Chair: Richard Walker), 'Theorising Identity'. European Association for Research on Learning and Instruction, Learning and Professional Development SIG Conference, Jvaskyla, Finland, 27–29 August.

Walker, R.A. (2010), 'Sociocultural issues in Motivation', in P. Peterson, E. Baker and B McGaw (eds), *International Encyclopaedia of Education*, 3rd edition, vol. 6, Oxford: Elsevier, 712–17.

Walker, R.A., Pressick-Kilborn, K., Arnold, L.S. and Sainsbury, E.J. (2004), 'Investigating Motivation in Context: Developing Sociocultural Perspectives', *European Psychologist*, 9: 245–56.

Walker, R.A., Pressick-Kilborn, K., Sainsbury, E., and MacCallum, J. (2010), 'A Sociocultural Approach to Motivation: A Long Time coming but here at last', in T. Urdan and S. Karabenick (eds), *Advances in Motivation and Achievement: The Next Decade of Research in Motivation and Achievement.*, vol 16B, Bingley, UK: Emerald Group Publishing, 1–42.

Wright, P.R. (2011), 'Agency, Intersubjectivity and Drama Education: The Power to be and do More', In S. Schonmann (ed.), *Key Concepts in Theatre/Drama Education*, Rotterdam: Sense Publishers, 111–15.

Part III

The Dynamics of Meaning Making through Drama Processes in the Classroom

7.

Dramatic Play and Process Drama: Towards a Collective Zone of Proximal Development to Enhance Language and Literacy Learning

Robyn Ewing

Introduction

The making of meaning was central to Vygotsky's theory of thought and language development. Importantly he gave close attention to the relationship between affect and intellect (Mahn and Steiner, 2002: 369; Vygotsky, 1986). This chapter asserts that both early dramatic play and the embedding of educational or process drama strategies across the early childhood and primary curriculum can facilitate work in a collective Zone of Proximal Development (ZPD) and link directly to children's language and literacy learning. Furthermore, it is also argued that classroom professional learning models, like the *School Drama Programme* (Ewing *et al.*, 2011, 2014), have the potential to encourage collective ZPD opportunities that can extend educators' and children's understandings alike and facilitate their deeper learning. Language and literacy learning is the particular area focused on for this discussion, but the principles can and should be applied across the early childhood and school curriculum.

Unfortunately these kinds of learning opportunities are threatened by the increasingly rapid pace of many twenty-first century lives. Less time and space is made available for such learning opportunities as young children are caught up in the complexities of adults' busy lives, as well as political and policy demands for overly structured transmissive learning programmes in the belief that this will improve academic success. Time for imagination and creativity can be squeezed out (Elkind, 2008; Zigler and Bishop-Josef, 2009). Hirsh-Pasek *et al.* (2003) describe this trend in the United States as a crisis for children in terms of their cognitive, social, spiritual, emotional and physical development. In many early childhood classrooms, it seems that so-called play activity centres are aimed at learning specific content in a particular area (e.g. number bingo, flashcards of common vocabulary or story recount exactly as told by the teacher) and are heavily dominated by the teacher rather than the children, with little allowance for messy experimentation or exploration made possible through drama (Graue, 2011: 15). Researchers also express concern that children are becoming *over-protected*. Lindon (2001) argues that children must have the right to take risks as part of play if they are going to learn how to assess and manage play in the many life situations they will confront.

The emphasis in this chapter is on the notion of a collective ZPD (Moll and Whitmore, 1993) rather than solely an individual one. It is argued that imaginative play more generally and dramatic play in particular help children co-construct knowledge with peers as well as teachers, caregivers or other experienced older children and adults, to demonstrate and practise what they already know while learning more about their world. Observing children engrossed in such activities also shows us *how* they are learning and thinking about language.

This chapter initially defines the concept of Vygotsky's ZPD and briefly outlines how it has been subsequently extended by other researchers to demonstrate how the concept can embrace symmetrical as well as asymmetrical relationships (Fernandez *et al.*, 2001). It then explores why dramatic play and process drama can be valuable in facilitating work in a collective ZPD that enhances language and literacy development. Finally, it asserts that the teacher professional learning co-mentoring model used in the *School Drama* (SD) programme can be theorized as a collective ZPD for the teachers, professional actors or teaching artists and students involved. In fact, in all probability there is more than one collective ZPD in the teacher professional learning communities that are developed through programmes like SD.

Defining the ZPD

In Vygotsky's own words:

> What we call the Zone of Proximal Development ... is a distance between the actual developmental level determined by individual problem solving and the level of development as determined through problem solving under guidance or in collaboration with more capable peers.
>
> (Vygotsky, 1978: 86)

From the outset then, interacting with others is a critical component of a child's learning and, subsequently, their development. Despite the importance of Vygotsky's original concept of the ZPD, it has been more recent researchers who have expanded our understanding of its potential. Wells (1999) emphasizes that the ZPD is created through the interaction between the student and co-participant. He notes that the quality of this interaction is critical. Building on Vygotsky's constructivist theorizing, Wood *et al.* (1976) and Bruner (1990) closely align the ZPD concept with what they described as 'scaffolding', a metaphor for the temporary role played by the teacher, parent or more experienced peer in providing intellectual support. And Jerome Singer (2006) comments that the value of scaffolding:

> ... seems especially true for imaginative play since its delicate, internalized structure seems to feed on a combination of parental approval and support, guidance into plot content and, at least initially, modelling of parental playfulness and story-telling.
>
> (Singer, 2006: 428)

Moll and Whitmore (1993) referred to the interwoven processes involved as complementary and envisaged a 'collective zone of proximal development'. They stress that it is the *quality* of cooperation between the child and the adult (my emphasis), requiring a mutual trust and active involvement that is central to the scaffolding process. Stone (1993: 178) extends this perception by arguing that scaffolding does not occur in singular social interactions, but rather through ongoing relationships. Furthermore, Petrick-Steward (1995: 13) suggests that the ZPD should be conceived of as being mutually and actively created by the child and the teacher during the activity of learning and teaching: not 'as a characteristic of the child or of teaching, but of the child engaged in collaborative activity within specific social environments.' Swain (2000: 113) similarly sees collaborative dialogue as joint problem solving and hence the opportunity to build knowledge. Snapshot 1 illustrates this collaborative dialogue.

Snapshot 1

'And what would you like to eat today, madam?' three-year-old Timothy asks his grandmother from the window of the makeshift cubby house in the playground. Jordy, Timothy's twenty-month-old brother, mimics him with not quite the same precision but a similar expression and inflection.

'Pancakes with maple syrup please.'

After 'madam' places her pancake order both boys disappear inside the cubby to prepare it. After serving it with a flourish they ask about a drink and following her request they will also prepare a rather sandy latte in an old paper cup retrieved from the sandpit. When madam finishes her coffee she asks: 'And how much is the bill, please?' She is informed that the cost is six dollars. 'Delicious and very reasonable,' she comments as the boys watch her count out the imaginary money.

Vygotsky (1966) suggests that children who are beginning to assign symbolic meaning (as Timothy and Jordy are doing in the snapshot from the café scene above) are already able to take on roles and are thus displaying the markers of the early stages of abstract thought.

The Importance of Imaginative Play

In Australia, *The Early Years Learning Framework (EYLF)* (Commonwealth of Australia, DEEWR, 2009) for early childhood educators, parents and policymakers emphasizes play-based learning and the importance of creative play in enabling children to become confident and active learners. It asserts that:

Play provides opportunities for children to learn as they discover, create, improvise and imagine. When children play with other children they create social groups, test out ideas, challenge each other's thinking and build new understandings...

(Commonwealth of Australia, DEEWR, 2009: 5)

Similarly, when they involve adults in their play, their shared memories of previous café experiences with their grandmother are replicated and extended. Imaginative and creative play is thus critically important in enabling children to explore multiple ways of knowing and being. Such joint adult-child imagining has been described as 'playworlds' (Lindqvist, 1995). Chapter 3 provided an example of adults and children creating and entering a common fantasy together.

Hughes (1996) suggested a number of different types of play that in actuality flow into each other and resonate with the playworld concept. Those that relate specifically to our discussion are summarized in Table 7.1 below.

Writing out of her research with young children's stories, Carol Fox (1993) suggested that another term could be developed to describe 'imaginative *play*',

Table 7.1 Types of play adapted from Hughes (1996) in Ewing (2012)

Creative Play – allows for a new response, the transformation of information, awareness of new connections, and may incorporate an element of surprise. Examples can range from creating a new use for an everyday object, to taking the rules of traditional games and making up new ones.

Communicative Play – playing with words, nuances, facial or gestural expression to communicate ideas. Miming an action for someone else to guess as in charades, telling a joke or riddle or sharing a poem, are all examples of this kind of play.

Dramatic Play – events are dramatized by children even though they may not have been direct participants – they may dramatize an event they observed at school or at a play.

Fantasy Play – rearranges the world in the child's way to create a fantasy situation – being incredibly strong like Pippi Longstocking or Popeye or Superman and able to perform amazing feats. Invention of an imaginary person or animal.

Imaginative Play – pretending that the conventional rules do not apply. Animals, elements and objects can talk; a child may insist that they have an invisible friend.

Object Play – uses infinite and interesting sequences of hand-eye manipulations and movements with objects to explore their uses or use them in a novel way. Wands emerge from sticks, lego bricks are shaped into swords or bridges.

because she believed the word 'play' tries to encapsulate such a conundrum: a serious and intense activity requiring much thinking and linguistic effort on the part of the child engaged but simultaneously ephemeral and often viewed by observers as trivial. She recommends that imaginative play be termed 'serious play' or 'play for real' (Fox, 1993: 190). This view of the importance of imaginative play links strongly with the notion of extending learning through the notion of a collective ZPD as defined above. Dramatic play further develops these possibilities.

From Imaginative to Dramatic Play

Vygotsky viewed what he termed 'pretend' play as allowing a child to take the next developmental leap to become 'a head taller than himself'. He provided the example of a child pretending that a broomstick is a horse. The child's ability to do this means that he or she can separate the object from the symbol. This is seen as marking the beginning of thinking abstractly. Building on Vygotsky's work, many others (Bergen, 1998) noted strong relationships between a child beginning to engage in 'pretend' play and the beginning of their receptive and expressive language development. Engaging in pretend play requires a child to be able to transform objects and actions symbolically and depends on interactive social dialogue and negotiation between those involved in the play. The child must take on a role and be able to improvise and portray appropriate emotions for that role. Such play should be seen as a continuous moving backwards and forwards through various realities – it is an attitude or orientation to the world (Garvey, 1991).

Dramatic play usually emerges seamlessly from other forms of play as children build on their own lives, opportunities and experiences to imagine and create new worlds and possibilities (Ewing, 2012). Often children's spontaneous make-believe experiences and adult facilitated process drama activities link very directly to the sharing of oral and written stories, picture books and films. In these kinds of situations, children's understanding of narrative is being developed and extended. Bruner (1990) suggested that the construction of imaginary narratives helps children think sequentially while also enhancing their creative capacities. Language plays a critical role in the making of meaning from using such 'lived experience'.

Snapshot 1 above demonstrates that dramatic play is not about acting as someone else: it is about suspending disbelief to *be* someone else for a few moments in time. After several iterations of the dialogue described above, problems or dramatic tension began to arise, initially scaffolded by the adult:

'Oh no, these pancakes are cold. I don't like them cold!'
'We will put them in the microwave, madam,' offered Timmy.
'In the microwave,' echoed Jordy.
'Thank you, I'm rather cross about this.'
'You're werry, werry angry now?' asks Jordy.

This extension of the playworld was not a replication of an earlier shared café experience. Rather the two children and their grandmother were developing the fictional context further and the boys were able to use other experiences to suggest a solution and to understand that the customer was now feeling cross.

The opportunity to explore an imagined context enabled Timmy and Jordy to suspend their real-world persona, draw on earlier experiences and make meanings from the perspective of the 'other', in this case the waiters in the café. Over time the two boys replaced the above café scenarios with the invention of a camping vignette using two old towels over a chair as a tent and introducing new ideas reminiscent of events during a recent holiday with their parents. Balancing opportunities for children to initiate and manage their own dramatic play alongside gently scaffolding further drama experiences requires sensitivity to each child's developmental needs and cultural background.

The power of dramatic play to engage children in creative thinking and problem-solving, and to help them make emotional connections, is demonstrated through evidence of improved thinking and literacy outcomes. A large research base documents the impact of drama and theatre activities on learning, particularly in the areas of language and expressive skill development (Bolton, 1984; O'Toole *et al.*, 2009). Process or educational drama strategies can encourage collaboration, problem-solving, the development of empathy and reflection (Baldwin, 2012; Bird *et al.*, 2012; Bolton, 1984; Ewing, 2010b; Miller and Saxton, 2004; Neelands, 1992). Enactment or walking in someone else's shoes (Ewing and Simons, 2004) should be regarded as the essence of educational drama. Heath (2000) underlines the power of moving from physical enactment or embodiment of an idea or event to visual and then written representation. Storytelling and imaginative writing have been shown to be greatly enhanced through the use of process drama strategies (Baldwin, 2012; Booth and Neelands, 1998; Crumpler and Schneider, 2002; Ewing, 2006, 2010b).

Furthermore, many case studies document the power of drama to change traditional classroom discourse to enable students to think for themselves, rather than trying to play 'guess what's in the teacher's head' (Ewing, 2006; O'Mara, 2004; Sinclair *et al.*, 2012). Through dramatic play, children can put their own world on hold, step into the shoes of others and behave 'as if' to solve the problem (Ewing and Simons, 2004). Drama enables us to suspend our disbelief and bend time and space to create a place for exploratory interactions, dialogues and representations out of which new thoughts, ideas and ways of looking at/seeing the world may emerge.

In any game or structured activity, the more experienced person initially takes most of the running in explaining or demonstrating the process in the first instance. Gradually, however, the player/learner takes more and more of the lead in such situations and, in time, not only assumes full control of the game, but invents other rules and ways of playing it, as with the much documented way the child learns to play the game 'peek-a-boo' for example (Bruner and Sherwood, 1976), it is often an adult or older child who takes responsibility at the beginning for introducing and modelling the procedures/rituals of hiding their face and then re-appearing. And so with dramatic play, the child will stretch and extend initial ideas and traditional games and activities to create new ones. Later they will push the different drama strategies introduced by the educator to modify them for their own purposes.

Parents, caregivers and educators have a pivotal role in ensuring there is time for such activities and providing the space and resources to encourage children to engage in dramatic play. They can collect materials and items relating to particular areas or themes around which dramatic play might develop. Time to build, make or create, dress up, play with puppets, provide opportunities to talk, cooperate and establish trusting relationships and contexts. For example, a Christmas gift of a magic set for 7-year-old Alexander immediately enabled him to transform into a magician who performed a diverse range of magic tricks. He enlisted his two cousins as his assistants. All three participants in the magic show visited the family dress-up box to find costumes appropriate to their assigned roles in the performance.

Over more than two decades, William Corsaro studied children's communicative strategies during this kind of what he termed 'fantasy play' (Corsaro, 1985, 2003). He particularly observed this play in areas set aside for lego or blocks or around sand tables/pits and hypothesized that through this play the children manipulated toy animals, blocks, lego bricks and people and other objects to build a shared history that enabled improvised cooperative fantasy play. Interestingly, three recurring themes were identified as most prominent during these episodes:

- danger-rescue;
- lost-found; and
- death-rebirth.

These themes are illustrative of the big philosophical issues children are interested in from an early age and often ask questions about. Corsaro and Johannesen (2007: 448) note that these themes are also seen in fairy tales and popular children's media, as well as in everyday stories. They are also common themes in contemporary computerized simulation and fantasy games. Extending these findings, Sawyer (1997) compares children's 'social pretend play' in which children's imaginations are given 'free rein' to improvisational performances:

> They manipulate dinosaur figurines to create a drama of panic after an earthquake. They play out a story in which a duck and a dinosaur are best friends. They build spaceships with elaborate systems of weaponry and controls, and go on adventures to exotic planets.
>
> (Sawyer, 1997: xviii)

Sawyer concludes with the assertion that such conversations are more improvisational than the average adult conversation.

From Dramatic Play to Adult Facilitated Drama Experiences

Very young children are aware of an adult or caregiver's approval through their exclamations of pleasure at their creative achievements through play. They will overhear their activities recounted to others who have been absent during this experience or respond to the adults' affirmation or clapping at the conclusion of an impromptu performance. Listening to such talk assists children in their own reflecting on their dramatic play, even before they can clearly articulate this. Making time for children to think about and, where appropriate, to talk about their imaginative experiences, thoughts and feelings – or to represent them in another media – is also an important part of the whole process of learning and understanding through play. This can be done informally, perhaps while children are engaged in other play activities or at meal or storytime.

In exploring how the educator can extend children's self-directed dramatic play as they transition to school, a range of process or educational drama strategies (O'Neill, 1995) can be introduced to children during the later stages of pre-school or early in their first year of school. At the same time it is important to ensure that children also have free time for their own spontaneous drama.

Process drama emphasizes the actual experience of the drama rather than any resultant performance or other formal outcome. In this way children can be encouraged to further experiment with taking on different roles and perspectives through walking in others' shoes. They will continue to develop their capacity to empathize and ability to collaborate. At times, the interested adult (or older child) may enter into the dramatic play as a co-player or more deliberately in role, to ask a question or suggest a focus or new direction. For scaffolding possibilities using mime, storydrama, sculpting, depiction, tapping in, hotseating and teacher in role, see O'Toole and Dunn (2002), Ewing and Simons (2004), Miller and Saxton (2004), Ewing (2012), Gibson and Ewing (2011) and Dunn and Stinson (2012). Well-loved children's literature provides an excellent starting point for mime and other drama activities.

Young children need many opportunities to control play situations, play out a story and pace activities themselves. In time they will be able to visualize these in their minds. Several months after the café and camping scenarios, Timothy articulated this internalization by explaining to his mother:

When I close my eyes I can make shows. And I can make any show I like.

Enabling play opportunities for young children are currently termed 'Developmentally Appropriate Practice' (Fleer, 2009) in many policies, articles and handbooks on early childhood education. They encapsulate a set of dispositions and practices that nurture children's curiosity, creativity and imagination. When so engrossed in such practices, young children are capable of long periods of intense concentration that far exceed what is generally expected of them. Adults should closely observe children during imaginative play to find more ways to encourage further creative interactions and the ongoing development of children's imaginations. Gonzales-Mena (2008) proposes five qualities aligned with such play:

- intrinsic motivation;
- active engagement;
- attention to the process rather than the outcome;
- non-literal behaviour;
- freedom from externally imposed rules.

Scaffolding may be in the form of tentative and open-ended questions asked by adults during such play.

Vygotsky theorized that dialogic and collaborative practices empowered learners to reframe a problem and then formulate a potential solution in their own words. He suggested that what begins as a collective work is transformed as students take up, or internalize, common language and knowledge of the collective to be used in their own individual work. Wink and Putney (2002) proposes that a way of further conceptualizing the ZPD as a potentially transformative classroom process is through these constructs of reformulation and internalization (Rieber and Carton, 1987; Vygotsky, 1978, 1986). Collaborative learning and development and individual learning and development are therefore integrally entwined with each other.

Snapshot 2: Towards a Collective ZPD: The *School Drama* Programme

This section moves the discussion from preschool to a snapshot from the school context. It reports on a professional learning model, co-mentoring (Ewing, 2002, 2006), which has the potential to encourage the development of a collective ZPD between teachers, teaching artists and students. This teacher professional learning process has formed the basis of the first five years of the SD programme developed in 2009 through a partnership with the Sydney Theatre Company and the Faculty of Education and Social Work, University of Sydney. In brief, the programme focuses on developing primary teachers' professional knowledge of and expertise about the impact of drama on children's English and literacy outcomes. Participating teachers are first introduced to the range of process drama strategies involved using contemporary literary texts. Actors or teaching artists work alongside classroom teachers to plan a programme focused on a particular English or literacy outcome identified by the teacher. The teaching artist then team teaches with the class teacher once a week for up to seven weeks in either term two or three of the school year. The teaching artist initially models the use of drama strategies (e.g. hotseating, sculpting, depiction, conscience alley, readers' theatre) with the chosen texts with the class teacher often modelling for other teachers. Over the timeframe the class teacher gains confidence and expertise in using drama strategies and choosing quality literature. At the same time the teaching artist develops an understanding of the classroom context. The students' literacy learning is enhanced.

The first year of the pilot programme involved 11 teachers, 250 students and 2 teaching artists in 2009 in 5 disadvantaged inner city Sydney primary schools. By 2013 the programme included 58 teachers, 10 teaching artists and 1500 children across 40 schools in the greater Sydney region and one rural and remote context. In addition, in 2013, a successful pilot programme was undertaken by the State Theatre Company in Adelaide working with teachers in five schools. The discussion below focuses on the notion of this model and its potential to facilitate the development of collective zones of proximal development. (For a more detailed outline of the programme itself see: *http://www.sydneytheatre. com.au/community/education/teacher-professional-learning/school-drama.aspx*)

Co-mentoring

The SD professional learning model is conceptualized as a co-mentoring approach. Instead of using the traditional conception of a mentor as *the* expert knower, the mentoring process is reframed as one of co-learning that positions the participants in a non-hierarchical or reciprocal relationship (Bona *et al.* 1995; 119; Le Cornu 2005). The different participants have different knowledge and understanding to share and each respects the expertise of the other. The teachers learn about the use of drama in enhancing literacy and English, while the teaching artists learn about adapting their professional theatre skills to a particular literacy focus in specific classroom and school contexts. The children benefit from the teacher's learning and ongoing use of drama strategies with literary texts to deepen understanding and improve the identified literacy outcome. The SD programme is thus dependent on the authentic partnership that develops between each educator and teaching artist as they use drama and literature to work towards improving student achievement in English and literacy in a particular classroom. Both must work to ensure a respectful relationship develops, one that appreciates the expertise of the other and can weather rigorous discussion about differences. The SD partnership is thus a significant departure from conventional artists-in-residence programmes. As one participating teacher explains:

> For me it was like mentoring in drama teaching ... [the teaching artist] broke it down in a way that made me realize I could do it. It was empowering. It was fantastic.

One of the teaching artists articulates this clearly, comparing his experience working with two teachers:

> It's really that building of the relationship between the teacher and the teaching artist that's so crucial. I realize now how important that is – because I've had the experience where it didn't happen ...

Overall, the participant teachers report a range of positive outcomes enabled by the implementation of drama strategies in their classroom English programme (Gibson, 2011, 2012, 2013; Gibson and Smith, 2013). These reported outcomes resonate with the concept of a collective ZPD discussed above. Participant teachers assert that the in-classroom professional learning that occurs during SD develops their confidence to use drama strategies as effective tools for learning and teaching particularly in English and literacy, but in addition more generally across the curriculum. Despite the short time frame, they report almost universally that student literacy outcomes in the focus literacy area are enhanced. The professional actors or teaching artists who work with the teachers report that the programme is just as valuable for them citing an understanding of the educative process as well as a heightening of their own skills as outcomes. Despite the short time frame, there is also a consistent reporting that children's literacy skills have improved as a result of the programme along with their understanding of different drama strategies. The improvement in literacy outcomes is also evidenced by analysis of the pre- and post-benchmarking in the literacy area identified.

Teacher survey and interview comments reflect the collaborative outcomes that eventuate and thus support the notion of a collective ZPD where there is active engagement of all participants. For example, one participant teacher reports that her kindergarten students:

have developed co-operative skills in working in small and large groups.

In addition she notes that the children's:

> ...language has improved in relation to using text knowledge and the metalanguage related to the story they have read. They can think beyond interpretive information contained in the story. By taking part in the drama lessons they have a deeper understanding of what is happening in the story and have developed more empathy for characters, by putting themselves in their position.

In terms of enhancing language skills and deeper learning and thinking, an English as a Second Language teacher responded in her post-programme survey:

> Removing the 'text' from literacy learning frees up students' minds and ways of thinking which facilitates greater expression, risk-taking and depth of appreciation. Drama allows students to take risks, express themselves orally, use their bodies and emotionally connect to the text. These are all important to deep learning...

Another post-programme teacher interview in 2011 noted that the opportunity of working with a professional actor resulted in improvement in students' 'use of higher level of language in dialogue activities. They were able to discuss in more depth the key issues in the text.'

The meta-analysis of the first five years of evaluation of the SD programme (Gibson and Smith, 2013) highlights the development of teacher 'understanding and skills in using process drama strategies to impact student literacy learning in participant schools.' In turn the students gained an 'understanding of process drama strategies...and confidence in using these.' Another teacher reflected on her students' increased willingness to push their own boundaries. In her words, her students demonstrated:

> a lot more confidence to express an opinion, to have a go at something that's outside their comfort zone and I think the process has given them a framework to build a story around.

Students themselves observed and reflected on the collective mentoring underpinning the programme: 'You didn't just teach us – you taught Ms V' (student comment to actor). A student letter to the teaching artist commented on the value of being allowed to 'totally express our emotions'.

The scaffolding provided for both the teachers and the students in the learning of drama strategies helped develop the dialogue about the themes and characterization in literacy texts. Both teachers and students commented on their deeper knowledge of children's literature, enabling a collective ZPD. At the same time the teacher and teaching artist create another collective and reciprocal ZPD. The group of teachers in the learning community undertaking the SD programme in any one year also experience another kind of collaborative learning as they begin to discuss experiences, share resources and texts and in some cases jointly programme future learning experiences based on embedding quality drama experiences in the English and literacy curriculum.

Conclusion

Child-directed imaginative and dramatic play opportunities in Snapshot 1 and co-constructed drama activities in Snapshot 2 allow children to learn how to work in groups, to share, to negotiate, to resolve conflicts, and to learn self-advocacy skills. When we allow children to be co-creators along with teachers and teaching artists, they can develop decision-making skills, move the activity at their own pace, discover their own areas of interest, and ultimately engage fully in the action.

Dramatic play and process drama can encourage adults and children to work in a collective ZPD and enhance children's language and literacy development, as well as their collaborative skills and their understandings of others. At the same time teacher professional learning can be extended and teaching artists can develop their understanding of classroom literacy. Learning situations that foster the development of a collective ZPD can allow everyone, not only the young child, 'what if' opportunities to play, create, imagine and learn.

References

Baldwin, P. (2012), *With Drama in Mind*, London: Continuum.
Bergen, D. (1998), 'Stages of Play Development', in D. Bergen (ed.), *Readings from Play as a Medium for Learning and Development*, Olney, MD: Association for Childhood Education International, 71–93.
Bird, J., Donelan, K., Freebody, K., O'Toole, J. and Sinclair, C. (2012), 'Drama: Social Dreaming in the 21st Century', in C. Sinclair, N. Jeanneret and J. O'Toole (eds), *Education in the Arts: Teaching and Learning in Contemporary Curriculum*, 2nd edition, Oxford: Oxford University Press, 65–90.

Bolton, G. (1984), *Drama as Education: An Argument for Placing Drama at the Centre of the Curriculum*, London: Longman.

Bona, M., Rinehart, J. and Volbrecht, R. (1995), 'Show me how to do like you': Co-mentoring as Feminist Pedagogy', *Feminist Teacher*, 9(3): 116–24.

Booth, D. and Neelands, J. (eds) (1998), *Writing in-Role: Classroom Projects Connecting Writing and Drama*, Ontario: Caliburn Enterprises.

Bruner, J. (1990), *Acts of Meaning*, Cambridge, MA: Harvard University Press.

Bruner, J. and Sherwood, V. (1976), 'Peekaboo and the Learning or Rule Structure', in J. Bruner, A. Jolly, and K. Sylva (eds), *Play: Its Role in Development and Evolution*, New York: Basic Books, 277–85.

Commonwealth of Australia, DEEWR (2009), *Belonging, Being and Becoming. The Early Years Learning Framework for Australia*, Canberra: Australian Government, Retrieved from: *http://foi.deewr.gov.au/system/files/doc/other/belonging_being_and_becoming_the_early_years_learning_framework_for_australia.pdf*

Corsaro, W. (1985), *Friendship and Peer Culture in the Early Years*, Norwood, NJ: Ablex.

Corsaro, W. (2003), *'We're Friends, Right?': Inside Kid's Culture*, Washington, DC: Joseph Henry Press.

Corsaro, W. and Johannesen, B. (2007), 'The Creation of New Cultures in Peer Interaction', in J. Valsina and A. Rosa (eds), *The Cambridge Handbook of Sociocultural Psychology*, Cambridge: Cambridge University Press, 444–58.

Crumpler, T. and Schneider, J. (2002), 'Writing with Their Whole Being: a Cross Study Analysis of Children's Writing from Five Classrooms using Process Drama', *Research in Drama Education*, 7(2): 61–79.

Dunn, J. and Stinson, M. (2011), 'Dramatic Play and Drama in The Early Years: Re-imagining the Approach', in S. Wright (ed.), *Children, Meaning-making and the Arts*, 2nd edition, Frenchs Forest, NSW: Pearson/Prentice-Hall.

Elkind, D. (2008), *The Power of Play: How Spontaneous, Imaginative Activities Lead to Happier, Healthier Children*, Cambridge MA: De Capo Lifelong.

Ewing, R. (2002), 'Framing a Professional Learning Community: An Australian Case Study', *Curriculum Perspectives*, 22(3): 23–32.

Ewing, R. (2006), 'Reading to Allow Spaces to Play', in R. Ewing (ed.), *Beyond the Reading Wars. Towards a Balanced Approach to Helping Children Learn to Read*, Sydney: Primary English Teaching Association.

Ewing, R. (2010a), *The Arts and Australian Education: Realizing Potential*, Melbourne: ACER.

Ewing, R. (2010b), 'Literacy and the Arts', in F. Christie and A. Simpson (eds), *Literacy and Social Responsibility*, London: Equinox.

Ewing, R. (2012), 'The Role of Dramatic Play in Developing Confident, Creative Learners,' in R. Ewing (ed.), *Creative Arts in the Lives of Young Children: Play, Imagination, Learning*, Melbourne: ACER.

Ewing, R. and Simons, J. (2004), *Beyond the Script. Take Two: Drama in the Classroom*, Sydney: Primary English Teaching Association.

Ewing, R., Gibson, R., Hristofski, H., Campbell, V. and Robertson, A. (2011), 'Using Drama to Enhance Literacy', *The School Drama Initiative. Literacy Learning: The Middle Years*, 19(3): 33–9.

Ewing, R., Gibson, R., Hristofski, H., Campbell, V. (2014), 'School Drama: Towards State of the Art in Teacher Professional Learning', in M. Anderson and C. Roche (eds), *Drama: State of the Art IV*, Sydney: University of Sydney Press.

Fernandez, M., Wegerif, R., Mercer, N. and Rojas-Drummond, S. (2001), 'Reconceptualizing "Scaffolding" and the Zone of Proximal Development in the Context of Symmetrical Collaborative Learning', *Journal of Classroom Interaction*, 36(2): 40–54.

Fleer, M. (2009), 'A Cultural-historical Perspective on Play: Play as a Leading Activity across Cultural Communities', in I. Pramling-Samuelsson and M. Fleer (eds), *Play and Learning in Early Childhood Settings*, Dordrecht, The Netherlands: Springer, 1–20.

Fox, C. (1993), *At the Very Edge of the Forest: The Influence of Literature on Storytelling by Children*, London: Cassell.

Garvey, C. (1991), *Play. The Developing Child*, London: Fontana Press.

Gibson, R. (2011), *Evaluation of School Drama, 2010*, Unpublished Report, Sydney: University of Sydney.

Gibson, R. (2012), *Evaluation of School Drama 2011*, Unpublished Report, Sydney: University of Sydney.

Gibson, R. (2013), *Evaluation of School Drama 2012*, Unpublished Report, Sydney: University of Sydney.

Gibson, R. and Ewing, R. (2011), *Transforming the Curriculum through the Arts*, Melbourne: Palgrave Macmillan.

Gibson, R. and Smith, D. (2013), *School Drama Project Meta-Evaluation 2009–2012*, Unpublished Report, Sydney, University of Sydney.

Gonzales-Mena, J. (2008), *Child, Family and Community: Family Centred Early Care and Education*, 5th edition, London: Pearson.

Graue, E. (2011), 'Are we Paving Paradise?' *Educational Leadership*, April: 15.

Heath, S. (2000), 'Seeing our Way into Learning,' *Cambridge Journal of Education*, 30(1): 121–31.

Hirsh-Pasek, K., Golinkoff, R. with Eyer, D. (2003), *Einstein Never Used Flashcards: How our Children Really Learn – And Why They Need to Play More and Memorize Less*, Emmaus, PA: Rodale Books.

Hughes, B. (1996), *A Playworker's Taxonomy of Play Types*, London: Playlink.

Le Cornu, R. (2005), 'Peer Mentoring: Engaging Pre-service Teachers in Mentoring One Another,' *Mentoring and Tutoring*, 13(3): 355–366.

Lindon, J. (2001), *Understanding Children's Play*, Cheltenham and London: Nelson Thomas.

Lindqvist, G. (1995), *The Aesthetics of Play: A Didactic Study of Play and Culture in Preschool*, vol. 62, Uppsala: Acta Universitatis Upsalensis.

Mahn, H. and John-Steiner, V. (2002), 'The Gift of Confidence: A Vygotskian View of Emotion', in G. Wells and G. Claxton, *Learning for Life in the 21st Century: Sociocultural Perspectives on the Future of Education*, London: Blackwell, published online: 14 January.

Miller, C. and Saxton, J. (2004), *Into the Story. Language in Action Through Drama*, New York: Heinemann.

Moll, L. and Whitmore, K. (1993), 'Vygotsky in Classroom Practice: Moving from Individual Transmission to Social Transaction', in E.A. Forman, N. Minick and C. Stone (eds), *Contexts for Learning: Sociocultural Dynamics in Children's Development*, New York: Oxford University Press.

Neelands, J. (1992), *Learning through Imagined Experience*, London: Heinemann.

O'Mara, J. (2004), 'At Sunny Bay: Building Students' Repertoire of Literacy Practices through Process Drama,' in A. Healy and E. Honan (eds), *Text Next: New Resources for Literacy Learning*, Sydney: Primary English Teaching Association, 119–36.

O'Neill, C. (1995), *Drama Worlds: A Framework for Process Drama*, Portsmouth, NH: Heinemann.

O'Toole, J. and Dunn, J. (2002), *Pretending to Learn. Helping Children to Learn Through Drama*, Frenches Forest, Sydney: Pearson.

O'Toole, J., Stinson, M. and Moore, T. (2009), *Drama and the Curriculum: A Giant at the Door*, London: Springer.

Petrick-Steward, E. (1995), *Beginning Writers in the Zone of Proximal Development*, Mahwah, NJ: Lawrence Erlbaum Associates.

Rieber, R.W. and Carton, A.S. (1987), *The Collected Works of L.S. Vygotsky*, vol. 1: *Problems of General Psychology*, translated by Sochinenii, New York: Plenum.

Sawyer, R.K. (1997), *Pretend Play as Improvisation: Conversation in the Preschool Classroom*, Mahwah, NJ: Lawrence Erlbaum Associates.

Sinclair, C., Jeanneret, N. and O'Toole, J. (eds) (2012), *Education in the Arts*, Melbourne: Oxford University Press.

Singer, J. (2006), 'Learning to Play and Learning through Play', in D. Singer, R. Michnick Golinkoff and K. Hirsh-Pasek (eds), *Play = Learning: How Play Motivates and Enhances Children's Cognitive and Social-Emotional Growth*, New York: Oxford University Press.

Stone, A. (1998), 'The Metaphor of Scaffolding: Its Utility for the Field of Learning Disabilities', *Journal of Learning Disabilities*, 3(4): 344–64.

Swain, M. (2000), 'The Output Hypothesis and Beyond: Mediating Acquisition through Collaborative Dialogue,' in J.P. Lantolf (ed.), *Sociocultural Theory and Second Language Learning*, Oxford: Oxford University Press, 99–116.

Vygotsky, L.S. (1966), 'Play and its Role in the Mental Development of the Child', *Voprosy Psikhologii*, 12(6): 62–76.

Vygotsky, L.S. (1978), *Mind in Society*, translated by M. Cole, Cambridge, MA: Harvard University Press.

Vygotsky, L.S. (1986), *Thought and Language*, Cambridge, MA: MIT Press.

Wells, G. (1999), *Dialogic Inquiry: Towards a Sociocultural Practice and Theory of Education*, Cambridge: Cambridge University Press.

Wink, J. and Putney, L. (2002), *A Vision of Vygotsky*, Boston, MA: Allyn & Bacon, 102–12, retrieved 28 December 2013 from: *http://www.joanwink.com/vov/vov_pgs102-112.phphttp://www.joanwink.com/vov/vov_pgs102-112.php*

Wood, D., Bruner, J. and Ross, G. (1976), 'The Role of Tutoring in Problem-solving', *Journal of Child Psychology and Child Psychiatry*, 17: 89–100.

Zigler, E. and Bishop-Josef, S. (2009), 'Play under Siege: An Historical Overview', *Zero to Three*, 30(1): 4–11.

8

Sociocultural Theory, Process Drama and Second Language Learning

Penny Bundy, Erika Piazzoli and Julie Dunn

Strains of children singing a traditional song in a language unknown to us are heard as we lug video cameras, tripods and drama props up a flight of stairs. We walk towards the beginner English as a Second Language classroom to continue our research work examining the value of using process drama to support language learning. Fifteen children, all newly arrived immigrants and refugees, are lined up in two neat rows. They employ a range of actions to reinforce the ideas within the lyrics of the song. They seem proud of their performance and are keen to impress. With the dance over, the children excitedly point to the work they have done with their teacher, Katie, since our last visit – the creation of a detailed map of the Island of Plenty Fish.

Introduction

While there is substantial work connecting the fields of *sociocultural theory* and *drama*, as well as *sociocultural theory* and *second language (L2) learning* (Lantolf, 1994; 2000; Lantolf and Thorne, 2006), consideration of how *process drama* and *sociocultural theory for L2 learning* work together has received minimal attention. Within this chapter we attempt to address this gap by applying four Vygotskyan concepts to analyse the action and interactions occurring during a process drama conducted in the L2 classroom introduced in the vignette above. This drama work was part of a larger refugee resettlement research project designed to support newly arrived children and young people from a range of cultural backgrounds.

Sociocultural theory for second language learning is an orientation to language teaching and learning based on the theories of Vygotsky. It emerged in the 1990s through the work of Lantolf (1994; 2000), Donato (2004), Swain (2000) and others, who were dissatisfied with approaches where isolated chunks of interaction were examined without considering the context in which they occurred. In contrast, in a sociocultural perspective, context and dialogue are considered crucial to generating language learning.

Vygotsky argued that all learning is *mediated*. The source of mediation can be a tool (e.g. a pen or a computer), a system of symbols (most notably, language) or another individual in social interaction. In the context of second language learning, symbolic mediation (through objects, systems or persons) transforms spontaneous impulses into higher-order functions (i.e. voluntary attention, voluntary memory and second language learning strategies). Thus unfocused learning actions become focused, based on how learning is *mediated* in the L2/ESL classroom (Donato and MacCormick, 1994).

Process drama as a pedagogy offers a particular way of mediating learning. Meaning is created through the participants' spontaneous collaboration, with learning further mediated through the elements of drama, including but not confined to role, tension, language, time, space, place, symbol and contrast. Context also mediates the development of meaning in process drama, as it does in language learning. While we recognize that context is critical to the development of meaning in a range of learning contexts, within process drama this is made more complex by the presence of at least two worlds that operate simultaneously – the actual world and the dramatic one. Drama participants respond to both worlds and to the juxtaposition of the two.

The process drama we analyse here was created to support the classroom teacher's language programme and involved members of our team working with the children on a weekly basis for most of a school term. Data collection included video recording and still photographic images of all lessons, samples of children's work (including writing and drawings), our lesson plans, audio recordings of our collaborative planning and debrief sessions for each lesson, audio recordings of the children's responses to specific tasks and audio recordings of interviews with the classroom teacher and the children at the conclusion of the series of lessons.

Four Vygostkyan Concepts

The four Vygotskyan concepts chosen to frame our discussions within this chapter are zone of proximal development (ZPD), dual affect, the cycle of imagination and *perezhivanie*. They were selected because they provide a useful framework for understanding the specific ways that process drama and its associated strategies and conventions mediate learning within L2 classrooms. We also argue that they are closely interrelated across the cognitive, affective and social dimensions of learning.

Later in this chapter we refer to a segment of action, taken from the third process drama lesson, to analyse these concepts and understand their contribution in action. First, however, we introduce these concepts, noting the differences in how they are understood and applied in sociocultural theory for L2 and process drama. These differences are especially apparent in relation to 'dual affect', a term not used at all within the second language literature but crucial for drama writers and practitioners. We begin with an examination of the ZPD.

Zone of Proximal Development

Vygotsky uses the term Zone of Proximal Development (ZPD) to describe how collaboration with, or support from, a more capable peer can produce learning that an individual would not be able to achieve alone. It is a process where learning leads development – 'what a [learner] can do with assistance today she will be able to do by herself tomorrow' (Vygotsky, 1978: 87).

Within sociocultural theory for L2 learning, ZPD has been variously interpreted, from 'collective scaffolding' (Donato and McCormick, 1994) to 'collaborative dialogue' (Swain, 2000) to co-authoring (Kinginger, 2002). In this chapter, we adopt Lantolf and Thorne's (2006) perspective of ZPD as language learners engaging in forms of dialogic interaction, where they draw on their collective potential as well as the experience and knowledge of more capable peers and adults, to form 'something of a collective expert' (Lantolf and Thorne, 2006: 283). In adopting this view we are also aligning ourselves to Holzman's work (2009: 29), as she sees ZPD as a 'collective activity of creating'.

Regulation is central to understanding how ZPD operates in social interaction. According to Ohta (2000), Vygotsky believed that learning occurs first through *inter*personal regulation, before moving to an *intra*personal level. To illustrate this, when children learn a language they first repeat an utterance they have heard before making it their own. As Ohta explained, in the L2 classroom, through social interaction, language structures (vocabulary, grammar, idioms, etc.) are processed on two psychological planes: first, on the *inter*psychological, and then the intrapsychological, or mental plane. Thus, 'social processes allow the language to become a cognitive tool for the individual' (Ohta, 2000: 54).

Vygotsky describes three types of regulation: object-regulation, other-regulation, self-regulation. In the L2 classroom, *object-regulated* language is constrained and limited by the grammar rules available; the speech of the *other-regulated* speaker emerges as a response, dictated by others (usually the teacher). Only a *self-regulated* speaker can freely express ideas and feelings in the target language (Kao and O'Neill, 1998: 45). This does not necessarily relate to proficiency: a beginner language learner can be self-regulated, but not grammatically accurate. Significantly, the *transformation* from other-regulation to self-regulation requires the creation of a ZPD.

While the sociocultural L2 literature has focused on self-regulation in relation to ZPD, the process drama literature has tended to focus on Vygotsky's ideas linking play and dual affect. He (Vygotsky, 1976) asserted that *play* creates opportunities for ZPD to occur:

> Play is the source of development and creates the zone of proximal development in the child. Action in the imaginative sphere, in an imaginary situation, the creation of voluntary intentions and the formation of real-life plans and volitional motives – all appear in play.
>
> (Vygotsky, 1976: 552)

Vygotsky's ideas about play are relevant to both ZPD and dual affect.

Dual Affect

Dual Affect is understood here as the notion that, when an individual is playing, a dual affective plan occurs with the emotional state of the 'play context' being different from the 'actual context'. Thus the child simultaneously 'weeps in play as a patient, but revels as a player' (Vygotsky, 1976: 549). Vygotsky therefore saw play as a purposeful activity triggering a 'dual affective' plan, or response (Vygotsky, 1976: 548). In drama education, the concept of dual affect, originally drawn by Vygotsky from Nohl, but then from Vygotsky by Bolton (1979), has received considerable attention. Our understanding of dual affect in the context of process drama is derived from Bolton's work and suggests that a participant is capable of having two different affective responses simultaneously, with one being generated by the actual world while the other is generated by the dramatic one.

By contrast, within sociocultural theory for L2 learning, the concept of dual affect is relatively unexplored. It appears that the expression 'dual affect' has been lost in translation. Our research indicates that it first appeared as '*dvoinoj affektivnyj plan*' (dual affective plan) in a lecture given by Vygotsky, in 1933, at the Leningrad Pedagogical Institute. This lecture was published in 1966 in *Problems of Psychology* (6), 62–76 and then republished in *Play: Its Role in Development and Evolution* (1976), which was edited by Bruner *et al.* (1976). Notably, this lecture was included (slightly modified) in the popular volume *Mind in Society*, edited by Cole *et al.* (1978). Although the two versions are similar, in the 1978 version some paragraphs have been omitted, including the phrasing 'dual affective plan'. Wherever 'affect' appears in the 1976 version, in the 1978 version it appears as 'desire' and 'impulse' (Cole *et al.*, 1978: 99–100 with Bruner *et al.*, 1976: 548). While the drama education corpus, following the work of Gavin Bolton in particular (1979), draws on the 1976 version, the sociocultural theory for L2 learning corpus relies on the 1978 version, resulting in a different focus.

While the idea of dual affect is relatively absent in Second Language Acquisition research, 'affect' as a trait of the language learner receives particular attention (Ellis, 1994). Working within a sociocultural perspective, Imai (2010) framed emotions as 'socially constructed acts of communication that mediate one's thinking, behaviour and goals' (Imai, 2010: 279). Emotion, and its impact on learning and engagement, is central to participation in process drama (Bolton, 1984; Courtney, 1995; O'Toole, 1992) and to collaborative learning within L2 development.

Cycle of Imagination

The third concept we consider is Vygotsky's notion of the cycle of imagination (Vygotsky, 2004). The cycle of imagination explores the relationship between 'imagination' and 'reality', with the cycle being understood as a two-fold, mutual interdependence between imagination and experience. It positions imagination as 'a function essential to life' (Vygotsky, 2004: 13). In *Imagination and Creativity in Childhood*, Vygotsky (1930/2004) argued that imagination is 'the basis of all human creative activity' (Vygotsky, 1930/2004: 9). A 'creative act' is any human act that gives rise to something new, with creativity being driven by both *emotion* and *thought*. In explaining the operations involved in a creative act, Vygotsky describes the relationship between *imagination* and *reality*. Through imagination, we take elements from reality, which are 'transformed and re-worked' (Vygotsky, 1930/2004: 16). Emotion is central to this.

For Vygotsky (1930), the relationship between imagination and reality is bi-directional. While emotions influence imagination, imagination also has an effect on emotions (Vygotsky, 1930: 19). Thus, on the one hand: 'Emotions possess a kind of capacity to select impressions, thoughts, and images that resonate with the mood that possesses us at a particular moment in time' (Vygotsky, 1930: 17–18). On the other hand, 'every construct of the imagination has an effect on our feelings, and if this construct does not in itself correspond to reality, nonetheless the feelings it evokes are real' (Vygotsky, 1930: 19). Vygotsky used this to claim a two-fold relationship of mutual dependence between imagination and experience.

Vygotsky (1930/2004) argued that imagination (the basis of all creative activity) is an important component of all aspects of cultural life, enabling artistic, scientific and technical creation. He saw creativity as underpinning the human condition: 'Creativity is present, in actuality, not only when great historical works are born but also whenever a person imagines, combines, alters and creates something new.' He saw creativity as 'an essential condition for existence' (Vygotsky, 1930: 11). He claimed: 'It must not be forgotten that the basic law of children's creativity is that its value lies not in its results, not in the product of creation, but in the process itself' (Vygotsky, 1930: 72). This view is highly compatible with the philosophy of drama education where the role of imagination and creativity is critical. While this is discussed frequently by arts educators (Eisner 2002; Greene, 1995), the term 'cycle of imagination' is seldom used within the process drama literature.

In L2 learning, attempting to express ideas in another language can be viewed as a creative act. For over two decades, researchers have explored the connection between creativity and foreign language speaking, finding positive correlations between the two (Simondon, 2008). 'Mushfaking' (Rothwell, 2013) is a creative language strategy used by L2 process drama participants to make use of whatever language they have in order to participate in an imagined world. In the *Island of Plenty Fish* drama, the children lacked the lexical knowledge for the term volcano, referring to it as 'the broken mountain'. Rothwell suggests that when second language learners 'mushfake' like this, they are using language creatively.

Perezhivanie

The Russian term *perezhivanie* (which cannot be translated directly into English but see earlier chapters in this book for lengthier discussions), refers to an intensively lived experience in a social context. In particular, perezhivanie encompasses the relationship between affect and cognition in an individual *and* the environment. It acknowledges that the same situation may be 'interpreted, perceived, experienced or lived through by different [individuals] in different ways' (Vygotsky, 1994: 354).

In an ESL context, Mahn and John-Steiner (2002) described perezhivanie as the process through which 'interactions in the ZPD are individually *perceived, appropriated*, and *represented*' by the language learner (Mahn and John-Steiner, 2002: 49, our emphasis). They drew on their research with ESL students compiling dialogue journals to argue that an essential part of students' *perezhivanijia* is provided by inter-personal relationships in the classroom, particularly for L2 language learners, who face further cultural and linguistic challenges.

A key component of interpersonal relationships in any communicative context is how embodiment influences perezhivanie as felt experience. Embodiment involves gesture and speech. McNeill (1992) and Vygotsky (1986) posited that speech and gesture develop interdependently. Gesticulation (spontaneous gestures that accompany speech) and emblems (culturally specific gestures) are co-expressive with speech. The act of gesturing carries meaning and mediates understanding. The opportunities for embodiment offered by participation in process drama support *self-regulation* in the target language.

Haught and McCafferty's (2008) research on embodiment analysed drama from an L2 sociocultural perspective, concluding that ESL learners self-regulate and create a collective ZPD through dramatic play. Here, we support their findings. However, while Haught and McCafferty worked with theatre games and short scripts, the dramatic approach we used is different.

Process Drama

In this section we focus on process drama as an aesthetic and pedagogical approach. While process drama shares the key elements of other staged theatre events (e.g. role, focus, tension, etc.), it lacks a predetermined script and separate audience. It is a collaborative, improvised art form and pedagogical approach. The text is generated in action by the teacher/facilitator and participants who engage physically, intellectually and emotionally to explore a particular dramatic question or focus. This is not the same as engaging in a series of games or dramatic activities designed to build skill or group cohesion. Rather, the group works together to explore and collaboratively create dramatic meaning. The outcome is often unpredictable.

The action of process drama is triggered by a pretext (O'Neill, 1995), a stimulus that has particular qualities that invite cognitive, affective and physical engagement. The participants explore the pretext and the meaning within and beyond it using a number of dramatic conventions.

In the following section, we begin by providing information about the drama's participants, then move on to offer an overview of the drama and detail relating to the work that occurred in the lead-up to the focus lesson.

Participants

The children involved in this study were students of a primary school in a major regional city bordering Brisbane, Australia. This school has more than 700 students, including almost 150 from a range of refugee backgrounds. The children involved in the work described within this chapter were recent arrivals from Sudan, Congo, Burundi, Burma, Laos, El Salvador and Macedonia. Aged between 9 and 13 years of age, they were all members of the new arrivals group, with minimal English. Although none appeared to arrive directly from war zones, many had spent considerable time in refugee camps.

In this chapter, we focus on the responses of six children, selected because they most usefully illustrate the four concepts under discussion. These children are Jelani (aged 10) from Burundi, Rishi (aged 12) from Congo, Boris (aged 13) from Macedonia, Dara (aged 10) from Burma, Thi Oo (aged 10) from Burma and Charuni (aged 10) from Sudan (the names are all pseudonyms). The first four children are boys, while the last two are girls.

The Island of Plenty Fish Drama

We planned the beginnings of a process drama based on a legend about an island and its people. One night there was a terrible storm and all the fish disappeared. In roles as the islanders, the children must solve this problem. To build belief in this context and to assume role, the children engaged in a number of writing, drawing and drama activities. For the first two weeks, they focused on creating the island, imagining and drawing its geographic features on a map. They created and took role as the islanders. Importantly, these roles were not predetermined by the drama facilitators, but were developed by the children as they interacted though a range of drama activities.

In the classroom time between our weekly visits, the children worked with their teacher to expand upon the initial ideas developed with us. They engaged in further writing and drawing tasks. They named the island (somewhat ironically) the 'Island of Plenty Fish'. By the third lesson, which is the focus of our analysis, the children were taking control of the direction of the narrative, displaying high-level critical thinking skills through the spontaneous introduction of creative ideas.

A vignette, describing a key section of this third lesson, follows:

Penny enters in-role as a villager from a nearby island seeking fish for her people as theirs have mysteriously disappeared. One child, Boris, appearing not to understand the narrative agrees to her request. The other children, recognizing that they have the same problem, chorus 'no'. Almost immediately, another child who has adopted the role of Baboo the Magic Man, claims that he can create fish by magic. Penny challenges Baboo stating that as she has no magic man on her island, she needs another solution. Thi Oo suggests that a slow dance might make the fish reappear. The children are excited by this idea and along with Penny, try it without success.

Penny then mentions that she has heard that the people of this island have 'a special dance'. Immediately the children look knowingly at each other and chorus 'yes', before arranging themselves for the performance we witnessed on arrival. This time however, the dance is playful. As it continues the children begin to sing. No fish appear. At the end of the dance, Dara falls to the floor melodramatically, claiming that he is hungry.

Penny begins to say farewell to the islanders, thanking them for their attempts when Boris, who previously appeared to misunderstand the narrative, declares that the dance has worked. He hands Penny a rolled-up piece of paper representing a fish. Soon all the children are handing Penny fish.

Later in this same session, Rishi (in role as the King) suggests that the arrival of the fish is due to Baboo's actions and that the fish will only continue to appear so long as the people dance and sing all day and all night – even as they work. The children have created their own narrative and are taking it in new directions.

In the section below we draw upon this episode, together with interview transcripts, to examine our four Vygotskyan concepts in action.

ZPD in Action

From the outset of this action, the creation of a ZPD is evident. Initiated by a pretext that establishes the context and invites participation by implying roles and situations, it is then extended through the spontaneous action of the drama. To exemplify this we focus on Boris whose contributions across the episode demonstrate growth in comprehension, confidence and engagement. Initially, as illustrated above, Boris lacks comprehension of the narrative of the drama, but by the conclusion of the episode his offering provides a new turn that other children follow. His initial response to Penny's questioning is noted in more detail in the transcript below:

> PENNY (*as villager*): ... I'm hoping you might be able to help me. I come from another island. We had a terrible storm and all of the fish and all of the animals have gone. Can you give me some of your fish to take for my people?
> BORIS: Yes!
> OTHER CHILDREN: Nooo ...
> PENNY: (*to Boris*) You have fish?
> BORIS: Yes.
> PENNY: You have fish on this island?
> BORIS: Yes.
> OTHER CHILDREN: Nooo! (*Loudly to drown out Boris*)
> PENNY (*as villager*): You don't have fish either?

While the other children have internalized the story sufficiently to deny the request for fish, Boris complies with the teacher's request, by suggesting that he has fish. This response appears to be other-regulated; he is simply agreeing with the teacher, rather than responding to the narrative. The other children, having internalized and understood the story, are able to self-regulate to offer a negative response.

However, following the dance sequence where the children attempt an embodied strategy to make the fish return, Boris's responses reveal a shift in understanding. Somewhat surprisingly, he is the one who indicates that the dance has worked. Here it seems that the collaborative and creative processes of the drama scaffolded Boris's understanding, allowing him to make a contribution that advanced the drama and showed self-regulation. In other words, the narrative mediates Boris's learning, with embodiment through the adoption of role supporting his comprehension.

Dual Affect in Action

To illustrate dual affect in action, we turn to the moment where Penny asks to be shown the special dance:

PENNY: Show me.
CHARUNI: Face this way! Ready, go!

They begin the dance we had seen earlier, but without singing. It is different though as the actions normally follow the lyrics. Charuni leads the way with actions. Some of the others copy. Rishi does not join in, sitting in his original spot without moving. There is much laughter. Penny as the visitor from the other island looks on in amazement.

PENNY: But some people aren't dancing ... will it still work?

Someone starts singing the rehearsed song that goes with the actions. There is more commitment from everyone, with even Rishi singing along and doing some actions. The 'performance' is louder and more playful than this morning's one and is punctuated with laughter. The singing finishes and Dara falls to the floor.

DARA: I'm hungry!

All the children laugh.

Here we see dual affect in action: as villagers, the children are pretending to be hungry and exhausted from dancing and singing in order to make the fish return; but as children, they enjoy the opportunity to spontaneously parody their school performance, developing it in playful new directions. The ending of the dance is a further example of dual affect in action, with Dara revelling in his playful performance of falling to the ground through hunger.

The value of dual affect for language learning is that it encourages children with limited English knowledge, to make a contribution in the target language. In this context, Dara's contribution is loud, improvised, unprompted and crucial to advancing the narrative. His desire to speak is motivated, at least in part, by the affective dimension of his role (as villager), as well as his affective responses as a learner. At times, the affective responses of their roles enabled the children to contribute, interact or engage in circumstances where their affective responses as learners might normally inhibit contributions.

The affective dimension in drama is created through the teacher's and children's management of the dramatic elements including role, tension, language and movement. For example, the use of role allows the teacher to lower her status in relation to the children and this has an impact on their confidence in using the second language. Similarly, dramatic tension (the force which drives the drama) stimulates the children's desire to engage and communicate.

Cycle of Imagination in Action

Within this lesson segment, the child's suggestion that the villagers need to 'slow dance' in order to bring the fish back could arguably be an example of Vygotsky's cycle of imagination. In making this suggestion, the child may be drawing on previous cultural experiences, including the slow and sedate traditional Burmese 'Bagan' dance. Although the children were rehearsing a dance at school, her suggestion was specific and was initially enacted quite differently from this class dance.

Later, Penny's mention of a 'special dance' may have triggered new imaginative associations for the children, with these being collectively understood and promptly enacted. Having experienced this dance, they could imagine it being 'recycled' for the purpose of the drama. The re-enacted dance (a parody of what they earlier learned) engaged the children in moving the narrative forward in a direction of their choosing.

Perezhivanie in Action

The following transcript, and indeed aspects of those offered previously, also provide useful examples of perezhivanie in action. They highlight the individual nature of each child's response, with their participation being dependent upon how they have perceived and interpreted the drama, and upon the relationships that exist in the classroom. Penny asks the children to show her what the island life might look like if the people must sing and dance continuously.

> PENNY: I want to see what this island looks like when you all have to sing when you have to work!
> CHARUNI: Everyone, let's do our job!
> PENNY: Yes . . . let me see everyone doing their job and singing.

The children immediately start getting into pairs and small groups. Jelani again adopts his very straight posture as the magic man, Boris begins to fish, two girls who have not been major participants verbally, begin a complex sequence of occupational mime in the corner, three girls sit (as childcare workers) holding hands, one girl stirs a cooking pot. Dara begins to waltz with another boy. Everyone is singing and working. Jelani gathers up the pieces of paper symbolizing the fish and positions himself in the middle of the other children (still in his very upright posture). Playfulness and excitement are apparent, with many of the children continuously smiling and laughing as they enact this scene.

PENNY: Very good (claps).

Jelani positions himself at the front of the group to formally announce

JELANI: Hello, my name is King Mannis and I bring all your fish back!

From the vignette and transcript above, we wish to highlight in particular Jelani's experiences in adopting the role, for throughout the drama he offers perhaps the clearest expression of how cognition, emotion and social relationships impact on learning. His work across the drama also reveals why embodiment is such a key dimension of perezhivanie.

When adopting the role, Jelani always embodies a specific 'magic man' stance. Described in the transcripts as 'upright' and 'extra straight with his hands by his side and his eyes looking off into the distance', this appears to be a physical representation of his newfound status as an important character. However, this status within the dramatic world is in direct contrast with the actual one, for Jelani is a low-achieving student whose progress in school has been slowed by the minimal formal education he received prior to resettlement. Within the drama, the role of Baboo appears to have boosted his self-image, offering him new ways to connect interpersonally with the other children, especially Rishi (who he admires). In addition, this role seems to have provided him with the opportunity to embody a new emotional state – confidence.

Insights into perezhivanie in action can also be gained by examining the interview data for this project, including Charuni's comments about her experience:

PENNY: What was it like to learn like that?

CHARUNI: I was looking the children, I said to him to sing the song, and everyone start singing. And sing, sing, sing, sing, and the food, that was um [...] there was Penny come, and said no food in her island, and she come to our island, and she said, 'Can you help us to find a food?' And she said ... and the magic man said, 'We have to sing' and we start singing, sing, sing, sing. And we give her our food and she go back to her island of ...

PENNY: I've forgotten about that bit! You have a good memory! Did you enjoy that part? How did it make you feel?

CHARUNI: Better.

PENNY: It was your idea, wasn't it, to sing too?

CHARUNI: Yeah. I said, 'let's think'.

Here Charuni is asked to comment on what it was like to learn through drama – to reflect on her learning. Instead, she describes her active *experience*, possibly due to a lack of comprehension of the interview question, and/or a lack of strategies to meta-analyse her learning. Yet, an alternative reading is that, for Charuni, learning *is* the lived-experience itself.

The experience, as she recalls it, was *socially constructed*. She frames her recollection in relationship to *others* within the drama (I was looking *the children*; I said to *him*; *everyone* starts... etc.). Interestingly, although this interview occurred several weeks after this episode, Charuni remembers her exact words ('Let's think'). This, she states, made her feel 'better'. It is not possible to ascertain in what way Charuni was made to feel 'better'. It may have been within the drama (as a villager helping her fellow-islanders), in the context of the class (as a successful learner), on a personal level (as a leader, or problem-solver) or in another way. However, Charuni's vivid recollection suggests that it was an *intensively lived-experience*. She adds:

PENNY: Do you ever play island of plenty fish at lunchtime or with your friends?

CHARUNI: Ah, one day, there was a people, she take me to school and back to home. And she was have a party, and I go there, I draw the island of plenty fish. She saw, wow, this was good. And she say me that. I draw.

Having internalized the drama, Charuni created a map to communicate with other people who had not been in the drama. Through this mediational means (the creation and sharing of the map), she was able to extend the dramatic world in a social context. Charuni's lived-experience (perezhivanie) of the drama is further extended on a social level.

On a final note, her choice of wording in the final line (I draw) suggests a self-perceived sense of agency: she places the focus on personally being the agent in the act of drawing. This sense of empowerment is made possible by the active, lived-experience (perezhivanie) afforded by the drama.

Conclusion

Across this chapter we have drawn upon four Vygotskyan concepts to illustrate how our approach created meaningful contexts for ESL learners, offering them ways to communicate that are not normally available to them through other pedagogies. While we discussed them separately, it is also important to understand the ways they overlap and work together within the L2 process drama classroom.

We argued that language learners' experiences were mediated by the use of process drama, especially through the adoption of role. We also suggested that role supports the introduction of new vocabulary. For example, earlier we discussed the children's use of the phrase 'the broken mountain' when referring to the volcano.

Working in role is a key dimension of ZPD. However, and perhaps more importantly, in the context of second language learning, role offers opportunities for embodied action. Significantly, these experiences also have a strong emotional component, for unlike language learning approaches where roles are used in a more functional way, serving merely to introduce context specific vocabulary, within a process drama approach, dramatic tension is used to imbue these roles and experiences with emotion. These emotions in turn impact on the physical responses of the participants, including gesture and facial expression, with embodiment being made more complex by the experience of dual affect.

In traditional ESL classrooms, where drama approaches are often superficially applied, emotions are *enacted* rather than *experienced*. Collaboration and co-construction are limited to sentence formation, conversation practice and shallow role-plays. This denies participants the chance to use their critical thinking skills, together with their imaginations, to achieve meaningful outcomes. By contrast, within process drama, language is authentically embodied and emotional connections and new opportunities for critical and imaginative thinking are made possible. Learner experience is therefore enriched because of creative collaboration.

Within *The Island of Plenty Fish* drama, the mediating influence of role and other elements supported the children to learn the English language, and also enabled them to apply their English to other areas of the curriculum. As the children's classroom teacher remarked:

[Through the process drama] you create a story, and lots of new language is learnt, so they learn lots of vocabulary, and lots of new concepts, and interestingly, you can see it transfer across to other learning areas [...] it's provided a good basis for them – for *us* – to build on it. And I can see lots of the language coming out, and the concepts, you know ... because they *knew* more, they were able to express their ideas.

(Teacher's interview, p. 1)

This quote also illustrates how the dramatic context supported Vygotsky's cycle of imagination. Within the various roles of the drama, individuals drew on experiences from both the actual world and the dramatic one to move the action forward, with the drama itself feeding into the cycle of imagination, enabling individuals to create more ideas than they might have been able to without their involvement. As such, the dramatic context supported the cycle of imagination, and contributed to the creation of a collaborative ZPD.

Our point is that across this drama experience, we saw the four Vygotskyan concepts in action. We saw how they supported these ESL learners to communicate in a way that might not normally be available to them outside of this experience. This occurred in spite of the children's beginner language status, their diverse cultural and historic backgrounds, their inexperience in drama work and their lack of a shared language beyond the target one itself. Looking at the work through this lens allowed us to see the value of sociocultural theory in action within a process drama, second language learning context.

References

Bolton, G. (1979), *Towards a Theory of Drama in Education*, Essex, UK: Longman.

Bolton, G. (1984), *Drama as Education: An Argument for Placing Drama at the Centre of the Curriculum*, Essex, UK: Longman.

Courtney, R. (1995), *Drama and Feeling: An Aesthetic Theory*, Montreal: McGill-Queen's University Press.

Donato, R. (2004), 'Aspects of Collaboration in Pedagogical Discourse', *Annual Review of Applied Linguistics*, 24: 284–302.

Donato, R. and McCormick, D. (1994), 'A Sociocultural Perspective on Language Learning Strategies: The Role of Mediation', *The Modern Language Journal*, 78(4): 453–464.

Eisner, E. (2002), *The Arts and the Creation of Mind*, New Haven and London: Yale University Press.

Ellis, R. (1994), *The Study of Second Language Acquisition*, Oxford: Oxford University Press.

Greene, M. (1995), *Releasing the Imagination: Essays on Education, the Arts, and Social Change*, San Francisco, CA: Jossey-Bass Publishers.

Haught, J.R. and McCafferty, S.G. (2008), 'Embodied Language Performance: Drama and the ZPD in the Second Language Classroom', in J.P. Lantolf and M.E. Poehner (eds), *Sociocultural Theory and the Teaching of Second Languages*, Oakville, CT: Equinox, 139–162.

Holzman, L. (2009), *Vygotsky at Work and Play*, East Sussex, UK: Routledge.

Imai, Y. (2010), 'Emotions in SLA: New Insights for Collaborative Learning from an EFL Classroom', *The Modern Language Journal*, 94(ii): 278–92.

Kao, S.M. and O'Neill, C. (1998), *Words into Worlds: Learning a Second Language through Process Drama*, London: Ablex Publishing Corporation.

Kinginger, C. (2002), 'Defining the Zone of Proximal Development in US Foreign Language Education', *Applied Linguistics*, 23(2): 240–61.

Lantolf, J.P. (1994), 'Sociocultural Theory and Second Language Learning', *Modern Language Journal*, 78(4): 418–20.

Lantolf, J.P. (ed.) (2000), *Sociocultural Theory and Second Language Learning*, Oxford: Oxford University Press.

Lantolf, J.P. and Thorne, S.L. (2006), *Sociocultural Theory and the Genesis of Second Language Development*, New York: Oxford University Press.

Mahn, H. and John-Steiner, V. (2002), 'The Gift of Confidence: A Vygotskyan View of Emotions', in G. Wells and G. Claxton (eds), *Learning for Life in the 21st Century: Sociocultural Perspectives on the Future of Education*, Malden, MA: Blackwell Publishers, 46–58.

McNeill, D. (1992), *Hand and Mind: What Gestures Reveal About Thought*, Chicago, IL: University of Chicago Press.

Ohta, A.S. (2000), 'Rethinking Interaction in SLA: Developmentally Appropriate Assistance in the Zone of Proximal Development and the Acquisition of L2 Grammar', in J. Lantolf (ed.), *Sociocultural Theory and Second Language Learning*, Oxford: Oxford University Press, 51–78.

O'Neill, C. (1995), *Drama Worlds: A Framework for Process Drama*, Portsmouth, NH: Heinemann.

O'Toole, J. (1992), *The Process of Drama: Negotiating Art and Meaning*, London: Routledge.

Rothwell, J. (2013), *Let's Eat the Capitain! Thinking, Feeling, Doing. Intercultural Language Learning through Process Drama*, PhD Dissertation (unpublished), Faculty of Education, Queensland University of Technology: Brisbane.

Simonton, D.K. (2008), 'Bilingualism and Creativity', in J. Altarriba and R.R. Heredia (eds), *An Introduction to Bilingualism: Principles and Processses*, New York: Taylor and Francis, 147–66.

Swain, M. (2000), 'The Output Hypothesis and Beyond: Mediating Acquisition through Collaborative Dialogue' in J. Lantolf (ed.), *Sociocultural Theory and Second Language Learning*, Oxford: Oxford University Press, 97–114.

Vygotsky, L.S. (1930/2004), 'Imagination and Creativity in Childhood', *Journal of Russian and East European Psychology*, 42(1): 7–97.

Vygostky, L.S. (1976), 'Play and its Role in the Mental Development of the Child', in J. Bruner, A. Jolly and K. Sylva (eds), *Play: Its Role in Development and Evolution*, Harmondsworth: Penguin Books, 537–54.

Vygotsky, L.S. (1978), *Mind in Society: The Development of Higher Psychological Processes*, M. Cole, V. John-Steiner, S. Scribner and E. Souberman (eds), Cambridge, MA: Harvard University Press.

Vygotsky, L.S. (1986), *Thought and Language*, Cambridge, MA: MIT Press.

Vygotsky, L.S. (1994), 'The Problem of the Environment' in R. Van Der Veer and J. Valsiner (eds), *The Vygotsky Reader*, Oxford, UK: Blackwell, 338–54.

Vygotsky, L.S. (2004), 'Imagination and Creativity in Childhood', *Journal of Russian and East European Psychology*, 42(1): 7–97.

Prolepsis and Educational Change through Drama: Bringing the Future Forward

Patricia Enciso

Introduction

In our country we did not have peace.
This is a place where we can make peace.

Get out of my country.

You don't belong here.

Why would you do this?
Do you hate yourself too?

I don't like the way you live.

Maybe you want a better life than me.
Maybe I have a better life than you.

The opening lines of this chapter are excerpted from a dramatized exchange between myself, as a teacher-in-role representing a bigot and students-in-role as community members, who challenged the bigot's hateful, dismissive nationalist discourse. Although the voice of bigotry, based in a fear of difference, is often available in news reports, media discourses and government policies, the corresponding voice of immigrants, living in diasporic communities, is often silenced or unavailable for deeper consideration. In US schools, and around the world, educators are grappling with the needs and perspectives of immigrant and non-immigrant youth in relation with longstanding institutional practices that often reinforce stereotypes, segregation and miseducation (Moll, 2014; Valenzuela, 1999). Education through drama, developed in relation with multiple narratives and resources, may provide a temporary setting for mediating and supporting the perspectives of global peers as they participate in shaping a changing society.

In this chapter, I describe and analyse a sequence of dramatic inquiry events (Edmiston, 2014; Edmiston and Enciso, 2002) that I facilitated in a US Midwestern middle school with two groups of 12- and 13-year-olds who were identified, in one class, as urban Appalachian White, African American and multi-ethnic youth (5 boys), and in another class, as first- and second-generation immigrant youth from Cambodia, Jordan, Somalia, Kenya, Mexico and Dominican Republic (3 girls and 8 boys). Across their classrooms, the youth and I drew on our past experiences and knowledge to shape a dramatized moment, in the present, with the potential to mediate a possible, more humanizing and equitable future for one another in the school and community. Using the sociocultural concepts of prolepsis, 'telos' and motivated setting (Cole, 1996; Smagorinsky, 2001, 2011; Wertsch 1985) and interpretation of 'sense' (Vygotsky, 1987), I analyse how dramatic activity interrupts familiarity by introducing and mobilizing new material with the potential to change existing social structures. I am interested, overall, in the ways drama can initiate new practices in school settings that value the cultural repertoires and potential of immigrant and non-immigrant youth as they become actors within the changing political and demographic landscapes of their communities (Gutiérrez and Rogoff, 2003; Maira and Soep, 2005). I present one exploratory case of dramatic inquiry that illustrates how a telos or underlying assumption of culture clash (Ngo, 2008) can be interrupted through the formation of a specific, motivated, imagined setting.

Prolepsis: A Mechanism for Cultural Continuity and Change

Prolepsis has been defined in narrative and film studies as a rhetorical device used to indicate that a future event can be anticipated, based on knowledge from the present. For example, a flashback will suggest that all of the events unfolding for a character in a present moment were established by a decision made in her childhood. In sociocultural theory, prolepsis is also tied to relationships among the past, present and future, but these are directed towards the social mediation and mutual constitution of cultural continuity and change. According to Cole (1996), prolepsis '... brings the end [future] into the beginning [present], by representing a future act or development as being presently existing' (Cole, 1996: 187). In other words, present interactions should be interpreted as though everyone already knows what they need to know and how they should act. The past is also implicated through prolepsis, when ongoing present experiences accrue as though they constitute a shared familiar past. In summarizing his review of specific instances of cultural-historically formed beliefs and actions across generations, Cole (1996) states, 'Only a culture-using human being can "reach into" the cultural past, project it into the future, and then "carry" that conceptual future "back" into the present to create the sociocultural environment of the newcomer' (Cole, 1996: 186).

Such a process would seem to preclude any options for change as daily life is quickly coordinated and made meaningful among people who tacitly agree (and use their authority to insure) that the values of a common past and agreed-upon future will continue for themselves and others in the present. For example, a teacher may pose a question in anticipation of fostering learning; in response, students will raise their hands to indicate their readiness to participate in learning. Initiation and response practices in classrooms such as these are seamless, in many cases, because teachers and students share an understanding of past interactions, as well as a shared 'reach' into an idealized future that assumes an already agreed upon connection between question posing, hand raising and school success.

Without questioning or interruption, classroom interactions run smoothly, in part because they are proleptic; children and teachers act as though they understand and accept the implied conceptual past and future as it is enacted in the present. However, for many children entering school for the first time, hand raising and other forms of being a student are not 'already known', making them vulnerable to adults' judgment that they are not prepared for learning, or worse, not intelligent and capable of engaging in complex and creative learning experiences. Prolepsis, then, is a ubiquitous feature of cultural life and yet, due to the constructed nature of social life, each interaction is also potentially available for contestation and improvisation. Families with diverse histories of immigration and migration introduce new ways of participating in everyday life and thus call attention to futures and pasts that are no longer reliable reference points for cultural continuity. Such questions about continuity lead to uncertainty about the future that often intensifies references to the past ('This is how it has always been'); and yet, uncertainty also opens possibilities for learning and change ('How might we value and learn multiple languages?') (Kumashiro, 2004). Thus, prolepsis is not as stable as it seems, as new perceptions and taken for granted daily interactions and institutional norms of inclusion and exclusion become subject to struggle and negotiation.

Prolepsis and Drama: Making Change Visible

Drama, like other art forms, brings everyday life into focus, and because of its enactive, playful and experimental nature, shows us how the world works in the present and how our actions, beliefs and relationships might create a different world in the future (O'Neill, 1995; Vygotsky, 1978). I argue that drama makes proleptic activity visible, by creating the setting for new interpretations of life and by situating these interpretations in immediate and emotional human relations. As Heathcote (1969) argued, through dramatic activity a group's ideas are modified and formed '... in "heated" not "cold" circumstances for it draws directly upon the individual's life and subjective experiences as its basic material ...' (Heathcote, 1969: 54). She continues, 'Dramatic activity is concerned with the crises, the turning points of life, large and small, which cause people to reflect and take note ...' (Heathcote, 1969). 'Subjective experiences' and the 'turning points of life' are, in many respects, precisely what interested Vygotsky as he developed a sociocultural theory of the relationship between human cognition and cultural change. Vygotsky (1986) and his colleagues planned formative experiments so they could observe children in the midst of learning about and solving unfamiliar problems with new mediating materials. Vygotsky's questions about learning and cultural change are akin to those that are often asked through drama.

As the opening lines of this chapter suggest, questions of cultural change in drama may be situated in the 'heated circumstances' of human relations and everyday life, while they are also distanced from the actual events that form ongoing assumptions and relationships in schools and communities. Dramatic inquiry, defined by Edmiston (2014) as collaborative inquiry into the 'competing perspectives in and on the imagined events in narrative worlds', allows teachers and students to move between imagined and actual circumstances as they construct the specific form and focus of a problem. Through embodying and 'living through' a problem, new mediating ideas and language may become available that alter perceptions of what has happened in the past, what is happening in the present, and what might be possible in the future.

In the following sections I describe the constraining functions of prolepsis and telos in the everyday learning of immigrant and non-immigrant children in the school where I participated as a co-teacher and researcher. I argue that principles of sociocultural theory and dramatic inquiry can work together to 'bring the future forward', so that oppressive proleptic cycles of activity are interrupted and new forms of anticipated [future] social interaction might be introduced in classrooms and schools.

Reproducing the Past in the Present: Prolepsis and Telos Limiting Voice and Learning

During one school year, I co-taught and observed students in three settings: the classroom for the students who needed additional educational support, the class next door designated for immigrant students whose heritage language is not English (ELL), and a weekly story club meeting in the school library for immigrant and non-immigrant youth. Across these settings I could begin to identify and interpret different, related forms of proleptic activity that were unquestioned, and yet mediated the meaning and value of students' cultural repertoires, especially their language, knowledge and relationships among themselves, within the school, and across their transcultural experiences outside of school (Enciso, 2011). All of these observations informed my relationships with the students and our co-construction of a dramatized setting for naming and responding to discrimination against immigrant youth and families in the United States.

According to Wertsch (1985), a guiding narrative or telos defines what activities mean and how materials, tasks, rules, relationships and evaluations should be organized over time in a particular setting. Such narratives establish the cultural goals of a group, whether that group is a classroom, school, community or society. Prolepsis, on the other hand, refers to the actions, materials and organization of rules, time and spaces that accrue to form the daily, taken for granted, practices that shape our lives together. Through the functions of telos and prolepsis, daily interactions are mediated by histories of shared activity and by accompanying narratives and goals. Narratives will be contested and resisted, but still guide the formation and interpretation of cultural belonging, continuity and change. Reframing the telos in an activity is critical for reframing learning to support historically marginalized youth.

Prolepsis and Recitation Scripts: Constructing the Absence of Inquiry and Voice

In both classrooms, during the first three months of school, the literacy curriculum required a focus on predetermined answers rather than exploration of a range of possible interpretations or perspectives. Although discussion was often encouraged, students rarely listened to or built on one another's ideas, and only a narrow range of cultural knowledge and linguistic repertoires were understood or developed among teachers and students. Gutiérrez and Larson

(1994) describe the absence of students' voices during literacy classroom discussions as the 'borderlands' within recitation scripts. Here, recitation scripts function as proleptic activities, creating a 'border' that effectively anticipates an already known and familiar pattern of participation for children whose cultural resources are familiar, while excluding or 'missing' the voices of youth whose cultural knowledge and resources are not well understood or valued.

Similar to recitation practices, teachers in both language arts classrooms selected literature that would engage students, but also created packets of materials for students to complete that featured teachers' questions and already determined approaches for answering questions. This meant that in both classes, youth had almost no experience of developing their own questions and meanings or working towards a collective understanding, whether in agreement or contestation of story interpretations, within or across classrooms (Enciso, 2011). The continuity of teachers' past experiences and students' implicit daily lessons in how to be a student in school, reinforced a telos that valued individual, monolingual, monocultural learning, while precluding a vision of students as transcultural youth with rich cultural repertoires for interpreting human experiences and engaging collectively with one another's ideas.

Culture Clash and Cultural Pluralism: Telos as Possibility in School Spaces

In addition to observing their language classrooms, I also facilitated a cross-cultural lunchtime story club that invited youth to co-narrate (Ochs and Capps, 2001) personal stories and tales based in their family traditions. In both classrooms and story club, my mediation of learning was intended to disrupt what Ngo (2008) calls a 'culture clash narrative' that validates segregation and reinforces silencing. Cultural clash narratives focus on cultural differences as static traits, language differences as deficits, and academic success or failure as an anti-Western refusal to adapt to Western beliefs. As a counter to the culture clash telos, my teaching was informed by a narrative of cultural pluralism, based on an assumption that culturally diverse youth are receptive and creative in the presence of one another's heritage languages, linguistic variations, knowledge, beliefs and norms (Paris, 2012). This telos is not an idealized version of cross-cultural harmony, but assumes contradiction and struggle. As Hansen (2010) contends, settings dedicated to the formation of new relations and identities across cultural differences entail 'the fusion, sometimes tenuous and tension-laden, of receptivity to the new and loyalty to the known' (Hanson, 1010: 5).

Although these sessions reduced the barriers of isolation between immigrant and non-immigrant youth, the real issue for everyone was the pervasive structures and practices in the school that reinforced stereotypes and deficit perceptions of immigrant youth, in particular. For example, the English Language Learning (ELL) classroom was located on the opposite side of the building from all other language arts classrooms. In order to move to their classroom, immigrant students had to walk in the opposite direction to their peers and visibly mark the distance between their knowledge and the 'proficient' knowledge of native English speakers in the school. Due to the location of the ELL classroom in relation with other special education services, walking down this hallway was also associated with cognitive disabilities and difference.

Not surprisingly, many students were subject to taunts and teasing about their racial and ethnic identities, language and clothing. Although immigrant students described adults and peers who were helpful and understanding when they were confused or felt threatened, they acknowledged having to defend themselves nearly every day inside or outside the school building. Their individual attempts to challenge taunts, however, did not lead to change in their own sense of agency or in the ongoing practices that reinforced culture clash narratives. Youth make many strategic decisions about how and when they will respond to slurs and teasing; but the experience of being silent or silenced is still profoundly significant for understanding oneself as a valued person in school. I did not expect to change longstanding, school and district practices; however, based on our talk together and students' emerging friendships in the lunchtime story club, it seemed possible to 'bring a future forward', guided by sociocultural theory that values cultural repertoires as mediating resources for learning, and a telos of cultural pluralism that values youth creativity and 'tenuous but tension-laden' engagement with one another's lives.

'Sense' and Uncertainty in Everyday Meaning Making

Finding new ways to intervene in culture clash practices and narratives is especially important for youth who experience silencing. In his analysis of the ways some voices are authorized and included and others excluded, Blommaert (2005) traces language practices across an 'itinerary of normative spaces ... filled with codes, customs, rules, and expectations ...' (Blommaert, 2005: 73). Normative spaces and attendant codes and rules form the 'exacting and restraining conditions' under which people struggle for voice. Blommaert argues further that voice will be produced and heard 'under conditions of empowerment' (Blommaert, 2009: 271).

While seeking to be understood within a deficit or culture clash telos, youth may not trust themselves to find the words and images that represent their 'voice' and their meaning. However, dramatic inquiry may invite the joint construction of a new telos where uncertainty and improvisation are valued and voices are able to be heard in an unfolding possible present and future.

Vygotsky's concept of 'sense' offers a useful theoretical bridge between the potential for voice and the empowering conditions that mediate or reconstitute normative spaces. Sense, in Smagorinsky's (2011: 136) analysis of Vygotsky's concepts, represents the '... set of images and associations one makes with a sign such as a word in the area of consciousness,' *prior to* enunciation or representation. Sense may be felt through the pauses, hesitations, shifts in expression, tone and body orientation among people, but is akin to 'a storm cloud of thought' rather than a fully articulated concept. Voice is imminent in the experience of 'sense', but is not yet available for further mediation among others. These nascent formations of ideas and meanings require a shared interest in what is possible rather than what is finalized. Indeed, finalized meanings are often associated with repeated proleptic activities such as recitation scripts, and are further reinforced by unquestioned guiding narratives or telos based on deficit views of youth linguistic and cultural resources.

Bringing a Future Forward: Design and Change in Proleptic Activity

Despite the repeated and unquestioned nature of everyday life in schools, proleptic cycles of activity are not as stable as they may seem. If prolepsis is essentially an anticipation of the future in the present, it is possible to imagine a counter-hegemonic future and design settings that bring the ideas and possibilities of a more inclusive future forward into the present.

In Smagorinsky's (2011) analysis of classroom life, the concepts of *motive* and *setting* point to the specific mechanisms for transforming how learning is accomplished. Drawing on Wertsch's (1985) interpretation of power in sociocultural theory, he argues that setting is formed, not because of a particular space it occupies, but because of the historically formed *motives* that define purposes for materials, time, organization and relationships. The motive, according to Wertsch, '... specifies what is to be maximized in that setting'

(Wertsch, 1985: 212). Smagorinsky concludes that, 'Without widespread agreement on the motive and meditational means, a setting could not exist' (Smagorinsky, 2011: 21).

Dramatic activity relies on the selective use of images, materials and other signs, including language to focus participants' explorations of meaning and viewpoints in a particular situation. Furthermore, the setting is formed through an agreement among participants that familiar objects and relations will be temporarily renamed in order to bring a different world into focus, a world that is deliberately formed or motivated for collective inquiry. In a classroom-based dramatic inquiry experience, the motive and setting can be planned by the teacher, but also negotiated with students so the purpose of inquiry is clear and the elements or mediating artifacts and relationships are made significant in the imagined setting. As Smagorinsky (2011) argues, a motivated setting maximizes resources in service of a guiding telos.

Settings, designed to maximize students' access to complex problems, have long been the focus of sociocultural research. For example, Cole (1996) and his colleagues designed settings that could 'bring the end into the beginning', whereby familiar proleptic practices were displaced or re-mediated and new mediating materials, social relations and problems were introduced.

Thus, an activity has to be carefully defined so that the setting is maximized for access to the fullest possible range of meditational means for analysing and solving the problems they encounter and consider alternatives for the future. This includes the consideration that youth will share responsibility for the roles required to bring new ideas and practices into being. As Cole and other sociocultural researchers have argued, when youth bring their knowledge and cultural resources to practices that are organized for their full participation, they may begin to see, think, feel and act in new ways, with recognized competence.

Bringing a Future (for Intercultural Voices) Forward through Dramatic Inquiry

In April 2009, as I worked on literature studies in both classrooms, I introduced stories of immigrant experiences in the United States and created multiple opportunities for youth to raise questions about events, characters' insights and the forces that motivate immigration. The students and I were interested in the characters' experiences in *Something about America* (Testa, 2005), a fictionalized account of true events that erupted in 2002 in Lewiston, Maine, a small East Coast town in the United States, when the town's mayor published a letter in the local newspaper informing all Somali community members that additional family members would not be welcome. The immigrant population, in his view, had grown too large and was upsetting the balance and traditions of their predominately white middle-class community. Told in free-verse poetry, the story's narrator, a young Kosovan girl, witnesses her parents' perceptions, reactions and stories as they, and especially Somali families and community leaders, become targets of a neo-Nazi organization whose members plan and stage an anti-immigrant rally in their town. As the students read this story with my guidance, over several class sessions, they also viewed and interpreted primary documents and videos from the actual event.

Something about America offered a window into a young girl's growing awareness of the pain and sense of loss her parents feel after being forced to flee their home country, resettle in the United States, and then defend their rights as citizens following the 9/11 attacks on the World Trade Center in New York City. The novella offered a compelling sense of uncertainty and anger in the face of discrimination, inviting readers to wonder, along with the narrator, about the effort required to prove one's belonging in a community and nation that is full of contradictions about democracy and freedom.

Among non-immigrant youth, the beginnings of interest in and empathy for actual immigrant peers became visible in relation with more nuanced interpretations of characters and events depicted in literature. For example, after reading a different story, based on the memoir of a young Somali boy and his family's experience of resettlement in the Midwest, a student imagined the constant hard work and loss of identity felt by the family's father. The father sought dignity in his labour but was distressed and angry about the constant dehumanizing interactions he had with people around him. The student wrote an essay from the father's point of view, recognizing, in the end, 'I am someone, you just don't know me.' During our discussions as a group, however, the story's underlying questions about who belongs and who stands up for dignity and humanity seemed to be the characters' problem rather than an immediate concern in the school. In many ways, the study of literature was still informed by proleptic activities of answering someone else's (the teacher's) questions, even though we were working with new ways of showing interpretations through visual art, enactments of character emotions and personal story telling.

The story's plot, and concern for immigrant rights, pointed to an initial setting and telos for 'bringing a future forward' that might engage all of us in the 'heated circumstances' of discovering what we feel and believe in the face of racism. I established an expert framing (Heathcote, 1984) for the beginning of our work together, so students could be offered both a situation that needed attention and a particular perspective and responsibility in relation to that problem. As reporters in the small town of Lewiston, they could function within the invented setting of a newsroom and community, to ask what it means to be a bigot and what it means to be an advocate. What words and tones represent these stances? What do we know and what can we say that can resist bigotry? In many ways these same questions were part of the daily experiences of both immigrant and non-immigrant youth, but were never the focus of a collective analysis and response.

These inquiry questions allowed us to enter the viewpoints of the main characters in the story as well as establish a way to question the everyday proleptic activities and culture clash narratives in the school culture. By 'maximizing resources' through drama, that is by focusing attention on a shared problem and reframing the setting for a new inquiry and purpose, we could loosen the hold of familiar proleptic activity that kept immigrant and non-immigrant youth experiences and resources separate and undervalued.

My intention with dramatic inquiry was to create the 'conditions of empowerment' for voice through practices that valued uncertainty, collective effort and multiple, intercultural repertoires of knowledge and experience. Drama strategies such as teacher-in-role and framed expertise would allow me to negotiate the intensity and meaning of our work, as well as our relationship to the problem situation. As I introduced elements of the dramatic setting, we could identify what mattered most as a point of interest and problem solving. The drama work would allow us to participate in the 'whole act' of using our voices together in response to bigotry.

Setting One: A Small Town Newsroom

In the class of boys, all non-immigrant, I began by writing the words 'bigot' and 'advocate' on the chalkboard and asked if they had any ideas about their meaning. The boys had heard of bigots and knew it was not good and probably prejudiced; and suggested that an advocate was probably someone who was good and listened. After asking the same question in the adjacent classroom, it was clear that neither group was definite about the meaning of these words. I wanted to use these words as foci or 'maximizing resources' for our inquiry, so I suggested that bigots were looking for reasons to exclude people and advocates were looking for ways to defend and support people who were being excluded. Students then added to the list of what these words evoked for them, including racist, haters, bullies, Nazi and, on the other hand, helper, citizen, friend and leader. I wondered with the students if they could think of the ways bigotry and advocacy entered into their everyday lives, sometimes within the same person or event.

Through this opening, I suggested that we work together taking on roles as reporters in Lewiston, to find out what people were thinking about the community members who were immigrants. What did people really believe about the people who lived and worked together each day? In anticipation of this initial framing of their relationship to the problem of bigotry, I had asked their teacher to represent a community member (in-role) who was not sure that immigrants were 'fitting in' to Lewiston. Their teacher agreed to respond to a question on digital video so it could be shown and reviewed on a computer as often as the students needed, as they developed their own directions for inquiry. At first, the boys, who were not used to drama, were unclear about the imagined and actual stance taken by their teacher. She was working with us and was able to assure them, as I had, that this was a pretend video so we could imagine what it must sound like when someone seems kind and reasonable but is actually saying things that are hurtful. They agreed that she was convincing, but wanted to hear what she-as-teacher really believed, at which point it was possible to place her imagined bigotry image in juxtaposition with her actual stance of advocacy. We returned to the words on the board and the boys wanted to know how someone could really feel so mean and want people to go away.

The fictionalized setting of a newsroom and beginnings of an expert frame as news reporters made it possible to suggest that they could 'go into the town' and find out what people were thinking. Using the computer and video camera I showed them how we could videotape interviews and upload these to the computer for review. I told the boys that we would be sharing these same interviews over our town's evening news report. I also suggested that these interviews could be shared with the class next door, where all of the students and their families were immigrants to the United States. The presence of an imagined and actual audience became a key, motivating focus, as we considered who should be interviewed and what they should be asked. Should we talk to the (imagined) mayor of Lewiston? We already knew his views; so perhaps we should seek another person who expressed bigoted views. However, giving more attention to such views could make non-immigrant people in the community angry and resistant to immigrant perspectives. They decided to seek a local business owner, someone who had worked with Somali adults over the past few years. Another teacher in the room served as the interviewee and made a factual, positive report on her employees and their contributions to her business and community. In the time remaining, the boys wondered what a 'kid' would have to say who was not an immigrant (like the boys in this room). One of the most vocal boys was interviewed about what it meant to 'be American' and how he knew he was American. Following his interview, we uploaded the video clips to the computer and reviewed them again so they could be edited for the evening news.

I wondered if they might also want to ask their peers, next door, what it had been like for them to be newcomers in the United States. One of the boys wanted to ask if anything or anyone had ever hurt them when they were in school. Another boy wanted to ask if they had been helped by anyone in school. I videotaped the boys asking these questions, then showed all of the video clips that would be aired next door and on the imagined 'evening news'.

Although the work we did together as reporters in a newsroom may seem to be an elaborate or even unnecessary way to engage students in asking questions about bigotry and advocacy, the focus of our work shifted away from a teacher-directed discussion in a classroom context to a slightly removed, fictional collective effort in an attempt to solve a problem that was equally engaging for teachers and students. By mediating the answers and ideas about bigotry and advocacy through interviews and video clips, students also had a chance to review and 'slow down' the images and words so they could interpret them and begin to move through *sense* into *meaning*. By working between the imagined world of a small town's conflict and their peers' presence in the room next door, the boys could also begin to sense the relationship between words expressed by adults and the feelings experienced by youth. Finally, through the drama frame, the students were offered some authority over the direction and interpretations of bigotry and advocacy, and how related images and expressions would be presented to others.

In the next room, I followed the same pattern of introducing the words bigot and advocate, and invited students to be editors in a newsroom setting for a special show on immigrant families in Lewiston. Although this was a very 'light' framing that was not developed due to time constraints, the video clips themselves suggested that their actual viewpoints were valued for interpreting the words of the interviewees. As I showed the video clips of the class next door, students moved out of their seats to lean in to hear the voices of three people whom they recognized, but had not seen in an imagined role as advocates or bigots. The feeling in the room shifted from passivity to interest and attention and an urgency to speak. One of the girls, whose family is Somalian and who was closest to the screen began to talk about how hard it is to find a job and then pay credit card bills. 'People don't know,' she said. Another boy pointed out that people are citizens even if they are immigrants.

The next videos, in which their peers asked questions about living in the United States, elicited a series of stories. For the first time, immigrant youth began to tell stories among themselves about their experiences as young children arriving in school and their memories of hardships in refugee camps and in war torn villages. All of these stories were videotaped and shared the next day in the room next door.

While viewing their peers telling stories via a computer screen, the boys became witnesses to real-life immigration stories as they also registered the feelings conveyed by their peers' voices and facial expressions. As one student said of his peer: 'He looks so worried and he's trying to be happy.'

In this exchange of questions and stories, a barrier was lowered between immigrant and non-immigrant youth so they could begin to understand themselves as global peers, living in the same place in the presence of bigotry, but with the possibility for advocacy. In terms of prolepsis and telos, they were no longer educated separately due to a guiding narrative that cultural differences precluded cultural understanding. Rather, they were located in the same imagined world, with actual concerns for one another's histories and futures.

Setting Two: Can We Resist Bigotry?

Towards the end of the story *Something about America*, the narrator discovers a flyer on her front door, left by a neo-Nazi activist that declares anti-immigrant views and the time and place of an anti-immigrant rally. The narrator wonders what will happen next. Will her parents act or retreat? What can be done?

In each classroom, I invited students to imagine that I could represent the bigot portrayed in the story as a neo-Nazi, with the intent to foment hate and fear among community members. We agreed to test out the meaning of bigotry and advocacy through an imagined encounter that takes place before the person/neo-Nazi places the flyer on the doorstep. What can we say to stop him/her? What could persuade her/him that this is wrong, that we are advocates in the face of bigotry? I was not sure if the students would actually be able to speak up as advocates; however, based on the previous days' drama and video exchanges, as well as the growing friendships and familiarity developing among some students through the weekly story club, I thought that if they could hear their voices collectively they would gain a sense of the strength of all of their ideas and be able to 'break' the actions of the bigot.

I knew that I would have to represent the bigot in order to insure control over the intensity and interplay of fictional and real voices. Together we imagined and practiced the degree to which my representation of this figure would be hateful and mean: what would she sound like, what would she say, how might she walk towards people's doors. They offered suggestions and I made the representations of the bigot-in-role so they could clearly see that I was creating a representation, not presenting my personal views. Once the bigot-in-role was clear, I gave the students post-its and asked them to write 2–3 responses to the bigot if she came directly to you and said 'This is MY America' or 'Go back to your country!' Students wrote notes to remind them of their responses so they could be prepared when I addressed them as the bigot-in-role.

Using the signal of putting on a beaten-up leather coat to indicate that I would begin representing the bigot, I walked slowly to the first student and declared one of the statements they had agreed would be said by the teacher-in-role/bigot. Once I/Bigot spoke, I stood near one of the students and waited for a response. At first, a few students responded with nervous giggles, but as I repeated the statement and sounded firmer in my views, one student, then the next, read from their notes in an effort to stop the bigot's verbal attacks. In some interactions I added another statement to press for more intensity in the students' response. The problem of responding to a bigot was game-like in some respects – to see if they could silence me in-role. As students heard one another's ideas and counters to bigotry though, they began to improvise beyond their written responses and added on to or echoed what others spoke. The students' words, excerpted from the full event in both classrooms, and transcribed as a poem below, reflect their confidence and insights as they expressed their views and inferred the perspective of the bigot.

This is my America.

But people come to
America for freedom.

Get out of my country.

Maybe your ancestors were immigrants.

I am American.

You have no right
to say all of those mean things.
It's wrong.

We all should be treated the same way.
It doesn't matter where you came from.

>*I don't like the way you live.*

Nobody is different.
Even if we are different colors,
religions
and nationalities.
> We are all the same.
> We are all human.

>*You don't belong here.*

Why would you do this?
Do you hate yourself too?

>*I don't like the way you live.*

Maybe you want a better life than me.
> Maybe I have a better life than you.
> I live the same way you do.

After students read transcriptions of their audio recorded voices, I guided them in reading aloud their words in a readers' theatre forum, using multiple voices, inflections and gestures to emphasize meaning. Some students decided that their words should be read more widely in their school. Their teachers and I helped them edit and transform their words into a large poster that was displayed in the school hallway.

The use of a teacher-in-role and student-in-role enabled youth in both classrooms to draw on the reality of their experiences of actual bigotry while imagining and enacting a future in which they could identify the feeling and form of advocacy. Through drama conventions such as 'slowing time' and negotiating and rehearsing how a problem might be addressed, we could condense the proleptic time frame, and 'bring forward' materials and resources motivated by a telos based on cultural pluralism. Our embodied interactions and initial ways of considering the meaning of cultural change in the present could become new material resources that might enter and become juxtaposed with the ongoing proleptic and teleologic encounters of everyday life in school.

Implications for Teaching and Research

Prolepsis is an ongoing part of everyday experience and learning and must be taken seriously as a mechanism for continuity and change. In research, as in teaching, it is possible to plan a motivated setting, or a formative experiment, that accounts for decisions about the selection and use of resources, in service of a defined telos. This new setting, animated through the principles and practices of dramatic inquiry, must also be understood in relation with a defined, ongoing proleptic activity cycle, which is also completed in relation to a defined telos. Constructions of settings and negotiations over resources, ideologies and identities are well-documented in literacy research, through the use of qualitative research methods and discourse analysis. These studies identify students' agency along with institutionalized constraints on change that exclude cultural resources and opportunities to learn (Lewis *et al.*, 2007; Ngo, 2010; Maira and Soep, 2005). In this chapter, I briefly described unquestioned institutional norms that positioned immigrant and non-immigrant youth in terms of a culture clash narrative. Like many researcher-educators, I am hopeful that change and inclusion are possible in schools. However, I also want to be clear that change can only be understood and sustained when settings are not only motivated for learning but also open to 'sense' and uncertainty and experimentation and reflection are supported as a collective effort.

References

Blommaert, J. (2005), *Discourse*, Cambridge, UK: Cambridge University Press.

Blommaert, J. (2009), 'Ethnography and Democracy: Hymes' Political Theory of Language', *Text and Talk*, 29(3): 257–76.

Cole, M. (1996), *Cultural Psychology: A Once and Future Discipline*, Cambridge, MA: Belknap Press.

Edmiston, B. (2014), *Transforming Teaching and Learning with Active and Dramatic Approaches: Engaging Students Across the Curriculum*, New York and London: Routledge.

Edmiston, B. and Enciso, P. (2002), 'Reflections and Refractions of Meaning: Dialogic Approaches to Classroom Drama and Reading', in J. Flood, D. Lapp, J. Squire and J. Jensen (eds), *The Handbook of Research on Teaching the English Language Arts*, New York: Simon and Schuster Macmillan, 868–80.

Enciso, P. (2011), 'Storytelling in Critical Literacy Pedagogy: Removing the Walls between Immigrant and Non-Immigrant Youth', *English Teaching: Practice and Critique* 10(1): 21–40.

Gutiérrez, K. and Larson, J. (1994), 'Language Borders: Recitation as Hegemonic Discourse', *International Journal of Educational Reform*, 3(1): 22–36.

Gutiérrez, K. and Rogoff, B. (2003), 'Cultural Ways of Learning: Individual Traits or Repertoires of Practice', *Educational Researcher*, 32: 19–25.

Hansen, D. (2010), 'Cosmopolitanism and Education: A View from the Ground', *Teachers College Record*, 112(1): 1–30.

Heathcote, D. (1969), 'Dramatic Activity', *English in Education*, 3(2): NATE.
Heathcote, D. (1984), *Dorothy Heathcote: Collected Writings on Drama and Education*, L. Johnson and C. O'Neill (eds), London, UK: Hutchinson.
Kumashiro, K. (2004), *Against Common Sense: Teaching and Learning for Social Justice*, New York: Routledge.
Lewis, C., Enciso, P. and Moje, E. (eds) (2007), *Reframing Sociocultural Research on Literacy: Identity, Agency and Power*, Mahwah, NJ: Erlbaum.
Maira, S. and Soep, E. (eds) (2005), *Youthscapes: The Popular, the National, the Global*, Philadelphia, PA: University of Pennsylvania Press.
Moll, L. (2014), *L.S. Vygotsky and Education*, New York: Routledge.
Ngo, B. (2008), 'Beyond Culture Clash Narratives of Immigrant Experiences', *Theory into Practice*, 47(1): 4–11.
Ngo, B. (2010), *Unresolved Identities: Discourse, Ambivalence, and Urban Immigrant Students*, Albany, NY: SUNY Press.
Ochs, E. and Capps, L. (2001), *Living Narrative: Creating Lives in Everyday Storytelling*, Cambridge, MA: Harvard University Press.
O'Neill, C. (1995), *Drama Worlds*, Portsmouth, NH: Heinemann.
Paris, D. (2012), *Culturally Sustaining Pedagogy: A Needed Change in Stance, Terminology and Practice. Educational Researcher*, 41(3): 93–7.
Smagorinsky, P. (2001), 'If Meaning is Constructed, What is it Made From? Toward a Cultural Theory of Reading', *Review of Educational Research*, 71(1): 133–69.
Smagorinsky, P. (2011), *Vygotsky and Literacy Research: A Methodological Framework*, Boston, MA: Sense Publishers.
Testa, M. (2005), *Something about America*, Somenville, MA: Candelwick.
Valenzuela, A. (1999), *Subtractive Schooling: US-Mexican Youth and the Politics of Caring*, Albany, NY: State University of New York Press.
Vygotsky, L.S. (1978), *Mind in Society*, Cambridge, MA: Harvard University Press.
Vygotsky, L.S. (1987), 'Thinking and Speech', In L.S. Vygotsky (ed.), *Collected Works*, vol. 1, R. Rieber and A. Carton (eds), translated by N. Minick, New York: Plenum, 39–285.
Wertsch, J.V. (1985), *Vygotsky and the Social Formation of Minds*, Cambridge, MA: Harvard University Press.

10

Interactive Drama with Digital Technology and Tools for Creative Learning

Susan Davis

Introduction

Within educational contexts there is a dominant discourse at play that asserts the importance of embracing digital technologies as essential for preparing students for the future. This often translates to a focus on the provision of more computers and technology, with a strong emphasis on Information and Communications Technologies (ICTs). The rhetoric about this focus leading to improved educational outcomes and economic superiority is not matched by the reality, with an ever-growing number of researchers and academics identifying the importance of social practices and technology rather than just the technology in itself (Buckingham, 2007; Greenhow *et al.*, 2009; Kritt and Winegar, 2007; Seiter, 2005; Thurlow and Bell, 2009).

Drama educators, like others, often desire to, or are pressured to embrace the use of ICTs in their classrooms. As prior research has identified, there are a range of issues involved including limited access to technology in areas not perceived to be core curriculum or ICT focused, and there is also a reluctance by some drama teachers to shift their focus from historical practices of drama education which prioritize live human interactions (Flintoff, 2005).

This chapter will therefore outline a project and related research, which explored student learning and creative practice using Information and ICTs, in a secondary school drama education context. An activity systems approach was applied to data analysis drawing on Cultural-Historical Activity Theory (CHAT) and the theory of expansive learning to understand the impact of an intervention.

Expansive Learning, Activity Theory and Contradictions

For the purposes of this research project, tools drawn from CHAT were utilized to inform the methodology and analysis of data. There have been minimal applications of activity theory to drama research to date (Davis, 2010; Grainger Clemson, 2011). Several studies have focused on dramatic play and early childhood settings (Gulpa, 2007; Van Oers, 2008) and more general application of cultural-historical analysis has been applied to the analysis of playworlds and arts-based practice (Connery et al., 2010). Activity Theory is readily applicable to drama educational research, but may require ongoing interpretation and consideration in the new research context.

CHAT emphasizes recognition of the historical dimensions of the evolution of human development and cognition. In this branch of theory and research, human activity is identified as the basic unit of analysis. This recognizes the situated and enacted nature of phenomena: the inter-related nature of internalized subject thinking and externalized interactions with others and the environment. As Engeström has pointed out, human activity is the bridge between the individual and society. It is the smallest and simplest initial unit, but within it are all the component elements to be found within a complex totality (Engeström, 1987). Activity therefore becomes the focus for analysis.

The theory of expansive learning was further drawn upon to inform thinking about the developmental process and research methodology. This theory was initially developed by Engeström (1987) as a model for conceptualizing and guiding developmental learning processes and innovation. It has since been further explicated (Engeström, 2001, 2009; Engeström and Sannino, 2010) and used to inform practical work and research in a wide range of settings such as health, computing, building construction and more. The theory of expansive learning is often used as an interventionist research methodology, where the researchers are both facilitators and participants in collective journeys of learning and change.

The different phases of expansive learning (Figure 10.1) provide an overview of the process. The cycle begins with a primary need state and questioning. Contradictions, cracks or disruptions in activity are then identified and used as sites for analysis. These contradictions may be traced as emerging from within or between the components of the activity. The process of analysing activities and their history can inform an understanding of potential solutions and the creation of a zone of proximal development (Engeström, 1987). The development of new models or solutions and their implementation inevitably calls for adjustments

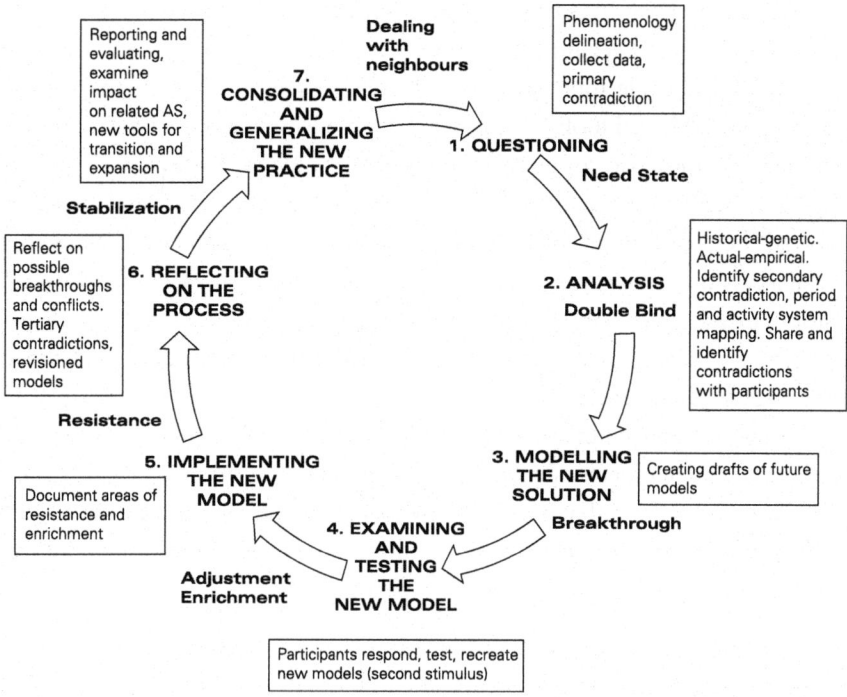

Figure 10.1 A representation of the cycle of expansive learning (Engeström, 2009)

and modification and these in themselves may lead to new contradictions and resistances emerging. Reflection upon these leads to further modification, realignment and then eventual consolidation of a new practice. However, this cycle is not linear and often there are mini-cycles of activity and the full cycle may not be completed.

To explore the potential for expansive learning within a contextual domain requires an understanding of the units of analysis, which are *human activity* and the components of the activity system. Understanding this activity system is fundamental to being able to identify the potential for intervention and shifts.

Activity Theory Background and Key Concepts

CHAT builds on the foundational work of Vygotsky and so it is important to revisit relevant concepts from his work. Vygotsky believed that learning was a social and individual process and that learning emerged out of a range of interactions with the historically accumulated knowledge of cultures (Cole,

1985; Daniels, 2008; Vygotsky, 1962, 1978). Direct experience of the external world and bodies of accumulated knowledge can be experienced and mediated through other people, tools, signs and artifacts. Of relevance to this chapter and work with ICT-based tools are the notion of mediation and the important role meditational tools play for humans acting within and upon the world (Vygotsky, 1978). Human *subjects* engage in the world enacting motives or what are called *objects*. The object or idea of what a person wants to achieve may be held within a subject's mind; however, realization of this relies upon *mediation* through various means – these are variously called tools, instruments, artifacts and signs. These may include physical tools and artifacts, but also culturally learned processes and signs such as language.

Leontiev developed the concept of activity and the object further particularly elaborating upon aspects of collective activity (Leontiev, 1978, 1979). The notion of object is a key term that is worth elaborating upon. He pointed out that while individual actions may have goals, to understand collective human activity requires an understanding of objects or motives:

> It is exactly the object of activity that gives it a determined direction ... the object of an activity is its true motive. It is understood that the motive may be either material or ideal, either present in perception or existing only in the imagination or in thought. The main thing is that behind activity, there should always be a need, that it should always answer one need or another. Thus the concept of activity is necessarily connected with the concept of motives.
>
> (Leontiev, 1978: 62)

Leontiev further identified features of collective activity such as the division of labour or work between participants and social relations, but did not represent these diagrammatically. Engeström's version of CHAT recognizes these elements and also includes other key elements beyond the basic subject object tool mediation triangle. A key feature of Engeström's work with CHAT has been the use of what has been called the 'triangle', a tool he created to help depict the different factors at play in human activity. To help illustrate how a community engages in collective activity, the bottom half of the activity triangle (Figure 10.2) includes *communities, rules* and a *division of labour*. These are mediating means, which inform the coordination of various subjects' actions within collective activity.

One of the purposes of using activity triangles for mapping the elements of activity is to help understand the nature of the activity and ways that people are

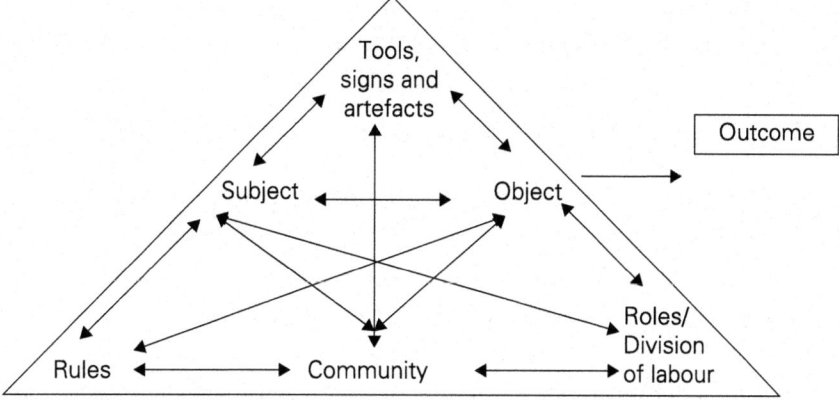

Figure 10.2 A representation of activity system components (based on Engeström, 1987 and 2001)

working and making meaning. Furthermore, they can be used to help identify various contradictions that may exist, for example between the historical and present versions of activity, for different elements of the triangle as the object shifts, or between the objects for different subjects. This is of major importance as contradictions are seen as signalling potential for development, the testing of new models and expansion. As Engeström explains, contradictions are not the same as problems or conflicts, but are structural ruptures and in response, organizational shifts can occur:

> Contradictions are historically accumulating structural tensions within and between activity systems ... When an activity system adopts a new element from the outside (e.g. a new technology or a new object), it often leads to an aggravated secondary contradiction where some old element (e.g. the rules or the division of labour) collides with the new one. Such contradictions generate disturbances and conflicts, but also innovative attempts to change the activity.
>
> (Engeström, 2009: 57)

It is important to acknowledge at this point that the philosophical roots of this understanding of contradictions and development is informed by dialectics, with movement between seemingly opposing forces or states of being as being central to notions of becoming, truth or synthesis. In using activity theory for analysis, it therefore becomes important to identify and analyse possible contradictions, particularly when new tools or practices are introduced into an activity system. Likewise, positive motivations, engagement and actions need to be acknowledged as well, though perhaps these are not so explicitly evident in CHAT and expansive learning models to date.

The Project, Research Design and Mapping of Activity

The specific school context for the research project was a selective public secondary school that had a specialist focus on educating students with particular interests in the arts and careers in the creative industries. This was a metropolitan secondary school and drama was taught as part of the formal school curriculum. The project was enacted with a class of eighteen 15–16-year-old students enrolled in a Theatre Arts subject. The students were in year 10 and the work that they were producing would be assessed as a component of their formal curriculum studies. The school was new, had wireless Internet access across the campus and all students had their own computers as well as access to a range of other digital technologies. The focus for this case was therefore to be on exploring what might occur and be learnt from operating in this 'ideal' ICT in-schools environment.

To determine the focus for the drama, the teacher canvassed opportunities to link ideas for the drama to other areas in the curriculum. The decision was made to make the connection to a Science unit about the 'Future Body'. The drama focus was to be that of our human and spiritual futures and considering concepts of mortality and immortality. The intention was to create a dramatic context, which allowed for strong symbolic and metaphoric explorations and so the focus became the question 'What would you do if you were offered immortal life?'

The dramatic form for the work can be conceived of as a type of *process drama* (Haseman, 1991; O'Neill, 1995; Wagner, 1976) or what Carroll and Cameron called interactive process drama (Carroll *et al.*, 2006; Carroll and Cameron, 2003). This includes teachers and students working in role and responding to situations and hence creating the drama through improvised action, often across a number of sessions and which are called *dramatic frames*. This work was also conceived of as a *cyberdrama*, drawing on Janet Murray's descriptions of such as a reinvention of storytelling through digital story forms, using different formats and styles that allow for participation (Murray, 1997).

For this particular project it was decided to launch the process through creating and sharing what O'Neill (1995) called a *pre-text*. A pre-text suggests possible problems to be solved; characters, places and situations but leaders leave it open as to how each frame of the drama progresses. They lay trails to begin with and see what participants respond to and where they take it, before reflecting on developments and considering the next frame of the drama. For this drama, a pre-text, which comprised of an email and video clip, was created and then emailed and shared live with students. This invited participants to accept the gift of immortality and join a group called *The Immortals*.

An overarching model including learning focus and dramatic conventions was created in collaboration with the teacher. This was organized around four modules, each of which was allocated 1–2 weeks worth of lessons.

As students created roles and responded to the pre-text, the story developed over several weeks through live and online interactions, with digital products uploaded for each module. At the conclusion of the unit, a performance event was held with parents and friends attending. At this event, students performed and presented in role and invited the audience to participate. The use of technology in performance included sharing video clips, the use of mobile phones and live Instant Message chat, which was projected onto a screen.

Table 10.1 Learning focus for each module

Learning Focus	Drama (tool and sign use)	The dramatic idea or concepts
Module 1 – Enrolling in the drama/who are you?	Roleplay and improvisation Role development Monologue Skills of performance – acting for film	Immortality – what does it mean? Different accounts in literature Individual and group responses to the pre-text
Module 2 – The news is out (building the narrative)	Dramatic tension Language of media presenters Narrative structure Improvisation skills – building and extending on offers	Scientific accounts – current research about immortality Incorporating responses to the question through the characters
Module 3 – There is something strange about ... (metaphor and analogy)	Symbol and metaphor Poetic devices and conventions	Comparing different beliefs about what is being offered to characters, impact on lives
Module 4 – Presentation	Skills of live performance Creating back-stories Improvisation Audience engagement and interaction	Contemporary views of immortality – personal, scientific, dramatically conveyed

Research Design

The type of research methodology was informed by CHAT and Activity Systems Analysis (Yamagata-Lynch, 2010), using methods such as document analysis, interviews and classroom observations, but also creative work and documentation of processes including photographs, video evidence, journals and computer-mediated communications.

The process of data analysis and case study writing was based on identifying experiences of contradiction and potential opportunities for expansion and emergence. As key incidents and shifts were identified, data for each was triangulated across the surveys, journals, interviews, observations and other sources to substantiate the issues. Accounts in the form of narrative case studies were created, with a particular focus on subject and systemic responses to specific interventions and contradictions.

Analysing the Activity System

To contextualize the application of activity theory to a practical example, the key components of the activity system are identified in Figure 10.3 as they related to 'The Immortals' project.

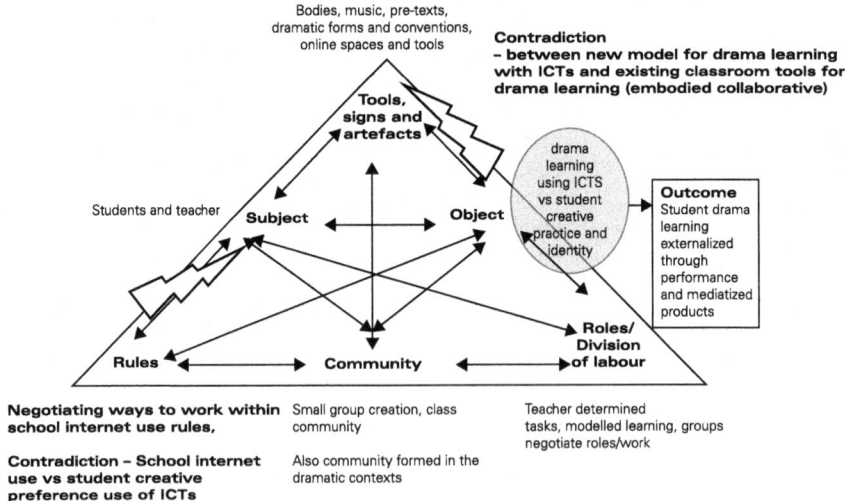

Figure 10.3 Activity system for *The Immortals* drama project

For this project, the main subjects were the secondary school students enrolled in a drama subject for that semester. The collective *object* of the activity was to create dramatic products and evidence. The *tools* and *artifacts* used included the primary tools of the drama process, which were the bodies and experiences of the participants. They also included cultural tools and literary texts including poetry and mythology about immortality. Procedural processes and scaffolding tools were created to stimulate the work processes and to organize and channel the student experiences. Digital tools and technologies used for this project included video cameras, mobile phones, i-pods, computers and the various tools students used to create mediatized dramatic products. Students were also required to work across a range of online spaces, including the e-learning platform *Blackboard* and a social networking site on *Ning*.

The students were part of one class *community* and this was broken down into smaller working groups of three to five students. These communities were operating within the wider context of the school community and the *rules* of this particular school and government schools in general. *Rules* regarding Internet access and use were of particular relevance, with students and parents having to sign forms about such at the start of the school year.

The roles and *division of labour* operated on different levels as well. In the overarching context, the teacher and I designed the task parameters and the requirements for the student activity. However, the tasks were open-ended and students were able to create their own responses within flexible constraints. Each group was set up to ensure a spread of skills but the final division of labour was negotiated within each group (they decided who would act, record action, edit it, post digital material to the Internet and so on). Of relevance to this being a drama project, was that roles and division of labour can also be considered within the context of a dramatic frame. Students and teachers took on fictional character-based roles throughout the course of the project.

In seeking to identify the potential for learning and development, it became clear that it was important to consider how contradictions might be expressed at a subject level as well as collective level. It is possible that contradictions can be identified through subject-level experiences of tension which might actually signal more systemic-level contradictions. So for this case study, through reading student journal entries and examining survey responses, it became apparent that there were some subject-level contradictions that were in fact significant for the entire system and these will be the focus for tracking the potential for expansive learning in this case.

One of these contradictions emerged as the project began and highlighted issues around the use of certain digital tools and spaces within a school context. The second emerged in relation to the implementation of this new form of drama and subject level expectations about preferred models for drama learning.

Contradiction and Subject Vignette 1 – Digital Tool Use in Schools

Harrison sees himself as a bit of an outsider and likes it that way. His preferred creative forms are comedy and creating various kinds of media. His comedy is often quite satirical and dark. He enjoys playing around with different computer programs to make humorous video clips and animations. At his former school he once made an animation using PowerPoint that included 700 frames. He also made a humorous film which was shown at a school assembly for Book Week. It challenged the boundaries of acceptability for a school presentation as it included a dog doing a poo on a carpet and then being attacked by Harrison. He likes looking for the humour in situations and being subversive. At his new school he has been one of a number of students who have posted video clips to YouTube and engaging in some online rivalry with another school. Students from both schools have been posting clips where they 'sledge' the other school and Harrison is proud of the fact that his clips are more humorous and show more skill than those from the other school.

During the introductory phases of the project, Harrison was called to the Principal's office. Other students revealed that they believed it would be about the latest video clip Harrison had posted to *YouTube*. They excitedly discussed the online rivalry between their school and another and that Harrison had recently posted a very funny clip to *YouTube*. After the lesson Harrison came back and spoke to the teacher about what had happened and revealed that he would perhaps be suspended from the school because of his *YouTube* postings.

Harrison showed us the clip he had uploaded as well as other student clips. We could see that his video was quite amusing and clever in part, but it was also problematic. He had clearly identified the names of the schools and used the logo and colours of his school in the clip. Some of the language was also derogatory and it was clear that members of the other school community might find it offensive. Harrison was concerned that he might be suspended; however, the Principal was providing him with the opportunity to made amends. The teacher encouraged Harrison to take the initiative and work out a strategy for addressing this. The solution involved him saying he would take the clip down from *YouTube* and apologize to the Principal of the other school. He was also to promise his Principal that he would no longer make clips with any reference to either school and would not use the school logo, name or uniform in any other clips.

After this incident, the teacher suggested that we would have to rework our cyberdrama project proposal. The idea for the project had been to promote the use of available web 2.0 applications to engage students in creative production and real world creative practice. In light of the incident with Harrison, the teacher suggested we modify the proposal and reconsider the use of *YouTube* and any other social networking spaces outside of Education Department's *The Learning Place* and *Blackboard*. This involved prioritizing the use of the official educational spaces proposing that she, as the teacher, would have to upload video material and moderate content on any external sites such as *YouTube*.

In terms of the activity system, what occurred was a contradiction in relation to the rules for possible ICT tool usage. There was also a contradiction between the tools and the object of the activity for creative practice. What was apparent was that the kinds of tools and spaces that students such as Harrison used for creative purposes outside of school hours were problematic for use within school. Contradiction was emerging largely from the context of the project being situated within the school organizational setting and authoritative power structures inherent therein. The system and its rule structure were not going to change and so shifts had to occur at a subject and operational level. The shift involved modifying the use of some tools, and a division of labour, which saw teachers/leaders playing a gate-keeping role.

It is pertinent to consider other data, which elaborated on student use and preferences for incorporating digital technologies and online spaces in drama. What was evident from the survey data and focus group discussion was student preferences for video recording technologies and online spaces where they could interact in-role. Students were also attracted to the idea of using sites such as *YouTube* to allow them to share their work with a wider audience than their class group. Students were not as enthusiastic about the use of educational spaces and did not regularly use those spaces out of school time. Their preference was for those spaces where they could be creative and which allowed them to show identity markers, control design elements and engage in creative practice. The types of tools they preferred for creative expression were blocked or restricted within school. Expansive learning could only occur through shifts within the parameters set by the institutional setting.

Contradiction and Subject Vignette 2 – New Models of Practice and Expectations about Drama

> *Jaida has been studying drama, as she is very keen on a future career in the performing arts, specifically in opera. She has realized that there are many talented girls at the school and if she wants to succeed she needs to stand out from the crowd. To be a serious singer she feels that drama skills will be useful, though she has no time for a lot of the drama games and improvisation type activities that often count for drama. She doesn't feel comfortable engaging in these activities, she feels self-conscious and that they are a waste of time. She would much rather focus on learning a role and rehearsing for a high-quality polished theatrical performance.*

From Jaida's journal and interactions in class it was apparent that she had trouble accepting a shift in the object and model of practice being proposed for this project. She believed that the use of the online components represented an engagement with popular culture and everyday forms of dramatic practice, whereas she was more interested in specific virtuosic forms of performance:

> I don't think I'll like it very much because it looks a little too much like drama back in mainstream schools, which I really hated because it was all fun and games and wasting time, etc. So, I really don't know what this is going to turn out like, but from the outset, I may not actually like it very much.
>
> (Jaida's Journal, 19.10.07)

It was apparent that for Jaida, her overall object was driven by her personal object and interest in live performance and singing. She saw her creative practice as being realized in this form primarily, with technology and the Internet as subsidiary tools used by the 'masses', not those that aspire to be true performing artists. The feedback she provided, though, was one form of feedback that was considered by the teacher and myself and informed the shift in activity outlined as follows.

About half-way through the project implementation, it became apparent that the nature of the tool use and activity emerging from the focus on using ICTs was leading to some shifts in social practices in the drama classroom.

The teacher indicated that she believed that students were feeling isolated in their groups. The weekly tasks required students to work most of the time in smaller groups and had led to minimal full class contact and co-present physical engagement. This presented a contradiction for the activity system and the teacher so she wanted to discuss ways of changing the activity to address these concerns. She felt that we needed to re-engage the whole group, to help them share their understandings of where the various narrative threads were at, with more opportunities to physically collaborate and engage. She proposed that we create some live process drama experiences and work in-role with the students.

This led to the creation of a whole class live improvisation in a face-to-face context. This experience proved to be a powerful one, with many students commenting at the end of the process that this had in fact been their favourite part of the whole process.

> Sian: Yeah, the live interaction. The way we sat down in our room and all of a sudden our Principal came in and gave this serious speech about what was going on and how our teacher had been taken away.
> ... and then the teachers burst through the door in character and then we all got thrown into this big improvisation process which really helped in the end ...
> (Interview transcript, 4 December 2007, lines 228–40)

What happened therefore was a contradiction arising from the intervention into regular drama activity, once again over tool use, but also the object and expected outcomes some subjects believed *should* emerge from creative practice in drama. The teacher was able to respond to student feedback and negotiate a shift in the tools used and the social practices. This led to a solution, which focused on using the corporeal body and the whole group as a community. The technological tools were still used (the lesson was videoed and material from this was edited and made into a video clip that was uploaded online); however, the focus shifted and the live drama and the face-to-face interactions determined the next stage of activity.

The expansive learning that emerged from this contradiction highlighted the importance of the corporeal experience and the body as the tool of expression and students' valuing of these practices as special to the drama classroom. This shift in activity is represented in Figure 10.4, as well as expansive learning that had emerged from the earlier contradiction, concerning Harrison and the use of ICT spaces.

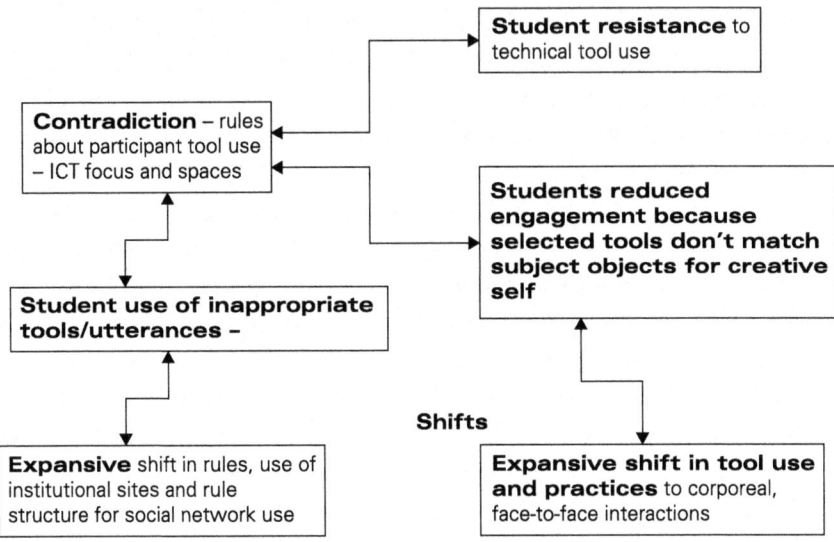

Figure 10.4 Shifts in activity for *The Immortals*

Learning and Expansion Arising from the Intervention

CHAT theorists identify the significance of contradiction as being a stimulus for shifts in activity and learning. The potential for learning within an activity system depends on contradictions being identified and then resolved through the creation and implementation of appropriate models or actions and expansions.

In terms of the activity system for this project, one of the initial contradictions that arose was in relation to the rules regarding the possible tools that could be used by students. In terms of the technology, what was apparent was that the kinds of tools and spaces that students were familiar with using outside of school hours were blocked or created problems within an educational context. This situation highlighted a contradiction in the activity system, but we were able to negotiate some shifts to enable moderated ICT-based activity to occur. The shift involved creating a new model including modified use of some tools and rules about tool use. The enactment of the activity required a division of labour, which saw teachers/leaders playing a gate-keeping role in moderating and uploading the material that could be shared with a wider audience.

Through implementing this model another contradiction became apparent related to tool use and subject-level objects of the activity. The shift of focus from the performative space being predominantly in the live face-to-face mode to the Internet and cyberspace indicated a key shift and intervention into the activity system that met with mixed responses. At the conclusion of the project, while all the students acknowledged they had learnt a lot about the use of technology and making videos, in the end some of them said 'I would still have preferred to do a straight drama performance.' Several spoke passionately about their enjoyment of the live performance experience, how it made them feel alive – and for those students in particular, the online experience did not really match it. It therefore seemed that the digitally mediated tools and processes could be used to extend young people's experiences in drama, but students did not want to see them replace the live ones. What this study suggests is that many students appreciate the experiences of collectively creating imaginative symbolic work and sharing corporeal drama work. These students do not wish to sacrifice these experiences at school if they are to be replaced by the use of ICTs that they consider inferior. In terms of possible future expansive learning, in such a context it may be possible then to create new models that carefully consider the balance of tool use and activity to ensure that there is still a primary focus on embodied physical performance.

To represent the journey of this project and relate it back to the theory of expansive learning, Table 10.2 maps the different kinds of contradictions for this project, the phase of expansive learning (middle column) and cites examples and evidence in the third column. This table draws on one included by Engeström in his 1987 work.

Table 10.2 Sequential structure of learning by expanding

Contradiction	Phase	Content from the activity
Primary contradiction within the components of the old activity	Need state	Subjects positioned within educational institutions requiring compliance to systemic rules determined by employment requirements or (for students) education act.
		Contradiction: Subjects desire to engage in creative practice for personal goals and fulfilment VS
		Subjects required to engage in educational activity with a focus on systemic success markers and compliance to rules
		(*Continued*)

Table 10.2 Continued

Contradiction	Phase	Content from the activity
Secondary contradictions, between the components of the old activity	Double Bind Object/motive construction	*Contradiction*: Rule structures of schooling restrict teacher/student decision making about ICT tools they can access and use VS the systemic limits on use of ICT tools that student want to use
		Existing model: Limited use of ICTs in drama, and limits on use of certain technological tools and spaces
		Springboard: Inappropriate student use of social networking sites
		New general model: Scaffolded learning model for creating different creative products using approved ICT tools/spaces, teacher moderation of content uploaded to outside sites
Tertiary contradiction between the old and the *given* new activity/motive	Application, generalization; component actions of the given new activity	*Contradiction*: Emerging new ICT tool use, incorporated into drama VS student expectations about drama being an artform that typically focuses on use of the human body and human interactions
		New activity focusing on using live interactions and performance as well as mediated
Quaternary contradiction – between the new activity and its neighbour activities (other subjects)	Activity 2: Reflection, consolidation	Engage in reflection activity with students to identify relevant subject-producing outcomes as well as collective arts product outcomes utilizing digital technologies.

What this analysis suggests is that the use of ICTs in the classroom involves various repertoires of practice and cultural tools, and these practices extend beyond using digital technologies and tools. However, related to these are sets of social practices and toolkits that are centred on subject relations, conceptual development and versions of self as leading activity.

Conclusion

This research work indicates several key findings and also possibilities for further research and applications. The project on which the research was based sought to explore the potential for using ICTs within school-based drama programmes. Through the analysis of data regarding student involvement and learning, it was identified that the introduction of digital technologies and use of online spaces within the drama curriculum project represented significant intervention into the usual activity for drama learning and the objects for some subjects. The ways that various participants responded indicated that some of the discourses around ICT use, which promote the idea that education through ICTs is superior to embodied classroom practice, need to be problematized. Perhaps it is more useful to consider the ways that technology can be used in combination with *quality* live learning experiences that students cannot readily replicate outside of school, and how the two can be used to leverage each other. It is unlikely otherwise that drama students and teachers will be willing to trade the dynamic live processes of the drama classroom with what they perceive to be sedentary online experiences of a restricted nature. ICTs can be used to facilitate learning; however, their use must be seen in the context of quality, engaging activity and social practices, not as a positive end just for the sake of it.

Another significant learning arising from this project was students affirming that there are certain special features about the nature of learning in drama that they hold dear. Students value the creative, collective experiences afforded through embodied dramatic action at school and these experiences are more engaging for most drama students than those they can experience through school-based ICTs or at home by themselves. Many students see drama as a vehicle for affirmation and recognition of identity and these opportunities to perform, be seen and recognized are important to them. The experience of drama at school can provide that recognition and these motives and drives are also important to recognize in discussions about meaningful and relevant education provision.

In terms of the application of CHAT and the theory of expansive learning to drama education, it is clear that Activity Theory can provide a useful framework for analysing challenges, experiences of contradiction and identifying what elements might need to be considered to move on to more productive learning. This is just one example; however, there is scope for a range of future work including mapping the negotiation of collective objects and also in analysing the relationship between learning and development that occur within the different frames of activity – such as in role and out of role – within a drama process. This signals the enormous potential there is for further applications in Activity Theory to drama and education research as a means of understanding human systems, dynamics and learning.

References

Buckingham, D. (2007), *Beyond Technology: Children's Learning in the Age of Digital Dulture*, Cambridge, UK: Polity Press.

Carroll, J. and Cameron, D. (2003), 'To the Spice Islands: Interactive Process Drama', *Fine Arts Forum*, 17(8).

Carroll, J., Anderson, M. and Cameron, D. (2006), *Real Players? Drama, Technology and Education*, Stoke on Trent, UK and Sterling, USA: Trentham Books.

Cole, M. (1985), 'The Zone of Proximal Development: Where Culture and Cognition Create Each Other', in J.V. Wertsch (ed.), *Culture, Communication, and Cognition: Vygotskian Perspectives*, Cambridge, UK: Cambridge University Press, 146–61.

Connery, M. C., John-Steiner, V. and Marjanovic-Shane, A. (eds) (2010), *Vygotsky and Creativity: A Cultural-historical Approach to Play, Meaning Making, and the Arts*, New York: Peter Lang.

Daniels, H. (2008), *Vygotsky and Research*, London and New York: Routledge.

Davis, S. (2010), *ICTs for Creative Practice in Drama: Creating Cyberdrama with Young People in School Contexts*, Doctor of Philosophy, Brisbane: Queensland University of Technology (QUT).

Engeström, Y. (1987), Learning by Expanding: An Activity-Theoretical Approach to Developmental Research, accessed 4 March 2013 at: *http://lchc.ucsd.edu/mca/Paper/Engestrom/expanding/toc.htm*

Engeström, Y. (2001), 'Expansive Learning at Work: Toward an Activity Theoretical Reconceptualization', *Journal of Education and Work*, 14(1): 133–56.

Engeström, Y. (2009), 'Expansive Learning: Toward an Activity-Theoretical Reconceptualization', in K. Illeris (ed.), *Contemporary Theories of Learning*, Abingdon and New York: Routledge.

Engeström, Y. and Sannino, A. (2010), 'Studies of Expansive Learning: Foundations, Findings and Future Challenges', *Educational Research Review*, 5: 1–24.

Flintoff, K. (2005), *Drama and Technology: Teacher Attitudes and Perceptions*, Master of Education thesis, Edith Cowan University, Mt Lawley Campus, accessed 2 April 2014 at: *http://ro.ecu.edu.au/theses/565*

Grainger Clemson, H. (2011), *The Social Drama of a Learning Experience: How is Drama Appropriated as a Pedagogical Toolkit in Secondary Classrooms*, Doctor of Philosophy thesis, Oxford: University of Oxford, accessed 2 April 2014 at: *http://ora.ox.ac.uk/objects/uuid%3A0d142ed9-9fe3-4185-86bc-05fc01d22582*

Greenhow, C., Robelia, B. and Hughes, J.E. (2009), 'Web 2.0 and Classroom Research: What Path Should We Take Now?' *Educational Researcher*, 38(4): 246–59.

Gulpa, A. (2007), 'Vygotskian Perspectives on using Dramatic Play to Enhance Children's Development and Balance Creativity with Structure in the Early Childhood Classroom', *Early Child Development and Care*, 1–13.

Haseman, B. (1991), 'Improvisation, Process Drama and Dramatic Art', *London Drama*, 1991(July): 19–21.

Kritt, D.W. and Winegar, LT. (eds) (2007), *Education and Technology: Critical Perspectives, Possible Futures*, Lanham MD: Lexington Books.

Leontiev, A.N. (1978), *Activity, Consciousness, and Personality*, Englewood Cliffs, NJ: Prentice-Hall.

Leontiev, A.N. (1979), 'The Problem of Activity in Psychology', in J.V. Wertsch (ed.), *The Concept of Activity in Society Psychology*, Armonk, NY: Sharpe. 37–72.

Murray, J. (1997), *Hamlet on the Holodeck: The Future of Narrative in Cyberspace*, Cambridge, MA: MIT Press.

O'Neill, C. (1995), *Drama Worlds: A Framework for Process Drama*, Portsmouth, NH: Heinemann.

Seiter, E. (2005), *The Internet Playground: Children's Access, Entertainment and Mis-Education*, New York: Peter Lang Publishing.

Thurlow, C. and Bell, C. (2009), 'Against Technologization: Young People's New Media Discourse as Creative Cultural Practice', *Journal of Computer-Mediated Communication*, 14: 1038–49.

Van Oers, B. (2008), 'Inscripting Predicates: Dealing with Meaning in Play', in B. Van Oers, W. Wardekker and E. Elbers (eds.), *The Transformation of Learning: Advances in Cultural-Historical Activity Theory*, New York: Cambridge University Press, 370–9.

Vygotsky, L.S. (1962), *Thought and Language*, Cambridge MA: MIT Press.

Vygotsky, L S. (1978), *Mind in Society: The Development of Higher Psychological Processes*, Cambridge MA: Harvard University Press.

Wagner, B.J. (1976), *Dorothy Heathcote: Drama as a Learning Medium*, Washington DC: National Education Association of the United States.

Yamagata-Lynch, L.C. (2010), *Activity Systems Analysis Methods: Understanding Complex Learning Environments*, New York: Springer.

Part IV

Practice and Research Inspired by Sociocultural Approaches to Drama, Education and Learning

A Theatre Company's Development, Cultural-Historical Activity Theory and Developmental Work Research: Movement between Archetypes

Satu-Mari Jansson

Introduction

This chapter demonstrates how cultural-historical activity theory (CHAT) can be utilized to investigate learning and developmental processes within a professional theatre setting. The subject of the study is one regional theatre company, the Rovaniemi Theatre, in Finnish Lapland. Over time the theatre has introduced an audience development and applied theatre function with the help of Regional Theatre Curators (RTCs) using participatory and applied theatre toolkits. The chapter also introduces new concepts to analyse practices of theatre companies. Organizational archetype (Greenwood and Hining, 1993) is understood as a way to describe an organizational form that carries out certain ideas, beliefs and values, and can inform an interpretative schema. This analysis demonstrates how professional theatre, especially institutional theatre, could be defined as an established organizational archetype of which the main goal has been to build performances on stage out of text. An understanding of organizational archetype provides a model, which enables the study of development in the logic of human activity. This chapter shows how one particular theatre company developed a hybrid form next to the historically-formed organizational archetype, as they started introducing applied theatre professionals and methods. As the activity became more diverse, it caused developmental contradictions as established knowledge and practices were challenged.

The data analysis draws on two theoretical realms: first, from the cultural-historical field including activity theory, contradiction, methodology of DWR and Engeström's (1987, 1991) interpretation of Vygotskian concepts such as the Zone of Proximal Development (ZPD); second, the organizational archetype concept is drawn from organizational change literature. Activity Theory and Developmental Work Research (DWR) have had limited application in the field of theatre, in Finland or elsewhere in the world (Kallinen, 2001; Engeström and Kallinen, 1988). In addition, organizational archetype theory has not been related previously to activity theoretical concepts. However, I have combined these two theoretical concepts, in order to conceptualize and analyse the Rovaniemi Theatre's challenges as an example of the developmental phase of institutional theatres.

The purpose of the research featured in this chapter was to answer two questions:

1. How can the current development challenges of the Rovaniemi Theatre be characterized as movement between archetypes? and
2. What kind of contradictions did RTCs experience when activities were changing?

The account includes a micro-historical narrative describing how multifunctional activities have grown in the specific case study theatre. The analysis shows how contradictions were experienced between established forms of archetypical activities and the new, more hybrid types of activities. Some theatre artists were expected to start the journey to understanding new types of theatre making and processes without sufficient preparation. This expansion of the theatre's aims caused changes in the actors' work, their toolkits, their traditional divisions of labour and their rules. I begin by introducing the two separate theoretical concepts, which will then be merged in order to analyse the developmental phase and challenges for institutional theatre.

The Idea of Organizational Archetypes

The field of organizational design and study has used the term 'organizational archetype' to understand more about the qualitative level of changes in activity. For example, in the public sector there is often a rigid organizational structure, although gradually there have been some concept level changes (Greenwood and Hinings, 1993). The term organizational archetype means 'a form or gestalt', with Greenwood and Hinings arguing that organizational structures and management systems should be viewed through a holistic perspective instead of just through a narrow analysis. Organizations are structural and systemic solutions for fulfilling a certain, interpretative scheme, and always function on the basis of certain ideas, beliefs and values, or 'components of an interpretative scheme' (Greenwood and Hinings 1993: 1052).

For organizations, it is easier to stay within one archetype than to move among a few. If the focus is directed towards one particular sector or field, there will be variation, but institutionally there are only a few archetypes that are legitimated. According to Greenwood and Hinings, 'In a heavily institutionalized sector, there may be only one or two institutionally approved forms at a given time' (Greenwood and Hinings, 1993: 1059).

Brock et al. (2007) have also written on organizations and archetypes, and suggest that institutionalized archetypes can change and exist even in a parallel solution. According to them, archetypical change is very difficult since 'deeply held beliefs and values' have to be restructured (Brock et al., 2007: 225). The whole interpretative scheme therefore has to be rethought.

Similarly to DWR researchers, Brock et al. (2007) are committed to dialectical thinking:

> One phase of any historical development tends to be confronted and replaced by its opposite. This opposite, in turn, tends to be replaced by a phase that is somehow a resolution of the two opposed phases.
> (Brock et al., 2007: 233)

This suggests the coexistence of two different archetypes may be possible, for example, when the objective is to meet different needs in the market, moving from the old and new. The solutions can then be called hybrids and the analysis of new public management in the UK public sector has identified how and why hybrid organizational structures and systems have emerged (Brock et al., 2007). For example, traditionally acted public services have been forced to take on new business models and this has caused a need for organizational development. In such cases a hybrid form has meant a coexistent organization of different archetypes. An organization is considered a hybrid when its:

> ... structure consists of diverse sub-units, each with its own internal structures and with different relationships with headquarters and other affiliates, sharing information and resources where appropriate but retaining quite distinctive local organizational structures
> (Brock et al., 2007: 231)

An Introduction to Cultural-Historical Activity Theory (CHAT) and Developmental Work Research (DWR)

The development of institutional theatre is conceptualized in this chapter through the lens of CHAT and DWR. This approach recognizes that work activities tend to change over time. When historically formed conventions and activities are questioned and developed by a community, this creates contradictions. Development happens dialectically as different forces push and pull in different directions. These frictions, challenges and push/pull effects are theorized in DWR as development contradictions (Engeström, 1987). Contradictions can be viewed as problems but also innovations.

Contradictions emerge when some parts of an activity change, for example, the object or motive of work. A contradiction in this type of situation would mean that even though the purpose of work has changed, people still act according to the old divisions of labour or rules. These types of situations mean that many problems are experienced in the work activity. On a personal level, contradictions can be experienced as conflicts, dilemmas and processes of qualitatively new kinds of sense-making (Engeström and Sannino, 2011). When contradictions have been resolved, it is called expansive transformation or expansive learning (Engeström 1987). An expansive transformation requires innovations being adopted in work activities. These could be new practices, new tools and new modes of collaboration. Contradictions, as well as work activities, are historical, so to comprehend the forces that affect the present phase, in research, their historical origins should also be traced (Engeström, 1987).

CHAT (Engeström, 1987; Leontjev, 1978; Vygotsky, 1978) helps us to comprehend movement from one stage or model to a different one. This may involve new forms of activity and this transition will also impact on the work of professionals. Change crystallizes in everyday life and work. Change is always contradictory and requires repeated problem solving. The historicity of archetypical theorizing brings a new dimension to the analysis of activity and development. The concept of organizational archetypes has further informed the framework used within this chapter to analyse the transition experienced by theatre workers hired to represent and build new functions in one theatre company.

Viewing the Developmental Phase of Finnish Institutional Theatre through the Lenses of DWR and Organizational Archetypes

To conceptualize the contextual field for the development experienced in this case study, a matrix has been created which aims to depict the sphere of operation typical within the Finnish theatre industry. This process is commonly undertaken by DWR scholars to help represent the wider development challenge that is faced in the field and scope out the potential ZPD. The matrix is a typology of Finnish theatre archetypes (Figure 11.1) and it provides a working hypothesis for analysing potential ongoing development. The matrix is created by combining elements of archetypical theory (Greenwood and Hining, 1993) and the way DWR scholars (Haavisto, 2002) create matrices to describe the essence of the developmental phase at hand. The matrix is created as a hypothetical tool in order to test developmental contradictions and describes the established activity model and the new one that is evolving.

Figure 11.1 illustrates how multifaceted the theatre field is and how funding, drama theatre tradition and ideas of new audiences affect theatre forms. The vertical axis is related to finance as it affects established forms of theatre. The one end describes project-based funding and non-stable activity and the other end sustainable funding and established form. The horizontal axis describes the diversity of activity. The left side relates to single format theatre and the right side to a hybrid form of activity.

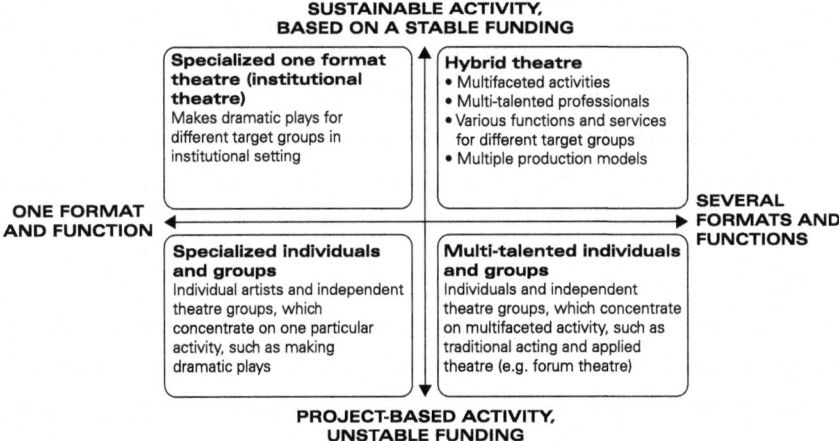

Figure 11.1 Typology of theatre archetypes in Finland

The top left quadrant represents the *status quo* for professional theatre companies in Finland. Regular theatrical activity in Finland dates back to the early nineteenth century, with institutional theatres gradually becoming municipally funded after the Second World War. Finnish institutional theatres created an established model of making theatre, playing psycho-realistic dramatic plays in traditional theatre performance styles and it has been difficult to change that model. The funding, schedule and rehearsing models are almost the same all over Finland and this institutional theatre model can be conceptualized as a predominantly single format theatre. Single format here refers to the logic of the product's construction and the main purpose of a theatre organization. Institutional theatres, in a traditional sense, present performances on a theatre stage and everything in the theatre serves that purpose. Institutional theatres have a broad annual repertoire that can consist of musicals, contemporary drama and operettas as well as classical plays. In the last five to ten years, some Finnish institutional theatres have become favourable to change, probably because of changing artistic concepts in the theatre field, governmental funding and interest in building new audiences.

The historical situation among independent theatre groups, represented in the bottom left side of the matrix, is different from that of the institutional ones because of funding, practices and their whole idea of theatre. Institutional theatres are generally bound to concrete buildings. However, independent groups do not necessarily have their own space and they are free to choose their working methods. Most of these theatre groups are committed to one type of form and artists are specialized to build such productions and performances (see lower left field). The common factor between institutional theatre and independent theatre groups is often their commitment to playing psycho-realistic plays. They fulfil, in this sense, a traditional drama theatre paradigm (Lehmann, 2006).

In spite of the variety of artistic expressions by individual directors, the activity depicted in both the left-hand quadrants can be perceived as homogenous types of activity, if we think of the knowledge and practices associated with the archetypical form. Theatrical performances are built with a rigid dramatic method and toolkit, with text orientation and director-led activity, even though every director and actor has his or her distinctive way of practising. What separates these two theatre forms, specialized groups and one format theatre, is the level of institutionalization, meaning the form of organization and the level of stable public financing. The more structural organization there is, the more formal the system will be, because the group tends to have a more fixed division of labour.

The lower right field describes more hybrid theatre groups and their professionals. To this field belong those independent groups in which actors or performers use diverse traditions to build their performances. For example, some theatre groups build performances based on participatory theatre methods, but actors still perform in more traditional fields, such as in film and theatre. Circus groups that perform within more traditional contexts and in hospitals (hospital clowning) also belong to this field. These type of activities falls into this category of 'multi-talented individuals and groups' in the matrix.

Single format institutional theatre is a systematic constellation that has developed along with the theatre politics and expectations of Finnish audiences. However, some of the institutional theatres are, in fact, moving towards hybrid theatre form, depicted in the upper right quadrant of the matrix. The difference between single format theatre and hybrid theatre is that the latter is built to fulfil several functions and activities. For large theatre organizations it is, however, easier to maintain these as separate activities, because then actors do not have to be multi-talented or hybrid actors.

Data and Methods of Analysis

To further understand the development and contradictions that emerge, the analysis of the Rovaniemi Theatre is conducted through two complementary phases. These include historical analysis and empirical analysis, both recommended by Engeström in his theory of expansive learning and DWR (Engeström, 1987) as important for being able to understand the historical emergence of contradictions.

The first, *micro-historical analysis*, shows how multifunctional activities were built for the Rovaniemi Theatre during several theatre managerial periods. Generally, in the field of theatre, the theatre's history is divided by managerial periods and the separate visions of different managers. The same phenomenon was witnessed in Rovaniemi when I interviewed the personnel. However, in this micro-historical analysis, the focus is on newer activities that are traced back in time. The second, 'actual-empirical analysis' (Engeström, 1987) aims to show problematic areas relating to the new functions that arose within the theatre. Here, special attention will be paid to the opinions of the RTCs, since they were the ones who had to live between the established theatre practice and more communal, participatory theatre function. The analysis shows contradictory areas of institutional theatre when it begins to diversify its activities to a multifunctional theatre format. It is important to view the developmental phase through the individual perspectives and personal learning tasks of these professionals, especially if we think of where the potential for widening theatre practices actually lies. This type of analysis gives us an idea as to what kind of learning challenges emerge.

The data analysis commences with a short micro-historical narrative on how the present developmental phase has been achieved in the Rovaniemi Theatre and what kind of developmental contradictions can be found. This will act as a foundation for further analysis when I build the hypothesis of the development phase of the Rovaniemi Theatre. I then move to actual-empirical analysis to connect the historical phase and contradictions experienced in the theatre. The micro-historical analysis is built from three key informants' interviews. Two of them were theatre managers, of whom one was a former manager and the other was then the manager (in 2008). The third interviewee had been employed in the theatre as the first RTC. I have also used secondary literary sources to construct the micro-history. The micro-history begins from the start of the regional theatre activity and ends with the period when the RTCs were hired at the Rovaniemi Theatre. In the second phase, I conduct the actual-empirical analysis by examining the dilemma and conflict appearances identified in the interview data from the RTCs themselves. This draws on interviews with two working RTCs.

Rovaniemi Theatre's History and Theatre's Expanding Hybrid Form

The Rovaniemi Theatre, which is also Lapland's Regional Theatre, is both the northernmost theatre in Finland and the northernmost regional theatre in the European Union. It has been a professional theatre company since 1962. The regional theatre branch was established during 1969–1978, when the theatre received an additional discretionary grant from the Finnish state. In different phases, 15 theatres in total were involved with this phase of experimentation. There were not any readymade plans or terms for experimentation given by the government. Instead, it was the theatres' decision as to how they would run their regional theatre (Niemi and Ojala, 1983: 39–41). In the case of the Rovaniemi Theatre, the aim for the regional theatre was to go touring with the same dramatic plays that were performed in the theatre building. The tour group of the Rovaniemi Theatre sometimes travelled up to 800 kilometres outside of Rovaniemi.

The regional theatre initiative brought more funding to the Rovaniemi Theatre and this provided more resources for the theatre to plan and fulfil its public assignment. The regional theatre function can be interpreted as one of the initial steps towards hybrid theatre, since being a regional theatre meant new resources for the theatre and an expanded audience group from city people to regional audiences all over Lapland. In this way, they were beginning to form new audience development functions and sets of applied theatre practices. With these new regional theatre resources, the theatre manager was able to hire the first RTC who handled audience development, and the job of regional theatre producer.

The regional theatre was built alongside the basic drama production model to deliver performances to Lapland's municipalities. In 1995, the first Theatre Curator (TC) was hired by the theatre to focus on audience development with the help of apprenticeships and grants organized by the local employment authority. The theatre manager at that time stated: 'We ... [the theatre] had set a goal to build the theatre education (function) and perceive youngsters as one of our main audience groups' (Ahonen, 1997: 20). The TC handled theatre tours, toured with the regional tour group and helped people to study manuscripts and plays, organized rehearsal visits, coordinated actors visits in schools and visited kindergartens and schools. In kindergartens, he told stories and performed. His main target group was youth and children. The theatre provided employment for him for two years. After that, the theatre took on another TC through an apprenticeship (Ahonen, 1997: 20–1).

The next important phase was witnessed less than 10 years ago, when one of the theatre managers began her job in the theatre and noticed immediately that the success of the regional theatre was in a state of decline. She believed that they could solve this by developing the functions of regional theatre. Around 2005, in her first year, she hired a new professional to the theatre with the working title of RTC. The role of the new RTC was to handle the brief of producer, such as planning and organizing the regional theatre function and regional tours, besides other duties such as performing and directing participatory performances and offering workshops to different communities by using applied theatre. The manager hoped that the young professional would bring new types of ideologies, methods, tools, practices and competences to the established text-based theatre activities, while also working with several performances in house and touring along with the theatre's own artists. The RTC used, among other forms, 'a Forum theatre derivative' (Boal, 1996), as she called it. She had several actors who worked with her. The theatre also introduced a new kind of service called

'Spotlight' to local firms and communities, which she organized and fulfilled. The idea was to sell workshops for non-theatre organizations to build team spirit and train speaking professionals. She also helped with amateur dramatics, and taught and worked with audience development. Her time in the house was not easy. She expressed her feelings about the role as follows:

> My theatre acts were 'weak' performances and too open structurally, since spectators had an almost equal chance to affect things. It was hard to make a good production that would have convinced the theatre's professionals. It must have been strange to watch. (In the performances) there was a beginning, but where was the middle point and ending? The will and direction of activities of characters were often inconsistent.
>
> (Kallio, 2008: 6)

This discussion identifies some contradictions emerging related to the RTC's 'toolkit' and working processes being unfamiliar.

As activities expanded, it became clear that the theatre would need two RTCs. The manager of the theatre then hired another RTC, whose role stayed the same, with them also organizing regional tours and running workshops. As the first RTC did not continue her employment, a third person was hired. The same RTC practices were still very similar and very much alive. One of the RTCs illustrated her job with one example of a project:

> *Basics of Alchemy* is part of the bigger media collaboration project. Children come here to see the performance called *Basics of Alchemy*, and they try out how to do a critique, an interview, a cultural story, and then later on, during the spring joint features from the children's writings will appear in *Pohjolan sanomat* and *Lapin kansa* [local newspapers].
>
> (Regional Theatre Curator, 25 February 2008)

The theatre had been shifting more and more towards a hybrid form (Figure 11.2), as first the regional theatre function, audience development work and later on participatory theatre practices grew side by side with those related to dramatic play productions. The transition had taken place under the influence and input of several theatre managers. In Rovaniemi Theatre, the various steps towards the hybrid theatre form had been taking place over five decades.

So far this narrative has described how complicated it had been to create an audience development function in the Rovaniemi Theatre, even though the hired people were well trained and had applied theatre methods in their toolkits. The narrative also brings forth how participatory theatre approaches created a

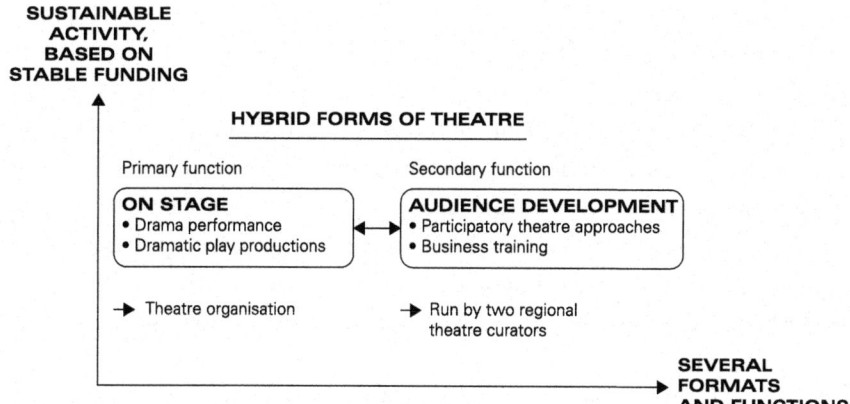

Figure 11.2 Moving to hybrid forms of theatre as audience development and participatory theatre comes to Rovaniemi

challenging situation for theatre actors, since the primary function initially was the theatrical performances acted on the stage, and audience development was seen as the minor activity on the side (Figure 11.2).

It was important for the Rovaniemi Theatre to grow possible future audiences and educate children to read different kinds of performances. This function had been marginal in the theatre since the theatre did not possess enough resources. When the new job title, RTC, was taken on as a regular part of the theatre's function, new theatre conceptions and practices stepped in. RTCs had to live between the old (the one format theatre) and newly formed activity model (a hybrid model). This change from a single format theatre towards a hybrid theatre caused contradictions as new diverse activities expanded the theatre's missions, its audiences and the toolkit of skills required by the practitioners.

Contradictions Emerging from the Shift towards Hybrid Forms of Theatre

To be able to understand the nature of contradiction involved in this development, a number of dilemmas and conflicts were identified in the interview data from those actually experiencing the change. This work draws on detailed interview data analysis around the RTC's functions. In order to identify organizational contradictions, Engeström and Sannino propose the study of both dilemmas and conflicts in speech. They define dilemma as a discourse where contrary issues are presented and which represent 'the materials through which people can argue and think about their lives' (Billig *et al.*, 1988: 8). Dilemmas can be found by focusing on hesitations such as 'on the one hand ... on the other hand' and 'yes, but' (Engeström and Sannino, 2011). Conflicts are more straightforward, as conflicts take the form of resistance, disagreement, argument and criticism in speech and discourse (Engeström and Sannino, 2011: 6). Conflicts may be recognized by triggers such as 'no', 'I disagree' and 'this not true' (Engeström and Sannino, 2011: 6). Both dilemmas and conflicts are cues to find developmental contradictions, as they show the problematic issues in conversations about people's working life.

Having identified them in the interview transcripts, I classified the dilemmas and conflicts within the data according to their content. From the first interview, 15 dilemmas and conflicts were identified and in the second one, 19 dilemmas and conflicts. All dilemma and conflict remarks were then grouped together under categories with identified commonalities and descriptive names. From there, descriptions of the top categories were formed and connected with 'theoretically developed contradictions'. These dilemmas and conflicts describe the developmental contradictions related to movement between organizational archetypes. Contradictions from single format theatre towards more hybrid forms were found in different forms:

1. theatre's expanded object versus traditional division of labour;
2. theatre's expanded object versus subjects established working methods; and
3. theatre's expanded toolkit versus old established rules.

Theatre's Expanded Object versus Traditional Divisions of Labour

The first contradiction relates to movement between archetypes, from single format to hybrid form, and is about theatre's expanded object versus traditional divisions of labour in theatre. Traditionally, the object of activity of institutional theatre is the dramatic play that the theatre collective is producing. This means that for actors and other artists in the production, the aim is to build a dramatic performance that consists of several elements, such as acting, directing, lights, costumes and so on. The focus is directed towards the work of art that is in progress. As the traditional territory of theatre was expected to expand, it meant opening up production processes to society more than before. Theatre professionals were expected to collaborate more with amateur theatre groups, artists from different art fields, local novelists, composers and fine artists.

The theatre's role was changing, which meant that play productions carried on as usual, but there were new audience groups that were also identified as a target. The change meant that theatrical tools, methods and performers may have to act as a servant for the theme at hand. Here 'to serve' means to take part in societal or important social issues, whether they concern school bullying or the well-being of elderly people in retirement homes. However, expanding the object contradicted the established institutional concept of theatre, since professional theatres had fixed territory traditionally. This caused some theatre professionals to question why they, as theatre practitioners, should have to collaborate more profoundly than before.

Some members of staff were scared at the thought of theatre being a collaborative organ, open to outsiders. There had also been rumours that RTCs were stealing actors' jobs. The role of the theatre was more to act as a link to the outside world as they served amateur groups, schools, kindergartens, retirement homes and social groups that were not able to come to the theatre building. One RTC said that if she had the power to choose, she would have built much stronger relationships with local residents, and across all of Lapland. However, RTCs did not have enough time to do so, since their job description was so wide: taking care of touring productions, touring planning and the entire field of participatory theatre:

> Well, I feel, that we should build much stronger connections to local residents, theatre amateurs, theatre creators out there, and that is what I sort of try to enhance. But then again, my job description is so broad that I'm not able to contact them, even though I want to.
> (Regional Theatre Curator, 25 February 2008)

The challenge was that the RTCs could not perform their jobs as they themselves wished. This meant that the planned expansion of the audience development activity, in the worst case scenario, faded away to a minimum. In other cases the theatre company community recognized these activities as their new regular working habit only after a huge crisis. The situation emerging was that the RTC's job description was so broad that it was leading to what they saw as an impossible situation if a resolution could not be found.

Theatre's Expanded Object versus Subjects' Working Methods

The second contradiction relates to movement between archetypes: from single format to hybrid form, as the theatre's expanded object contradicted with subject perceptions of their working methods. The object expansion for RTCs also included their work, now including business training and services (e.g. team building), which the theatre offered to local organizations as organized and led by the RTCs. Corporate services also included the possibility of renting the theatre building out for private performances. These services were called 'Spotlight' and when the idea was introduced to personnel, a fierce debate occurred. Some expressed negative judgements about the proposal, insisting that these new services did not represent any traditional ideology of theatre.

Even though local companies wanted to buy theatre-based trainings, the theatre did not have enough skilful professionals to present them. One RTC said that they needed a discussion about how they could involve more actors in the corporate training:

> And using actors in these trainings and others, you could form an idea, how they could take part. I am especially interested in how you could do this kind of forum theatre type of thing.
>
> (Regional Theatre Curator, 12 May 2008)

The function of audience development and applied theatre knowledge and methods were mostly used in touring, participatory productions and business training sessions. Even though the same methods could be used for both purposes – participatory theatre and business training – these two activities were, however, different and some of the personnel had not had a good opportunity to explore and discuss the similarities and differences between these two.

Theatre's Expanded Toolkit versus Established Rules

The third contradiction relates to movement between archetypes: from single format to hybrid form as the theatre's expanded toolkit challenged established rules. By using the theatre's established methods, initially peoples' actions were routinized and most of the rules related to work were taken for granted. Taking in new methods and tools for theatre caused situations where methods did not sit well with assumptions about how the new work and actions should happen.

One RTC explains that it was difficult to perform outside the theatre when, due to financial reasons, it was still important to fill the large auditorium:

> At the moment, I'm very interested in doing children's theatre and also making performances for elderly people. The centre of the theatre isn't that interesting for me, even though from the theatre's perspective it is most important, to think about how to fill the large auditorium.
> (Regional Theatre Curator, 22 February 2008)

The RTCs saw that they could take performances to other places, even to churches or barns. However, the more performances that were taken outside the auditorium, the more it became an issue of finance, such as renting transport, and paying daily allowances. In addition, public sector organizations were not able to pay for the performances and workshops.

The applied toolkit also required very different kinds of rules and practices. Rules on how to build a play were very different, for example the focus might be on the theme that the work group wanted to handle. The text was not the most important tool anymore – instead the rules of methods were more important, such as the logic of Forum Theatre. These rules dictated the work, and other professionals in the theatre had a hard time comprehending the differences between two separate ideologies of theatre. In addition, it was expected that participatory theatre methods would be learned through trial and error, something that overwhelmed some of the professional actors in the house.

For many of the actors, participatory theatre methods were felt to be a 'heavy method', as actors did not have proper training. Some actors had fears that they had to do something that they could not handle. RTCs often found themselves in a situation where they had to allay the fears of the actors about the performance expectations:

> If we think of the participatory theatre, there is interaction with the audience. For the actors who are not aware of the process or have not done it previously, it is difficult to imagine how they are able to handle it. But there are so many working techniques. For example, in Forum theatre, which is the most familiar to me, there is almost a readymade play, and after you have watched it you start breaking down the performance (with the audience) and there are very specific rules about how you get it working.
> (Regional Theatre Curator, 12 May 2008)

Conclusion

The aim of this chapter was to study organizational development in Finnish theatre and the type of learning that might emerge. In this case it can be seen that theatre activity was shifting between two archetypes, which led to the emergence of contradictions and potentially expansive development. In the Rovaniemi Theatre, where the activities of the RTC became a part of the theatre, they started to develop the audience development function with the help of participatory theatre approaches. The aim and target groups of the theatre expanded and began to affect the work of the theatre's artists. However, these types of changes have not just happened in Rovaniemi, as the same type of expansion is notably occurring in other Finnish institutional theatres.

Single format theatre began to move towards a hybrid type of theatre organization when audience development became a steady function of theatre. An expansion of the theatre's aims caused changes in actors' work, toolkits and traditional divisions of labour and rules.

For the Rovaniemi Theatre, it was clear that the theatre's role was visibly changing, with a broadening of activities for the institutional theatre and that has been conceptualized as a hybrid form of theatre. The movement from the established single mode format theatre to an expanded offering, delivering knowledge and education alongside performing dramatic plays, caused growing pains for actors, because some established practices in the theatre were expected to change (Figure 11.3). The theatre opened up to other parts of society with the work contribution of the RTCs; however, that development entailed contradictions that were experienced in their daily work.

Even though the hybrid form was created within the theatre, the work field

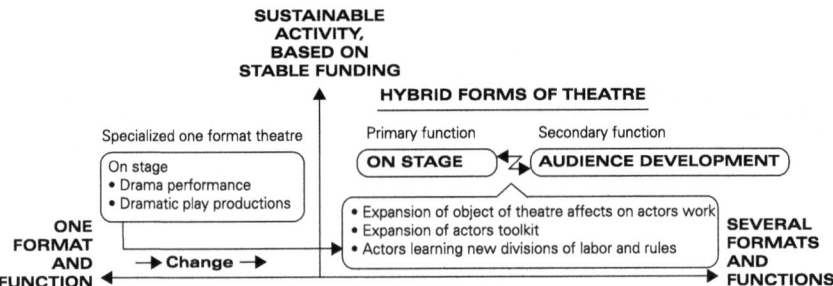

Figure 11.3 Contradictions related to the movement between a single-format theatre archetype to hybrid forms of theatre

of the RTCs and issues emerging for more traditional theatre and actors were not solved. Most of the contradictions were related to actors' toolkits and routines, since their work practices were expected to change. Actors were put in a situation where they were required to do work, even though they did not know how to do it. As there was no ready-made model of how to combine theatre actor functions with the participatory theatre function, it became an enormous challenge for the actors who had traditional acting training. In order to follow through on the change and development, these problem areas needed to be addressed. The work in this regard is ongoing.

I hope the work of this chapter may open up some new possibilities for researching the development of creative organizations such as theatre companies. I have combined two separate theoretical constellations in order to analyse the developmental phase of institutional theatres: organizational archetype and contradiction. While organizational archetype theory and DWR have been previously related to the study of activity of theatre companies, I believe this work can open up new perspectives on how to study the developing activity of theatre companies, exploring the potential for expansion in relation to embracing applied and participatory theatre functions. This could lead to further robust research into change and development in creative organizations and companies.

References

Ahonen, A. (1997), 'Iloisesti umpihankeen! (Happily into Unbroken Snow!)', in R. Airaksinen and M. Eerola (eds), *Teatterikuraattori – silta tekijän ja kokijan välillä (Theatre Curator – a Bridge Between Authors and Interpreters)*, Helsinki: Teatterikorkeakoulun julkaisusarja, 27: 20–1.

Billig, M., Condor, S., Edwards, D., Gane, M., Middleton, D. and Radley, A. (1988), *Ideological Dilemmas; Social Psychology of Everyday Thinking*, London: Sage Publications.

Boal, A (1996), *The Rainbow of Desire. The Boal Method of Theatre and Therapy*, translated by A. Jackson, New York: Routledge.

Brock, D.M., Powell, M.J. and Hinings, C.R.B. (2007), 'Archetypal Change and the Professional Service Firm', *Organizational Change and Development*, 16: 221–51.

Engeström, Y. (1987), *Learning by Expanding: An Activity-Theoretical Approach to Developmental Research*, Helsinki: Orienta-Konsultit

Engeström, Y. (1991), 'Developmental Work Research: A Paradigm in Practice. (Introduction)', *The Quarterly Newsletter of the Laboratory of Comparative Human Cognition*, 13(4): 79–80.

Engeström, Y. and Kallinen, T (1988), 'Theatre as a Model System for Learning to Create', *The Quarterly Newsletter of the Laboratory of Comparative Human Cognition*, 10: 54–67.

Engeström, Y. and Sannino, A. (2011), 'Discursive Manifestations of Contradictions in Organizational Change Efforts: A Methodological Framework', *Journal of Organizational Change Management*, 24(3): 368–87.

Greenwood, R. and Hinings, C.R. (1993), 'Understanding Strategic Change: The Contribution of Archetypes', *Academy of Management Journal*, 36(5): 1052.

Haavisto, V. (2002), *Court Work in Transition. An Activity-Theoretical Study of Changing Work Practices in a Finnish District Court*, academic dissertation, Helsinki: University of Helsinki, Faculty of Education, Department of Education.

Kallinen, T. (2001), *Näyttämötaiteilijasta teatterityöntekijäksi – Miten moderni tavoitti suomalaisen teatterikoulutuksen (From Stage Artist to Theatre Maker – How Modern Theatre Came to Finnish Theatre Education)*, Acta Scenica, Helsinki: Theatre Academy.

Kallio, P. (2008), 'Kokemuksia kairoilta – Lapin yleisöä oppimassa. Mitä alueteatterikuraattori tekee? (Experiences from Backwoods. Learning Lapland's Audience. What Regional Theatre Curator do?)', *Teatteri – Esitystaiteen aikakauslehti (Theatre – Performing Arts Magazine)*, 4.

Lehmann, H-T. (2006), *Postdramatic Theatre*, translated and with an introduction by Karen Jürs-Munby, London and New York: Routledge.

Leontjev, A.N. (1978), *Activity, Consciousness, Personality*, Englewood Cliffs, NJ: Prentice Hall.

Niemi, I. and Ojala, R. (1983), 'Suomalainen alueteatteri: tausta-toiminta-vaikutus (Finnish Regional Theatre: Background-Action-Affect)', *Helsinki: Valtion taidehallinnon julkaisuja*, 23.

Vygotsky, L.S. (1978), *Mind in Society: The Development of Higher Psychological Processes*, Cambridge MA: Harvard University Press.

Vygotsky, L.S. (1987), *The Collected Works of L.S. Vygotsky*, vol. 1, *Problems of General Psychology*, New York: Plenum.

12

How Environment Affects Learning: School Teachers Engaging with Theatre-based Pedagogies

Anton Franks

Introduction

The problem examined here is how socio-spatial environments affect learning. The notion of a socio-spatial environment is intended to evoke a sense of the dialectical nature of the relationship between social and physical aspects of the environment. As a setting for human activity, physical space is shaped by the social and, conversely, physical space has a role in shaping patterns of activity. It is a perspective that, in its concern with the materiality of environment as a setting for human activity, aligns with ethnographic approaches to material culture which examine what physical stuff means in the lives of diverse social groups (Miller, 2010). A view on the effects of physical setting on consciousness, social arrangements and activity is to be concerned with material aspects of cultural environment, visible stuff, and focus on exteriorities and what they might indicate about the nature of the learning.

The broad question guiding the inquiry is about how the materiality of particular socio-spatial environments frames, mediates and affects learning. An interpretative framework drawing from the work of Vygotsky on learning, in particular social, cultural and historical contexts, Goffman's work on frame analysis and Kress's work on multimodal social semiotics are applied to an example of teachers working in a Royal Shakespeare Company (RSC) rehearsal room. The teachers were enrolled on a professional education programme developed by education practitioners from the RSC and teacher educators from the University of Warwick (UoW). The example is taken from observational and interview data generated from a research project evaluating the programme.[1] Multimodal semiotics will assist in describing how the surfaces or exteriorities of interaction located in particular environments are involved in meaning-making processes. Linked to the semiotic perspective, frame analysis concentrates on how interaction is interpreted by social actors as the participants in located encounters. Vygotskian theory allows insight into how located and framed encounters might be internalized by participants and interpreted as a learning experience that is mediated by environment.

Environment in Vygotskian Approaches

At a first pass, the role and effect of the environment might not appear to be a new problem in Vygotskian studies of learning. In much of his work, Vygotsky was interested in schooled and unschooled learning (Vygotsky, 1987). In one paper, he concentrates specifically on the problem of the environment and its relationship to learning, noting that as children grow and develop, not only does their environment change (e.g. from home to school), but their perception and sense of their environment changes (Vygotsky, 1994: 339). Differentiating between sense and meaning towards the end of his substantial work on the role of 'word' in learning and development, he proposes that the sense of a word develops only in living speech as it 'absorbs intellectual and affective content from the entire context in which it is entwined' (Vygotsky, 1987: 276). The dynamics of sense making and its place in learning are not straightforward but are part of a process in which there are 'varied direct and reverse movements and transitions' (Vygotsky, 1987: 283).

In a later paper on the psychology of actors' creative work, Vygotsky elaborates on the role of affective and intellectual aspects of context and the complexity of the ways in which, mediated by techniques actor training, they interact through indirect means (Vygotsky, 1997). Vygotsky observes that the training that actors undergo is situated in and produced out of particular cultural and historical circumstances. From age to age, techniques of actor training change alongside theatrical conventions and spaces (Vygotsky, 1997: 239). Through examining the refractory processes of actor training techniques, his focus on emotion shifts away from individuated psychology towards a view of technique as indicative of prevailing ideologies of particular cultural historical circumstances. Taken all together, Vygotsky's concern with the cultural contexts for learning – that learning is entwined with a sense of the 'whole context', his interest in the active and physicalized techniques of actor training – demonstrates that he recognized the implication and affect of material environment on learning, yet it appears not to be an aspect of his work that was explicitly developed.

Subsequently, in post-Vygotskian perspectives, terms such as 'contexts for learning' (Forman *et al.*, 1993) and 'situated learning' (Lave and Wenger, 1991) have become commonplace, each connoting the sense of a learning environment. Lave and Wenger write of *situatedness* as being concerned with the 'relational character of knowledge and learning, about the negotiated character of meaning, and about the engaged and dilemma-driven nature of learning activity for the people involved' (Lave and Wenger, 1991: 33–4). Situatedness, taken to be largely synonymous with context, is about specific events in particular circumstances. In their introduction to *Contexts for Learning*, Forman *et al.* (1993) define context as layered, comprised of institutional contexts, language in use, human interactions and modes of thinking, the latter evolving as an integral system of motives, goals, values and beliefs closely connected with 'concrete forms of social practice' (Forman *et al.*, 1993: 6). Environment as context is defined in terms of its social and cultural organization, its rule systems and the forms and processes of mediation. The surfaces, the exteriorities and material circumstances of social arrangements and the physicality of environments, however, remain peripheral to social, cultural and historical perspectives on learning.

Post-Vygotskian researchers rightly emphasize the social and cultural aspects of the learning situation; locations of learning are institutional, social and socially constructed over time, subject to social processes and systems. At the centre of descriptions, analyses and explanations of learning is socially organized human activity. The use of the term 'environment' in relation to learning perhaps denotes too naturalized a view of learning and development, emphasizing bio-physical aspects of learning over the sense of learning as fundamentally a socially organized process. However, in looking at learning in drama, the lack of attention to the physical aspects of the environment is somewhat anomalistic; the situation of drama – its settings, costume, lighting effects and so forth contribute to the making of dramatic meaning. So, environment as physical setting is likely to have its part in the patterns and processes of dramatic learning. The purpose of this chapter is to make a case for the inclusion of environmental factors in sociocultural and cultural historical explanations of learning and to suggest that the physicality of socio-spatial contexts are pertinent to learning in drama, particularly on the view that the meaning of environments is socially generated.

Framing Socio-Spatial Environments: The Work of Erving Goffman

If the material aspects of environment are shadowy in, or absent from, Vygotskian accounts of contexts for learning, cultural perspectives drawn from other fields of interest might assist in providing a more concrete sense of the part that environment plays in learning. The work of sociologist Erving Goffman on 'frame analysis' assists in helping to define environment as a context for learning (Goffman, 1986). In looking at Goffman's work, 'frame' is a means for describing the ways that learning in drama delineates and relates to social arrangements, themes and ideas and how, in combination, these serve to provide a context for drama and the playing of roles (Heathcote, 1984; O'Toole, 1992). Here again, such approaches tend not to be concerned with materiality of settings for drama.

Goffman's focus is on face-to-face interaction, yet the sense of the physical location of such interaction appears to be peripheral. Goffman's claim is that the concept of 'frame' can be employed as a way of understanding face-to-face interactions. He acknowledges that the term and concept is derived and developed from the earlier work of Bateson (2000). Bateson's frame is both material and abstract: it is as material as a frame around a painting and as abstract as the borders of a conceptual category. In its combination of materiality and abstraction, a frame is the way in which we are able to make sense of what is happening in particular situations. A frame, writes Goffman, can tell us something about the organization of experience, 'something that an individual actor can take into his mind' (Goffman, 1971: 13). Goffman reserves a special place for drama amongst a range of other human activities. In earlier work, he tends to use dramatic references in a metaphorical sense (Goffman, 1971); in later work, however, drama becomes an object of study in itself:

> ... dramas and contests provide engrossables – engrossing materials which observers can get carried away with, materials which generate a realm of being. The limits placed on this activity are limits placed on activities that can become engaging and entrancing. The history of these limits is the history of what can become alive for us.
>
> (Goffman, 1971: 57–8)

Goffman's concept of frame therefore provides an analytical tool that can approach both material and mental aspects of social encounters, allowing insight into how particular material situations and environments for learning can be understood by participants and described by observers.

The Multimodal Social Semiotics of Socio-Spatial Environments

In focusing on the materiality of environment, its meaning and effects on human interaction, Gunther Kress's work on multimodal social semiotics makes up the final strand of the framework employed here in examining the effects of environment on learning (Kress et al., 2005, 2010). Kress defines semiotic mode as a 'socially shaped and culturally given semiotic resource for making meaning', shaped and regularized over time (Kress, 2010: 79). Speech, handwriting, print, speech images, colour, layout, music, gesture and so forth, have developed as modes of communication, as have significant aspects of architecturally-shaped environments that comprise the settings for interaction. 'Multimodality' promotes the notion that meanings are generated out of the combination and articulation of diverse modes. The articulation of spatial settings, the ways that constituent aspects of the environment are orchestrated, serve as resources for meaning making (Franks, 1997; Franks and Jewitt, 2001; Kress, 2010; Kress and Leeuwen, 2001;).

The learners I will be concentrating on in this chapter are school teachers on a course of professional education jointly devised and organized by the RSC and drama education specialists from the UoW. Coming from all over England, a cohort of teachers recruited to the scheme work in an RSC rehearsal room in the Company's hometown of Stratford-upon-Avon. Over the course of a residential weekend designed to launch them into the project, the teachers participate in a two-day programme of workshops in the rehearsal room and take in a production in the RSC's theatre. Later in the project, the teachers will be asked to involve colleagues and students in their own and neighbouring schools to mount a production of a Shakespeare play. These teachers become part of the RSC's 'Learning Performance Network' (LPN). Initiating the project in the RSC's home territory, the intention is that the teachers will carry with them not only the learning from the set of workshop activities and their experience of a production, they will also carry with them some sense of this very specific learning environment. Subsequently, in teaching through workshop activities, it is hoped that they will be able to evoke a sense of this learning environment in themselves and will be able to mediate this to their students and colleagues.

The purpose and intention of such activity is clearly not that they will be able to become members of the RSC ensemble, but to encourage them to engage with, be inducted into and adopt certain practices to enhance their teaching, specifically their teaching of Shakespeare. It is the way that teachers might carry the learning experience of Stratford-upon-Avon with them – an experience with physical, social and psychological aspects and how this is given substance and form in the ways in which they subsequently work with school students and teaching colleagues that interests me here.

The data are taken from a funded research project and is in the form of detailed observational field notes of a workshop that initiated the LPN project at the RSC's rehearsal space with a newly recruited group of teachers. In an attempt to give a full and coherent sense of how this learning environment is constructed, there follows below a fairly lengthy narrative adapted from field notes. Excerpts of transcript from interviews conducted with teachers from previous cohorts will follow to give some sense, from teachers' and students' points of view, of the ways in which the environment of the RSC's rehearsal room might have been transferred and enacted in classroom spaces.

Learning in Socio-Spatial Environment: The Case of Teachers at an RSC Rehearsal Room

In the middle of a rehearsal room in Stratford-upon-Avon, across a green from the main auditorium of the home of the RSC, sitting in a wide circle of chairs are a group of 25 teachers. In among them is an RSC set designer, an RSC education practitioner and a drama education academic from the UoW. The room has no windows, a high ceiling, a gallery painted matt-black running around the room above the group, pinewood wall panels and black rubberized flooring. It is March, and although it is still cold outside, the room is warm and warmly lit. The floor area is about the size of a large main stage. It smells of wood dust and rubber, with a slight note of sweat coming through – as a working, rehearsal room space ought to smell. It feels to me, as observer, that there is a faint echo, a buzz of recent and past activity in the room. The previous day, the teachers have worked in this same space. In the evening, the teachers have been to see a production of *Romeo and Juliet* in the main auditorium.

The teachers, mixed in age and gender, appear to be engaged but relaxed. Some are English teachers, some teach drama or teach both in secondary schools, and some are primary school teachers. Tuning into the talk, it appears that the animated person holding the floor in the discussion is the set designer of the previous night's production. This – the practical drama workshops, production and discussion with theatre practitioners – is all part of the introductory two-day workshop for the teachers recently recruited into the LPN.

The designer says that he thinks that the play 'boils down to people who don't fit the world'. He wants 'to reclaim something of the story from *West Side Story* and Baz Luhrman's film version of *Romeo and Juliet*'. At the same time, he wanted to design something that is 'accessible and identifiable for modern youth'. The set is sparse and white. He is asking how the teachers responded to the overall concept behind the design, wondering whether the set design 'detracts from the sense of the story'. A teacher responds that she liked the 'simplicity' of the production, which she sees as 'enough to carry the story'.

Another figure, the director, enters and draws a chair into the circle. He slips into the discussion, talking about the ways in which the design fits with the overall production concept. 'It's the RSC's mantra,' he says, 'bodies in space.' His easiness in the context appears to relax the group even more. They are not being lectured at; it is a conversation in which the theatre practitioners appear genuinely interested in soliciting direct feedback on their work, relishing the opportunity to engage directly with an interested group of people. Not only are the teachers an immediate audience, they are also responsible for the education of future audiences.

The discussion continues for a few more minutes and, through the door, two more people appear, at which point the designer takes his leave. They are actors, here to demonstrate something of the RSC ensemble's rehearsal room techniques. 'Ensemble' and 'rehearsal room pedagogy' emerge as important practical concepts. The actors and director pick up scripts and the director introduces the scene in which Friar Lawrence exercises his persuasive powers in trying to convince Romeo that he needs to leave Verona, complying with the banishment order and avoiding a sentence of death. It is a scene of tension, with the rebellious, hot-headedness of youth showing through strongly in Romeo's speeches. They play the scene through, scripts in hand, dancing around and confronting each other. The director then calls for assistance from two volunteers. They are instructed to face each character respectively and to push hard against them, providing physical resistance and embodying the tension of the scene.

After the scene is played through a couple of times, each time using different volunteers to push against the actors, the RSC education practitioner asks how such a rehearsal exercise is realized in the production. 'Obviously, we can't use it in the scene ... we feel things that will settle in your body,' one of the actors responds. The other adds, 'It makes it very live, riffing off each other, pulling up on someone else's performance.'

'So, that's ensemble?' asks a teacher. The director adds a point about ensemble work into the discussion, 'Yes, we create together. For other companies it's just a day job. This work sets you free rather than binds you.'

As he sits back in the circle and the actors depart the studio, he confesses that, when he was younger, he felt that Shakespeare was not for him.

'It's what happens in our classrooms,' a teacher responds, 'building a relationship with the text from the ground up. It's just happened through the process [of the workshop activities]. I feel my own relationship with the text develop, to own the text but relinquish its authoritativeness.'

Using rehearsal room techniques and being part of an ensemble is key to the RSC's way of doing things, reflects the director. 'If it's not in the body, nourishing mind, body, intellect and imagination, it's academic,' he says.

'It's like he said,' says a teacher, indicating another teacher in the circle who had spoken earlier, 'layering, layering in our classrooms, a layering process. They [the students] are teaching us.'

It is nearly lunchtime and the teachers take a break. Afterwards, they return to the rehearsal room and engage in a range of exercises that allow them to engage with the narrative structure of Romeo and Juliet and to speak the lines of the text as they move around the space of the rehearsal room in various group formations.

Multimodal Social Semiotics of the Space and Place

The sense of place is immediately apparent. It is a very distinctive social and cultural environment, an exceptional space located in the heart of Shakespeare's birthplace and adjacent to the RSC's première venue for Shakespearean production and emerging out of a very specific history. It is a place populated by individuals who form particular social arrangements, interacting in very specific ways. It is a complexly layered environment with physical, emotional and intellectual aspects.

The experience of physical space can be seen to be one that is meaningful in its sign-value, its semiotic, one that is multimodal and multi-sensory. The semiotics of the environment that form the setting for activity are layered too, working inwards from the exterior topographies of the town and architecture of the RSC's campus in its midst. The teachers spend an evening in Stratford-upon-Avon, a town that derives status from being known as Shakespeare's birthplace, in which its preserved and restored Elizabethan architecture, its souvenir shops and eateries are gathered around the RSC's complex of rehearsal rooms and theatre buildings. It is a place of cultural pilgrimage, populated with tourists and practitioners of Shakespearean arts. Arriving in the town, walking between their overnight accommodation to the rehearsal rooms and across the green to the theatre the previous evening, the teachers are immersed in the multiple semiotics of the town, its streets and buildings layered over time. Everywhere there are images of Shakespeare, there are signposts, shops and specialist buildings attached to the RSC, the Shakespeare Birthplace Trust and so forth, advertising and underlining the Shakespearean character of the town at every turn.

Then there are the interior spaces – the auditoria and workshop spaces – that, in their part, shape patterns of movement and the social arrangement of bodies in space. The qualities of places, how they look from various viewpoints, the decoration, internal design, acoustic properties, lighting, even the smell of places affect and shape particular interactions between specific individuals and groups. Inside the studio, sitting in a circle at its centre, the teachers experience some sense of transposition and transformation: the circle is a familiar arrangement for drama work in schools. Here, instead of being surrounded by the architecture and sensory aspects of schools and schooling with its familiar smells, sounds and patterns of movement, they are in a distinctive space that admits little sound from outside. Lit by floodlights, the space is brightly washed with light. The smell of lantern-heated dust, the rubberized flooring, the pine panelling, the slight lingering odour of bodies engaged in physical exercise, are sensed differently from school spaces; it is at the same time familiar but different, differentially accented and inflected from schooled spaces. Learning activity in this place, too, is different. For example, the sense of the circle arrangement, and their position in it as teachers, is shifted. Interacting with theatre practitioners in the circle, discussing the play and participating in workshop activities, they are addressed by theatre practitioners first as critically responsive audience and then as workshop participants; temporarily they are invited to sense themselves as part of the RSC ensemble.

Their arrangement in space, the forms of address and response in speech, gesture and positioning brings about shifts in sensibility. Later, involved in the workshop activities, working the space in various groups and formations, they are encouraged to work and move through the whole space available to them, to explore the potentials of the space for movement, to experiment with ways of moving whilst listening to themselves and others, to experience the different qualities of sound and speech in different locations around the studio. Music is played as an accompanying soundtrack. They are given excerpts of Shakespearean text to speak aloud as they huddle in small groups and then move out into and around the space and, located in the RSC's rehearsal room at the heart of the town, the sense of the script and the utterance of its words accrue differently accented meanings.

Experiencing different social arrangements and practical activities whilst moving through the different environments of the town outside and into the situation of the theatre and the rehearsal room, engaging with theatre practitioners and the genres of theatrical speech and movement, constitute the multimodal social semiotics of this very particular environment. It is a specialized environment in which this group of teachers is immersed, an environment for socially organized activity that accrues meaning not from one aspect or another, but through the intersection and combination of multiple sensory modes that comprise the socio-spatial environment for this instance of learning.

The Framing of Socio-Spatial Environments: Rehearsal Room and Schools

Seen through the lens of frame analysis, different aspects of the way that environment works to make meaning come into view. At the outer layers, there are its historical dimensions and associations with Shakespeare, his life and work – a sense of its heritage that is inescapable as soon as one enters the town of Stratford-upon-Avon. At the centre of the town is the theatre, at which the teachers had been audience to a production on its main stage after the first day's workshop, a five-minute walk across the green from the theatre in the rehearsal room. The previous evening, the teachers had been in the role of audience. The morning of the workshop, they had travelled 'backstage', behind the scenes, in the very rehearsal room in which preparations for the production had been made, and they were engaging with the designer and director of that very production.

Over the period of a day and night, the LPN teachers' sense of the place was emerging and developing as they had arrived to stay in the town and had moved between rehearsal and performing spaces. Over time, they had adopted different roles as workshop participants, theatre audience and interlocutors interacting with each other, with RSC education practitioners, the designer, theatre director and actors. The nature and sense of the words they were using, the conversations they were having, were also changing and developing. They were being invited to enter and engage with a peculiarly situated Shakespearean sub-culture, one that they shared with each other as members of the RSC's LPN. Over time, even in the period of hours observing the workshop in the rehearsal space, unrolls a process in which the teachers as participants are encouraged to become increasingly engrossed. Participation and engagement with RSC practitioners in this setting draws the teachers into inhabiting a physical and mental space. Sitting in a circle talking with the designer and director, walking the space and engaging in actors' exercises, increasingly involves them in the roles, rules and rituals of rehearsal and ensemble work.

However, their roles as teachers in classrooms along with their relationships with students, were still present in the teachers' minds, in their talk and, almost certainly, in their bodies. The evidence of the shifts between the frame of classroom teacher and workshop participant is evident in their talk of 'what happens in our classrooms' and 'building a relationship with the text'. The 'lamination' of frames, as Goffman terms it, is evident in the teacher's use of the metaphor of 'layering' and in the sense that relationships have to be 'built from the ground up'. These words give a sense of the experience that emerge for the teachers of the overlapping frames of the classroom, theatre and rehearsal room, and at the centre of which are particular social arrangements and specific practices working with Shakespearean text. Entwined in this sense of place is a historical thread – a sense of their past activities in classrooms with students working on Shakespeare, a sense of their present situation in the RSC's rehearsal room and theatre spaces and, forming in their thoughts and imaginations, a sense of possibility for future engagements with students in classrooms.

Environment and Physicality in Learning

The particular physical, social and cultural environment of the rehearsal room is significant, but importantly in the way that it provides the setting and shapes particular activities and interactions. The rehearsal room is seen as a socio-spatial setting, one in which there is an interaction between physical environment and the socially organized activity that takes place within it. At the same time, this sense of place is constituted in the nature of activity and interaction, which chimes with Vygotsky's assertion that particular techniques of actor training, especially in relation to the evocation and portrayal of emotion, are indicative of ideologies that prevail under particular historical conditions.

Initiating the LPN programme, RSC practitioners introduce the teachers to, and induct them into, practices that are indicative of the range of techniques developed over time by the Company working with Shakespearean text. According to its practitioners, these techniques embody a particular ideology that prevails at the RSC, one that promotes the openness to 'bodies in space' and exercises that allow feelings to 'settle in the body'. Such attention to the body in space is significant in terms of learning in particular socio-spatial environments. Working in ensemble, the director claims that, through its combination of physicality, intellect and feeling, 'sets you free rather than binds you'. It is an ideology that purports to liberate teachers from the quasi-religious authority of Shakespearean text, in the words of a teacher, 'to own the text but to relinquish its authority'. In the environment of the rehearsal room, the teachers, their conversation and practical activity, are drawn in and positioned as members of an ensemble working, as RSC practitioners do, through rehearsal room techniques of teaching and learning.

The set of techniques offered establish the text as porous, allowing a permeability of meaning and flexibility in its realization; through this, Shakespeare becomes a text for exploration and performance. Feeling for the text, in both physical and emotional terms, is seen as liberating, releasing groups and individuals to make their own sense and meaning from Shakespeare. Although there is some ambiguity in the status of Shakespearean text (in that it appears to be an object of veneration at the same time as being open to interpretation), an ideology of openness and experimentation is embedded in the approach to ensemble and rehearsal room techniques. Approaches that depend on an ethos of ensemble and experimentation through physicalized exercises do not work directly in interpreting text; rather they are designed to mobilize body, thought and feeling to work indirectly to realize meaning through collective action.

The Problem of Transfer: Learning in the Rehearsal Room to Teaching and Learning in School

So far, I have been constructing an argument about the nature and importance of environment in learning. It is an attempt to instate the role that practical activity located in concrete socio-spatial settings has in processes of learning and development. It is to suggest that the concreteness of activity in particular settings is an aspect of learning in culture that contributes to learning in sociocultural settings that have hitherto appeared as peripheral to social, cultural and historical accounts of learning. The semiotic modalities of space and social arrangements, the role of situated talk and physical interaction, the social and mental framing that allows sense to be made of encounters and interactions, and ideologies underlying particular patterns of situated activity, all constitute environment.

Ultimately, environment contributes to individual and group learning and development through both direct and indirect means. However, the question that remains is how is it possible to give evidence to the ways in which such learning is internalized? Since it is never possible to penetrate the interiorities of learning and development, or to suggest how teachers' subjectivity might be affected, the recourse is to look for ways in which such learning is talked about and ultimately translated into patterns of practical activity. It is with these questions in mind that I conclude by turning to some excerpts of interview data gathered from teachers who experienced the workshop (albeit, not the one described above) that initiated the LPN, followed by some responses from students. The extracts are selected because they give some sense of how, back in their schools, teachers have adapted particular socio-spatial environments in school as learning spaces for their students.

In the first extract below, the head of a primary school involved in the LPN describes how she and colleagues gave specific attention to spatial setting to create a specific environment for learning:

> So we focused on certain parts of [*Hamlet*] where the ghost appears on the battlements and the children were acting that out and being soldiers and standing guard and ... we did lots of things to create the atmosphere. We timetabled the hall so that they could go in there and ... we blanked all the windows off so that it was dark and we've got a big screen and we had on the screen a picture of a castle in moonlight ... We got the atmosphere and then the children acted out being a guard and being cold and rubbing their hands and hearing the wolves howl. We did lots of work on soundscapes to create the atmosphere and then we had the bit where [a character] arrives ... who has actually seen the ghost of the old king Hamlet and rushes off to tell Hamlet's friend what he's seen.
>
> (Primary Headteacher)

They do 'lots of things', she says, 'to create the atmosphere', and these things involve a shaping of the environment for learning. They have a projected backdrop, they blank out the windows, they create an eerie soundscape and, within that setting, they encourage the children to populate the whole space of the school hall, to act out being on guard, rubbing their hands to keep warm and so forth. It is dramatic activity shaped in and by the setting. It appears that part of the teachers' purpose is, through creating a setting that is in part material and in part imaginary, to enable children to feel their way into the story, to internalize it and then to externalize it through action and, subsequently, in writing.

Another teacher, this time the Head of English in a secondary school, describes how the LPN experience has enabled her to develop her thinking and practice in her pedagogical approach to Shakespeare. Previously, although she has had some training using drama techniques, she has not had the confidence to put them into her own practice, but this has changed:

> This project has enabled me to see how, even within an English classroom that's relatively cramped and full of tables, you can still create that environment that happens in rehearsals.
>
> (Secondary Head of English)

The teacher is creating, or recreating, the sense of the classroom as a rehearsal space, a place of possibility. She too feels that the modification or transformation of a classroom into a studio environment contributes to students' learning:

> I've seen the growth of students particularly in their confidence and how they are able to engage so much more easily with the language of the script ... I'm now taking those methods and incorporating them into other English lessons with poetry and other fictional texts.

Her students' responses corroborate the teacher's sense that transforming the classroom environment affects their sense of themselves and their learning:

> Well we're doing Romeo and Juliet at the moment in English ... it was more like drama than English.
>
> (Secondary school student)

Another student notices how active, rehearsal room approaches have not only affected their learning, but how their teachers' approach to teaching has changed:

> In English it's changed a lot because we are doing 'Much Ado About Nothing' ... maybe a couple of years ago we would have just sat down and talked about it but now we're actually doing exercises and being characters and understanding it together and doing more drama type work.

Conclusion

In much of what is written about teaching and learning, as for example, discussed above in relation to sociocultural approaches to learning, it seems that the notion of learning environment is a strangely abstract and empty space, unpopulated, without arrangements and movement of physical beings in and through particular locations and situations. As Bateson described the idea of frame as being neither totally abstract nor completely material, my argument has been that physical environments shape activity and learning as much as social activity and interaction shapes the physical environment. The classroom and the school hall are physical places that affect not just social arrangements, but also the learning of groups and individuals. Yet, they can be acted upon, made mutable through particular patterns of pedagogical activity, led by teachers who remain sensitive and amenable to the possibilities afforded by particular environments and how they might be modified through teaching and learning. The effects of environment, particularly in terms of setting, are clearly crucial to drama and ways in which it makes meaning.

In drawing together and elaborating on the concepts of frame and multimodality in relation to Vygotsky's work on learning, my aim has been to articulate a framework that brings into focus physical aspects of place as an environment for learning. It is a framework that might function both as an explanatory method, as a way of understanding how physical environments have effects on learning, but also as means for generating ideas and resources for pedagogic design. As a means of critical reflection, it might assist in realizing how particular environments have affected our own learning as teachers and how classroom environments affect students' learning experiences, how the sense of an environment might permeate and inflect perceptions and subsequent actions. As a constructive tool, it can draw attention to the ways in which physical arrangements in particular settings affect student learning and therefore how environments might be shaped and modified in the ways that teachers on the RSC scheme adapted their classrooms, school halls and so forth. Beyond the drama studio, the arrangements of other learning spaces might be also considered; how school science laboratories, art-rooms, or the everyday arrangements of desks, tables and chairs in classrooms affect the learning of students, thinking about how environments might either afford or delimit the learning experience. Ultimately, critical, theoretically informed reflection on spaces designated as environments for learning might, perhaps, be used to enhance learning experiences in particular socio-spatial environments.

Note

1 The research team comprised Pat Thomson (PI), Chris Hall and Deborah Thomas of the University of Nottingham, Ken Jones of Goldsmiths College University of London and myself, commissioned and funded by Creativity, Culture and Education.

References

Bateson, G. (2000), 'A Theory of Play and Fantasy', *Steps to an Ecology of Mind: Collected Essays in Anthropology, Psychiatry, Evolution, and Epistemology*, Chigago: University of Chicago Press, 177–93.

Forman, E.A., Minick, N. and Stone, C.A. (1993), *Contexts for Learning: Sociocultural Dynamics in Children's Development*, New York and Oxford: Oxford University Press.

Franks, A. (1997), 'Drama, Desire and Schooling. Drives to Learning in Creative and Expressive School Subjects', *Changing English*, 4: 131–47.

Franks, A. and Jewitt, C. (2001), 'The Meaning of Action in Learning and Teaching', *British Educational Research Journal*, 27: 201–18.

Goffman, E. (1971), *The Presentation of Self in Everyday Life*, London: Penguin.

Goffman, E. (1986), *Frame Analysis*, Boston: Northeastern University Press.

Heathcote, D. (1984), 'From the Particular to the Universal', in L. Johnson and C. O'Neill (eds), *Dorothy Heathcote: Collected Writings on Education and Drama*, London: Hutchinson, 103–10.

Kress, G.R. (2010), *Multimodality: A Social Semiotic Approach to Contemporary Communication*, London: Routledge.

Kress, G.R. and Leeuwen, T. v. (2001), *Multimodal Discourse: The Modes and Media of Contemporary Communication*, London: Arnold.

Kress, G.R., Bourne, J., Jewitt, C., Jones, K., Franks, A., Hardcastle, J. and Reid, E. (2005), *English in Urban Classrooms: A Multimodal Perspective on Teaching and Learning*, London: RoutledgeFalmer.

Lave, J. and Wenger, E. (1991), *Situated Learning: Legitimate Peripheral Participation*. Cambridge: Cambridge University Press.

Miller, D. (2010), *Stuff*, Cambridge: Polity Press.

O'Toole, J. (1992), *The Process of Drama: Negotiating Art and Meaning*, London: Routledge.

Thomson, P., Hall, C., Thomas, D., Jones, K. and Franks, A. (2010), *A Study of the Learning Performance Network an Education Programme of the Royal Shakespeare Company*, London: Creativity, Culture and Education, accessed 2 April 2014 at: http://www.creativitycultureeducation.org/a-study-of-the-learning-performance-network-an-education-programme-of-the-royal-shakespeare-company

Vygotsky, L.S. (1987), 'Thinking and Speech', *The Collected Works of L S. Vygotsky*, vol. 1, *Problems of General Psychology*, New York: Plenum Press, 39–288.

Vygotsky, L.S. (1994), 'The Problem of the Environment', in R. van der Veer and J. Valsiner (eds), *The Vygotsky Reader*, Oxford: Blackwell, 338–34.

Vygotsky, L.S. (1997), 'On the Problem of the Psychology of the Actor's Creative Work', in R.W. Rieber and J.L. Wollock (eds), *The Collected Works of L.S. Vygotsky*, vol. 6, New York and London: Plenum Press, 237–44.

Drama, Theatre and Performance Creativity[1]

R. Keith Sawyer

Introduction

As a creativity researcher I have been investigating different manifestations of creativity for several decades. The framework I have adopted is situated in a sociocultural tradition, with its historical roots in Vygotsky and in the American pragmatists G.H. Mead and John Dewey. In recent decades, the sociocultural approach has been significantly extended by the contributions of anthropologists and culturally inclined developmental psychologists, including Shweder (1990), Cole (1996), Hutchins (1995) and Rogoff (1990).

In creativity research, the most influential proponent of a sociocultural approach is Csikszentmihalyi (1996), who has proposed that creativity does not emerge from a single isolated individual, but instead emerges from a *systems model* that includes creator, creative communities and the accumulated body of created works. In this chapter, I use a sociocultural approach to analyse performance creativity, with a focus on performance forms that include elements of improvisation. The central topics of the chapter are a consideration of how individual and social aspects intertwine in group improvised performance, how such performances emerge from collaborative dynamics, how performers and groups attain a 'flow state' of peak effectiveness, how ideas form and develop on stage and the role of the audience. I conclude the chapter by exploring the potential of applying similar approaches in educational contexts.

Improvisation and Performance Creativity

In 1992 and 1993, I was the pianist for one of Chicago's most popular improvisational comedy groups, known as 'Off-Off-Campus'. While much of my early research was focused on creativity in music, this performance experience led me to realize that improvised theatre had many of the same characteristics of group musical performance. The underlying similarities are grounded in the interactional dynamics of the ensemble, and in the processes whereby individual contributions build on each other over time to result in a collective creative performance. In many ways, improvisational theatre – with interaction mediated by language and gesture – is easier to understand, and easier to connect with everyday social encounters, than improvised musical performance.

Although the cast rotated, Off-Off-Campus typically consisted of eight actors, the director and the pianist. I began each show by playing an up-tempo blues on the piano, as the stage lights came on and the actors ran to the stage. The show often began with a highly physical 'game' with a lot of movement, such as 'Freeze Tag'. To start the game, one of the actors asked members of the audience to shout out suggestions for a location or a starting line of dialogue. Two performers then used this suggestion to begin an improvised scene. The actors accompanied their dialogue with exaggerated gestures and broad physical movements. The audience was told to shout 'Freeze!' whenever they thought the actors were in interesting physical positions. Whenever anyone shouted Freeze!, the actors stopped talking and immediately froze in whatever body position they happened to be in. A third actor then walked up to these two and tapped one of them on the shoulder. The tapped actor left the stage. The third actor then copied that body position, and began a completely different scene with her first line of dialogue, justifying their body positions but interpreting them in a new way.

After five or ten minutes of these high-energy games, the actors would move on to *scene improvisation*. Example 1 is an improvised dialogue that I videotaped during a 1993 performance by Off-Off-Campus, the first few seconds of dialogue from a scene that the actors knew would last about five minutes. The audience was asked to suggest a proverb, and the suggestion given was 'Don't look a gift horse in the mouth.'

Example 1. Lights up. Dave is at stage right, Ellen at stage left. Dave begins gesturing to his right, talking to himself (Sawyer, 2003b):

1 DAVE   All the little glass figurines in my
         menagerie,
         The store of my dreams.
         Hundreds of thousands   *Turns around to admire.*
         everywhere!

2	ELLEN		*Slowly walks toward Dave.*
3	DAVE	Yes, can I help you?	*Turns and notices Ellen.*
4	ELLEN	Um, I'm looking for uh, uh, a present?	*Ellen is looking down like a child, with her fingers in her mouth.*
5	DAVE	A gift?	
6	ELLEN	Yeah.	
7	DAVE	I have a little donkey?	*Dave mimes the action of handing Ellen a donkey from the shelf.*
8	ELLEN	Ah, that's I was looking for something a little bit bigger,	
9	DAVE	Oh.	*Returns item to shelf.*
10	ELLEN	It's for my Dad.	

By turn 10, elements of the dramatic narrative are starting to emerge. We know that Dave is a storekeeper, and Ellen is a young girl. We know that Ellen is buying a present for her Dad, and because she is so young, probably needs help from the storekeeper. These narrative elements have emerged from the creative contributions of both actors. Although each turn's incremental contributions to the unfolding story can be identified, none of these turns fully determines the subsequent dialogue, and the emergent dramatic narrative is not chosen, intended or imposed by either of the actors.

Improvised dialogues like Example 1 demonstrate the key characteristics of what I call *collaborative emergence*:

- At each moment, the performance is *contingent*: The next action can greatly change the collective understanding of the prior performance, as well as the possible future paths of the performance.
- Performers often change the collective understanding of prior actions. This possibility of *retrospective interpretation* means that individual actors are not solely responsible for the meaning and effect of their own actions.
- Because of this moment-to-moment contingency and retrospective interpretation, the performance remains continually *unpredictable*. No performer can effectively plan ahead, but must always remain in the moment.
- Due to all of the above, performances *emerge* from the collective and sequential actions of multiple individuals.

When the above characteristics of collaborative emergence are found in a group, psychological analyses of individual group members can never explain the collective creation that emerges. The greatest explanatory power comes from an analysis of the interactional dynamics among the members of the group, because that is where the creativity emerges from. Such group interactions require a sociocultural and distributed approach.

Improvisation and Oral Traditions

The current predominance of scripted theatre on the professional stage makes it hard to imagine a time when *all* performance was improvised. But of course, this was the case at the beginning of human culture, when writing systems had not yet been developed. The idea that a playwright would write down a script for later performance is a relatively recent innovation in human history. Long before the invention of writing, human societies had musical and ritual performances, oral traditions that were passed from one generation to the next.

Oral traditions vary from one performance to the next. Every performance of a North Carolina tall tale or an Irish fiddle tune is a little different. Contemporary anthropologists, who study verbal ritual performance around the world, have documented variations even in the most sacred rituals. For example, in many performance traditions, only experienced elders have acquired the skills required to speak at important rituals. But even after a lifetime of performing prayers, incantations and sermons, they still repeat the ritual text a little differently each time. Folklorists initially viewed this as an annoying problem; their goal was to write down the correct version of the story or ritual, but each time they observed a performance, it was different.

In the 1970s, some anthropologists began to accept that oral traditions are not repeated verbatim, like the performances of a literate culture. These researchers began to study the improvisational creativity of the performer, and began to emphasize the ways that folklore was a living, practised tradition (Bauman and Sherzer, 1974). These new perspectives have changed the way we look at early European theatre. They have driven home the importance of a previously neglected fact. Until at least the late medieval period, many European actors remained illiterate. Some scholars, for example, believe that Shakespeare did not write scripts, but rather taught his actors their parts orally. Scholars argue that the scripts we have today are transcriptions of actual performances, done from memory by someone in Shakespeare's group (Delbanco, 2002). This helps to explain why different portfolios of the same play have different scripts (Sawyer, 2009).

Modern theatre is often traced to a popular form of entertainment called the *commedia dell'arte*, a partially improvised genre of plays originating in sixteenth-century Italy and thriving for the next 200 years throughout Europe. Scripts for commedia dell'arte performances were not fully written or adhered to. What historians have found are scenarios or rough outlines of plot, with brief descriptions of the characters. The actors developed their own versions of well-known archetypal characters and these capitalized on their particular performance skills. They could easily memorize these rough outlines and scenarios, but all of the dialogue was improvised in front of the audience. The success of a commedia dell'arte performance depended on the individualized internalized knowledge and history of the form and the ensemble's improvisational creativity.

Literacy became more widespread in Europe during the same years that improvisation was fading out of our performance tradition. Over the 200-year period that commedia dell'arte was popular, literacy became much more common among actors, and the scenarios developed into more highly scripted plays. By the eighteenth century, this form of early improvisation had been largely replaced by scripted theatre.

In the 1950s, improvisation returned to the professional theatre scene. Chicago inspired an improvisation revolution in modern theatre that has influenced directors, playwrights and actor training. Chicago-style improvisation is widely considered to be America's single most important contribution to world theatre.

Creativity in the Performance of Scripted Plays

It is fairly easy to identify the creativity of the performer when the performance is fully improvised. It is perhaps more difficult to identify the more subtle forms of performer creativity to be found in the performance of scripted texts; this is also worthy of further analysis and research. In scripted theatre, the actors do not have to improvise the words. But the actors still have to deliver the lines so that they sound like natural human dialogue. For example, when one actor stops speaking and the next one starts, the two actors have to make the transition sound natural, and this requires a subtle form of collaboration. They have to monitor the other performers' actions at the same time that they continue their own performances. As they hear or see what the other performers are doing, they immediately respond by altering their own actions. They implicitly and subconsciously communicate with subtle facial expressions and gestures (Caudle, 1991: 50–51).

The script does not specify every element and feature of everyday conversation; how it is realized in performance includes a host of other factors beyond pronunciation of the words themselves. To research the creative actions and decision-making evident in performance it is possible to draw on fields such as *conversation analysis* to examine the detail and techniques being used. To make this more obvious, theatre director Brian K. Crow (1988) transcribed everyday conversation (Figure 13.1) using the extremely detailed techniques of conversation analysis. Note in particular the detailed representation of pauses, overlaps and subtle changes in pitch and volume:

Normal scripts do not have this much detail – and consequently, actors have to decide where to pause, and how long each pause should be; whether there should be speaker overlap at various points in the dialogue; and how to deliver

```
K:      That was last night
J:      That's what I said last night
        (4.0)
K:      Well I –
   [
J:      Getting to know you
K:      ((laughs))
J:      You'll accept everything but you do nothing
K:      Wo:::::
           [
J:         No: that's not true
K:      Everybody's that way in certain instances (.) are they not?
J:      Not me:, =
K:      = Not you:, oh no
                  [
J:                ((laugh)) Wonderful me
                           [
K:                         It's your turn – It's your turn to
        get the tea
        Oh:: no (.) I did it six months ago it's
        your turn
                  [
J:                ((laughs))
                     [
K:                   he he he
J:      No
```

Figure 13.1 Transcript of conversation that was performed by a theatre group exactly as it was originally spoken. The punctuation marks indicate pitch changes, volume, emphasis and overlapping speech, which the actors were required to copy exactly[2]

each line – which words to emphasize, and with what tone of voice. A transcript like Figure 13.1 makes it clear how much information is left out of the typical script. Everything that is put back in by the actors involves performance creativity. And although a lot of those decisions are made in rehearsal, many of them are made improvisationally every night, on stage, in front of the audience.

To teach actors how to make their dialogue sound natural, a few directors and playwrights have used detailed transcripts like Figure 13.1 to generate their scripts. This style of theatre is called *everyday life performance* (Hopper, 1993; Stucky, 1988, 1993). Crow used detailed transcripts of everyday dialogues to create *Conversation Pieces: An Empirical Comedy* in 1987, a production in which actors performed transcripts like Figure 13.1 exactly as written (Crow, 1988). This removes a lot of actor creativity, but it is a useful exercise for teaching actors how much creativity a normal script requires. All of the unwritten aspects of the dialogue have to be improvised by the actors, and the improvisation is collaboratively managed by all actors.

Researching the Creativity of the Actor and the Ensemble

Psychological studies of performance creativity are rare. Partly this is because acting is an ensemble art form, and it is hard to isolate the creative contribution of any one actor (Sawyer, 2003a). But it is also due to the all-too-common belief that performance is not creative, but is just execution and interpretation (Kogan, 2002). A few studies of acting creativity have identified three stages: preparation, rehearsal and performance (Blunt, 1966; Nemiro, 1997). *Preparation* is when the actor learns the basics of acting through academic training, observing other actors in theatre and in films, and observing people interacting in everyday life. The preparation stage includes some solitary activities, but for the most part, actor training is social and collaborative.

The second stage, *rehearsal*, involves at least five activities:

1. Identifying something in the character that the actor can relate to;
2. Using personal experiences as substitutes for the character's feelings;
3. Discovering the character's objectives;
4. Creating a physical persona for the character – how the character walks and moves;
5. Studying the script to learn what the other characters think about the character.

The rehearsal stage is mostly collaborative; although actors spend some time alone to memorize their *lines*, most rehearsal is done with the rest of the cast. The third and final stage, *performance*, is the most collaborative of all. Performance involves at least five activities:

1. Focusing on the moment – what has just happened and how the character would perceive the situation at that moment, with no knowledge of how the rest of the play unfolds;
2. Adjusting to other actors;
3. Interacting with the audience;
4. Keeping the concentration and energy level high;
5. Improving the performance and keeping it fresh over repeated performances.

This third stage, performance, is what the audience sees; this is the most important for the final realization of acting creativity. In improvisational performance, preparation and rehearsal are much less obvious; the entire creative process is both rehearsal and performance every night on stage, in front of a live audience.

The Flow of Performance

Many actors believe that their performance is much better during public performance than in rehearsal (Konijn, 1991: 63). Social psychologists have known for decades that performance often improves in the presence of an audience; they call this *social facilitation* (Guerin, 1993). Konijn (1991) found that actors' heart rates were higher during public performance than rehearsal, indicating an elevated stress level, but the public performances were rated more highly by the actors and by expert observers, suggesting that an increased stress level improves performance. This may be why good actors welcome stage fright; it is good for performers to experience a little stress, because it increases the quality of the performance (Wilson, 1985). But there is an interesting twist. Although social facilitation studies show that an audience can facilitate performance on an easy task, they also show that an audience can reduce performance on a difficult one (Geen, 1989). This paradox can be explained by Csikszentmihalyi's theory of flow (1990), which proposes that individuals experience a flow state when the challenges of the task are perfectly matched to their own level of skill (Csikszentmihalyi, 1990). Actors are faced with a task that would be too challenging for most of us, but they have mastered the skills necessary to perform the task. They may not experience flow in a rehearsal because that context is not challenging enough.

The Creativity of the Ensemble

Theatre is an ensemble art. Explaining theatre creativity requires a sociocultural approach, because the explanation has to be based in the interpersonal dynamics among the actors. Focusing only on the inner mental states of the individual performers will miss the most fundamental aspects of performance creativity, the emergence of a unique performance from the unpredictable and always changing interactions among performers on stage.

If every group used a script like the one in Figure 13.1, there would be a lot less variability from night to night. But theatre seems to be more entertaining with an element of uncertainty and performer creativity. Groups attain their best performances by staying in a zone between complete predictability and being out of control. Improvisational actors have to be the most highly attuned to this zone. They cannot just develop the scene in a conventional way, because that would be boring. But they also cannot do something so radical that it just does not make sense, surprising all of the other actors and puzzling the audience. The challenge of staying in this improvisation zone leads to a flow experience, a peak mental state that performers get when they are in a particularly effective performance (Sawyer, 2001).

But improvisation's unpredictability makes it a risky way to attain flow. It does not always happen, even in a group of talented, well-trained performers. Many improvising actors talk about both the high they get from a good improvisation, and the terror they feel when a performance is not going well. The unpredictability of group creativity can be frightening because failure is public. If a painter fails, he or she can paint over the canvas; a writer can crumple up the paper and throw it away. But imagine if writers had to publish every single one of their manuscripts – that is the situation improv actors find themselves in every night. Mark Gordon, a director of and actor in The Compass Players said, 'It always felt to me like taking your pants off in front of an audience. A little terrifying' (Sweet, 1978: 110). Ted Flicker, director of the first St Louis 'Compass' and founder of the New York group 'The Premise', said, 'Unless you've actually tasted what improvising in front of an audience feels like, you can't *imagine* the horror of it' (Sweet, 1978: 162). Up to a certain point, this fear can contribute to the potential for a flow experience. But once it crosses a certain threshold, the actor moves from the flow zone into the anxiety zone.

The flow state that comes from a successful performance is 'something like a drug', which is the title of a book about the improvisational Theatresports league (Foreman and Martini, 1995). Improvisers keep doing it, in spite of the lack of money and fame relative to conventional theatre, television and movies, because of the high they get from the flow experience. Comparing improvisation to conventional theatre, Andrew Duncan felt that the flow experience was much greater in improvisation. After leaving *Second City* in 1963, he said that 'I really missed that kind of company – the community, working together, respect ... They were intense moments in your life that had meaning' (Sweet, 1978: 61).

Even if the individual performers are prepared and focused, a good group performance does not always emerge, because there are simply too many intangible factors that cannot be known until the performance begins. And a group might be in group flow even when the performers do not realize it. Improvisational musicians and actors alike often describe the experience of walking off of the stage at the end of the night, feeling that the performance had been really bad, and then hearing later that the audience had found it to be a stellar performance. Pete Gardner described how the improvisers always valued shows in which everything connected well, but 'the audiences absolutely love the shows where there was a mass confusion.' He described an experience where one friend compared a slick show with a confused show, explicitly noting that the confused and messy show was 'so much better' (Sawyer, 2003b: 46). Inversely, most group performers can tell a story of at least one night's performance that they thought was particularly good, but later as they were discussing the performance with knowledgeable, trusted colleagues who had been in the audience, they discovered that it was not one of their best.

Many Chicago improvisers refer to group flow using the term *groupmind*. Group flow helps the individual actors reach their own internal flow state. Comedian Jim Belushi famously said that the high that comes from a group performance was 'better than sex' (Seham, 2001: 64). Actor Alan Alda referred to this state, saying, 'You're actually tuned into something that's inside the actor's mind and there's a kind of mental music that's played and that everybody shares' (Sweet, 1978: 326). Improv actors often speak of group flow as 'a state of unselfconscious awareness in which every individual action seems to be the right one and the group works with apparent perfect synchronicity' (Seham, 2001: 64). No one actor can make this happen single-handedly; it requires a very special collaboration. The ensemble has to let it emerge from a group creative process.

Because these improvisational performances are collaboratively emergent, their analysis and explanation requires a focus on the dynamics of the interactions between group members, as well as the specific cultural context and the role of the audience.

Interaction between Actors and Audience

Peter Brook (1968) described a touring performance of *King Lear* by the Royal Shakespeare Company in the 1960s. The tour began by passing through Europe. Brook reported that 'the best performances lay between Budapest and Moscow' (Brook, 1968: 21) and that the audience profoundly influenced the cast, even though their mastery of the English language was not great. Yet, their experience of life under communism prepared them to connect with the play's difficult themes. The actors were in peak performance and became progressively more excited as they finished the European portion of the tour and then moved to the United States. Yet after a few weeks in the United States, the spirit had gone out of the company. Brook reported that:

> ... it was the relation with the audience that had changed ... This audience was composed largely of people who were not interested in the play; people who came for all the conventional reasons – because it was a social event, because their wives insisted, and so on.
>
> (Brook, 1968: 22)

The actors modified their performances in an attempt to engage this different type of audience, but with limited success.

Performers feed off of a good audience, and it leads the performers to rise to the best of their ability. Audiences can even affect specific moment-to-moment performance decisions. In a theatre performance, an unexpected audience chuckle might lead the actors to pause a split-second to let the laughter play out and die down, and they might exaggerate the next similar line by the same character, whereas on another night, an audience might not respond at that moment and the performance would be unaffected. In an improv comedy performance, a laughing audience lets the cast know they are performing well, but if there is no laughter, the cast knows they need to change something, perhaps to take the character and story development in another direction.

When other audience members react, whether with laughter, fear or sadness, we are more likely to experience that emotion or reaction as well. This group phenomenon is called *emotional contagion* (Hatfield *et al.*, 1994). This happens a lot with laughter and applause, and the larger the audience, the more extreme the effects. Examples include the extreme emotions that spread through the crowd at a sports event or a stadium concert. To understand the role of the audience, we need a sociocultural approach that explains group dynamics and communication.

The Creative Process made Visible

Most creativity research has focused on product creativity instead of performance (Sawyer, 1997, 2003a). In scientific disciplines, creative products include theories, experimental results and journal articles; in the arts, products include paintings, sculptures and musical scores. In product creativity, the creative process results in a finished, fixed product. In product creativity, the creative process usually takes place in isolation, in a studio or a laboratory. It can take months or years before the final product is completed. The creator has unlimited opportunities for revision, and does not have to release the product until he or she is ready.

Creativity does not happen all in the head, as individualist psychology would have it; it happens during the hard work of execution. That is why explaining creativity requires a focus on the creative process. No creative process is ever completely predictable; there is always some improvisation. Creative works emerge from a creative process that involves the creator, but also the materials being used and the unfolding and developing external representations of the creator's thought (John-Steiner, 1985). A painter constantly responds to his canvas and oils as he is painting. Each step of the painting changes the artist's conception of what he is doing – the first part of a painting often leads to a new insight about what to do next. Fiction writers constantly interact with the story as they write. A character or a plot line frequently emerges from the pen unexpectedly, and an experienced writer will respond and follow that new thread, in an essentially improvisational fashion.

Improvisation is most essential in stage performance because, unlike the painter or the writer, performers do not have an opportunity to revise their work. The improvisations of the painter can be painted over or discarded, and the writer has the power of a word processor to generate the next draft. But the improvisations that occur on stage are exposed to the audience. As a result, the audience gets to see the creative process in action, sharing not only in every unexpected inspiration but also in those disappointing attempts that fail. Fans of the popular improvisational rock-band 'The Grateful Dead' had a rule of thumb:

You have to go to five concerts to be assured of getting one really inspired performance. Even the most famous artists often destroy or paint over a significant number of their canvases, and these aborted attempts are generally lost to history. But actors can never take back a bad night.

We cannot explain performance creativity unless we focus on the collaboration and the emergence of the group. And studying performance can provide valuable insights into all creativity, because collaboration is important in all creative domains. In modern scientific research, these collaborations range from the group work that goes on in the laboratory to informal conversations over late-night coffee. The creative interactions of an improv theatre group are much easier to study, since the analyst can hear and transcribe how this interaction affects each actor's creative process. Performance can be viewed as the creative process made visible.

The individualism of academic psychology has led us to neglect performance creativity, even though it, of all forms of creativity, provides us with the best window onto the collaboration and improvisation of the creative process and collaborative learning processes. We now know that creativity is fundamentally social and collaborative, that it involves preparation, training and hard work, and that the process is as important as the product and the personality. By explaining performance, we can ultimately better explain all creativity.

Implications for Education

In educational contexts, participatory and improvised forms of drama began to rise in popularity in the 1970s, driven by influential work with participatory forms of improvised drama promulgated by educators such as Dorothy Heathcote in the United Kingdom (Heathcote, 1967; Heathcote and Bolton, 1995). In fact, the first improvised groups to form in Chicago, in the 1950s, were heavily influenced by Viola Spolin's work in developing improvised games for children during the 1930s and 1940s (Spolin, 1963).

The use of drama in education is solidly grounded in learning sciences research. In classrooms that use the effective forms of pedagogy suggested by constructivism and sociocultural theory, classroom interactions can be considered to be improvisational encounters. After all, the core insight of constructivism is that learning is most effective when learners creatively construct their own understandings. Constructivist learning consequently requires unpredictability, as the learners find their own path to discover key insights about the material (Sawyer, 2011). The most effective teaching, from a constructivist perspective, is that which guides and scaffolds learners as they engage in this fundamentally improvisational learning process – what I have called *disciplined improvisation* (Sawyer, 2004).

In these classrooms, the interactions that emerge between teacher and students are characterized by collaborative emergence. As such, the study of these classrooms requires a sociocultural approach, one that analyses the moment-to-moment contingency of classroom dialogue, one that focuses on the unfolding process and not only the ultimate product, the desired learning outcome.

Conclusion

This chapter has provided an overview of the sociocultural elements that need to be considered in understanding and valuing performance creativity. It has demonstrated that highly advanced forms of collaboration and distributed creativity are realized in improvisation and theatrical performance. It has identified how interactional dynamics, audience and context all play an important role in the successful realization of the improvised act. It has suggested that all effective pedagogy can be viewed as a form of collaborative improvisation, guided by an expert teacher. Finally it highlights how further research of these processes in professional and educational contexts is required, and will assist in further expanding human understanding of distributed creativity and learning.

Notes

1 This chapter is a revised version of Chapter 19 from *Explaining Creativity* (second edition), 2012.
2 Originally from *TDR/The Drama Review*, 32:3, 23–54 T119–Fall 1988. Bryan K. Crow, *Conversational Performance and the Performance of Conversation*.

References

Bauman, R. and Sherzer, J. (eds) (1974), *Explorations in the Ethnography of Speaking*, New York: Cambridge University Press.

Blunt, J. (1966), *The Composite Art of Acting*, New York: Macmillan.

Brook, P. (1968), *The Empty Space*, New York: Atheneum.
Caudle, F.M. (1991), 'An Ecological View of Social Perception: Implications for Theatrical Performance', in G.D. Wilson (ed.), *Psychology and Performing Arts*, Amsterdam: Swets and Zeitlinger, 45–57.
Cole, M. (1996), *Cultural Psychology: A Once and Future Discipline*, Cambridge: Harvard.
Crow, B.K. (1988), 'Conversational Performance and the Performance of Conversation', *TDR*, 32(3): 23–54.
Csikszentmihalyi, M. (1990), *Flow: The Psychology of Optimal Experience*, New York: HarperCollins.
Csikszentmihalyi, M. (1996), *Creativity: Flow and the Psychology of Discovery and Invention*, New York: HarperCollins.
Delbanco, N. (2002), 'In Praise of Imitation', *Harper's Magazine*, July: 57–63.
Foreman, K. and Martini, C. (1995), *Something Like a Drug: An Unauthorized Oral History of Theatresports*, Alberta, Canada: Red Deer College Press.
Geen, R.G. (1989), 'Alternative Conceptions of Social Cacilitation', in P.B. Paulus (ed.), *Psychology of Group Influence*, 2nd edition., Hillsdale, NJ: Erlbaum, 15–51.
Guerin, B. (1993), *Social Facilitation*, New York: Cambridge University Press.
Hatfield, E., Cacioppo, J.T. and Rapson, R.L. (1994), *Emotional Contagion*, New York: Cambridge.
Heathcote, D. (1967), 'Improvisation', *English in Education*, 1(3): 27–30.
Heathcote, D. and Bolton, G. (1995), *Drama for Learning: Dorothy Heathcote's Mantle of the Expert Approach to Education*, Portsmouth, NH: Heinemann.
Hopper, R. (1993), 'Conversational Dramatism and Everyday Life Performance', *Text and Performance Quarterly*, 13: 181–3.
Hutchins, E. (1995), *Cognition in the Wild*, Cambridge: MIT Press.
John-Steiner, V. (1985), *Notebooks of the Mind: Explorations of Thinking*, Albuquerque, NM: University of New Mexico Press.
Kogan, N. (2002), 'Careers in the Performing Arts: A Psychological Perspective', *Creativity Research Journal*, 14(1): 1–16.
Konijn, E.A. (1991), 'What's on Between the Actor and his Audience? Empirical Analysis of Emotion Processes in the Theatre', in G.D. Wilson (ed.), *Psychology and Performing Arts*, Amsterdam: Swets and Zeitlinger, 59–73.
Nemiro, J. (1997), 'Interpretive Artists: A Qualitative Exploration of the Creative Process of Actors', *Creativity Research Journal*, 10(2&3): 229–239.
Rogoff, B. (1990), *Apprenticeship in Thinking: Cognitive Development in Social Context*, New York: Oxford University Press.
Sawyer, R.K. (ed.) (1997), *Creativity in Performance*, Greenwich, CT: Ablex.
Sawyer, R.K. (2001), *Creating Conversations: Improvisation in Everyday Discourse*, Cresskill, NJ: Hampton Press.
Sawyer, R.K. (2003a), *Group Creativity: Music, Theater, Collaboration*, Mahwah, NJ: Erlbaum.

Sawyer, R.K. (2003b), *Improvised Dialogues: Emergence and Creativity in Conversation*, Westport, CT: Greenwood.

Sawyer, R.K. (2004), 'Creative Teaching: Collaborative Discussion as Disciplined Improvisation', *Educational Researcher*, 33(2): 12–20.

Sawyer, R.K. (2009), 'Writing as a Collaborative Act', in S.B. Kaufman and J.C. Kaufman (eds), *The Psychology of Creative Writing*, New York: Cambridge University Press, 166–179.

Sawyer, R.K. (ed.) (2011), *Structure and Improvisation in Creative Teaching*, Cambridge: Cambridge University Press.

Seham, A.E. (2001), *Whose Improv is it Anyway? Beyond Second City*, Jackson, MS: University Press of Mississippi.

Shweder, R.A. (1990), 'Cultural psychology – What is it?' in J.W. Stigler, R.A. Shweder and G. Herdt (eds), *Cultural Psychology: Essays on Comparative Human Development*, New York: Cambridge University Press, 1–43.

Spolin, V. (1963), *Improvisation for the Theater*, Evanston IL: Northwestern University Press.

Stucky, N. (1988), 'Unnatural Acts: Performing Natural Conversation,' *Literature in Performance*, 8(2): 28–39.

Stucky, N. (1993), 'Toward an Aesthetics of Natural Performance', *Text and Performance Quarterly*, 13: 168–80.

Sweet, J. (1978), *Something Wonderful Right Away: An Oral History of the Second City and the Compass Players*, New York: Avon Books.

Wilson, G. (1985), *The Psychology of the Performing Arts*, London: Croom Helm.

14

Building a Workplace Theatre: Forum Theatre and Developmental Work Research as Developmental Resources in Interventions

Satu-Mari Jansson

Introduction

Drama and applied theatre processes are being increasingly practised beyond traditional educational contexts. New contexts might affect drama methods as tools for facilitating and assisting change and the applied theatre processes themselves. I have been involved in many such applied theatre processes, including several that involved techniques drawn from drama and theatre and the methodology of Developmental Work Research (DWR) (Engeström 1991). My interest in intertwining developmental resources started because I was involved as a script facilitator and project manager for several Forum Theatre projects. Experiences taken from these projects made me realize that there are similar types of developmental logics behind the two developmental resources, Forum Theatre and DWR. I see both developmental resources as tools for intervention. Intervention is defined by Midgley (2000: 113) as 'purposeful action by a human agent to create change'. The word 'intervention' comes from Latin and means *inter*, between, *venio*, to come, meaning 'to come between'. 'The interventionist comes between an actor's actions so that the activity finds a new direction' (Virkkunen and Newnham, 2013: 3).

This chapter studies the relationship between Boal's (1995) Forum Theatre and the methodology of DWR, developed by Engeström (1991), the first created in the field of theatre and the second in the field of workplace development. The hypothesis is that an overlap exists between the two developmental resources and that drama educators could readily combine the two resources. This chapter demonstrates how a research-oriented approach (DWR) was used in play-building that focused on the conceptual development at hand.

This chapter outlines the theoretical foundations of the two developmental resources and discusses their similarities, differences and complementary aspects. It does so through presenting a case in which the methodology of DWR helped to create a Forum Theatre type of narrative and 'anti-model'. The narrative depicted development that was in progress in the case organization, and the narrative was used to prompt the challenges of change management. The research question that underpinned the process and research was: 'How can Forum Theatre and the methodology of DWR be used as intertwined developmental resources?'

The pilot project was conducted as part of a project titled: *Arts Developing Quality and Innovation Capabilities in Work Life*, which was financed by the EU and the Ministry of Education and Culture in Finland. Several other projects were organized throughout Finland, which involved providing workshops run by artists and arts-based facilitators that utilized drama, fine arts, movement improvisation, dance, music, literature, handicrafts and photography. The aim of the project was to develop arts-based ways of working in new contexts, as parliamentary ministries have indicated that the role of the creative industries for the future is crucial for achieving a better working life and improved worker well-being. The project, at the same time, presented a chance to test two different kinds of developmental methods that I had used separately in earlier projects. Underpinning this work was the hypothesis that both of the developmental resources were needed to create a narrative and 'anti-model' that presents conceptual development. I named the combination of these two developmental resources *Workplace Theatre*.

Developmental Work Research – Knowing through an Analysis of Research Data

To begin, I will explain both developmental models, and then introduce the way they were intertwined in a concrete pilot case. The methodology of DWR is based on Cultural-Historical Activity Theory (CHAT) (Engeström, 1987, 1991, 1999). The theory and methodology are used in a special intervention model called Change Laboratory (Virkkunen and Newnham, 2013). Change Laboratory is used in various contexts, such as in the media field (Helle, 2010) and the Central Surgical Unit of a University Hospital (Kajamaa, 2011; Virkkunen and Newnham, 2013).

The idea of Change Laboratory is that a work community, with the help of an researcher-interventionist, analyses the development of its activity including the object of the activity, their tools, rules and division of labour (Virkkunen and

Newnham, 2013). The development process is participative in its nature and the aim is to support a work community in questioning their previous and present work practices and helping them to develop their actions.

Researcher-interventionists try to identify the historically formed nature of the activity, the development phase of the activity, what factors may have caused contradictions (Figure 11.1; Chapter 11) and how contradictions are experienced as disturbances in daily work. The aim of the developmental process is to help the work community to design a new kind of activity concept, which resolves experienced contradictions (Chapter 11). During the developmental process, new solutions are iteratively tested and implemented as they arise. Testing starts gradually changing the object of activity, and the way participants see their work, as they try out new ways of working and make new rules on how to collaborate (Virkkunen and Newnham, 2013).

During an intervention, one or more researcher-interventionist works with the planning group to identify the focus for the research and development. Every intervention project consists of an ethnographical phase, as the researcher-interventionist conducts interviews, possibly records workplace interactions via video or audio, and makes observations about the work community and their typical ways of working (Virkkunen and Newnham, 2013). Researchers then collect research data from the daily work activities and look for disturbances, meaning disruptions, to the workflow in order to identify developmental contradictions (Figure 14.1).

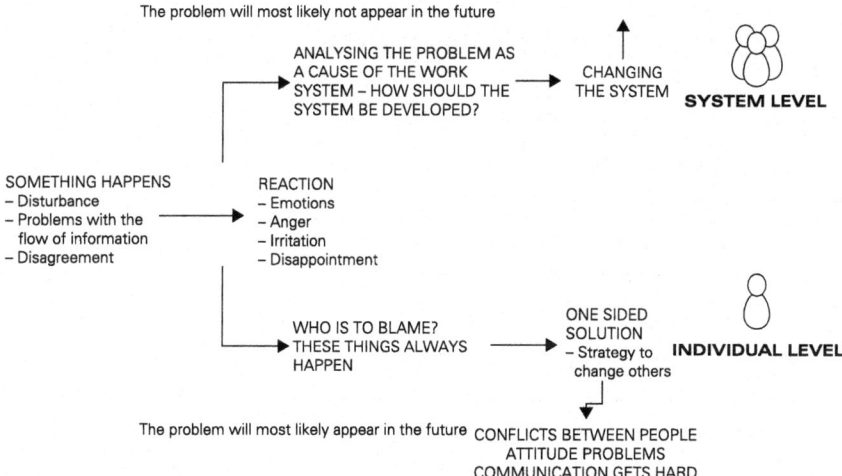

Figure 14.1 Two different types of problem handling strategies (modified from Mott, 1992: 114)

Collected data is then analysed with the help of various tools taken from the methodology of DWR. These tools could be, for example, analysing an activity system and any contradictions, and identifying the development trajectory using a model of expansive learning (Virkkunen and Newnham, 2013). During the intervention, the model of expansive learning is used to identify the historically formed developmental phase in which the organization finds itself at that moment in time. The goal of the researcher-interventionist is to work with and support the community by bringing in a 'mirror' showing data about their work. The data should concretize the problems experienced in the work that are related to the present activity. In the subsequent intervention sessions, the interventionist designs analytical tools to make the connection between daily work, the systemic level and future possibilities. Typically, this type of intervention takes place across ten two-hour sessions, the whole process lasting over several months (Virkkunen and Newnham, 2013).

The aim of the method is to create an environment that enables collective, expansive learning to take place. In the end, the work community must own the outcomes and future actions, so the purpose of the process is to support them in analysing their own work practices with analytical tools (Engeström 1999; Virkkunen and Newnham, 2013). For the purposes of this case study, these tools were complemented by drawing on aspects of Boal's theatrical form Forum Theatre, so the following section will introduce the philosophical approach and this form.

Forum Theatre – Knowing through an Aesthetic Space

Forum Theatre was created by Boal (1931–2009) in Brazil, during the 1950s and 1960s, a period that was marked by an oppressive political atmosphere. Boal's aim was to change undesirable power relations and support citizens in gaining awareness of their role in maintaining those relations. Subsequently they would rehearse change in concrete interaction situations. Forum Theatre was just one strategy or convention that was developed to enable change and show that people can change their oppressed situation. He also identified that the oppressor does not have to be an outside person, and that oppression can appear as a 'cop-in-the-head', which appears in the form of taken-for-granted ways of thinking. Boal aimed at giving people a voice and having them develop models for change and action (Boal 1995; Schutzman and Cohen-Cruz, 1994; Taussig and Schechner, 1994).

Boal (1995) himself saw the theatre as enhancing action – a place to rehearse the revolution. Therefore, Forum Theatre is a participatory theatre method that brings forth the multiple voices of a social and cultural community. It may be a safe and efficient method for fictional experimentation regarding how different decisions and reactions affect outcomes.

During Forum Theatre, oppression is made visible through dramatic scenes. The aim is to provoke, by presenting the situation and the people behaving in an exaggeration or caricature of a potential reality. This is called an 'anti-model' and is the core scene in Forum Theatre (Schutzman and Cohen-Cruz, 1994: 236). This is used to arouse the feelings of the audience with a desire to protest and change the situation (Boal, 1995).

In Forum Theatre, the play introduces a story with a problem, the 'anti-model', which is then changed. After that, the spectators suggest different solutions to the conflict situations. Actors then try to achieve the outcomes suggested by the audience. When actors show how they are trying to solve the situation, it is possible that it may become even worse before other alternatives are explored (Boal, 1995).

Forum Theatre differs from a standard theatre performance in that it is led by a Joker, someone who is a host, a facilitator and provocateur. The play is watched once and then, with the help of the Joker, the spectators, or spect-actors, have a chance to talk about what they see. Afterwards, individual scenes are changed and repeated and tried out according to comments and ideas for resolution. This logic changes the role of spectators as they become spect-actors who both watch and may also participate, stepping up and actually taking on the roles of the oppressed to explore different alternatives and possible action. Scenes can be repeated again and again, which means several different attempts can be made to explore different solutions through drama (Boal, 1995; Schutzman and Cohen-Cruz, 1994; Taussig and Schechner, 1994).

Forum Theatre has been applied in various contexts. There are plenty of case descriptions in several of Boal's legacy books (Schutzman and Cohen-Cruz, 1994; Taussig and Schechner, 1994). Even though Boal's method is a strategy developed within the context of political oppression, it has been used a lot in workplace contexts – maybe because the 'anti-model' technique provides a concrete tool as the catalyst for changing actions.

The method brings fiction and reality into a dialogue and uses the power of drama. An aesthetic space (Boal, 1995) may be formed by the spect-actor when they view the Forum Theatre play. The aesthetic space stimulates knowledge and discovery, cognition and recognition. As Boal (1995) defines it: '... in the aesthetic space one can be without being. Dead people are alive, the past becomes present, the future is today, duration is dissociated from time, everything is possible in the here-and-now, fiction is pure reality, and reality is fiction' (p. 20). Boal also describes how reality and fiction interact:

> The emotion of the characters penetrates us, the moral world of the show invades us, osmotically; we are led by characters and actions not under our control; we experience vicarious emotion – I am not penetrated by the emotion of others; instead I project my own. I guide my own actions, I am the subject. – Here we see the phenomenon of metaxis; the state of belonging completely and simultaneously to two different, autonomous worlds: the image of reality and the reality of the image. She (the oppressed) shares and belongs to these two autonomous worlds: her reality and the image of her reality, which she herself has created.
>
> (Boal, 1995: 42–43)

For understandings to become meaningful beyond the world of the drama, the process of what Boal identified as *metaxis* needs to occur. The played image has to become independent from, but connected to, the reality to form metaxis. When this happens, 'the image of the real, is real as the image'. The audience are playing with the reality of the images they are observing. During the dramatic process it is up to the audience to make an extrapolation from their current reality and the image (the reality, also, but of a different kind), which he calls a fiction. Through this the audience have to make another extrapolation in another direction, from the fictional image to social reality.

The Forum Theatre Narrative and Anti-model, the Mirror of Concept Development and Management Actions

There are several key differences, similarities and complementary factors inherent in Forum Theatre and DWR. DWR is a methodology rather than just a method, because the theoretical background combines the use of several analytical tools. DWR especially offers theoretical and analytical tools to understand the historical development phase and ways to solve the contradictory phase in which the work community is placed. Development is viewed on the systemic level, occurring through individual actions, even though work practices are developed collectively. What Forum Theatre helps to create is a strong theatrical and aesthetic space in which the spect-actors may have a chance to experience the contradictions through a frame that is removed from the 'real' through the creation of the fictionalized model or anti-model. This provides a layer of protection which can allow them to interpret and respond to the narrative and anti-model and place themselves in particular situations and reflect upon them without being directly exposed to having their own actions the immediate focus for analysis.

The DWR projects and developmental sessions, in particular, are usually compressed and filled with sharing actual-empirical data analysis from the work (Figure 14.2). The data is presented in a way that helps participants to connect daily work with systematic analysis of activity, for example in the form of video.

In DWR, the researcher and participants might identify a gap between the existing state, the ideal future state and imagining new actions related to the implementation of organizational transformation. Engeström (2007) highlights that during interventions it is one thing to have innovative and creative ideas and to build models for activity and another to shift them into practice. He illustrates this by giving an example of an investment banking case in which, during one of the developmental sessions, there was a moment where they actually could bridge this connection between ideas and activity by enforcing experiences – or more simply the act of experiencing. Two managers acted and simulated a situation where one of them played an investment manager and the other played a client. Engeström writes, 'The simulation sparked an unusually intense and engaged discussion that contained no less than eight significant ideas or suggestions formulated by the participants' (Engeström 2007: 26).

Characterisation	Forum Theatre	Developmental Work Research
Overall aim	Realize the oppression and rehearse new actions	Realize the developmental phase and form a new object in order to change one's own actions
Aim of workshop	To be a challenger and provocateur with the play and facilitation	To be a challenger and provoker with mirror data, analytical tools and facilitation
The role of author	Joker – subjective power during workshop	Researcher-interventionist subjective power during workshop but uses objective analytical tools
Aim of content	To build a powerful play which demonstrates the oppression	To build a mirror data which concretizes the contradiction
Content of scenes	Group of theatre people, forming on a basis of their knowledge and experience	Researcher-interventionist collects actual-empirical data and analyses data with the help of analytical tools

Figure 14.2 Comparison of Forum Theatre and DWR

Given Engeström's idea of bringing experience into intervention, one possible way would be to put the DWR type of analysis into narrative and dramatic form. Presenting the results of analysis in such a form could help people to question their situation and develop their activity. Blunden (2010) writes:

> ... instead of situating concepts of things in a taxonomy of attributes, or as nodes in a semantic network or as the units of a theory, our ideas of things may present themselves as character, situations or resolutions of a narrative. Narrative can be seen as an alternative to description and exposition as means of presentation of concepts as well as a mode of communication of ideas.
>
> (Blunden, 2010, para. 2)

Blunden (2010) presents that narrative is a 'meaningful presentation of human action, situating concepts in vicarious experience and providing the material from which conceptual knowledge can be abstracted as the "truth" of narrative.' Narrative is a conceptual form of knowledge or dialogue. The question is how then to form the narrative out of the analysis? According to Blunden (2010: para. 11), the plot is central as it brings 'events into a meaningful whole, by placing events in chronological order and suggesting a connection between them.' The plot presents the concept and, more precisely, the predicament represents the concept (Blunden, 2010).

In Forum Theatre, the narrative focus is on depicting an oppressive situation and relationship between oppressor and oppressed. Oppression is demonstrated through the enactment of narrative and anti-model. The narrative and anti-model are most often created by the theatre group itself or by a scriptwriter or director if there are such roles available. The narrative is built from a type of research process, utilizing the group's own knowledge, experience or understanding.

Forum Theatre provides the opportunity to demonstrate what DWR-researchers see as the way that contradiction is felt personally. Often in DWR when practitioners meet a mirror that reflects their own actions and disturbances, they experience them on a personal level as a failure. Through this process powerful 'cognitive, emotional and social dissonances are triggered' (Engeström, 1999: 7). In DWR processes, the researcher-interventionist analyses the data, and in this way is subjectively connected to the data. However, the data is being analysed with the help of objective analytical tools.

The similarity between the two approaches is that the facilitator (researcher-interventionist and Joker) is the chair. In the developmental session, the researcher-interventionist reveals the results of the data analysis and tries to get people to analyse activity on a system level. In Forum Theatre, the narrative and anti-model is presented and the Joker helps people to find changeable parts of the play. It is part of Forum Theatre's working method that the Joker does not say to the audience 'you should see the play or character like this' or say 'no' to any suggestions. Instead comments should openly test and ideas be rewound as they are suggested from the audience. The goal is to have a discussion forum that is established through the participants and the Joker.

During Forum Theatre, the presentation of the model allows a certain distance initially, for the spect-actors and the Joker to discuss possibilities for overcoming the problematic situation. The research-based viewpoint in DWR helps to connect history, the present and the developmental solutions that overcome the present situation. There are clearly aims that overlap in the two developmental resources and that is why they were entwined for the purposes of this case. The process for collecting data, forming hypotheses, building a narrative and anti-model, and making visible the role of the researcher-interventionist-Joker now follows.

Case: Leading Conceptual Change

The Workplace Theatre, meaning a combination of Forum Theatre and DWR, was applied in the polytechnic field. Next I introduce briefly the developmental state that Finnish polytechnics have been facing. In 1990, Finland's higher education sector experienced significant reform as various colleges were merged to form new institutions called polytechnics, or universities of applied science. The task of these universities was to 'carry out research and development that supports education, the development of working life, and regional developments in the geographical area in which they operate' (Virkkunen, et al., 2008).

The next reform occurred several years ago as the government legislated to increase the autonomy of all universities and polytechnics. The polytechnics have since taken the form of limited companies as opposed to public organizations (*http://www.okm.fi/OPM/Koulutus/koulutuspolitiikka/Hankkeet/Yliopistolaitoksen_uudistaminen/index.html?lang=en*). This created a turning point for these organizations and their personnel. It is argued that being a limited company increases independence and the ability to answer more flexibly to the developmental needs of working life. Polytechnics have been given a role, by the Ministry of Education and Culture, as a partner for developing business and working as regional educators and developers.

The goals emphasize the concept of 'innovation pedagogy', which aims at generating new social innovation and renewing existing operating models. Innovation pedagogy means that education is supposed to be integrated into research, development and new practices. However, the new model and practices are not proving easy to adopt. The idea is to support and create learning environments for students that are directly related to working life. It means creating projects that are to be carried out in workplace contexts and aims at developing workplaces with teachers and students. All the study projects, or most of them, are to be carried out in workplaces in different sectors. Polytechnic teachers are expected to apply for funding and collaborate and integrate new areas and themes for these projects and their teaching practices. Innovation pedagogy is seen as being fulfilled when teachers from different subject areas and units combine their competencies and create integrated courses based on new teacher collaborations. Meeting the goals of a polytechnic entails the creation of new competencies for teachers.

Because of the reforms, teachers are expected to collaborate more, generate research ideas, lead development and innovation, and obtain funding for projects. This stimulates questioning related to their previous knowhow. Teachers also need to expand their knowhow and practices in order to manage new types of collaborative networks. They have to familiarize themselves with different funding agencies and their needs, write funding applications, coordinate projects and combine practical studies and assignments for the students in these projects. In this case, change pressures are concretized in the work of Degree Programme Managers (DPMs). They manage teachers and guide the content development of their own degree programmes. At the same time they need to support teachers to change their concept of what it means to be a teacher in this new context – this change profoundly affects the teacher and the DPMs' professional identity and the way they practise.

In our discussions, unit leaders and DPMs said they felt the change pressure quite overwhelmingly, as the process of change had been a constant over several years. Teachers were tired and some of them rejected the idea of engaging in funded projects, refusing to see anything positive about the new aims that had been thrust at the polytechnics. The DPM role became visible as they were expected to help and support teachers in developing their working practices.

One particular unit wanted to support the DPMs' leadership skills in situations of change. A contact person approached me and asked to take part in a pilot project. The idea of Forum Theatre and DWR was then presented to the unit's leader and to the executive boardroom. In the pilot project we were then given the task of developing the DPMs' change management and leadership skills, as this was felt to be a crucial issue in the change process. The object of the development was specifically the 11-member executive board. Half the executive board were DPMs. The developmental process were only conducted with the executive board, so no teachers were involved in the actual intervention workshop.

Building a Play that Depicts the Developmental Phase

The process lasted several months altogether and began with my meeting with the unit's leader and discussing the aim of our project. I then started an initial inquiry and interviewed 21 people within the organization, half of whom are managers and the rest teachers and other personnel. Each of the DPMs led their own degree programme. All the DPMs are also part of the executive board.

Before the interview I had planned the questions in order to understand more about the challenges of DPM's work and 'change management'. The interviews were semi-structured interviews focusing on what was challenging in the manager's work and what was not. I was interested in finding concrete problems and ideas and identifying the bigger challenges that were part of examining how activity could be developed towards innovation pedagogy.

After the interview period, I read through the data several times and formed hypotheses. The idea was to create hypotheses of 'real life' and especially the most problematic situations. I formed hypotheses out of *opposing forces* and *problem areas* that were mentioned during discussions and interviews. I then brought the methods and analytical tools of DWR to the play-building process for developing the anti-model. When creating the story, ideas from DWR were taken into dramatic action, especially collective activity and contradictions. This helped to reveal problems, challenges and ideas that the DPMs faced in their work, and to understand what kind of themes could be brought to a Forum Theatre process and play. In our intervention, the logic of Forum Theatre was applied in the work context without an embodied characterization of the oppressed and oppressor. Instead, there was an interpretation of the contradiction that teachers and DPMs felt on a personal level.

I went through the data and formed an initial idea about the contradiction. As the unit's leader wished that the performance would deal with change management, I tried to also focus on that. The polytechnic was already trying out a new activity model, as some already worked according to 'innovation pedagogy' and some of the personnel felt a double bind in their work. They felt a contradiction; the old way of working was not effective enough and the new way of working was still too far away to imagine.

Through considering the nature of these problematic issues identified from the data, I formed three hypothesizes as tools to build a narrative. The three hypotheses were:

1. The new activity, innovation pedagogy, contradicts previous work practices and the term itself is felt to be abstract; it does not give direction with regard to everyday actions.
2. Familiar practices and dynamics of the executive board were preventing innovation.
3. DRMs required more time and further change management competencies to lead interaction situations.

The first hypothesis was a contradiction between present activity and innovation pedagogy. The other two were 'hypotheses of real life' focused on the action level (Engeström 1987), as more about challenges in interactions. The last scene was built as the anti-model, a scene that would be changed with workshop participants depending on discussions.

The first hypothesis concerned a new activity and the fact that there was a gap between vision and practice. Managers were being encouraged to apply innovation pedagogy practices; however, this term was interpreted by the DPMs and teachers as an abstraction that did not provide answers to questions such as 'what should I do differently?' Managers wondered how the content and meaning of innovation pedagogy could be communicated so that new practices would be comprehensible and therefore innovative pedagogy could be observed as a potential positive vision.

An example taken from an interview with a DPM demonstrates the gap between present activity and future innovation pedagogy work practices:

> Throughout this multiyear project, we have learned a lot and we even got follow-up funding again. There are significant things that we have done, but our degree programme still lacks the volume of these funding projects. And there is also a little resistance against this kind of activity, because teachers feel that they have come here to teach and not to do these projects and get money for the school, as they say 'we're hired as teachers.'
>
> (DPM 1)

The second hypothesis dealt with the dynamics of the executive boardroom. Many felt that they, as a group, did not act in innovative and supportive ways.

The members themselves said that they knew each other so well they could actually finish each other's sentences, and because of that they felt that new and fresh ideas were lacking. A second example taken from DPM's interview outlines that issue:

> Our executive boardroom's challenge is, that when somebody opens up his or her mouth and says something on their mind, its meaning is pigeonholed immediately – 'click'. You sort of decide not to listen, you don't ask them to specify and you draw the conclusion quite directly.
>
> (DPM 1)

The third hypothesis was about the change the DPMs, as leaders, experienced in face-to-face situations with teachers. Many of the teachers resisted taking part in innovation projects, because applying for funding and other extra work was seen as a burden. The DPMs felt that they did not have enough understanding or tools to be real change leaders and they were also very busy. The point that is highlighted through this extract from a DPM's interview is as follows:

> Your own physical state affects how you can keep your emotions under control. The more tired you are the more you get irritated. I don't like persuading others, I don't want to talk like this: 'we have to do these (projects), but what good can we get out of them?' or 'You should probably know that we include these and these in these courses...'
>
> (DPM 1)

After forming the ideas about the contradiction and hypotheses, I devised a rehearsal process with two professional actors. First we discussed my findings and initial ideas. Later we started improvising on the basis of developmental contradiction. By engaging in improvisation I felt it was an opportunity for me as a director, or viewer, to examine the direction in which the plot was going and whether or not it was relevant to our case. We did not bring real characters into the story nor use any other dramatic techniques.

Our rehearsals also acted as a way to further analyse the data, because I was responsible for the narrative development but had also conducted the interviews. It was my duty to continue to identify and highlight important issues and clarify our mission – the picture became clearer during rehearsals.

With the actors we therefore created a fictional polytechnic. The polytechnic was named MultiPotentia and the story was about a new degree programme where physical education, gastronomy and homeopathy were integrated. We wanted to highlight the idea of contradiction between present activity and future innovation pedagogy in terms of collaboration between teachers. We brought the fictional teachers of Potentia, which was part of the larger polytechnic MultiPotentia, into the narrative. Teachers tried to figure out how they should change their work in order to fulfil innovation pedagogy, and how difficult it was for managers to support the change.

We did not need to get approval for the workshop and content of the story. The unit's leader was briefed and told about the process, as well as being assured of the confidentiality of interview material. I talked with the unit's leader beforehand and he wished for us to concentrate on leadership in change. He also requested that nobody would have to step on stage and act, as members of the executive boardroom had expressed the wish to not do so. Of course, if participants had stepped up, we would have happily made changes to our initial plans. In our 3-hour workshop, every 15 to 20 minute scene was discussed separately. The executive board – 11 people – sat in a horseshoe formation.

Several extracts follow and these demonstrate examples of the resulting scenes and anti-model. They depict discussions between two teacher characters who are trying to figure out what innovation pedagogy means and how their work should be changed:

TERO: We have big changes coming up. Homeopaths are integrating with our profit unit and the administration of Potentia has a vision that we should develop customer-oriented services for firms. Service orientation is the word of the day. We should think of the customer of our customer, meaning our student's customer. And also we should produce large well-being services. We can't do it without entering each other's fields and combining our knowhow and working practices. It won't be easy. BTW, did you receive my text via email?

TARA: Oh no, that sounds very demanding! I'm a bit terrified about all this, but I'm happy that I came back. But what happens to our courses? I think that there is only one right way to make a cinnamon bun and you don't learn it in any other way than participating in a baking course.

TARA: And what do they mean by saying 'we teach together'? No we don't! We have our own courses, I have mine and you have yours. I don't get it. How do you integrate baking a bun to someone massaging a calf?

TERO: Our work is changing, I guess you can't help it. Different degree programmes are forced to get funding for projects and I don't know . . . you have to figure this all out a bit differently. Haven't you read the bulletins?

The following section includes an extract from the last scene, an anti-model, in which a resistant physical education teacher was talking with her DPM. The scene worked as a tool for us to change and develop the DPM's actions and behaviour. The anti-model was created to concretize and discuss how DPMs could change their own behaviour and give support to teachers. In this scene the DPM 'Tero' is not giving his best in the interaction situation and is not, in fact, listening to teacher 'Kaisa's' problem and cannot support her because of that:

KAISA: Yeah, I know, I promised, but things have changed and actually I don't remember talking about any special project, but anyway, I don't have any time for these types of projects and besides I'm not a project person at all!

TERO: You can do it, you can do it! When we work together we can score, that's for sure!

KAISA: And besides, what is this innovation pedagogy? Explain it to me in Finnish?

TERO: Innovation pedagogy simply means that you operate in the concrete field, not in school, and create different service products with local companies. In this way we effectively get study points for our students, they graduate from school and we get more money for the school! That's it.

KAISA: (*upset and aggressive*) You know, I'm very distressed even by thinking of this funding stuff and I'm very tired, I don't have energy to do that! I don't understand why I have to do these projects!

The workshop was run in order for the DPMs and executive board to develop and question their action strategies in the polytechnic's change processes. The ideas of the DWR were not directly discussed with the audience. As I was leading the discussions I fielded viewpoints from the audience and started the dialogue between the audience and the players. In the play, the focus was on the work of the DPM.

Afterwards, the workshop received positive feedback and during it we had good discussions on the developmental challenges that relate to the DPM's work. I interviewed some of the DPMs after six months of the intervention and it became clear that some saw the intervention as very interesting and memorable, while others had started questioning their management actions and developed their interaction skills.

Conclusion

This chapter reflected on two intervention resources; one originally created in the field of theatre and the other in the field of workplace development. Both resources are tools for development that aim to emancipate and develop social actions. Behind this pilot project there was a presumption that in the long run the strongest parts of these resources could be brought together and intertwined – and this case provided the opportunity to test out this proposition in order to learn more. This chapter raises discussion about the resource's similarities, differences and complementary aspects. It also demonstrates how a research-oriented approach (DWR) was used in play-building that focused on the conceptual development at hand.

The intertwined development resources in this study were called 'Workplace Theatre'. Workplace Theatre differs from Forum Theatre in a way that the narrative is built with the help of a DWR toolkit, especially analysis of contradiction. The narrative is constructed in collaboration with the researcher's data and devising rehearsals. The main idea is to form a narrative that works as a mirror of daily work and demonstrates the contradictions that are caused by the development at hand that are experienced at personal level.

The DWR's theoretical tools were helpful in the research, analysis and play-building phase. The DWR offered analytical tools for understanding development. The manager's actions were related to understanding and supporting the teacher's actions towards a new activity model. Forum Theatre, on the other hand, provided a form that helped to create a strong theatrical and aesthetic space, where the managers and executive boardroom had a chance to experience and interpret the play – to place themselves in particular situations and reflect upon them. Three scenes were built with the help of actual research data, analysis and a devising process. The results of the analysis were formed as hypotheses of real life problems, which informed the narrative construction and story building.

Forum Theatre helped the intervention to be experimental with regard to imagining the possible future horizons. Since differing realities were simulated in front of everybody, it was easier to analyse and discuss them. Testing and simulating helps people to understand reactions and the consequences of their actions through the testing out of 'what happens if?' In this way the intervention is actually more experiential, making it easier for participants to remember rehearsed actions if and when the 'real' interaction occurs. The pilot project showed that there could be value in further explorations of fusing Forum Theatre and DWRs together, and also more study into what ways these resources can together to help work communities to question and develop their activities and actions.

References

Blunden, A. (2010), *Concepts, a Critical Approach*, Chicago: Haymarket Books. URL, accessed 30 March 2014 at: *http: http://home.mira.net/~andy/works/concepts-narrative.htm*

Boal, A. (1995), *The Rainbow of Desire. The Boal Method of Theatre and Therapy*, translated by A. Jackson, London: Routledge.

Davis, S. (2014), 'Interactive Drama with Digital Technology and Tools for Creative Learning', in S. Davis, B. Ferholt, H. Grainger Clemson, S. Jansson and A. Marjanovic-Shane, *Dramatic Interactions in Education: Vygotskian and Socio-Cultural Approaches to Drama, Education and Research*.

Engeström, Y. (1987), *Learning by Expanding: An Activity Theoretical Approach to Developmental Research*, Helsinki: Orienta konsultit.

Engeström, Y. (1991), 'Developmental Work Research: A Paradigm in Practice', (Introduction), *The Quarterly Newsletter of the Laboratory of Comparative Human Cognition*, 13(4): 79–80.

Engeström, Y. (1999), 'Perspectives on Activity Theory, Innovative Learning in Work Teams: Analyzing Cycles of Knowledge Creation in Practice', in Y. Engeström, R. Miettinen and R.L. Punamäki, (eds), *Perspectives on Activity Theory*, Cambridge: Cambridge University Press, 377–404.

Engeström, Y. (2007), 'Putting Vygotsky to Work The Change Laboratory as an Application of Double Stimulation', in H. Daniels, M. Cole and J. Wertsch, (eds), *The Cambridge Companion to Vygotsky*, Cambridge: Cambridge University Press, 363–82.

Helle, M. (2010), *Toimitustyö muutoksessa. Toiminnan teoria ja mediakonsepti tutkimuksen ja kehittämisen kehyksenä. (Changing Journalism. Activity Theory and Media Concept as Tools for Understanding and Developing Work Practices in Newsrooms)*, Tampere: University of Tampere.

Jansson, S (2014), 'A Theatre Company's Development, Cultural-Historical Activity Theory and Developmental Work Research: Movement between Archetypes', in S. Davis, B. Ferholt, H. Grainger Clemson, S. Jansson and A. Marjanovic-Shane, *Dramatic Interactions in Education: Vygotskian and Sociocultural Approaches to Drama, Education and Research*.

Kajamaa, A. (2011), *Unraveling the Helix of Change – An Activity-theoretical Study of Health Care Change Efforts and Their Consequences*, Helsinki: University of Helsinki.

Midgley, G. (2000), *Systemic Intervention: Philosophy, Methodology, and Practice*, New York: Kluwer Academic/Plenum.

Mott, L. (1992), *Systemudvikling. Den menneskelige dimension*, Köpenhavn: Förlaget Samfundslitteratur.

Schutzman, M. and Cohen-Cruz, J. (1994), 'Introduction', in M. Schutzman and J. Cohen Cruz, (eds), *Playing Boal. Theatre, Therapy, Activism*, London: Routledge.

Taussig, M. and Schechner, R. (1994), 'Boal in Brazil, France, the USA. An interview with Augusto Boal', in M. Schutzman and J. Cohen Cruz, (eds), *Playing Boal. Theatre, Therapy, Activism*, London: Routledge.

Virkkunen, J. and Newnham, D.S. (2013), *The Change Laboratory, A Tool for Collaborative Development of Work and Education*, Rotterdam: Sense Publishers.

Virkkunen, J., Mäkinen, E. and Lintula, L. (2010), 'From Diagnosis to Clients – Constructing the Object of Collaborative Development between Physiotherapy Educators and Workplaces', *Activity Theory in Practice: Promoting Learning Across Boundaries and Agencies*, 9–24.

Index

abstract thought 47, 139
acting
   actor training 230, 239
   all humans as actors 8–9
   creativity of the actor 245–58
   'objectives' and 'units' 45–7
   organic vs representational 22, 26
   and perezhivanie 41–2
   Problem of the psychology of the actor's creative work (Vygotsky, 1932) 26–9, 41, 48
   teachers co-mentoring with professional actors 145–8
   Vygotsky on 24–5, 26–9
Activity Systems Analysis 196
Activity Theory 5, 212 *see also* CHAT (Cultural-Historical Activity Theory)
activity triangles 192–3, 196–8
Actor's Work, An (Stanislavski, 2008) 46
actual-empirical analysis 217
adolescence 31
adults
   facilitating children's drama experiences 143–5
   involvement in children's play 58–9, 81, 138, 140, 141
aesthetics 20, 264–6
affect *see also* emotion
   affective-volitional tendency behind thought 49–50
   dual affect 155, 156–7, 162–3
   emotion linked to cognition xviii–xix, 57, 62–3, 72, 157
   and intellect 135
   Vygotsky on 230
affinity groups 118
Afinogenov, A. 39, 40, 50
Ahonen, A. 219
Alda, A. 254
Alvarez, A. xvii
anthropology 248
'anti-models' 265, 267–9, 272, 275

applause 79, 256
archetypes, organizational 211, 212–13, 215–17, 222–7
art
   and 'not not' 68
   Vygotsky on 20, 48, 54, 67, 69
Art as Experience (Dewey, 1934) 72
artists-in-residence programmes 146
Arts Developing Quality and Innovation Capabilities in Work Life project 262
'as if' modes 64–5, 81, 141
Aspelin, J. 72
audience
   actors' sense of 'audience' 47
   audience development functions 219, 220–1, 223
   audience-actor interaction 255–6. *see also* participatory theatre
   blurring of spectator-audience boundary 109
   classroom drama doesn't have a separate 'audience' 79–80
   as motivating factor 182
   participatory theatre 217, 224, 225, 265
   understanding social signs 54
Australian Early Years Framework 138
authoring 103, 106
Ayers, W. 81

Bakhtin, M.M. 4, 48, 53, 84–5, 87, 89, 90, 91, 92, 94, 102
banning of Vygotsky's work 53
Basics of Alchemy 220
Bateson, G. 64, 232, 242
Baumer, S. 7, 58
behaviour
   'restored behaviour' 64–5, 68
   stages of performance related to behaviour 65–6
   students with 'behaviour problems' 118
   'twice behaved behaviour' 64–5

Bekhterev, V. 45, 51
Belushi, J, 254
Berducci, D. 49
Berry, C. 91
bigotry 171, 181–2, 184–6
Billig, M. 222
Blommaert, J. 177
Blunden, A. 268
Boal, A. 8–9, 109, 123, 219, 261, 264–5
Bolton, G. 6, 79, 104, 108, 156, 157
Bottomore, T. 27
Boyd, M. 83
Bozhovich, L. 33, 63
Brock, D.M. 213
Brook, P. 255
Brown, J.S. 102
Bruner, J. 80, 137, 140, 157
Buber, M. 71, 72
bureaucracy 44–7

Cameron, D. 194
canalization 122
Carnicke, S.M. 22
Carroll, J. 194
categorization of children 97
catharsis 20
Chaiklin, S. 101
Challenge the Gap 97
Change Laboratory 262–3
change management 269–71
characterisation, and perezhivanie 62
characterization
   and metaxis 123
   Vygotsky on 5, 25
CHAT (Cultural-Historical Activity Theory) 4, 5, 64, 190–4, 196, 211, 214, 262
Chekhov, A. 42
Chelpanov, G. 45
child development
   drama as a meta-frame for 31–4
   of imagination 47, 54
   symbolic meaning 138, 140
   and the theory of expansive learning 190
   Vygotsky on 105
circle layouts 105, 237
circus groups 217
clarification 84
cognition
   and cultural change 174

   linked to emotion xviii–xix, 57, 62–3, 72, 157
Cohen-Cruz, J. 265
Cole, M. 4, 73 n.4, 101–2, 157, 172, 173, 179, 245
collaborative working
   in classroom drama 79, 82, 115, 124, 125
   collaborative emergence 247–8, 255, 258
   collaborative play reading 91
   collective creativity 103
   and *contracting* 105
   in dialogic inquiry 82–3
   drama as collaborative process xx
   enaction vs experience of emotions 167
   expanding the role of the theatre 223
   and improvisation 255, 257
   and intersubjectivity 121–2
   and motivation 126–7
   and performance creativity 252
   in scripted plays 249–50
   and the ZPD 83–4
collectivity
   and activity theory 192
   collective ZPD for literacy learning 136–48
   collective ZPD for second language learning 155
   and identity formation 103
Collie, R.J. xviii, xix
co-mentoring 144–8
commedia dell'arte 249
communities, in activity theory 192–3, 197
communities of practice 102, 118
Compass Players 253
computers *see* ICT (Information and Communications Technologies)
Concrete Human Psychology (Vygotsky, 1986) 32
conditioned reflexes 45
conflicts (vs dilemmas) 222
Connery, C. xvi
conscience alley 145
consciousness
   Bakhtin on 85, 92
   and 'eventness' 91
   and perezhivanie 63–4
constants 70–1
constructivist learning 257–8
continuum 91, 92, 93

contracting 105–6
contradictions, in activity systems
  in digital technologies study 193, 196, 197, 199, 201, 202–4
  in theatre company development study 212, 214, 221–5
  in workplace theatre study 263, 271–2, 273
conversation analysis 250–1
Corsaro, W. 142
Creative Collaboration (John-Steiner, 2000) xx
creativity
  children as co-creators 148
  the creative process 256–7
  and dramatic play 141
  and imagination 157–8
  performance creativity 245–58
  in schooling 99–100
  squeezed out of childhood 135–6
  and the transformative potential of drama on identity 97–111
  Vygotsky on xx, 2, 54, 99–101, 103, 106
Crime and Punishment (Dostoevsky, 1866) 65–6
critical historical perspectives 24
Crow, B.K. 250, 251
Csikszentmihalyi, M. 245, 252
cultural clashes 171–87
Cultural-Historical Activity Theory (CHAT) 4, 5, 64, 190–4, 196, 211, 214, 262
cyberdrama 194, 199
cycle of imagination 157–9, 164, 168

Daigle, E.A. 61
Daniels, H. 41, 45
Davis, D. 2
Davis, S. 108
Del Rio, P. xvii
Delpit, L. 106–7
democratic classrooms 106, 124
depiction 143, 145
despair, overcoming 63–4
'Developmentally Appropriate Practice' 143–4
Dewey, J. 2, 67, 72, 245
Dezuanni, M. 116
dialogue

dialogic inquiry 82–3, 84–5, 86, 92–4
  scaffolding as dialogic interaction 155
  as social transaction 48
  ZPD as collaborative dialogue 137–8
D-identities 117–18, 119
Diderot's paradox 27
dilemmas 221–2
disadvantaged students 98–111
disbelief, suspension of 6
disciplined improvisation 258
discourse communities 118
Discourses 118
division of labour, in activity systems 192–3, 197, 202, 214, 222–3, 262
dog in rehearsal room 46–7
Donato, R. 154
Donnellan, D. 46–7
Dostoevsky, F. 65–6
double negativity 68–9
double voicing 81, 87
double-sidedness 70
drama
  as educational subject 1–2, 6
  key concepts in drama education 5–9
  vs theatre 6
  Vygotsky's drama of life 29–34
dramatic inquiry
  and cultural change 172, 179–86
  described 80–4, 174
  and telos 178, 179
  via *The Tempest* 79–94
dramatic play (children's) 7, 139–42
Driagins, V. 61
dual affect 155, 156–7, 162–3
Dubna Psychological Journal 19
Duffield, J. 97
Duguid, P. 102
Duncan, A. 254
Dunn, J. 92, 143
DWR (Developmental Work Research) 212, 213, 214–17, 261–77

edinitsy ('units') 45
Edmiston, B. 80, 81, 82, 87, 93, 174
Eisenstein, S. 40
e-learning platforms 197, 199
Ellis, V. 5
Ellsworth, E. 88
emblems 159

embodiment 54, 159, 167, 174, 186, 201, 205, 235–6, 239
Emerson, C. 90
emotion *see also* affect
  and acting 48
  and art 69
  emotional contagion 256
  and imagination 157–8
  linked to cognition xviii–xix, 57, 62–3, 72, 157
  and thought 49–50
empathy 54, 143, 147
empowerment, through drama 181
enculturation 121
Engeström, Y. 4, 190, 192, 193, 212, 214, 217, 221, 222, 261, 264, 267
ensemble 124, 235, 236, 239, 251–2, 253–5
environment
  creating environments for learning and developing 83–4
  socio-spatial environments 229–43
  Vygotsky on 230
ESL (English as a Second Language) 147, 153–68, 175
eventness 91–2
everyday world
  drama of everyday life 3, 29–34
  drama reflects 109
  everyday life performance 251
  vs 'figured' worlds 103, 104
  vs play 81
  and prolepsis 178
Ewing, R. 139, 143
expansive learning, theory of 190–4, 201, 202–4, 214, 264, 267
'experiential learning' 7 *see also* process drama
Experimental Study of Concept Formation, An (Vygotsky) 47
experimental theatre movement 42
expert framing 181, 182

fairy tales 52, 142
Fear (*Strakh*) (Afinogenov, 1931) 39, 40, 45, 50–3
feedback and reflection
  critical reflection 123
  drama teachers' 116
  and identity formation 116
  from 'outside' 92
  on physicality of environments 243
  in process drama 7
  the 'reflecting "I"' of adolescence 31
  reflection-in-action 123
  reflective dialogue in dramatic inquiry 89
  and the theory of expansive learning 191
Ferholt, B. 60, 66, 71
figured worlds 102–3
Fleer, M. 143
Flicker, T. 253
flow 69, 70, 71, 144, 252–4
Forman, E.A. 231
Forum Theatre 8, 109, 219–20, 224, 225, 261–77
Fox, C. 138–9
frame analysis 229, 232, 238–9, 242–3
framed expertise 181, 182
free time, children need 142, 143
Freebody, K. 119
'Freeze Tag' 246
Freire, P. 8
FSM (free school meals) 97–8, 107–8, 111

Gallimore, R. 101
Gardner, P. 254
Gaughenbaugh, L. 82
Gee, J. 117, 118–19
general genetic law of cultural development 30
gesture 159
Gibson, R. 143, 146, 147
'Given Circumstances' 42
Glăveanu, V.P. 98–9
goal-directed thought 45
goal-oriented action 47
Goffman, E. 229, 232, 239
Gomel, Vygotsky in xv, 21, 43
Gonzales-Mena, J. 144
Gonzalez Rey, F. 33, 63
Gordon, M. 253
Graue, E. 136
Greene, M. 81
Greenwood, R. 211, 212–13, 215
Griboedov, A. 49
Griffin, P. 101–2
groupmind 254

guided participation 84
Gutiérrez, K. 175–6

Hamlet (Shakespeare)
  in *The Psychology of Art* xv, 20–1
  teachers in RSC rehearsal room 241
  and 'verbal thinking' 34
Hamsun, K. 42
hands, bodily memory of 63, 70
Hansen, D. 176
Hapgood, E.R. 45
Harré, R. 86
Harste, J.C. 107
Haught, J.R. 159
Heath, S. 141
Heathcote, D. 6, 90, 107, 108, 109, 174, 181, 232, 257
Hickey, D.T. 119
Hinings, C.R. 211, 212–13, 215
Hirsh-Pasek, K. 135
History of the Development of Higher Mental Functions, The (Vygotsky, 1931) 30, 31, 32
Holland, D. xvii, 102–3, 104, 110
Holzman, L. xviii, 82, 83–4, 155
hotseating 143, 145
Hughes, B. 138, 139
Hutchins, E. 245
hybrid organizations 213, 217, 219, 220–1

ICT (Information and Communications Technologies) 189–205
identity
  construction of identity in drama classroom 115–29
  disadvantaged children's identities 97–111
  and metaxis 123
  sociocultural perspectives on identity (overview) 117–22
  Vygotsky on 102, 115
IDIERI (International Drama in Education Research Institute) 3
I-identities 117–18, 119
imagination
  cycle of imagination 157–9, 164, 168
  and emotion 157–8
  imaginative enquiry 7, 54. *see also* process drama
  imaginative play as 'serious play/ play for real' 139
  importance of imaginative play 138–9
  and play 81
  in Soviet society 52
  squeezed out of childhood 135–6
  in Stanislavski's theatre 43
  transformative potential of drama 109
  Vygotsky on xx, 1, 9, 47, 54, 81, 157
Imagination and Creativity in Childhood (Vygotsky, 1930) 2, 157
Imai, Y. 157
immigrant children 160, 171, 173, 179–80, 181–4
immortality dramatic inquiry 194–201
improvisation
  in children's play 142
  and identity formation 104, 123–4
  and oral traditions 248–9
  and performance creativity 245–58
  process drama 159–60
  to shift expectations and models of practice 201
independent theatre 216
individualism, vs co-existence 72, 120
'infecting' the audience 23
initiation-response interactions 173
innovation pedagogy 270, 271–5
Instant Messaging 195
institutional theatres 216
intentionality 85
internal and external self within environment 68, 81
internal dialogue 83, 84, 93, 94
internalization 121–2, 143, 144, 155, 162, 166
intersubjectivity 121, 123, 125
interventionist research methodologies 190, 262–3, 266–9
interventions 261, 263, 267
Invisible Theatre 8
ISCAR (International Society for Cultural and Activity Research) 3
Island of Plenty Fish drama 158, 160–6
I-You (I-Thou) relationship 71, 72

Jackson, T. 8
Jetnikoff, A. 116
Johannesen, B. 142

Johnson, L. 90
John-Steiner, V. xvi, xx, 99, 159, 256
Joker (in Forum Theatre) 265, 268–9

Kallio, P. 220
Kao, S.M. 156
Karpov, Y.V. 19
King Lear (Shakespeare) 255
Konjin, E.A. 252
Kozulin, A. 50
Kress, G.R. 229, 233–4
kusok ('bit'/ 'units') 46

L2 learning 147, 153–68, 175
Lachiotte, W. xvii
Langemeyer, I. 5
Langenhove, L.V. 86
language
    classroom language 54
    as cultural tool/ 'mediated action' xvii, 44, 98–9, 154
    dramatic play and language/literacy learning 135–48
    external language as process of understanding 54
    in identity construction 117
    second language learning 147, 153–68, 175
    Vygotsky on theatrical language 21–2
Lantolf, J.P. 153, 154, 155
Larson, J. 175–6
Lave, J. 102, 231
layering processes 236
learning
    and identity formation 102–4
    linked to emotion xviii–xix, 57, 62–3, 72, 157
    Vygotsky on 107, 108–9, 154, 191–2, 230
Learning Performance Network (LPN) 233, 234–43
Leland, C. 107
Leningrad theatre 50–1
Leontiev, A. 33, 45, 102, 192
Lewis, C.S. 59
'life of drama,' Vygotsky's 21–9
Lindon, J. 136
Lindqvist, G. 7, 8, 58, 138
Lion, the Witch and the Wardrobe, The (Lewis, 1950) 59

living theatre 24–6, 27–9, 42–4, 46, 51
longitudinal study 125–9
low SES (socio-economic status) children 97
Luria, A. 4, 45

Mahn, H. 41, 159
Mandelstam, O. 40, 105
Marjanovic-Shane, A. xvi, 58
Markarian, W. 83
Martin, J. 125
Marx, K, 43
Marxian-Hegelian dialectic 20, 27
'mask' metaphors 25
materialism 45
'maximizing resources' 179, 181
McCafferty, S.G. 159
McNeill, D. 159
Mead, G.H. 245
meaning
    child development of word meaning 47
    children developing symbolic meaning 138, 140
    collaborative meaning making in classroom drama 79
    and creative tools 99
    developing meaning from 'sense' 172, 177–8, 183, 187, 230
    dialogic inquiry 84–5, 92
    and gesture 159
    meaning-making via dramatic inquiry 80–2
    scientific vs spontaneous meaning 84
    thought mediated internally by meanings 33
    via mediating tools 82
mediation
    and ICT 192, 203, 205
    'mediated action' 44
    mediated learning 154
    of power and control relationships 98, 105, 106–8, 109
    Vygotsky on 4, 30–1, 33, 154, 192
mental function 100
Mercer, N. 84
meta-frame, drama as 31–3
metaphor, drama as 30–1
meta-theoretical perspectives 120
metaxis 123, 266

Meyerhold, V. 53
micro-historical analysis 217–18
middle schools 172
Midgley, G. 261
Miller, C. 143
mime 143
Minick, N. 4, 43, 45, 47
mirroring 63
mobile phones 195, 197
Moll, L. 137
monologic (vs dialogic) inquiry 84–5, 86
Moran, S. xvi, 99
Morson, G.S. 90
Moscow Art Theatre 40, 49, 50
Moscow Institute of Defectology 40
motivation
    actors revealing 51, 52–3
    and collaboration 126–7
    drama and social mediation of
        motivation development 116–29
    motivated settings 172, 187
    and play 144
    and proleptic change 178
    and thought 49–50
Mott, L. 263
multimodal social semiotics 229–30,
    233–4, 236–8
Murray, J. 194
'mushfaking' 158

narratives 88, 140, 141, 175, 194, 268 *see also* telos
naturalistic drama 5, 23, 40
Neelands, J. 105, 106, 124
negation
    double negativity 68–9
    negations of negations 27
negotiation 101, 104, 106, 110
neo-realism 23
new public management 213
Newman, D. 101
Newnham, D.S. 261, 262, 263, 264
newsroom dramatic inquiry example
    181–4
Ngo, B. 176
Niculin, D. 93
N-identities 117–18
Niemi, I. 218
Nissen, M. 5

non-school educational settings 8
'not not me' 68–9

'objective' – translation of 46
objectivist vs subjectivist perspectives in
    psychology 44–5
object-regulation 156
objects, of activity 192, 197, 222–4
Off-Off-Campus 245–6
Ohta, A.S. 155
Ojala, R. 218
O'Neill, C. 80, 90, 110, 143, 156, 159, 174, 194
online working 194–201
oppression 109, 181–6, 265, 271
oral traditions and improvisation 248–9
'organic' development 44
organic vs representational acting 22, 26
organizational archetypes 211, 212–13,
    215–17, 222–7
'other,' perspective of 85, 91, 92–4, 105, 140, 143
other-regulation 156, 162
O'Toole, J. 6, 92, 143, 232
Our Monday theatre reviews 21–9
'outside,' reflection from 92
over-protection of children 136

participation
    guided participation 84
    participatory theatre 8, 217, 224, 225, 265
    and the transformative potential of
        drama 107
Pavlov, I. 45, 46, 51
PDAs (Personal Data Assistants) 126
Pedagogy of the Oppressed (Freire, 1979) 8
Pedology of the Adolescent, (Vygotsky, 1930/31) 31
perezhivanie
    as 'anchor' 70–2
    applied to the study of play 57–73
    and co-existence 72
    defined by Stanislavski 40–1, 43, 62
    defined by Vygotsky xix, 57, 62–3, 71, 401
    defined within CHAT 64
    difficulty of translation to English 61–2
    Ferholt's working definition 71–2
    living theatre 24–6, 27–9, 42–4, 46, 51

and modern Western education 54
and 'not not me' 68
performance as perezhivanie 64–5
and second language learning 158–9, 164–6
theatrical/ psychological definitions of 61–72
and Vygotsky's theatre reviews 22–3, 24
performance
  and motivation 127–8
  performance creativity 245–58
  performance events as culmination of work 195
  in playworlds 64–72
personality 31–3, 34, 119
perspectives, differing 85, 91, 92–4, 105, 140
Petrick-Steward, E. 137
Piaget, J. 105
planning 84
Platonic dialogue 93
play
  and abstract thought 47
  ambiguity of the term 'play' 58–9
  common philosophical themes explored 142
  and dramatic inquiry 80–2
  imaginative play as 'serious play/ play for real' 139
  playworlds 7–8, 58–73, 138
  as root of drama 2–3
  in Soviet society 52
  types of play (Hughes' list) 139
  Vygotsky on xv–xvi, 81, 83, 101, 156
playworlds 7–8, 58–73, 138
pluralism, cultural 176–7, 186
polyphonic dialogue 93
'positionality' 86
positioning 86–7, 93, 104
Positioning Theory 86–7
'possible worlds' 80–1
power and control, relations of
  and dual affect 163
  mediated via drama lessons 98, 105, 106–8, 109
  in schools generally 97
preschool children 57–73, 143–4
present moment
  in dramatic inquiry 90–1
  and perezhivanie 69–70

Pressick-Kilborn, K. 121, 122
'pretend' play 139–40
pre-texts 159–60, 161–2, 194–5, 265
primary school drama 145–8, 160
Problem of the Psychology of the Actor's Creative Work (Vygotsky, 1932) 26–9, 41, 48
problem solving 83–4, 108, 137, 141, 144, 263
Problems of Method (Vygotsky, 1978) 43
process drama
  and the collective ZPD 141, 143–8
  and cycle of imagination 158
  vs dramatic inquiry 80
  and dual affect 156
  and embodiment 159, 167
  vs Forum Theatre 109
  and ICT 194
  and identity formation 115
  in introduction 7
  for L2 learning 159–60
  and mediation of learning 154
progressive education 6
prolepsis 65–7, 172–87
props
  in dramatic inquiry 82
  parents providing 142
  in playworlds 59
  as symbols 108
  toys akin to xv
Prospero 79, 87–8, 93, 94
psychology
  in Communist period 44–7
  drama as a meta-frame for psychological development 31–3
  psychology needs to address emotion-cognition link 57, 62–3
  theatrical psychology 26–9
Psychology of Art, The (Vygotsky, 1925) xv, 69
puppet/ marionette metaphors 25–6
Putney, L. 144

readers' theatre 145
recitation scripts 176
recordings, using 60, 154, 181–4, 186 *see also* technology
reflection and feedback
  critical reflection 123

drama teachers' 116
and identity formation 116
from 'outside' 92
on physicality of environments 243
in process drama 7
the 'reflecting "I"' of adolescence 31
reflection-in-action 123
reflective dialogue in dramatic inquiry 89
and the theory of expansive learning 191
reflexes, conditioned 45
refugee children 160
Regional Theatre Curators (RTCs) 211, 217–18, 219–21, 223, 225
regulation 155–6
rehearsals
 and perezhivanie 41, 42, 65–6, 68, 69
 and performance creativity 251–2
 rehearsal room pedagogy 235
 and Stanislavski's dog 46
 teachers in RSC rehearsal room 229–43
 and text-based drama 124
research
 cross-disciplinary research 3
 drama as a research tool 119
 drama education research often misses Vygotsky 2–3
 interventionist research methodologies 190, 262–3, 266–9
 longitudinal study 125–9
resistance 122
'restored behaviour' 64–5, 68
rituals, performance of 248
Robbins, D. 61, 64, 70, 71
Rogoff, B. 245
role-playing (vs collaborative drama) 167
role-taking 7, 108, 109–10, 123–4, 163, 165, 167 see also TIR (Teacher in Role)
Romeo and Juliet (Shakespeare) 234–5
Roper, B. 2
Rothwell, J. 158
Rovaniemi Theatre, Finnish Lapland 211, 217–27
Royal Shakespeare Company (RSC) 229–43, 255
rules, in activity theory 192–3, 197, 199, 214, 224–5, 262
Russian Revolution 21

Sainsbury, E. 121
Sannino, A. 190, 214, 221, 222
Saussure, F. de 43
Sawyer, R.K. 142, 246, 249, 251, 253, 254, 256
Saxton, J. 143
scaffolding
 of collaborative work 124, 125
 the co-mentoring approach 145–8
 of dramatic play 140, 141
 and educational drama 143
 and imaginative play 137, 144
 and the quality of interaction 137
 and second language learning 155, 162
 and the ZPD 101
Schechner, R. 64–6, 68, 69–70
School Drama Programme 135, 144–5
Schutzman, M. 265
scripted plays *see* text-based drama
sculpting 143, 145
second language learning 147, 153–68, 175
Seham, A.E. 254
self
 awareness of 47
 in imaginative play 140
 internal and external self within environment 41–2
 notions of self in conditions of categorization 108, 109
 self-regulation 156, 159, 162
self-canalization 122
self-confidence 128, 165, 242
semiotics 43, 45, 229, 233–4, 236–8
senior school students 194–201
'sense,' interpretation of 172, 177–8, 187, 230
set pieces in playworlds 59
settings 178–9, 181, 187
Shakespeare
 Hamlet 20–1, 34, 241
 King Lear 255
 Romeo and Juliet 234–5
 teachers in RSC rehearsal room 229–43
Shweder, R.A. 245
signs
 mediation via 33
 semiotics 43, 45, 229, 233–4, 236–8
 subtext and social signs 47–50, 51
 visual symbolism in theatre 51

silencing of certain voices 177–8
Simons, J. 143
Singer, J. 137
situated learning 231, 240
Sivan, E. 119
Slade, P. 6
Slavina, L. 33
'slowing time' 186
Smagorinsky, P. 34, 48, 61, 172, 178, 179
social constructivist perspectives 86
social determinism 120
social facilitation 252
social networking 197
social positioning 86–7, 92
socially imagined worlds 82
sociocultural reductionism 120
socio-spatial environments 229–43
Something about America (Testa, 2005), 179–80, 184
Spolin, V. 257
spontaneity in the theatre 51–2 *see also* improvisation
'Spotlight' 220, 224
stages, 'ladder' vs dramaturgical stages of development 105
Stanislavski, K.
   on the actor's and learner's work 39–54
   biographical details 42, 53
   definition of perezhivanie 22
   living theatre 24–6, 27–9, 42–4, 46, 51
   on perezhivanie 62
   and rehearsal processes 5
   and *stage* 105
   Stanislavskian binaries (table of) 26
   and subtext 48
   translations of 45–6
   and 'verbal thinking' 33–4
   Vygotsky on 24
State Theatre Company, Adelaide 145
Stern, D. 73 n.6
stick for a horse xvi, 47, 139
stimulus-response unit 45
Stinson, M. 143
Stone, A. 137
storydrama 143
Styan, J.L. 5
subtext and social signs 47–50, 51
Swain, M. 137, 154
Sweet, J. 254

Sydney Theatre Company 144
symbolic meaning
   children developing 138, 140
   and second language learning 154
synchronicity 69
systems model of creativity 245

tapping in 143
teaching *see also* scaffolding
   as assisted performance 101
   co-mentoring 144–8
   as polyphonic dialogic positioning 92–4
   pressure to change in Finnish polytechnics 269–71
   teacher and pupil talk 54
   teacher as facilitator in improvisation 124
   teacher as facilitator of drama experiences 143–5
   teacher as guide in dramatic inquiry 81, 82, 86, 94
   teacher-in-role (TIR) 108, 143, 171, 181, 182, 185–6
   teachers in RSC rehearsal room 229–43
   Vygotsky on 82
technology 189–205
telos 172, 174, 175–87
Tempest, The (Shakespeare) 79–94
tension, dramatic 3, 7, 39, 53, 105, 140, 163, 167, 235
text-based drama 123, 124, 216, 239, 249–51 *see also* Shakespeare
texts, Vygotsky's 19–21
Tharp, R.G. 101
theatre
   applied theatre 8, 261
   vs drama 6
   history of oral tradition in theatre 248–9
   living theatre 24–6, 27–9, 42–4, 46, 51
   Neelands' four conditions of theatre 106
   participatory theatre 8, 217, 224, 225, 265
   in schools 6
   theatre company development (Rovaniemi Theatre) 211–27
   Theatre in Education movement 8
   Vygotsky on old vs new theatre 23–4
   Vygotsky on 'social process' of 52
   workplace theatres 261–77

theatre reviews, Vygotsky's 21–9
Theatresports league 254
themes in children's play 142
Thinking and Speech (Vygotsky, 1987) 32, 33, 34
Thorne, S.L. 153, 155
Thought and Language (tr Kozulin, 1986) 50
throughaction 43
Tolstoy, L. 23
tools
  for creativity 98–100
  culturally construced artifacts 98–9
  culturally constructed artifacts xvii
  digital technology and interactive drama 189–205
  for mediated learning 154
  props as mediating tools 82
  socially constructed signs as xvii, 4
transformative power
  of drama 97–111, 125
  of ZPD in imaginative play 144
transitional objects 68
triangle, activity 192–3, 196–8
'truth,' onstage 5, 41, 42, 43, 46, 53
Tulviste, P. 43, 100
Turner, V. 64, 88
'twice behaved behaviour' 70

understanding, developing 84–5, 92, 94, 121
'units' 45–6

Vadeboncoeur, J.A. xviii, xix
Valsiner, J. xix, 101, 120
Van der Veer, R. xix, 101
Vasilyuk, F. 33, 63, 65–6, 67
verbal thinking 49–50
Veresov, N. 30
video clips 195, 198, 201, 267
Virkkunen, J. 261, 262, 263, 264, 269
visual, Vygotsky on the 43
voices silenced 177–8
voluntary attention 45
Vygotsky, L.
  on acting 24–5, 26–9
  on affect 230
  on art 20, 48, 54, 67, 69
  banning of Vygotsky's work 53

  biographical details xv, 20–1, 40, 43, 45, 53
  on characterization 5, 25
  on child development 105
  on creativity xx, 2, 54, 99–101, 103, 106
  definition of perezhivanie xix, 57, 62–3, 71, 401
  definition of ZPD (Zone of Proximal Development) xvi, 136–7, 155
  on environment 230
  on identity 102, 115
  on imagination xx, 1, 9, 47, 54, 81, 157
  influence on Western thought 53–4
  on learning 39–54, 107, 108–9, 154, 191–2, 230
  on mediation 4, 30–1, 33, 154, 192
  Our Monday theatre reviews 19–35
  on play xv–xvi, 81, 83, 101, 156
  on the problem of the actor's and learner's work 39–54
  on Stanislavski, K. 24
  on teaching 82
  on theatre 23–4, 52
  on theatrical language 21–2
  on the visual 19–35, 43

Walker, R.A. 119–21, 122
Way, B. 6
Wells, G. 82, 83, 137
Wenger, E. 102, 231
Wertsch, J. 43, 100, 172, 175, 178
West, D.W. 20
Western thought, influence of Vygotsky and Stanislavski 53–4
'what if?' scenarios 6, 42, 81, 87, 148, 276
Whitmore, K. 137
Wink, J. 144
Winnicott, D.W. 64, 67, 68
Woe from Wit (Griboedov) 49
Wolfson, B. 50–1
Wood, D. 137
Woolf, V. 70
workplace theatre 261, 269–77
Wright, P. 123

Yaroshevsky, M. 104–5
Yasnitsky, A. 20
YouTube clips 198–9

zadacha ('objective') 46
ZPD (Zone of Proximal Development)
   and creativity 101–2
   defined by Vygotsky xvi, 136–7, 155
   in drama classroom 125
   and dramatic inquiry 83–4
   dramatic play and literacy learning 135–48
   and DWR (Developmental Work Research) 215
   and play 156
   and role-taking 167
   and second language learning 155–6, 161–2
   and the theory of expansive learning 190

Lightning Source UK Ltd.
Milton Keynes UK
UKOW04f1140010916

281893UK00001B/35/P